Trauma and Transcendence

Trauma and Transcendence

SUFFERING AND THE LIMITS OF THEORY

ERIC BOYNTON AND PETER CAPRETTO

Editors

AFTERWORD BY MARY-JANE RUBENSTEIN

FORDHAM UNIVERSITY PRESS

New York 2018

Fordham University Press has no responsibility for the
persistence or accuracy of URLs for external or third-party
Internet websites referred to in this publication and does
not guarantee that any content on such websites is, or will
remain, accurate or appropriate.

Fordham University Press also publishes its books in a
variety of electronic formats. Some content that appears in
print may not be available in electronic books.

Visit us online at www.fordhampress.com.

Library of Congress Cataloging-in-Publication Data
available online at https://catalog.loc.gov.

Printed in the United States of America
20 19 18   5 4 3 2 1
First edition

CONTENTS

Trauma and Transcendence

The Limits of Theory in Trauma and Transcendence

Eric Boynton and Peter Capretto

Aporia and Intelligibility in Trauma Theory

Within the humanities, specifically in the past decade, trauma theory has become a robust site of interdisciplinary work. Trauma resonates with scholars in and across disciplines and has become a trope with a distinctive significance. Whereas philosophers and social theorists a generation ago drew almost exclusively upon classical trauma theory, derivative of the psychological and psychoanalytic traditions, recent studies have rooted themselves in a more immediate past. Researchers now turn to many late twentieth-century figures such as Jacques Derrida,[1] Cathy Caruth,[2] and Judith Herman[3] as touchstones for their own disciplinary insights. While this diaspora of theory has strengthened cultural and philosophical reflections on a subject matter once dominated by psychiatry, it has also made trauma's once unified subject matter variegated across disciplines, particularly in the humanities. Given the many conflicts among these disciplines and their methods, the very idea of trauma is becoming increasingly unclear. The scope of scholarship on trauma has always been challenged by the temporal, affective, and corporeal dimensions of trauma itself, yet it has recently been rendered all the more complex by theoretical and methodological issues that have emerged for these disciplines in their attempts to think trauma.

Trauma studies faces a recurrent challenge in so far as its efforts to delineate the field or make prescriptive claims on its future are easily shot down as reductive. Several competing narratives have vied for the fate and future of trauma studies since the field became formally recognized in the early to mid 1990s. The seminal contributions of Caruth, Shoshana Felman, and Dori Laub have foregrounded the sense that trauma ought to be distinguished by its non-assimilable character.[4] Though careful not to fall into the trap of deliberate obscurantism, these theorists caution against headstrong and totalizing definitions of trauma. Caruth, as a humanist working in trauma theory, is "interested not so much in further defining trauma, that is, than in attempting to understand its surprising impact: to examine how trauma unsettles and forces us to rethink our notions of experience."[5] Such governing interpretations have held substantive yet ambivalent influence over scholars in the social sciences and humanities working on trauma. Methodologically, those maintaining the irreducibility of trauma have simultaneously deployed and critiqued medical, anthropological, and psychoanalytic analyses of traumatic repression and testimony. Our inability to give adequate testimony does not necessarily refute reductive readings of trauma; more accurately, it may point out the ideological character of certain medical, psychiatric, or even historical reductions of trauma built on the promise of intelligibility.

The phenomenon of trauma as an aporetic event thus has a dual effect of unsettling reductive readings of trauma but also entrenching trauma studies in repetitions of the moment when thought reaches its limit. In either case, the aporia of trauma potentially forecloses rather than opens up prospects in thinking the claim that trauma is a non-assimilable event. As cultural and film theorists Ann Kaplan and Thomas Elsaesser both warn, a "realistic worry"[6] is that trauma will conceptually become "too handy a catch-all for resolving the aporias or lacunas of previous theoretical configurations" in their fields.[7] One consequence of this trend is that scholars become motivated to admonish those considering trauma in a defined or operationalized way typified by the psychiatric and medicalized community. Vincenzo Di Nicola, a contributor to the volume with training in both psychiatry and philosophy, goes to great lengths to parse out these dichotomies between what he terms the "psychiatric and cultural communities" of trauma theory. Across a spectrum of disciplines, ranging from emergency medicine to philosophy, fewer and fewer disciplines may have satisfactory ways of operationalizing trauma or arriving at a standard definition. Yet the mere fact of this spectrum should not mandate disciplines such as philosophy, literature, religion, and film to adopt a default position wherein trauma can only be theorized as an aporetic phenomenon to which one is drawn yet of which no one can speak.

By bringing together scholars at the intersections of trauma, social theory, and the continental philosophy of religion, one intent of this volume is to draw attention to the increasing challenge of deciding whether trauma's transcendent, evental, or unassimilable quality is being wielded as a defense of traumatic experience against reductionism, or whether it is promulgated as a form of obscurantism—a common critique against theory in contemporary continental thought. Here, the Freudian charge against religion as occultism takes on a new valence when directed toward trauma's transcendence: "What is in question is not in the least an invasion of the field of religion by the scientific spirit, but on the contrary an invasion by religion of the sphere of scientific thought."[8] Introducing the claim of unintelligibility into the field of trauma studies—a field already wrangling with an unclear object of study—may conceal the fact that humanities research is becoming increasingly irrelevant. The contribution of the humanities to trauma studies introduces a peculiar bind: Without deliberately obscuring progress in trauma studies, the humanities' future in trauma studies may become precarious or short.

One defense against this alleged double bind is to insist that fields like the continental philosophy of religion are not merely playing theoretical games with the phenomenon of trauma. No one is willfully obscuring potentially better understandings and definitions; the "material substance" of trauma *is* being responsibly sought; it just so happens that the ways the phenomenon of trauma is reduced or operationalized fails to capture the lived experience of trauma's "substance." In this view, trauma becomes not so much a transcendental concept or evental experience, but more accurately a heuristic around which scholarly disciplines and practices share their resources to better understand. Wherever the future of trauma studies is headed, these person-centered claims must be taken seriously to ensure its discourse remains closely tied to the concrete and material context of traumatic encounter. Yet for those in the humanities and cognate disciplines with training in the history of ideas, special scrutiny must also be given to the ways that personal suffering can be co-opted by a surreptitiously metaphysical defense of trauma. Disputes over what experiences pass as "traumatic" may help defend vulnerable populations, and their already thin identity as survivors of trauma, from being appropriated as unintelligible.

But interdisciplinary research in the humanities should also be cautious about the ways that these conversations are wedded to the idea that there really is an essence to trauma.

From a phenomenological perspective, the pursuit of intelligibility in trauma studies may seem to reaffirm the Husserlian principle of principles for philosophy to remain committed to the things themselves, or as the case may be with trauma, a commitment to bodilyness or *Leibhaftigkeit*. Trauma studies in the humanities could be distinguished by its *own* bracketing of the naturalistic attitude, which rejects medicalized and empirical approaches that presume to know how trauma operates in an unreflective way. The question then becomes whether, through this proprietary *epoché*, the foregrounding of trauma as an unassimilable event forecloses *or* broadens the phenomenological horizon of thinking. If allusions to transcendence and event only structure a critique against scientific operationalisms of trauma, then humanities research in trauma theory falls prey to the Freudian critique: Trauma studies in the humanities only protects itself by eviscerating all other constructive efforts to theorize.

Trauma and the Continental Philosophy of Religion

Disciplines often organize themselves around fundamentally enigmatic concepts, thereby constituting their academic discourse as the pursuit for greater clarity on basic yet fundamental terms: What is *wisdom*; how do we understand the *psyche*; what counts as *religion*; where does one locate *society*? Yet given the aporetic quality of trauma's intelligibility, disciplinary attempts to claim or monopolize trauma theory as its own quickly become problematic. The traps of reductionism and obscurantism in thinking trauma are partly a consequence of methodological incompatibility across disciplines: One discipline's careful analysis is another's theoretical violence. There are, indeed, broader arguments to be made, particularly against the empirical methods employed by scientific disciplines, which can only ever operationalize trauma; at the same time, these operationalizing disciplines can reasonably defend themselves on the grounds that, unlike more humanistic fields, they are actually stating their claims constructively enough to make themselves vulnerable to critique. This volume cannot hope to resolve these disputes, since, quite simply, not all scholars who invoke the name "trauma" are having the same conversation. Emphasizing the points at which the "shared problem" or approach of trauma reaches its limit, as this volume does, opens up, however, the potential for greater interdisciplinary progress in trauma studies.

Linked to the consideration of these disciplinary and methodological limits, recent developments in the continental philosophy of religion also focus on the aporetic analysis endemic to trauma studies. In and through such analysis, thinkers working within the context of continental thought not only have found the resources for and interest in encountering religious themes anew, but those themes are themselves encountered as disclosive phenomenological limit-experiences. Religion manifests itself in this approach as philosophically significant and able to "reorient philosophy,"[9] propose directions for fundamental questioning left unattended by philosophy, even direct thinking toward what would constitute first philosophy. The continental philosopher of religion finds herself *called* to explore the enigma of religious phenomena, and *addressed* by the themes of the suffering other. She seeks to expose philosophy to the exteriority of the religious, taking up the dominant obsession with otherness or difference that has gripped the continental tradition in philosophy. This obsession, inaugurated in French thinking of recent decades, turns thought toward the aporia of the gift or the enigma of the face thereby stretching the character of phenomenological inquiry.[10] Indeed, the continental reflection on religion appears less an investigation that takes religion as its object than a submission to the salutary shock of something different. In this approach, religion harbors an exteriority that becomes a source of amazement, an aporia for thought stretched to its limit. In the attempt to make thematic the encounter with the appearance of a phenomenon excessive of its very phenomenality, thought reaches its limits or is challenged by the logic of the claim. Indeed, religious themes and phenomena have become amazing (*thaumaston*) again.

Yet this amazement in the face of religious themes and phenomena— bent as it is toward aporias, wounds, paradoxes, sites of saturation, "impossibilities" paradigmatically religious—also has its detractors. Taking up the theme of the gift or givenness, some have pointed to the dependence upon hyperbole in establishing the significance of this amazement. Infamously, the conditions of possibility of the gift—that it is completely free and that it is present, or identifiable *as such*—are simultaneously its conditions of impossibility: No gift that is ever present is completely free, and if it is not present then we cannot know it as a gift. The gift structurally exemplifies what Derrida calls "the impossible," where conditions of possibility meet with conditions of impossibility in an aporia. One aspect of this aporia is the requirement that *ingratitude* constitute the proper response to the gift in order that it is not annulled by a return of the giving gesture in an economic exchange. To think the "pure gift" as such, ingratitude must be held as a condition. Such an argument about the impossibility of giving falls victim to the common problem in the continental philosophy of religion of being unhelpfully hyperbolic in its reliance on a particular rhetorical device. Adriaan Peperzak, for one, has argued that "such rhetorical exaggerations can be appreciated if their irony is obvious and if they are not overworked. [. . .] The numerous repetitions of this exaggeration have robbed it of its rhetorical charm and impact, but they have hardly strengthened the idea (or the *idée fixe*) contained in it."[11] This hyperbolic exaggeration of a rhetorical scheme only exacerbates an already opaque phenomenon. We are left uncertain of whether we can reflect on religion and avoid consigning the significance of religion to the secret of faith or sacrifice its significance at the threshold of intelligibility without reducing religion's relation to thought as extremity.

This rhetorical trend in turn risks creating an unproductive and foreclosing set of prospects for the continental philosophy of religion and its task of thinking the aporia of gift: "If the argument is right, it seems that one must choose between complete *cynicism* and a *fideistic* leap to the impossible possibility of generosity, giving, love, friendship and so on."[12] That is, rather than sustaining the aporetic quality of phenomena such as trauma and gift, the continental philosophy of religion potentially requires a more classically Kierkegaardian situation, a paradoxical Either/Or that forces an impossible response: "Either there is a paradox, that the single individual as the single individual stands in an absolute relation to the absolute, or Abraham is lost."[13] Such a perspective seems committed to the prior significance of the religious as a site of extremity *because* thought cannot investigate it.[14] In such a context, philosophy of religion, "if there were one," becomes an impossible task, attempting to think through the source or site of amazement that is simply beyond such scrutiny.[15]

This is precisely where the paradox that lies at the heart of trauma studies can inform debates and impasses in the continental philosophy of religion—the phenomenon of trauma cannot be left to itself as merely enigmatic but requires a therapeutic and ethical response if it is to be properly attended. This turn is inextricably linked to the question of ethics and the existence of the other person who "calls me into question" and places a demand of non-injury on me. The ethical engagement with alterity and the suffering other can thus be thought in terms of an engagement with the unconditioned as such, laying hold of questions traditionally issuing from a theological perspective.

If such a possibility constitutes the novelty of the continental reflection on religion, then trauma studies as an interdisciplinary investigation of such a double bind is instructive. How can we step back from hyperbolic claims that have *rightly* rendered the religious amazing in order to clear the space to think through this amazement *as* it finds expression? If we leave aside a "hyperbolic outbidding"[16] of two directions for discerning the "'pure' and proper possibility" of religion,[17] do the tensions at the heart of trauma studies provide a way of thinking the extremity of phenomena while recognizing that our amazement cannot be left merely as an unknowable secret before which one stands in awe? Can amazement be found in the striving between moments of appropriation and expropriation? Can the purity of a transcendent analysis locate its desideratum by attending to the unbearable brokenness of an immanent yet bottomless harm?

Interdisciplinary Approaches to a Transcendent Phenomenon

By naming the limits of intelligibility of trauma through interdisciplinary sources, this volume seeks to multiply ethical and methodological openings for trauma studies. While the need for institutional and disciplinary critiques of reductive analyses of trauma remain, critical reflections in the continental philosophy of religion frees up critical energy to scrutinize the looming specters of metaphysical reductionism within humanities research, not just outside of it. This also means that phenomenology, the philosophy of religion, and philosophical disciplines in the social sciences can focus on the pressing ethical issues of how to cultivate responses to racial, cultural, sexual, and colonial trauma. However, because this project focuses on the limitations of trauma theory within philosophical and interdisciplinary humanities settings, it does not purport to offer a systematic treatment of every profound instance of trauma. For instance, the volume offers a supplement to the saturated body of literature on war trauma and torture without directly addressing existing scholarship on war trauma and torture. By recognizing the evental and transcendent character of trauma, it contends that humanities research can begin thinking transcendence, truth, and event in ways that do not merely subsume trauma into categories which have, following Heidegger's warning, already been exhausted and entrenched in tired theoretical machinations.

This volume gathers scholars in a variety of disciplines to meet the challenge of how to think trauma in light of its burgeoning interdisciplinarity, and often its theoretical splintering. From a distinctive disciplinary vector, the works of philosophers, social theorists, philosophical psychologists and theologians consider the *limits* and *prospects* of theory when thinking trauma and transcendence. The primary arc of the assembled chapters names critically and responds generatively to the ways theory has been shaped, even conceptually isolated, by the disciplines invested in work on trauma. Toward this end, three areas of concern facing the disciplines and the humanities generally structure the volume: "Constructive Phenomenologies of Trauma," "Social and Political Analyses of Traumatic Experience," and "Theological Aporia in the Aftermath of Trauma."

In the first section, Vincenzo Di Nicola, Robert Stolorow, Donna Orange, Eric Boynton, and Eric Severson ask how the interdisciplinary reception of phenomenology problematizes trauma as a philosophical and ethical category, and propose avenues for constructive phenomenologies of trauma. For Vincenzo Di Nicola, while the goal of both clinical work and cultural research generally is the transformation and transcendence of trauma, these communities struggle to characterize trauma as a unified discourse even within one discipline. In his chapter, he makes three proposals that provide order for the concept of trauma through conceptual dichotomies that divide their discourses: First, the term has accrued a supplementarity or excess, which helps explain the variation between the clinical use of trauma and its cultural avatar; second, theorists must separate the ways the word "trauma" is deployed within the trauma process; third, trauma must be separated radically from Event, which is the subtext of a cultural trauma theory. This philosophical archaeology offers keys of translation between these competing cultural and psychiatric trauma theories, calls to deactivate the desubjectivation associated with trauma, and opens new prospects for interdisciplinary research in these intersecting fields based on the possibilities of the Event.

Beginning with a brief overview of his scholarship in intersubjective systems theory, Robert Stolorow considers the evolving conception of emotional trauma within the phenomenological-contextualist psychoanalytic perspective. Through reflections on his own traumatized states and studies of existential philosophy, he argues that trauma's essentially contextual features demand a ethics of finitude rooted in emotional dwelling, which embraces the unbearable vulnerability and context-dependence of human existence. Donna Orange, who has been an interlocutor and coauthor with Stolorow for decades, makes an independent though related claim regarding the infinite obligation demanded by the transcendence of traumatic experience. Focusing on the egoism that emerges from social domination and racial privilege, and the crisis of climate change, Orange makes the radical ethical claim that persons must allow themselves to be traumatized, persecuted, taken hostage by the starvation and homelessness of others. Her suggestion, which is both classically Levinasian and attuned to contemporary situations of social trauma, is that transcendence in trauma underscores our responsibility for all, which in turn is indispensable for facing up to the challenges of the climate emergency and continuing racial and colonial injustices.

The final two chapters in this opening section extend the Levinasian reflections on Trauma, more specifically on the problems of phenomenological unconcealment and commemoration. Responding to the recent attempts in modern thought to commemorate historical trauma in our genocidal age, Eric Boynton's chapter links the lingering enigmatic quality of evil as a theological term with recent trauma theory and the counter-monuments proposed and completed by the German installation artist, Horst Hoheisel. Linking Levinas's work with Hoheisel's constructions and trauma theory's characterization of trauma as non-assimilable with recent philosophical considerations of evil and suffering, Boynton offers a fundamentally different approach to commemoration. His claim is that Hoheisel's attempt to bring to presence that which is essentially absent opens up an alternative approach to evil and trauma issuing from the perspective of absence and loss, thereby granting the failure of therapeutic techniques an ethical significance.

Eric Severson's chapter considers how Levinas utilizes "trauma" to refer to the pre-original unsettling of the auto-identification of the ego, a project that takes center stage in his final masterwork, *Otherwise than Being*. Building from Plato's Allegory of the Cave and Heidegger's work on unconcealment, he argues that whereas for Heidegger and Plato trauma occurs through unconcealment of sensation, for Levinas trauma occurs as an interruption of sensation's appropriation into perception itself. His contribution focuses principally on the event itself, the encounter with the other, which at times he calls "inspiration" instead of trauma, and the way this event occurs in a time-before-time that initiates the very possibility of responsibility.

In the second section, Tina Chanter, George Yancy, Ronald Eyerman, and Peter Capretto interrogate what strategies might aid social discourse in the humanities to resist the pervasive tendency of politically entrenching traumatic encounters within racial, moral, and psychological categories that exacerbate their violence. Tina Chanter's chapter explores the context of Rancière's critique of Lyotard, particularly regarding the attenuation of any sense to trauma that accumulates a privileged status for its singular event. It is, in effect, deeply attentive to and critical of the question: "If everyone is traumatized, what specific meaning remains for trauma?" In highlighting Rancière's resistance to the absolutization of the other in politics and art, and Lyotard's tendency to turn alterity into the unrepresentable, the unassimilable, and the unthinkable, Chanter contends that the consequences for trauma theory are precisely what Rancière forebodes with the appropriation of the sublime: For all its talk of art witnessing that which is unrepresentable—and the holocaust as the unrepresentable per se—the ethical turn only manages to rejoin a discourse of purism.

In his chapter, George Yancy theorizes racialization as an interstitial process that becomes a site of trauma, wounding, and felt terror of both symbolic and existential annihilation. In the context of white supremacy, white privilege, and white power, he argues that whiteness functions as the transcendental norm that obfuscates its own racialization and normative constitution vis-à-vis Blackness, thereby marking the Black body within the socio-political matrix as "dangerous," "evil," "suspicious," and "disposable." The experience of trauma thus is the result of a violation and violence that attempts to reduce Black people to a state of pure facticity, the very absence of transcendence, where Black alterity is reduced to the white racist imago. By contextualizing the historical backdrop of anti-Black racism through the examples of Trayvon Martin, Eric Garner, Tamir Rice, and his personal experience with racial hate speech, Yancy demonstrates how the Black body has undergone a long and enduring history of racialized somatic trauma.

Through a sociological exploration of the My Lai Massacre as one of the significant atrocities of the American war in Vietnam, Ron Eyerman's chapter draws attention to an aspect of trauma easily overlooked in social analyses: the social pressure to individualize guilt and restrict any attempt to collectivize responsibility. With special attention to the traumatic character of the event of My Lai, his chapter introduces and develops perpetrator trauma as the moral injury that occurs when individuals and collectives feel they have acted in ways contrary to deeply held moral beliefs; as such, Eyerman contends that the mass murder of Vietnamese civilians at My Lai must be understood as traumatic among perpetrators as well, given its unquestionable shattering of individual and collective identity.

Responding to the double bind of the impossibility of witnessing and the necessity of advocating on behalf of survivors, Peter Capretto's chapter analyzes the potential problem in trauma theory of fetishizing the traumatic lived experiences of others. This begins with the examination of Freud's psychoanalytic understanding of the psychic economy of trauma and Heidegger's phenomenological critique of the concept of lived experience. Through this, Capretto argues that trauma theorists in philosophy and religion must be attentive to the fetishization of the traumatic lived experience of others, wherein the impossibility of satisfying the ethical demand of witnessing is replaced with one's proximity to the more visceral and embodied experience. That is, more quotidian attention to our psychic motivation supplements the transcendent task of conceptually understanding the psychic exteriority of others in trauma, thereby elevating the ethical standards the continental philosophy of religion sets for social research into trauma.

In the third section, theologians Shelly Rambo, Marcia Mount Shoop, and Hilary Jerome Scarsella reflect on how religious and Christian metaphysics work within the limits of their semantic, embodied, and violent histories while also pursuing the theological task of preparing the way for healing and recovery from trauma. Rambo's essay opens this section by examining the connection between poetics and transcendence in light of new trajectories of trauma studies and growing literatures in theopoetics. She argues that while many theologians recognize their work as situated within a "post-traumatic" context, poetics remains a more elusive challenge for trauma theology. Building from the insights of Rebecca Chopp on testimony and literary pedagogical theories of poetics, Rambo predicts that trauma will become the context out of which theology is done, poetics will be its new form, and transcendence will be rewritten in the process.

Using Christian theology's ambivalent historical relationship with embodiment as her point of departure, Marcia Mount Shoop examines the practical theological potential that embodied spiritual practices offer for healing after trauma. She argues that even as many core Christian institutions resist the incarnational symmetry between embodied practice and Christian theological professions, bodies explore and embrace healing modalities at the margins of Christian practice. Using the emerging wisdom of four particular healing explorations along the margins of Christian institutional life, Shoop's chapter explores the contours of Christian spiritual practices that fold out of trauma by attending to the possibilities for institutional transformation around trauma.

The recurrent problems of healing and retraumatization within theological contexts extend into the section's final chapter by Hilary Jerome Scarsella. There, Scarsella notes that, because the discipline of Christian theology is itself formed around the traumatic narrative of Jesus's crucifixion, investigating trauma in order to provide useful accompaniment to trauma survivors is theology's starting point, not merely a secondary interest. Holding the narrative of crucifixion at its center, her chapter asks whether a discipline constructed in response to traumatic rupture is bound to exacerbate systems of retraumatization or has the potential to empower trauma survivors toward recovery. Building upon the scholarship of late twentieth- and twenty-first-century womanist, feminist, and mujerista theologians and the significant risk of retraumatization, Scarsella engages contemporary psychoanalytic trauma theorists to argue that theology's strength with respect to trauma and contribution to the interdisciplinary task of supporting trauma survivors is its potential as a holding space for diverse stories of both traumatic rupture and recovery.

Because of the connections this volume and its scholars draw between trauma theory, philosophy, and religion, Mary Jane Rubenstein's afterword responds to the implications and prospects this volume poses to the continental philosophy of religion. With a particular eye toward the contemporary trends and future problems facing her discipline, Rubenstein's piece not only offers a capstone to this volume and its contributions, but more explicitly connects its labor and insights to the limits and prospects that face the philosophy of religion as it takes trauma as a serious subject of inquiry. Perhaps most importantly, because this volume was conceptualized and its chapters were written prior to the 2016 U.S. Presidential election, Rubenstein's afterword offers a brief but crucial reflection on a political event that many have experienced as traumatic for countless reasons. Like her, the editors recognize that the election has indeed changed the landscape of our scholarship in unforeseeable ways, particularly for those committed to reflecting on trauma.

The projects across the three areas return to roots and seminal moments in the authors' disciplinary considerations on trauma, parsing out the under-theorized traps that risk stagnating future efforts across their fields. The collection of the scholars as a whole and the structure of the sections in particular connect the interdisciplinary reader in trauma theory with overlapping but adjacent research on these shared limitations. One ambition of the volume is to point out the trends toward insularity within the humanities and social theory around discussions of trauma—a phenomenon owned by no discipline—and to create a forum for scholars to think the prospects and limitations of trauma theory in the humanities.

NOTES

1. Jacques Derrida, *Points: Interviews 1974–1994*, ed. Elizabeth Weber, (Stanford: Stanford University Press, 1992); Jacques Derrida, *Aporias*, trans. Thomas Dutoit, (Stanford: Stanford University Press, 1993); Jacques Derrida, *The Gift of Death*, trans. David Willis (Chicago: Chicago University Press, 1995); Jacques Derrida, *Hospitality, Justice, Responsibility* in *Question-*

ing Ethics: Contemporary Debates in Philosophy, ed. Mark Dooley and Richard Kearney, 65–82 (New York: Routledge, 1992); Jacques Derrida and Anne Dufourmantelle, *Of Hospitality*, trans. Rachel Bowlby (Stanford: Stanford University Press, 2000); Jacques Derrida, *The Work of Mourning*, ed. Pascale-Anne Brault and Michal Naas (Chicago: Chicago University Press, 2001); Jacques Derrida and Maurizio Ferraris, *A Taste for the Secret* (London: Polity, 2001).

2. Cathy Caruth, *Trauma: Explorations in Memory* (Baltimore: Johns Hopkins University Press, 1995); Cathy Caruth, *Unclaimed Experience: Trauma, Narrative, and History* (Baltimore: Johns Hopkins Press, 1996).

3. Judith Herman, *Trauma and Recovery: The Aftermath of Violence—from Domestic Abuse to Political Terror* (New York: Basic Books, 1997).

4. Shoshana Felman and Dori Laub, *Testimony: Crises of Witnessing in Literature, Psychoanalysis, and History* (New York: Routledge, 1992).

5. Cathy Caruth, Introduction to *Trauma: Explorations in Memory*, ed. Cathy Caruth (Baltimore: Johns Hopkins University Press, 1995), 4.

6. Ann Kaplan, *Trauma Culture: The Politics of Terror and Loss in Media and Literature* (New Brunswick, N.J.: Rutgers University Press, 2005), 69.

7. Thomas Elsaesser, "Postmodernism as Mourning Work," in "Trauma and Screen Studies: Opening the Debate," *Screen* 42, no. 2 (2001), 201.

8. Sigmund Freud, *New Introductory Lectures on Psycho-Analysis*, trans. and ed. James Strachey (New York: Norton, 1965), 210.

9. See, for example, Robert Gibbs, *Correlations: Rosenzweig and Levinas* (Princeton: Princeton University Press, 1992), 4.

10. With the figure of Levinas looming large in this discussion, a thinker such as Jacques Derrida, in his own way, has begun to approach the "impossible" site with reference to the religious and at times baldly in a theological idiom. See, for example, Jacques Derrida, "Force of Law: The 'Mystical Foundation of Authority,'" in *Deconstruction and the Possibility of Justice*, ed. Cornell, et al., trans. Mary Quaintance (New York, Routledge, 1992); Jacques Derrida, *Specters of Marx: The State of Debt, the Work of Mourning and the New International*, trans. Peggy Kamuf (New York: Routledge, 1994); Jacques Derrida, *The Gift of Death*; Jacques Derrida, "Faith and Knowledge: The Two Sources of 'Religion' at the Limits of Reason Alone," in *Religion*, ed. Gianni Vattimo and Jacques Derrida (Stanford: Stanford University Press, 1998).

11. Adrian Peperzak, "Giving," in *The Enigma of Gift and Sacrifice*, ed. Edith Wyschogrod, Jean-Joseph Goux, and Eric Boynton (New York: Fordham University Press, 2002), 162–63.

12. Peperzak, "Giving," 162–63.

13. Søren Kierkegaard, *Fear and Trembling*, trans. and ed. Howard V. Hong and Edna V. Hong (Princeton: Princeton University Press, 1983), 120.

With Hegel in his sights, Kierkegaard claims that this "position cannot be mediated, for all mediation takes place only by virtue of the universal; it is and remains for all eternity a paradox, impervious to thought. And yet faith is this paradox, or else [. . .] Abraham is lost" (Kierkegaard, 56).

14. See Kierkegaard, *Fear and Trembling*, 53. He contends that no thought can grasp the paradox of faith that "makes murder into a holy and God-pleasing act [. . .] because faith begins precisely where thought stops." Compare this to John D. Caputo and Michael J. Scanlon, Introduction to *God, the Gift, and Postmodernism*, ed. John D. Caputo and Michael J. Scanlon, 1–20 (Bloomington: Indiana University Press, 1999), 4. Caputo and Scanlon argue that Derrida's recent work is seeking out an alterity expressed religiously: "*Deconstruction is structured like a religion*. Like a *prayer* and tear for the coming of the wholly other (*tout autre*), for something impossible, like a messianic prayer in a messianic religion [. . .]. Like a *faith* in the coming of something we cannot quite make out, a blind faith where knowledge fails and faith is what we have to go on, which even believes in ghosts or specters." See a similar description in Caputo, *The Prayers and Tears of Jacques Derrida: Religion without Religion* (Bloomington: Indiana University Press, 1997), xxi–xxvi.

15. Proposing the impossibility of philosophy of religion, Marion states: "The field of religion could simply be defined as what philosophy excludes or, in the best case, subjugates. [. . .] The 'philosophy of religion,' if there were one, would have to describe, produce, and constitute phenomena, it would then find itself confronted with a disastrous alternative: either it would be a question of phenomena that are objectively definable but lose their religious specificity, or it would be a question of phenomena that are specifically religious but cannot be described objectively" (Jean-Luc Marion, "The Saturated Phenomenon," trans. Thomas A. Carlson, *Philosophy Today* 40 [1996]: 103). Philosophy of religion either consigns religious phenomena to a faith that knows not of what it speaks or constitutes them as phenomenon simply known, unless, for Marion, a broader range of "phenomena" are given the right to appear.

16. Derrida, "Faith and Knowledge," 21.

17. Derrida, "Faith and Knowledge," 58.

PART I

Constructive Phenomenologies of Trauma

Two Trauma Communities: A Philosophical Archaeology of Cultural and Clinical Trauma Theories

Vincenzo Di Nicola

Threshold—הַלְדָבַה—Havdalah: "Separation"

Open closed open. Before we are born everything is open in the universe without us. For as long as we live, everything is closed within us. And when we die, everything is open again. Open closed open. That's all we are.

YEHUDA AMICHAI[1]

Prologue: The Age of Trauma

In a catastrophic age, [. . .] trauma itself may provide the very link between cultures: not as a simple understanding of the pasts of others but rather, within the traumas of contemporary history, as our ability to listen through the departures we have all taken from ourselves.

CATHY CARUTH[2]

What has happened in our contemporary world such that the experiences of disaster and displacement, migration and exile, horror and terror, separation and loss, catastrophe and misfortune, humiliation and shame, "the nightmare of childhood" or "the state of exception," and other vicissitudes of life—what Freud called the discontents of civilization—have been reduced to the passive victimization subsumed under the rubric of trauma? Cultural trauma theorist Cathy Caruth calls it a catastrophic age. Why is our experience constructed this way in our time and why has trauma become the emblematic experience of contemporary life to the point that we may invoke the epithet "the age of trauma?"

It is difficult to characterize trauma as a unified discourse or as a spectrum, even within a given discursive formation such as psychoanalysis or psychiatry. The best strategy to find our way through this thicket of aporias is to discern a shifting, porous, and unstable dichotomy. The investigation of trauma in this chapter straddles both the clinical and cultural poles of this dichotomy; my task, in part, is to make each of them intelligible by placing them in their context through surveys of discourses and practices. In what follows, I describe the poles of this dichotomy under the rubrics of *aleph* and *beth*. While they are neither clearly delineated nor discrete, they offer a heuristic for understanding the *dichotomized* ways that trauma theorists approached the discourse at hand. This requires a different history of psychology and psychiatry and a different genealogy of trauma.

The age of trauma takes place in trauma's estate. To understand how trauma has become an emblematic clinical experience and trace its pervasive presence as cultural trauma, this chapter conducts a *philosophical archaeology* in the ruins of trauma's estate, excavating its many associated discourses and apparatuses.[3]

> Provisionally, we may call "archaeology" that practice which in any
> historical investigation has to do not with origins but with the moment
> of a phenomenon's arising and must therefore engage anew the sources
> and traditions.[4]

Philosophical archaeology allows us to discern the relationships among *rupture* (predicament, state of exception, evental site), *trauma* (the destruction of experience, of the possibility of experience), and *Event* (contingent, unpredictable, undecidable). I invoke the work of Giorgio Agamben and Alain Badiou to oppose trauma to Event, making an absolute distinction between them: trauma does not conduce to Event; Event does not arise from trauma. Human predicaments emerge in evental sites, where rupture occurs. Neither the rupture nor the predicament is predictable or decidable in advance. As trauma psychiatrist Lifton says of survivors of disasters and genocides, we may open out, porous and permeable to *novation*, or close down, emptied and evacuated, in a traumatized state.

By reading texts at the core of cultural trauma's preoccupations—fiction and poetry, memoirs and witnessing—through philosophy and critical theory, I illustrate how philosophical archaeology may approach and refresh our understanding of trauma. I contend that *trauma is not the generic name of a predicament or even of a particular experience but a generic name for the destruction of experience.* Yet it also offers keys for translation—if not paths of reconciliation—among the communities that address trauma and Event: those who hold by *trauma/Event* as a radical disjuncture, those who hope for a transformation of *trauma into Event*, and those who harbor the transcendent view of *trauma as Event*.

A Philosophical Archaeology of the Concept of "Trauma"

In her genealogy of trauma, Ruth Leys deploys *mimetic* and *antimimetic* theories of trauma.[5] From the perspective of cultural-intellectual history, Wulf Kansteiner, who cites Leys sympathetically, sees a *scientific–metonymic pole* and a *literary–metaphorical pole* of what he describes as a "trauma discourse spectrum."[6] Because "spectrum" suggests an underlying order, "dichotomy" or "dialectic" better captures the dynamic tensions among trauma discourses. Even that is only an approximate characterization as at times the two poles of a perceived dichotomy do not acknowledge or communicate with each other, as Kansteiner contends.

In their inquiry into the "empire of trauma," physician/social anthropologist Didier Fassin and psychiatrist/anthropologist Richard Rechtman trace a dual genealogy of "post-traumatic stress" which they characterize as being divided into *scientific* and *moral* strands. The scientific strand, in the domain of psychiatry, psychology, and psychoanalysis, addresses trauma both theoretically and in practice. The moral strand, related to social conceptions, "traces changes in attitudes to misfortune and to those who suffer it" and "towards the authenticity of such suffering."[7]

Fassin and Rechtman find the way these two strands interact most revealing. Posing a series of questions about how this occurred over time, across cultures, through disciplines and social discourses, they believe as I do that the key is in examining this dual genealogy at each crucial turning point. They see an underlying "*discontinuity* marked by the end of the historical era of suspicion that hung over victims of violence" (which I characterize as an epistemological shift away from the experiential cut of Karl

Jaspers' phenomenological psychiatry) and the more powerful *continuity* toward a moral affirmation of trauma as "the ultimate truth."[8]

In some articulations of trauma, these strands are so finely interwoven that separating them requires dexterity to discern the mesh of discourses and practices. This is the case with the influential presentation of cultural trauma by Caruth, which is criticized with precision and clarity by Wulf Kansteiner and Harald Weilnböck.[9] At times, the tissue falls apart in our hands as we do this work and we lose the very pattern we are trying to reveal.

A survey of the issues at stake in the history of academic psychology and psychiatry in defining trauma reveals that these revolve around: consciousness and phenomenology; the definition of the subject; and issues of language, memory, and representation. Consulting histories of psychology and psychiatry, we may eliminate the more partisan forays establishing sectarian claims. First, let us separate the history of madness from the history of psychiatry, which are not only two different maps, but altogether two different territories. For our purposes, the history of psychology revolves around the question of consciousness, both as a philosophical question and as a technical or methodological matter. The history of modern psychiatry, on the other hand, revolves around the crucial question of the experiential chasm, as Jaspers put it: Either we can or cannot cross an empathic bridge to understand psychosis, the most alienating experience that psychiatry had encountered at that time. And psychosis, constructed as schizophrenia, became in Angela Woods's resonant phrase, "the sublime object of psychiatry."[10]

We can line up all the approaches and contributions around this question: whether the subjective experience of psychosis is accessible to psychiatry or not. Those who agree with diagnostic categories (based on Kraepelinian *aetiopathology*—the so-called "medical model"—or Jaspers's *phenomenology* as a science of signs and symptoms) see a *phenomenological chasm* between the psychotic patient and the psychiatrist. Whereas those who are continually looking for other ways to understand alienating experiences (starting with Viktor Tausk's psychoanalytic interpretation of the "influencing machine") explicitly reject (as with R. D. Laing's social phenomenology) or reframe the question (as with John Watson's behaviorism or Gregory Bateson's systems theory).

With this map of the history of psychology and psychiatry, we may examine how another cut—rupture leading to trauma—is understood as psychopathology.

Trauma: A Confusion of Signifiers

It is an error to divide people into the living and the dead: there are people who are dead-alive, and people who are alive-alive. The dead-alive also write, walk, speak, act. But they make no mistakes, and they produce only dead things. The alive-alive are constantly in error, in search, in torment.

YEVGENY ZAMYATIN[11]

The psychiatry of trauma is the psychiatry of the "dead-alive" in Zamyatin's terms, of the "state of exception" and "bare life" in Agamben's philosophy,[12] and what Badiou calls the "reactive subject."[13] The discourse of psychic trauma is marked by a confusion of signifiers. There is a confusion among what we may separate conceptually into *predisposing, precipitating,* and *prolonging factors* of trauma, to which we may add *protective factors.* This is the model of the psychiatric formulation employing the biopsychosocial model. Furthermore, we need to separate direct, *immediate traumatic impacts* from delayed, latent, or *long-term consequences,* called *sequelae* in medical terms. Finally, we may call this schema a *trauma process.* The term process implies *diachronic* evolution over time with sequences and a *synchronic* interplay of factors at any given moment in time.[14] Thus, we may usefully separate the traumatic process into these factors: (1) predisposing traumatic contexts or situations that place individuals at risk—we may call these *distal determinants,* such as causes and influences; (2) precipitating traumatic triggers are *proximal determinants*; (3) prolonging factors amplify, augment, or extend the traumatic process synchronically or diachronically; (4) protective factors dampen, diminish or mitigate the traumatic process.

The key question then becomes: What makes trauma *traumatic*? Is it the threat that something hurtful may happen, the experience of the injury itself, or living with the consequences of the threat of injury? Which aspect is the trauma and which traumatic? Is this conflation of predisposing, precipitating, and perpetuating factors normal? Is this typical in medicine or psychiatry? Infections work like this; "flu," the common term for *influenza* means the virus, getting infected and suffering with the symptoms. Nonetheless, the very notion of medical progress means the clear identification of different phases of a disease process and its determinants. These are the psychiatric questions.

In philosophical terms, we need a vocabulary for what Agamben calls "desubjectivation"—the "dead-alive" (Zamyatin), "bare life" (Agamben), and "states of dissociation,"[15] but we also need to open space for what Foucault called "subjectivation"—for the Event and for the faithful subject, as Badiou has described them.[16] This distinction opens only the first of many dichotomies that emerge in every trauma discourse. In the onomasiology (from Greek, ὀνομάζω onomāzo, "to name") of trauma—how we name trauma—we encounter dichotomies and bivalent notions throughout.

A Dichotomy in Trauma Theories

I think that many philosophers secretly harbor the view that there is something deeply (i.e., conceptually) wrong with psychology, but a philosopher with a little training in the techniques of linguistic analysis and a free afternoon could straighten it out.
                                              JERRY FODOR[17]

At first sight, Caruth thus appears to define trauma in ways that are quite compatible with psychological research on trauma and post-traumatic stress. However, unlike most of her contemporaries who study the vicissitudes of mental suffering in a clinical context, Caruth goes on to celebrate the experience and the concept of trauma as providing unprecedented insight into the human condition.
                        WULF KANSTEINER AND HARALD WEILNBÖCK[18]

Two opinions emerge over cross-disciplinary research: One is from a philosopher who, true to the linguistic or analytic tradition, unveils the belief that some clear thinking can resolve the conceptual problems of a field like psychology. Jerry Fodor's self-deprecatory remark reflects the thinking of many empirically oriented psychologists and psychiatrists. Continental philosophers describe them as positivists although these same empiricists would update the term with the concept of "the evidence" (as in "evidence-based medicine").[19] The other opinion, more strongly expressed by two historians, is that literary and cultural theorists (including philosophers) who are not trained in clinical work and do not read psychotherapeutic literature carefully, have conflated "the traumatic and the non-traumatic, the exceptional and the everyday" and even "obfuscate the essential difference between the victims and perpetrators of extreme violence."[20] In my prologue, I observed that we cannot characterize trauma as a unified discourse or as a spectrum even with one discipline. What seems to bring conceptual order to the concept of trauma and to trauma studies is to *discern a dichotomy* as a separator or marker that divides the discourses along different axes and conceptualizations. This is a *meta-concept* that creates two groups, or two poles, around which certain notions or studies or emerging traditions congeal. Yet any given separator that creates a dichotomy is itself shifting, porous, and unstable.

In describing two theories of trauma she names *mimetic* and *antimimetic* theories, Ruth Leys lucidly demonstrates that "from the turn of the century to the present there has been a continual oscillation between them, indeed that the interpenetration of one by the other or alternatively the collapse of one into the other has been recurrent and unstoppable."[21] Furthermore, she notes that historically, the *mimetic/antimimetic* dichotomy constantly invites and defeats all attempts to resolve it. Leys predicts that our current debates are "fated to end in an impasse."[22]

Leys's genealogy becomes part of the *meta-concept of trauma*, such that her mimetic/antimimetic dichotomy confirms the notion of a dichotomy but does not exhaust it. Other dichotomies come into play and while we can separate their poles, they do not match evenly with each other and are sometimes even incongruent and incompatible. What I appreciate most about Leys's analysis is her conclusion that trauma has a historical structure, an idea that is congruent with Foucault's notion of a discursive formation or *épistémè*. Trauma, as a concept or theory with its associated practices, has become an apparatus. In *The Order of Things*, Foucault invokes "points of heresy"[23]—described by Étienne Balibar as opposing disciplines within an *épistémè* or paradigm that form a structured opposition.[24]

Not only has "trauma" been constructed and deployed as an apparatus describing something we want to name and explain, but as Kansteiner and Leys emphasize, it is hard not to reach for this apparatus as an explanatory model, with all its conflations and confusions. Secondly, Leys convincingly demonstrates that the two theories are intertwined not only *across* theories but *within* each individual theory or group of researchers. In concluding, Leys acknowledges the intractability of the dichotomy and eschews a meta-position from which one can assess the aporias that she sees as intrinsic to this field.

My meta-concept places Leys's approach within a larger one: Hers is one dichotomy among others. This is not to say that we can take a stand above the dichotomy but that if we see it as an apparatus, which is a discourse with a strategic function, we can discern that it functions not as one dichotomy, but an *epistemological cut* in any possible discourse about trauma. We see this in the bivalence of crucial terms in this archaeology, from the word "trauma" itself and the metaphors used to describe it, to the ways in which "wound" is deployed in Western culture. From Achilles's spear that both cuts and heals,[25] to Plato's *pharmakon*, which is both a poison and a remedy,[26] this bivalence reaches its apogee in the current cultural theory of trauma which I call *trauma as Event*.

Leys's analysis of a historically structured dichotomy and its repetition is a short step from Derrida's notions of *iterability* and *dissemination*.[27] Derrida's notion of iterabilility concerns *repetition* and *difference*—everything is a *trace*, a version of something else that both repeats and changes. Through dissemination, this process always creates a *supplement* to philosophy, both inextricable and intractible. In fact, I can think of no better examplar of Derrida's theory than Leys's repetitive, unresolvable mimetic/antimimetic dichotomy. Impregnated with traces and fostering supplementarity, the mimetic/antimimetic dichototomy continually disseminates.

Nonetheless, I eschew her pessimistic conclusion that it is intractable. Her advice is to be pragmatic and that clinicians should not fuss over an exact fit between theory and practice. While this is practical, as a clinician I maintain that there must be a minimal coherence in our interventions and as a philosopher I hold that it is provided by theory. The alternative is a kind of blind empiricism or positivist science cobbling together practical tools with an eye on behavioral outcomes and little regard for scientific merit on one hand and for subjectivity and meaning on the other.

The dichotomy in trauma theories will be intractable insofar as we unwittingly repeat it, a point Leys makes lucidly by observing that each generation rediscovers the notion of traumatic stress. Once we are aware of trauma as an apparatus, we may more consciously entertain other theories, as Kansteiner suggests, by finding a new lexicon for trauma.

Kansteiner calls for "low-density" psychological concepts that "avoid the moral and existential excess of the trauma claim," hoping that greater conceptual precision will allow us to differentiate between trauma and the culture of trauma.[28] Kansteiner wants to interrupt what philosopher Ian Hacking calls "looping effects" between professional and public or cultural discourses.[29]

My own proposal is more nuanced but also stronger and is the heart of my thesis. First, I believe that trauma has accrued a *supplementarity* or *excess* (echoing both Derrida and Kansteiner here). This supplementarity is "overdetermined," as Freud would say, or more simply, multiply determined. I suspect that a great proportion of the variation may be attributed precisely to the "looping effects" between the clinical use of trauma and its cultural avatar. Second, I believe that we must separate the various ways in which the word trauma is deployed and differentiate our vocabulary for these different aspects of the trauma process. Third, and most salient, I believe that trauma must be separated radically from Event, which is the subtext of cultural trauma theory.

Dichotomising Trauma

With this introduction, let us now examine some of the characteristics of the trauma trope according to two columns or groupings of dichotomies: *aleph* and *beth*. The reason that I do not simply offer a definition at the outset is to reveal the armature of the construction of the concept and how it is deployed as an apparatus. We need to know the structure of the armature so that when we examine what is built around it, we know why it has the shape it does. The list includes my characterizations of major contributors to trauma studies.

What this representative but not exhaustive survey demonstrates is that the word *trauma* has become too broad and inclusive, too vague and unfixed, too (am)bivalent and polysemous, too deterministic and fatalistic an idea. All the other descriptors set the stage for an emblem to emerge that then binds them into an explanatory notion; once an emblem appears, it retrospectively creates its own precursors, in the well-known process Freud called *Nachträglichkeit*, belatedness or deferred meaning, which Lacan crafted as *après-coup*. And while it is true that *trauma* also invokes the inverse of these terms, its deployment as a trope reveals fissures and contradictions that one term cannot contain.

As we see in the epigraphs from Fodor and Kansteiner and Weilnböck, most scholars read each other's domains but harbor strong opinions about their claims. Working on the threshold between disciplines I hear such confessions all the time. This is no less true for trauma studies. Philosophers such as Badiou do not believe that empiricism will resolve the aporias of ontology and many other domains, and he is dismissive of number crunching in medicine.[30] Culturally responsive researchers hold that empirical studies will clarify the picture of trauma, by conducting qualitative research with sophisticated methodologies that reach into subjective experience (for example, experience sampling methods) and personal narratives and are suspicious of what they see as abstract (read "distant") philosophical reflections.

The tension is not just between ontology and phenomenology. We could take the theme of trauma (or Event) and unspool a thread throughout all the major thinkers of the continental tradition (accepting this somewhat arbitrary classification with the caveats that Critchley enunciates in his treatment of the subject).[31] From psychoanalysis to phenomenology,

א—Aleph	ב—Beth
Oligosemia, asemia (Concreteness, loss of meaning and expression)	*Polysemia[a] (Sensory and expressive overload)*
Broad	Narrow
Vague, unfixed	Rigidly defined
Ambiguous	Clear
Subjective experience	Objective experience
Illness as metaphor	Metaphor as illness
Victims as emblems of social or political preoccupations	Phenomenological descriptions of victims' experiences
Resilience	Vulnerability
Process	Outcome
Vicarious traumatization	Direct exposure
Sequential traumatization	Discrete incidents, without accumulation
Freudian legacy	Kraepelinian legacy
Psychoanalysis	Psychiatry
Trauma as event	Event as trauma
Mimetic	*Antimimetic[b]*
Threat is incorporated	Purely external incident
Identification with aggressor	Assault from without
Response is determined by other life experiences	Response due to characteristics of traumatic incident
Doubts about veracity	Trauma victim not complicit in her trauma
Victim's status as witness doubted	Victim is aloof, a spectator of her trauma
Shatters or disables cognitive and perceptual apparatuses	Victim can see and represent the experience to herself and others
Memory doubtful	Memory preserved
Hermeneutic understanding	Positivist/scientist explanation
Difficult to recover memories	Memory of the incident recoverable
Object relations model	*Psycho-economic model[c]*
Collapse of internal object relations	Excessive arousal
Breakdown of internal communication	Uncontainable anxiety breaks through the stimulus barrier
The experience of total abandonment precludes integration of trauma by narrative means	"Pure trauma" which is "nameless"
Special class of "man-made disasters" such as the Holocaust, war, ethnic persecution, torture aims to annihilate historical-social existence	Naming trauma is a historicization after the fact; the analytic task is to recognize such screen memories and reconstruct the authentic story

Literary-metaphoric pole	*Scientific-metonymic pole[d]*
Cultural trauma	Psychological, psychotherapeutic conception of trauma
Lack of historical and moral precision	Historically informed accounts
Aestheticizes violence	Recognizes suffering
Conflates experiences (victims, perpetrators, spectators)	Accurate distinctions among those involved in trauma
Moral	*Scientific[e]*
Social conceptions	Psychiatry, psychology, psychoanalysis
Trauma as the ultimate truth	Discontinuity/era of suspicion

Dominick LaCapra	
Everyday psychological challenges	Extraordinary psychological ordeals of extreme violence

Lloyd deMause	*Philippe Ariès*
Childhood is a nightmare	Childhood is a cultural invention

Alice Miller	*Freud*
Ubiquitous childhood violence	Childhood sexual seduction is a fantasy

Richard Mollica	
Witnessing the trauma story	Traumatic experiences of everyday life
Resilience, self-healing of victims	

[a] The descriptors in these two columns are based on my reading. These are my terms: *oligosemia*, diminished meaning, and *asemia*, loss of meaning (seen in trauma literature as concreteness, loss of meaning and expression); *polysemia*, multiple meaning or surfeit of meaning (describing sensory and expressive overload).
[b] Ruth Leys, *Trauma: A Genealogy*.
[c] These are the key models in current psychoanalytic trauma theories. See Werner Bohleber, "The Development of Trauma Theory in Psychoanalysis," in *Destructiveness, Intersubjectivity, and Trauma: The Identity Crisis of Modern Psychoanalysis* (London: Karnac, 2010).
[d] Kanstainer, "Genealogy of a Category Mistake."
[e] Fassin and Rechtman, *The Empire of Trauma*.

from neo-Kantians to critical theorists, from post-modernism to post-colonialism, from feminism to cultural studies—everyone has something to say about trauma. The thoughts about trauma are rich, nuanced, allusive, suggestive, sometimes contradictory and enigmatic but quickly polarize in any discussion.

Leys has documented her thesis well, showing a dichotomy of trauma theories based on imitation or mimesis. Again, her analysis is powerful but not exhaustive. My greatest concern, however, is that *trauma* is too pre-conceived and, ultimately, too emblematic a condition. The fact that there are *mimetic* and *antimimetic* features within most theories belies the probability that this is the single differentiator. My argument is that complex, heterogeneous phenomena are bound to pique our interest and a wish to bring order to them. Sometimes, the order we perceive is a pragmatic heuristic to guide our thinking, like Wittgenstein's ladder that is used to climb then discarded. When we consider the emotional intensity of the subject of trauma and the social, academic, and political investments in trauma as an apparatus, meaning that it serves a strategic function, that renders it still more complex.

It is important to point out that most complex phenomena can be broken down into two or more groups, yet the question is to what extent does such a schema explain the phenomena in causal terms (this translates into the positivist values of reliability, predictability, and control), how does it advance a broader understanding on the level of meaning, and is it a practical plan for action? Several of the contributors cited address the practical or therapeutic aspects of a given conception of trauma. Leys does so explicitly, as does Kansteiner on a therapeutic level. Fassin and Rechtman address broader questions about social and public policy in terms of trauma victims as witnesses for such things as recognition of their status as sufferers and gaining refugee status. We could add the dimension of compensation and indemnification of victims of torture, violence, and genocide. Surprisingly, some commentators are transparently indifferent to the treatment of victims of trauma because they valorize the trauma trope on a cultural-symbolic level, concerned with philosophical or historical truths. Manfred Weinberg is cited as an example by Kansteiner and Weilnböck.[32] Again, the list items do not line up with complete coherence as they articulate different pivots or separators in different domains.

Threshold—הֲדִיקָע—The Akedah: The "Binding" of Isaac

Abraham made everything ready for the sacrifice, calmly and quietly, but as he turned away Isaac saw that Abraham's left hand was clenched in anguish, that a shudder went through his body—but Abraham drew the knife.

Then they turned home again and Sarah ran to meet them, but Isaac had lost his faith. Never a word in the whole world is said of this, and Isaac told no one what he had seen, and Abaham never suspected than anyone had seen it.

SØREN KIERKEGAARD[33]

John Gerassi: And Kierkegaard? [. . .] How did you react to god ordering Abraham to kill his son?

JPS: Not as I was supposed to. To me god was the state ordering its
subject to do as told.
JEAN-PAUL SARTRE IN CONVERSATION WITH JOHN GERASSI[34]

"Isaac-Machine"—The Akedah *as Apparatus for Children's Trauma*

One of my concerns in working with children and trauma is the use of
children as *emblems* of adult preoccupations. This is my rule of thumb:
The more that is said about abstract *childhood* and *development*, the less attention is given to *actual children* and their *growth*. A corollary is the use of
childhood and *development* as *metaphors*.[35] The word "development," along
with words such as "culture," "ideology," and "trauma," is among the most
complex words in European languages.[36] Neither illnesses nor stages of life
are properly understood metaphorically.[37] This approach risks the expropriation of experience and difference.

Teleological thinking, that is thinking about something in terms of its
end-state whether as a purpose, goal, or simply as an outcome, is particularly precarious with children. One of the great problems with the notion
of *resilience* is that we tend to value the outcome over the process, such
that the adult outcome is given more weight than the child's lived experience. In my reading of three novels about children during war[38] and Primo
Levi's account of the child Hurbinek in Auschwitz,[39] notions such as Adélia
Prado's *desdobravel*, "unfolding,"[40] and Agamben's *potenza*, "potentiality,"[41]
offer valuable alternatives to imagine children's experiences.

Two other issues with children are especially salient. One concerns
vicarious trauma. Can children be traumatized indirectly by witnessing
trauma? The hypothesis is that their attachment to caregivers renders
them more at risk to be indirectly traumatized if their caregivers are directly traumatized. The gamut includes being hurt in the same incident,
witnessing the incident against a caregiver, or having the incident about a
caregiver recounted to them.[42] Psychological and philosophical questions
include whether this is a question of dependency on adult caregivers, attachment processes between and among significant persons in the life of
the child, and empathy for the pain and suffering of others. These are far
from resolved and my review of this literature reveals a stark problematic:
Our current models of attachment, development, and empathy are woe-
fully inadequate. On the issue of development, the term has lost value as a

research question and we need other conceptions to understand children's emotional, cognitive, and philosophical growth.[43] Agamben's work is very intriguing and promising here: A subtext of much of his work has been language, *potenza*, infancy and indeterminacy, the threshold between *arthron* and *phone*.[44]

Finally, a crucial question with children concerns *sequential traumatization*.[45] Is it a single, overwhelming incident or traumatic context that triggers a traumatic response, or a series? Do they accumulate? Are there sleeper effects that lie latent, only to be expressed or become symptomatic later? Do they amplify each other? Are there mitigating factors that dampen the likelihood of a traumatic outcome? Is there a particular sequence of incidents or factors that is salient in some way for a given child? On the other hand, is each day a new life? Should we understand the child more in terms of his lifeworld in a social web at a given moment and concentrate on the relationships and incidents at that moment? Single incident or a series? A cross-section of the child's life now or over time? Some of these questions have been addressed in the historical and public health research discussed later.

We may add other concepts and theories of children's trauma to our list. There is a strong debate about the history of childhood and the family. In *Centuries of Childhood*, Philippe Ariès articulated the thesis that until the Enlightenment and modernity, children lived in a more undifferentiated state of being in a supposed golden age of family and social relationships in Europe. Ariès argued that childhood as a distinct phase of life was a relatively recent discovery in the West.[46] We could say that Ariès did for childhood and its allied institutions, the family and the school, what Foucault did for the clinic and the prison. Lloyd deMause attacked this thesis vehemently with his work on the history of childhood: "Ariès' thesis is the opposite of mine [. . .] a special condition known as childhood was 'invented' in the early modern period, resulting in a tyrannical concept of the family which destroyed friendship and sociability and deprived children of freedom."[47] DeMause called for historical research on the "untold story of child abuse."[48] In this view, there was never a golden age of childhood, children having been abused and punished since antiquity. I trace the origins of this story to the founding myth of the Judeo-Christian tradition, the *Akedah*, or "binding," of Isaac. In this story, when Isaac is bound on an altar for sacrifice by his father Abraham at God's command, an angel intervenes with the injunction, "Lay not thine hand upon the lad."[49] "Isaac-Machine" is the name we give to an apparatus that generates the myth of Isaac's sacrifice.[50] An *apparatus* is defined as something with "the capacity to capture, orient, determine, intercept, model, control, or secure the gestures, behaviors, opinions, or discourses of living beings."[51] Our collective unwillingness to recognize this social history was reflected in Freud's denial of sexual abuse as the sexual fantasies of his female patients.

The study of the relation between childhood adversity and its sequelae would have to wait a century for the pioneering study of adverse childhood experiences by Vincent Felitti and associates. The study "found a strong graded relationship between the breadth of exposure to abuse or household dysfunction during childhood and multiple risk factors for several of the leading causes of death in adults."[52] Furthermore, the "seven categories of adverse childhood experiences were strongly interrelated and persons with multiple categories of childhood exposure were likely to have multiple health risk factors later in life."[53] These results address the questions posed in the preceding paragraph about sequential traumatization and the cumulative effect of adverse events. This study spawned a cottage industry of research and reflection on the medical and mental health consequences of adverse childhood events and on health risk behaviors.

א—Aleph—*Trauma as a Trope*

One way to make sense of this, a hypothesis of the order of Leys's mimetic/antimimetic dichotomy, is to see the *aleph* list as the Freudian legacy.[54] Clearly, the positivistic sciences of academic psychology and psychiatry, which seek objective empirical data for causal explanations, could not tolerate this. This happens repeatedly in these fields—a creative and gifted clinician or scholar has an insight and then the "researchers," the accountants and bookkeepers of the academy, come along and define and research the idea to death.[55] The *beth* list is the Kraepelinian legacy. Narrower, more pathological in its discernments, neo-Kraepelinian psychiatry draws a sharp line between health and disease (if the investigator is biologically-oriented or given to evolutionary psychology, both of which favor categorical thinking) or health and illness (if the investigator is more given to the social sciences and a hermeneutic, socio-cultural or narrative approach).

It is also of note that this dichotomy reflects a split in psychiatry/psychoanalysis between the French and the American traditions.[56] In both traditions, trauma is an apparatus in Agamben's sense of the term. Each of these approaches engenders risks. Using trauma as a cultural trope means we have lost the specificity, the distinctness of the term. It no longer is simply the name of something, pointing to that something. It becomes a condition, an emblem of its own. It becomes reified.

As an apparatus, trauma is a rupture or cut, emblematic of many other types of cuts. Trauma as a psychiatric disorder is also an apparatus, an apparatus in a different discourse—it is a different kind of cut. Psychiatric trauma implies a dual cut: It conceives of a cut within subjective experience and places the subject herself in a different category across a chasm between trauma and normal experience. This is Jaspers's phenomenological cut—the chasm between the patient's experience and the psychiatrist's experience—and his lasting legacy. He single-handedly shaped and changed psychiatry. Ultimately, this is what R. D. Laing confronted in psychiatry in trying to bridge the chasm established within psychiatry about the nature of schizophrenia. His entire *oeuvre* may be understood this way. What is relevant from his work at this juncture are these thoughts from Laing's text: "The term schizoid refers to an individual the totality of whose experience is split in two main ways: in the first place, there is a rent in his relation with his world and, in the second, there is a disruption of his relation with himself."[57] In describing the dual rent or rupture of the schizoid experience, Laing offers an uncanny mirror of currrent descriptions of trauma. In fact, just as Leys despairs of resolving the rift in the mimetic/antimimetic dichotomy she delineated, Laing objected that the technical vocabulary of psychiatry "consists of words which split man up verbally in a way which is analogous to the existential splits we have to describe here."[58] Laing also remarked that no view of the person as a unitary whole existed in the language of psychiatry or psychoanalysis to address the existential splits he described. Now, whereas historian Leys does not perceive this possibility, another historian Kansteiner does in his suggestion of finding "low-density" psychological concepts. As a clinician, I believe this project worthwhile and promising.

ב—Beth—*PTSD Is a Psychiatric Disorder*

The *beth* list,[59] as already noted, is the Kraepelinian legacy: more defined, more circumscribed, a more objective etic description in anthropological terms.[60] This list has become the domain of Post-Traumatic Stress Disorder (PTSD) studies by academic psychiatry and psychology, and all that they imply. There are debates within this camp: "conceptual bracket creep" is a key one. Precisely because this approach wants to define criteria and use them for both theoretical and practical clarity in diagnosis and research, loose boundaries of the criteria whereby the brackets keep expanding (so-called "bracket creep") to accommodate more possible types of trauma is a conceptual threat.[61] As a response, psychiatry has created the concept of "complex PTSD" for really severe cases. This demonstrates Leys's thesis once again: Each pole reacts defensively to maintain its position and defeat resolution of the dichotomy.

Several more dichotomies are evident in the way that PTSD has been defined and deployed by the diagnostic manual of the American Psychiatric Association. The psychiatric approach emphasizes exposure to an extreme traumatic stressor that involves direct or indirect potential for serious injury or death to oneself or others. Initially (circa 1980), PTSD was constructed as a normal response to an abnormal situation and the stress was on the "trauma" (although clearly implied, the single term "trauma," meaning *traumatic insult, situation, or vector*, is not differentiated from *traumatic impact*, even today). Discussion of vulnerability factors was avoided as "blaming the victim." Just a decade later, given that most people do not develop PTSD in response to potentially traumatic incidents, specialists began to study differential responses. Rather than focus on the traumatizing incident or situation, research shifted to the qualities of the traumatized person. PTSD was declared psychopathology, a paradigm shift that clearly puts the study of trauma in the *beth* column as a psychiatric disorder, still considered exceptional but not because traumatic incidents are exceptional but because individuals who succumb are vulnerable. The most striking aspect of the definition of PTSD is that there are two distinct groups of signs and symptoms: One involves persistent vivid re-experiencing of the traumatic incident, the other is expressed in persistent fearful avoidance of the incident and everything associated with it, from thoughts to situations, accompanied by numbing, detachment, and withdrawal.[62]

This difference perceived in the clinical responses to extreme traumatic stressors is most puzzling. Either we have put together very different sorts of human experiences that might be better sorted out separately or, as Leys suggests, it is inherent in the nature of trauma and this generates the dichotomy she describes. While I see many other parallel dichotomies, my meta-concept is an observation of the bivalent history and deployment of the notion of trauma. It is difficult, therefore, to decide whether a dichotomy or cut is built into our way of perceiving or whether it is possible to establish by phenomenological (or other) methods what people experience in such predicaments to arrive at new ways of understanding trauma. I hold that it is exceedingly difficult to effect such changes by empirical studies, even with very sophisticated and nuanced ethnographic, context-sensitive methodologies. As we saw with the nineteenth-century notion of degeneration, trauma too will pass.[63] Theory, clinical practice, and social discourses interact in such complex ways, including Althusser's lacunar discourse, Foucault's épistémè and apparatus, Agamben's paradigm, Hacking's looping effect, and my notion of nested hegemonies (a complex apparatus whereby parallel or contradictory discourses coexist and subtly reinforce each other[64]), that trauma remains unpredictable, and in its current configuration, undecidable.

The notion of "looping effects" described by Hacking addresses the intertwined nature of theories of trauma. Looping effects are the reciprocal influences between discourses and apparatuses.[65] Hacking gives the example of diagnoses, which are created and used in practice: The patient identifies with the diagnosis and interacts with it, and this in turn loops back to the clinician. Repeated many times in a community, this looping exchange between professional and public discourses influences how trauma is perceived, deployed, and subtly reinvented over time.

Absent from my lists are Caruth's own assertions about her theory. While Kansteiner is critical of her approach, things are somewhat more complex and subtle. I see Caruth's approach and the cultural trauma theory more radically: *trauma as Event*. In this view, trauma is a limit experience, shattering known categories such that it becomes incommunicable, non-representable, beyond language. And yet, it opens something. There is a sense of awe in the face of life at the limits of life, a wish to "honor" the experiences there and not impose or demand an accounting of it. As Kansteiner says, there is an imperative not to disturb it and almost an interdiction of narrative. Again, the mimesis: The trauma is propagated in ways that cannot be known, even directly experienced; it is merely registered or imprinted somehow and transmitted through a community and down the generations. And again, the paradox: mimetic, unknowable, present at times in its absence, contagious yet incommunicable. Kansteiner is provoked by the idea that this should not be disturbed. Systemic family therapy calls this an isomorphism, whereby a relational process is mirrored in the observer.[66] Psychoanalytic theory names similar processes: transference and countertransference.[67]

I think it possible that this theory does describe part of the lived experience of trauma and for that reason we should know it, investigate it in order to identify its presence and ways of spreading as soon as possible, alleviate it as best we can, and prevent it if at all possible. This is the moral imprecision of which Kansteiner complains: Surely, no matter what truths and knowledge about life emerge from the testimony of trauma survivors, no one would wish torture, violence, and desubjectivation to receive it.[68]

Let us understand, however, that this risk inheres in the study of horror. The vicarious entering into another life—*lifeworld* as Husserl called it, simply *world* for Badiou, and *predicament* for me[69]—is the most precarious of things. Not for nothing did Jaspers introduce the phenomenological chasm we experience in the encounter with radical alterity. The tools available to surmount that alterity—analogy and metaphor, "fortunate confusion" and digression, contradiction and irrelevance, and many other tropes—are imperfect and should be used with caution.[70]

Trauma psychiatrist Mollica counsels us to listen to the "trauma story";[71] Miller wrote about being an "enlightened witness";[72] LaCapra suggests we can glean a faint echo of suffering even on the screen by a process he calls "emphatic unsettlement" (which sounds like the receptive version of Brecht's alienation effect), understood by Kansteiner as a "dispositional unease," based on our capacity for mimetic affection.[73] These efforts at empathy are worthwhile no matter their limits. My most important reservation is that we do not arrive at extreme or categorical judgments based on empathy, as Jaspers did. Above, I wrote that the phenomenological chasm reflects the difficulties of reaching others; thus we should avoid dichotomous thinking based on empathy alone. Amazingly, Caruth and cultural trauma theory seem to join Jaspers and phenomenological psychiatry on this point: trauma today brings us—victim and interlocutor together—to the limits of being and of communicability just as schizophrenia did for Jaspers.

Trauma Psychiatry

> The act of naming is the great and solemn consolation of mankind.
>
> ELIAS CANETTI[74]

Trauma psychiatry is the reconfiguration of the field of psychiatry around the "ubiquity of the contemporary politics of trauma," coalescing three emergent fields described by Fassin and Rechtman in *The Empire of Trauma* as "psychiatric victimology, humanitarian psychiatry, and the psychotraumatology of exile."[75] This reconfiguration naturalizes the concept of trauma, universalizes it, and demonstrating Hacking's "looping effect," trauma is no longer confined to psychiatric diagnosis, rather it is now "embedded in everyday usage."[76] In a chilling parallel of the concerns of thoughtful and incisive scholars such as Kansteiner and Weilbock, LaCapra and Leys, Fassin and Rechtman argue that *trauma is the new language of the event.*[77]

This new field is directed at a new public. Fassin and Rechtman observe that the new task of psychiatry is not to treat people who are sick but who are "suddenly affected by the impact of abnormal events."[78] In a very precise Foucauldian formulation, they note a dual social innovation: "the invention of new areas of knowledge and practices, and the discovery of new patients and subjects."[79]

This grasps my essential claim about the age of trauma. From its passionate advocates, above all Caruth who has articulated cultural trauma theory in an accessible and influential manner, with an anti-clinical spin by Weinberg where trauma is treasured and not to be trampled upon by remembrance and narrative, to its concerned critics ranging from Fassin and Rechtman's dispassionate sociocultural inquiry to more militant attacks from Leys, Kansteiner, and Weilnbock—trauma has become ubiquitous, embedded in the quotidian, and the subject of new fields. The invocation of *trauma's estate* reflects Andre Malraux's novel of the failed first Chinese revolution, *Man's Estate*. The failure in the case of trauma is a double one, of both politics and cultures.[80]

Trauma as Distributed Phenomena

There is a relationship between the definition of the subject and the definition of trauma. In Badiou's ontology, one becomes a subject through a tripartite process of recognizing, naming, and being faithful to an Event. In my work, the subject is not bounded by the skin of the individual but is defined as a distributed/relational subject.[81] In relational psychology, which is a cognate of intersubjective psychoanalysis and social psychiatry, subjectivity/identity is distributed, which means it is contextual, relational, dialogic.[82] Each of these terms is both distinct and overlapping. "Contextual" means that an individual is situated in a community, a *world* in Badiou's terms. "Relational" means that encounters and exchanges occur among subjects in their worlds. "Dialogic" means that encounters and exchanges take the form of language and form discourses.

In the tripartite process of the Event, something that arises from the evental site must be recognized and named before it can be pronounced an Event. Elisabeth Cathely, a character in Badiou's novel, *Calme Bloc Ici-Bas*, insists that even a terrorist gesture, an act of rebellion that is obvious, must be named: "What happens, everything that really happens, should be signed. Only nothing is anonymous."[83] Badiou's naming is very clearly a relational and dialogic process. In Badiou's ontology, as in relational psychology, naming implies a dialogue, as community. The third part of the process of the Event is fidelity. Elisabeth demonstrates fidelity even as the Event is emerging, which she insists on naming. It becomes a reciprocal process of recognition-naming-fidelity. From this process, the subject arises/constructs itself.

Not only is the subject situated and distributed, but trauma itself is a distributed notion. One word is inadequate to indicate the complex facets involved in trauma. For simplicity, we may describe them as *Tt, the Trauma trigger*, *Tp, the Trauma process*, and *Ti, the Trauma impact*:

Tt = *Trauma trigger* (aspects: incident, stressor, vector)
Tp = *Trauma process* (aspects: context, predicament, evental site)
Ti = *Trauma impact* (aspects: reactions, consequences, sequelae)

All three facets of trauma are distributed. It is not difficult to agree that trauma triggers (*Tt*) are potentially distributed across persons: they are in the environment, natural or human, e.g., an earthquake, a plague, terrorism or war. Nor is it difficult for relational therapists and child psychiatrists to perceive the predicament of trauma (*Tp*) as an interpersonal process where the burden of trauma is shared with significant others in a family or a community, sometimes amplifying (the horror of seeing a loved one attacked), sometimes mitigating (the reassuring presence of a significant person) the individual's suffering. Furthermore, social psychiatry, community psychiatry and public health—all of which adopt a group, community or popoulational approach—easily see trauma as distributed phenomena. Finally, trauma impact (*Ti*) must also be seen as distributed. The construction of trauma, from how it is experienced to how it is signified, is an interpersonal process as well. This does not deny individual experience but rather places it in a more comprehensive framework. This might appear to be at odds with more biological models—neurobiology and genetics for example—or some psychoanalytic models emphasizing individual history and psychic structure (see Werner Bohleber) but it is not: many genes are modulated by the environment and neurophysiology and biochemistry also respond to social context, not to mention pathophysiological processes. For example, blood pressure is exquisitely sensitive to social context and people have the physiological accompaniment of anxiety such as rapid respirations and accelerated heartbeats triggered by the slightest of stimuli.

Whereas Event opens possibilities, trauma closes them. Whereas the evental site (predicament, world) opens the possibility of the Event and through fidelity, too, the Event/subject comes into being (i.e., subjectivation), the closure of possibilities through trauma eclipses the subject (i.e., leads to desubjectivation). *A corollary is that if an Event can and must be named, trauma, through a process of desubjectivation, is nameless.* This is why

Levi feels compelled to witness and to allow those who cannot talk to "witness through these words of mine."[84] Is that what Adorno meant in his controversial declaration about poetry after Auschwitz? Is poetry a witnessing, a naming?

Let us not be confused or conflate matters. Even when careful documentation can unequivocally describe what happened, this is not the same as naming it.[85] To name something means to grasp its meaning deeply, to seize its decisive features, to know it ontologically. An external description cannot exhaust everything that can and must be said about it. It is not phenomenology, which is concerned with appearances, but ontology that confers a name. Ontologically, true trauma cannot be named; it remains nameless. Phenomenologically, we can describe it, seize its shape, and outline its borders. But, we do not enter it.

Returning to Adorno (and if we approach Auschwitz, we cannot avoid him) is neither an endorsement nor a criticism but rather an acknowledgement of the seriousness of the wager he made about Auschwitz. He is not a weather-forecaster, a diviner, or a soothsayer. He was looking at what occurred and had the decency to express shame and regret. There is a seriousness of purpose in Adorno, even if we define the aporias differently. And yet, there are difficulties with the construction "after Auschwitz." As Jean-François Lyotard notes, "'After' implies a periodization. Adorno counts time (but what time?) from 'Auschwitz.'"[86] Lyotard asks, "What era ends and what era begins with this event?"[87] We may make suggestions about where to place the brackets for the Event, attaching them provisionally to certain figures or circumstances. Like my meta-concept of dichotomising trauma or the phenomenological gesture of "bracketing," Adorno offers Auschwitz as a model, not an example. An example illustrates an idea but remains indifferent to it; a model "brings negative dialectics into the real."[88] Lyotard captures this presciently:

> This model responds to this reversal in the destiny of the dialectic: it is the name of something (of a para-experience, of a paraempiricity) wherein dialectics encounters non-negatable negative (*un négatif non niable*), and abides in the impossibility of redoubling that negative into a "result." *Wherein the mind's wound is not scarred over.*[89]

Let us pause on this a little longer. Wittgenstein posed the question, "How does one philosopher address another?" Answer: "Take your time."[90] Jean-François Lyotard expressed the namelessness of trauma with one of the most trenchant analogies about the camps: How does one measure an event when all the instruments for its measurement are broken? Geoffrey

Hartmann acknowledges this yet notes the aftershocks are felt and that new instruments must be built.[91]

One more thought from Lyotard reading Adorno which is related to how Lyotard imagines limit experiences. Lyotard makes much more accessible what others say in more abstract language. In place of Adorno's "after Auschwitz," Lyotard says "within Auschwitz":

> The Auschwitz model would designate an experience of language which brings *speculative discourse* to a halt. The latter can no longer be pursued *after Auschwitz*, that is, *within Auschwitz*. Here would be found a name within which we cannot think, or not completely. [. . .] It would be *a name of the nameless*. [. . .] It would be a name which designates what has no name in speculation, *a name for the anonymous*. And what for speculation remains simply the anonymous.[92]

Annotation on Trauma: Catachresis/Apostrophe

Let us consider the Greek definition of *catachresis* (or *abusio* in Latin) in the rhetoric of Aristotle: "in naming something that does not have a proper name of its own, metaphor should be used."[93] A classical deployment affirmed that *catachresis*, "ocurs when a new, bold, or improper name is used for the literal or proper one."[94] Catechresis is a supple rhetorical device often invoked in the Latin sense of abuse or misuse, but more interestingly in the sense of a place marker, "taking the place of" and "standing in for."

This is the sense that emerges from Thomas Zummer's discussion of Narcissus' reflex—"that initial, momentary, arrestment of the body as Narcissus stared, immobile and transfixed"[95]—where he takes his reflection to be another:

> It is this dual aspect in mediation—*suture et rupture*—that constitutes what one might call a *science-fictional body*, a body both technical and irreal which cohabits the spaces of the real. A body which, as both appearance and apprehension, partakes of the real, even as it forms a *catachresis*, a scar, sealing over, marking the place of the real, a space it cannot ever fully occupy, or fill.[96]

Building on this, we may elabroate trauma as a rhetorical configuration articulating the gestures "rupture/continuity" with the tropes "catachresis/apostrophe": *Trauma, defined as a rupture, fissure, negativity or absentation may be considered, from the point of view of a rhetorical configuration, as a form of* catachresis, *a trope which, in this case, means a "sealing over" or "covering" of a break, absence, or aporia. However, it is also the case that catachresis is neither wholly stable nor is it pure, which is to say that it is not unaffected by other forms of figuration. A more appropriate description of trauma, therefore, may be that it operates like a* catachresis, *which is at the same time also an* apostrophe *(a "turning away," Latin:* aversio, *French:* volte-face*). The catechretic "scar" or "cicatrice" turns away from itself—that is, from the wound—only to return again, as another form of address, possibly elsewhere.*

Trauma: The Destruction of Experience

You have therefore come to this house to destroy.
What have you destroyed in me?
You have destroyed, simply
—with all my past life—
the idea that I have always had of myself.
                        PIER PAOLO PASOLINI[97]

We can now weave various strands from Adorno and Lyotard together with Agamben and Badiou to define trauma and make a map of trauma's estate. Earlier, we said, *if Event must be named, trauma is nameless.* Badiou teaches us that the Event must have a name. Adorno teaches us the name-lessness of trauma. Agamben, in exploring desubjectivation in our time, is in a sense, the antipsychologist, the antiphenomenologist. Let me explain: If phenomenology, starting with Hegel is the "science of the experience of consciousness," which has been the core preoccupation of modern psychology—we see this manifestly in Maurice Merleau-Ponty's psychology of perception—then Agamben has explored repeatedly and in different ways in his *opere filosofiche* the destruction of experience. This is why as a child specialist I am so taken with his key work, *Infancy and History,* which is quite simply an *antiphenomenology of childhood.*[98]

In trauma's estate, trauma is not the generic name of a predicament or even of a particular experience but a generic name for the destruction of experience.

Understand: not the destruction merely of *a given experience* but of *a capacity for experience.*[99] This is what makes it the opposite of Event. With this definition, we can again examine the dichotomous columns of signs and symptoms of trauma and theories of trauma and begin to pose the larger and more significant question of the relation between trauma and Event. We may understand that trauma can mean the loss of memory and the coarsening and concretization of language (loss of symbolic meaning and metaphoric communication) and the diminution of conscious human being. In an essay on states of exception and states of dissociation, I catalogued a disquieting group of contemporary experiences from *alexithymia* to *cyranoids* and *zombies* with the concomitant increase of a passive, dissociative ventroloquism.[100]

Trauma evidences desubjectivation such that in the strict sense, one cannot speak of a traumatized subject. A traumatized person begins to lose his subjectivity, the nadir of which becomes the *Muselmänner*—such totally desubjectivated entities that they enter an indeterminate zone between the human and non-human, the dissociative dummies of the ventriloquism of power, living a bare life, denuded of the word.[101] In a reversal of our bodily nature where consciousness takes the form of the neurophysiological apparatus which we may call incarnated thought, in the state of exception trauma means bodies speaking words, like Hurbinek's meager *mastiklo* or *mass-klo*.[102]

Epilogue: Disarming the Desubjectivation Machine

The modern state functions [. . .] as a kind of desubjectivation machine.
GIORGIO AGAMBEN[103]

In the survivor experience, one can either close down or open out.
ROBERT JAY LIFTON[104]

Philosophical archaeology allows us to discern the relationships among *rupture* (predicament, state of exception, Evental site), *trauma* (the destruction of experience, of the possibility of experience), and *Event* (contingent, unpredictable, undecidable). In this investigation, I have invoked the work of Agamben as the philosopher of desubjectivation and Badiou as the philosopher of the Event. I have opposed trauma to Event, making absolute distinction between them; trauma does not conduce to Event, Event does not arise from trauma. The *Akedah* ("Isaac-Machine"), "Achilles' spear" and other apparatuses are located in what Agamben calls a "zone of indifference" or what Badiou calls an "evental site." Human predicaments emerge in evental sites, where rupture occurs. Neither the rupture nor the predicament is predictable or decidable in advance. As trauma psychiatrist Lifton says of survivors of disasters and genocides, echoing Amichai's poem, we may open out, porous and permeable to *novation*, or close down, emptied and evacuated, in a desubjectivated, traumatized state. This offers keys for translation—if not paths of reconciliation—among the communities that address trauma and Event: those who hold by *trauma/Event* as a radical disjuncture, those who hope for a transformation of *trauma into Event*, and those who harbor the transcendent view of *trauma as Event*.

In a boldly original doctoral dissertation with Badiou, Terrence Hands-comb proposes the theory of a subject-body in the form of an *abstract mu-tant automaton*: "Mutant automata are not the faithful subjects of events. Following the occurrence of a pseudodialectic turn of events, mutant-automaton-subjects instead suffuse the registers of the imaginary at the level of the symptom."[105] This philosophical proposition has already taken dramatic shape in the desubjectivated bodies of the *Muselmänner* of the Nazi death camps.[106] And we risk repeating it in dissociative states as *cyra-noids* and *zombies* in our current state of exception.[107]

Caveat: Poetry, prose, memoir can still express what must be said, give form and voice to what will not lie still, but *within Auschwitz*, to read Adorno through Lyotard, they will not redeem us. If we grant so much power to the word, why is it that writers who wield it with awe-inspiring capacities themselves despair of the word, and all-too-often, of life itself? When he was asked why he wrote plays when he despaired of saying some-thing of value, Samuel Beckett famously replied, "They're only words; it's all we have."[108] Eugene Ionesco wrote in his journal, "But not everything is unsayable, only the living truth."[109]

Beautiful words, sounds, and images are no longer adequate. They have, as Adorno anguished and warned, become entertainment.[110] They will not protect us, despite Mollica's moving appeal in his work, *Healing Invisible Wounds*. They may comfort us, make the pain more bearable and offer vis-tas of beauty that are possible in another life, "under another sky" in Levi's haunting phrase. Some of those who survived Auschwitz found the words to become a messenger, to express bitterness, to laugh darkly, or to become a witness. Yet poets Paul Celan and Jean Améry committed suicide. Ta-deusz Borowski committed suicide and Primo Levi's death was pronounced a suicide.

Isaac-Machine, the apparatus that governs child abuse, and other ma-chines—starting with what Agamben calls the "anthropological machine," followed by Auschwitz-Machine, Gulag-Machine, and all the machines for destruction and desubjectivation—will have to be dismantled and rendered inoperative.[111] If not, the minefield that I call predicament (where rupture occurs) and in which we may discern states of exception (or evental sites) will shut down our lives into trauma. In our current predicament, philo-sophical archaeology, sniffing out the apparatuses and the machines like a bomb-detector, must identify and disarm them. Only then can we pa-tiently wait to see if we will recognize the Events that are scattered around us like so many haphazard fragments of a puzzle.

Threshold— *"We Are All No More Than Haphazard Fractions"*

What if the world isn't scattered around us like a jigsaw puzzle—what if it's like a soup with all kinds of things floating around in it, and from time to time some of them get stuck together by chance to make some kind of whole? What if everything that exists is fragmentary, incomplete, aborted, events with ends but no beginnings, events that only have middles, things that have fronts or rears but not both, with us constantly making categories, seeking out, and reconstructing, until we think we can see total love, total betrayal and defeat, although in reality we are all no more than haphazard fractions.

Perfection, fullness, excellence are all rare exceptions—they occur only because there is such an excess, so unimaginably much of everything! The daily commonplace is automatically regulated by the world's vastness, its infinite variety; because of it, what we see as gaps and breaches complement each other; the mind, for its own self-preservation, finds and integrates scattered fragments. Using religion and philosophy as the cement, we perpetually collect and assemble all the garbage comprised by statistics in order to make sense out of things, to make everything respond in one unified voice like a bell chiming to our glory. But it's only soup [. . .] The mathematical order of the universe is our answer to the pyramids of chaos.

STANISLAW LEM, THE INVESTIGATION[112]

NOTES

This chapter is based on a presentation to the Harvard Program in Refugee Trauma, Harvard Medical School, Cambridge, Mass., October 15, 2012, and my doctoral dissertation, Vincenzo Di Nicola, *Trauma and Event: A Philosophical Archaeology* (Saas-Fee, Wallis, Switzerland: European Graduate School, 2012).

1. Yehuda Amichai, *Open Closed Open*, trans. Chana Bloch and Chana Kronfeld (New York: Harcourt, 2000), 6. Amichai's poem takes its inspiration from the Babylonian Talmud. "Threshold" is a key notion throughout my work on culture and trauma, inspired by anthropologist Victor Turner's work on liminality, transitional states, and threshold people. See Vincenzo Di Nicola, *On the Threshold. Selected Papers. Volume I: Culture, Families and Culture Change* (New York: Atropos Press, forthcoming). *Havdalah*, meaning "separation" in Hebrew, is a Jewish ritual marking the end of the *Shabbath* and the beginning of the work week. Like the Sabbath, *havdalah* is a *shibboleth*, a marker punctuating difference and change; it opens and closes, and

is itself on the cusp between the sacred and the profane. As such, the threshold is a zone of indistinction, a central theme in the philosophy of Giorgio Agamben. Cf. Entries on "Indistinction" and "Threshold" in *The Agamben Dictionary*, ed. Alex Murray and Jessica Whyte (Edinburgh: Edinburgh University Press, 2011).

2. Cathy Caruth, Introduction to *Trauma: Explorations in Memory*, ed. Cathy Caruth (Baltimore: Johns Hopkins University Press, 1995), 11.

3. Philosophical archaeology is a philosophical-historical method refined by Giorgio Agamben, in the footsteps of Michel Foucault. Agamben traces the term from Immanuel Kant. An archaeology of the term itself reveals it to be embedded in successive strata of thought from Nietzsche's "critical history" to Foucault's "epistemological field, the *épistémè*," where we see glimpses of Freud's "regression," Marcel Mauss's "historical a priori," Franz Overbeck's "prehistory," Georges Dumézil's "fringe of ultra-history," and Walter Benjamin's "prehistory and post-history." The link between psychoanalytic regression and archaeology was intuited by Paul Ricoeur, carefully elaborated by Enzo Melandri, and explicitly connected to the task of philosophy through Foucault by Agamben. Agamben constructs a genealogy from Kant and Nietzsche, connecting Freud and Foucault to forge a subtle and fertile method of philosophical inquiry. Adapted from my doctoral dissertation, Vincenzo Di Nicola, *Trauma and Event*. Cf. William Watkin, *"The Signature of All Things*: Agamben's Philosophical Archaeology," *MLN* 129 (2014).

4. Giorgio Agamben, "Philosophical Archaeology," in *The Signature of All Things*, trans. Luca D'Isanto and Kevin Attell (New York: Zone Books, 2009), 89.

5. Ruth Leys, *Trauma: A Genealogy* (Chicago: University of Chicago Press, 2000).

6. Wulf Kanstainer, "Genealogy of a Category Mistake: A Critical Intellectual History of the Cultural Trauma Metaphor," *Rethinking History: The Journal of Theory and Practice* 8 (2004).

7. Didier Fassin and Richard Rechtman, *The Empire of Trauma: An Inquiry into the Condition of Victimhood*, trans. Rachel Gomme (Princeton: Princeton University Press, 2009), 8.

8. Fassin and Rechtman, *The Empire of Trauma*, 9, emphasis added.

9. Fassin and Rechtman, *The Empire of Trauma*, 9; Wulf Kansteiner and Harald Weilnböck, "Against the Concept of Cultural Trauma or How I Learned to Love the Suffering of Others without the Help of Psychotherapy," in *Cultural Memory Studies: An International and Interdisciplinary Handbook*, eds. Astrid Erll and Ansgar Nünning (Berlin: Walter de Gruyter, 2008).

10. Angela Woods, *The Sublime Object of Psychiatry: Schizophrenia in Clinical and Cultural Context* (Oxford: Oxford University Press, 2011).

11. Yevgeny Zamyatin, "On Literature, Revolution, Entropy, and Other Matters," ed. and trans. Mirra Ginsburg, in *A Soviet Heretic: Essays by Yevgeny Zamyatin* (Chicago: University of Chicago Press, 1970), 110.

12. Giorgio Agamben, *State of Exception*, trans. Kevin Attell. (Chicago: University of Chicago Press, 2005).

13. Alain Badiou, *Second Manifesto for Philosophy*, trans. Louise Burchill (Cambridge, U.K.: Polity, 2011).

14. See Ferdinand de Saussure, *Course in General Linguistics*, ed. Charles Bally and Albert Sechehaye, in collaboration with Albert Reidleinger, trans. Roy Harris (London: Duckworth, 1983).

15. Vincenzo Di Nicola, "States of Exception, States of Dissociation: Cyranoids, Zombies and Liminal People," in *Letters to a Young Therapist: Relational Practices for the Coming Community* (New York: Atropos Press, 2011).

16. Badiou, *Second Manifesto for Philosophy*.

17. Jerry A. Fodor, *Psychological Explanation: An Introduction to the Philosophy of Psychology* (New York: Random House, 1968), vii.

18. Kansteiner and Weilnböck, "Against the Concept of Cultural Trauma," 230.

19. See: Alison Faulkner and Phil Thomas, "Editorial: User-led Research and Evidence-based Medicine," *British Journal of Psychiatry* 180 (2002): 1–3; D. D. R. Williams and Jane Garner, "The Case Against 'The Evidence': A Different Perspective on Evidence-based Medicine," *British Journal of Psychiatry* 180 (2002): 8–12.

20. Kansteiner, "Genealogy of a Category Mistake," 194.

21. Leys, *Trauma: A Genealogy*, 299.

22. Leys, *Trauma: A Genealogy*, 305.

23. Michel Foucault, *The Order of Things: An Archaeology of the Human Sciences* (New York: Pantheon, 1970).

24. Nicolas Duvoux and Pascal Sévérac, "Citizen Balibar: An Interview with Étienne Balibar," trans. Michael C. Behrent, *Books and Ideas* (November 26, 2012).

25. "Violence, like Achilles' lance, can heal the wounds that it has inflicted," Jean-Paul Sartre, Preface, in Frantz Fanon, *The Wretched of the Earth*, trans. Constance Farrington (New York: Grove Press, 1968), 30.

26. Jacques Derrida, "Plato's Pharmacy," in *Dissemination*, trans. Barbara Johnson (Chicago: University of Chicago Press, 1981).

27. Jacques Derrida, "Plato's Pharmacy," Cf. Niall Lucy, *A Derrida Dictionary* (Oxford: Blackwell, 2004); Simon Morgan Wortham, *The Derrida Dictionary* (London: Continuum, 2010).

28. Kansteiner, "Genealogy of a Category Mistake," 195.

29. Kanstainer, "Genealogy of a Category Mistake." The elaboration of

Hacking's "looping effects" is mine. See Ian Hacking, "The Looping Effect of Human Kinds" in *Causal Cognition: An Interdisciplinary Approach*, ed. Dan Sperber, David Premack, Ann James Premack (Oxford, U.K.: Clarendon Press, 1995).

30. Alain Badiou states, "We live in the era of number's despotism [. . .]. And medicine itself, apart from its pure and simple reduction to its scientific Other (molecular biology) is a disorderly accumulation of empirical facts, a huge web of blindly tested numerical correlations." *Number and Numbers*, trans. Robin Mackay (Cambridge, U.K.: Polity, 2008) 1–2 (emphasis in original).

31. Simon Critchley, *Continental Philosophy: A Very Short Introduction* (Oxford: Oxford University Press, 2001).

32. See Kansteiner and Weilnböck, "Against the Concept of Cultural Trauma," 231. "Weinberg states explicitly that 'the clinical aspect is precisely what does not interest me—or only in a marginal way—about trauma' (173)."

33. Søren Kierkegaard, *Fear and Trembling*, trans. Alastair Hannay (New York: Penguin Books, 2006), 13.

34. John Gerassi, ed. and trans., *Talking with Sartre: Conversations and Debates* (New Haven: Yale University Press, 2009), 54.

35. Vincenzo Di Nicola, "On the Rights and Philosophy of Children," *Transcultural Psychiatry* 32, no. 1 (1995).

36. See Raymond Williams, *Keywords: A Vocabulary of Culture and Society* (London: Fontana, 1983); Tony Bennett, Lawrence Grossberg, and Meaghan Morris, eds., *New Keywords: A Revised Vocabulary of Culture and Society* (Oxford: Blackwell, 2005); Barbara Cassin, *Vocabulaire Européen des Philosophies: Dictionnaire des Intraduisables* (Paris: Le Seuil / Le Robert, 2004).

37. Illness as metaphor has been explored forcefully by Susan Sontag: *Illness as Metaphor* (New York: Farrar, Straus and Giroux, 1978); *AIDS and Its Metaphors* (New York: Farrar, Straus and Giroux, 1989); *Regarding the Pain of Others* (New York: Penguin Books, 2003).

38. Gunter Grass's *The Tin Drum*, Jerzy Kosinski's *The Painted Bird*, Elsa Morante's *History: A Novel*.

39. Primo Levi, *The Truce*, trans. Stuart Woolf (Boston: Little, Brown, 1965), 23.

40. The affirmative ending of Adélia Prado's great mission poem, "*Com licença poética*," is "*Mulher é desdobrável. Eu sou.*" With poetic licence: A woman unfolds and unfurls. I do. In Adélia Prado, *Poesia Réunida* (São Paulo: Siciliano, 1991, my translation).

41. "Man is a being of *pure potentiality* [potenza pura], which no identity and no vocation can exhaust": Giorgio Agamben, *La Potenza del Pensiere:*

Saggi e Conferenze (Vicenza: Neri Pozza, 2005), 330 (my translation, emphasis added).

42. Vincenzo Di Nicola, "Ethnocultural Aspects of PTSD and Related Disorders Among Children and Adolescents," in *Ethnocultural Aspects of Posttraumatic Stress Disorder: Issues, Research, and Clinical Applications*, ed. A. J. Marsella, M. J. Friedman, E. T. Gerrity, et al. (Washington: American Psychological Association, 1996).

43. Gareth Matthews concluded that either children ask serious philosophical questions or philosophy is not a mature activity. Work on children's ethical and scientific thinking suggests we need new ways to think about "development." See Gareth B. Matthews, *The Philosophy of Childhood* (Cambridge: Harvard University Press, 1994); David Archard, *Children: Rights and Childhood* (London: Routledge, 1993); Di Nicola, "On the Rights and Philosophy of Children."

44. Giorgio Agamben, *Infancy and History: On the Destruction of Experience*, trans. Liz Heron (London: Verso, 2007).

45. Hans Keilson, "Sequential Traumatization of Children," *Danish Medical Bulletin* 27, no. 5 (1980).

46. Philippe Ariès, *Centuries of Childhood: A Social History of Family Life*, trans. Robert Baldick (New York: Vintage, 1962).

47. Lloyd deMause, "The Evolution of Childhood," in *The History of Childhood: The Untold Story of Child Abuse*, ed. Lloyd deMause (New York: Peter Bedrick Books, 1988), 5.

48. deMause, "The Evolution of Childhood," back cover.

49. Shalom Spiegel, *The Last Trial*, trans. with an Introduction by Judah Goldin. New Preface by Judah Goldin (Woodstock, Vt.: Jewish Lights Publishing, 1993).

50. Beyond referencing "apparatus" in the Foucault/Agamben sense, "Isaac-Machine" was inspired by German playwright Heiner Müller's extraordinary play *Die Hamletmaschine/*"Hamlet Machine." See Heiner Müller, *Hamlet-Machine and Other Texts for the Stage*, ed. and trans. Carl Weber (New York: PAJ, 1984).

51. Giorgio Agamben, "What Is an Apparatus?" in *What Is an Apparatus and Other Essays*, trans. David Kishik and Stefan Pedatella (Stanford: Stanford University Press, 2009), 14. Agamben's definition of apparatus follows a reading of Michel Foucault's work.

52. Vincent J. Felitti, R.F. Anda, N. Nordenberg, et al., "Relationship of Childhood Abuse and Household Dysfunction to Many of the Leading Causes of Death in Adults: The Adverse Childhood Experiences (ACE) Study," *American Journal of Preventive Medicine* 14, no. 4 (1998), 245.

53. Felitti, Anda, Nordenberg, et al., "Relationship of Childhood Abuse and Household Dysfunction."

54. In Hebrew, *aleph*, representing the number 1, is the first letter of the Hebrew alphabet and the word, *emeth*, meaning truth. The legend of the Golem has it that to deactivate the clay Golem, which had exceeded its mission, the Rabbi who created him erased *aleph*, the first letter of *emeth*, written on its foreword to animate it, leaving only *meth*, meaning death.

55. An example is René Girard's mimetic theory, which is rich in explanatory power and a goldmine for the analysis of a broad variety of social and cultural practices. Although he argued it was easy to verify rivalry in infants, such experimentation, Girard concluded, would be "of limited value. It would not be at the intellectual level of the theory [. . .] which cannot be subjected to empirical verification or falsification through empirical testing, or the canons of contemporary science, especially the principle of falsifiability. The complexity [. . .] is too great for that." See René Girard, "The Anthropology of the Cross: A Conversation with René Girard," in *The Girard Reader*, ed. James G. Williams (New York: Crossroad Herder, 1996), 277.

56. For a perspective on the evolution of psychoanalysis in France by an American, see Sherry Turkle, "French Anti-psychiatry," in *Critical Psychiatry: The Politics of Mental Health*, ed. David Ingleby (Harmondsworth: Penguin Books, 1981), 150–83. For a French perspective, compare Alain Badiou and Élisabeth Roudinesco, *Jacques Lacan Past and Present: A Dialogue*, trans. Jason E. Smith (New York: Columbia University Press, 2014).

57. R. D. Laing, *The Divided Self: An Existential Study in Sanity and Madness* (London: Tavistock, 1960), 17.

58. R. D. Laing, *The Divided Self*, 19.

59. In Hebrew, *beth* representing the number 2, functions as a preposition meaning in, at, or with. The name of the letter is a homonym for the Hebrew word for house. I associate it with this group, which is more enclosed or encased, "housed" within certain limits.

60. The *emic/etic* distinction originating in linguistics is used in anthropology and other social sciences to denote subjective *emic* descriptions of insiders versus objective *etic* descriptions from outsiders.

61. See Richard McNally, *Remembering Trauma* (Cambridge: Belknap/Harvard, 2003), 281.

62. See Richard J. McNally, "Posttraumatic Stress Disorder," in *Kaplan & Sadock's Comprehensive Textbook of Psychiatry*, 9th ed., vol. 2, ed. Benjamin J. Sadock, Virginia Alcott Sadock, and Pedro Ruiz (Philadelphia: Lippincott, Williams and Wilkins, 2009).

63. Daniel Pick, *Faces of Degeneration: A European Disorder, c. 1848–1918* (Cambridge, U.K.: Cambridge University Press, 1989).

64. In Primo Levi's witnessing of Auschwitz, I discerned *nested hegemonies*, a complex apparatus where "parallel (e.g., the eugenics movement, the New Man, Nazi anti-Semitism) or even apparently contradictory (e.g., Aryan superiority, Ashkenazi exclusivity) discourses may not only coexist but subtly reinforce each other." Vincenzo Di Nicola, *Trauma and Event*, 36.

65. Hacking, "The Looping Effect of Human Kinds."

66. See "Isomorphism" in *The Language of Family Therapy*, ed. Fritz B. Simon, et al. (New York: Family Process Press, 1985).

67. See: Jean Laplanche and J.B. Pontilis, *The Language of Psycho-Analysis*, trans. Donald Nicholson-Smith. (London: The Hogarth Press and the Institute of Psycho-Analysis, 1973).

68. For examples of such searing and pained testimony, see Primo Levi, *Survival in Auschwitz*, trans. Stuart Woolf (New York: Collier, 1961); Paul Celan, "*Sprich Auch Du*," in *Selected Poems and Prose of Paul Celan*, trans. John Felstiner (New York: Norton, 2001), 76.

69. Vincenzo Di Nicola, *A Stranger in the Family: Culture, Families, and Therapy* (New York: Norton, 1997), 119.

70. These tropes are drawn from William Empson's *Seven Types of Ambiguity* (London: The Hogarth Press,1984). Recall Sontag's concerns about the uses of metaphor.

71. Richard Mollica, *Healing Invisible Wounds: Paths to Hope and Recovery in a Violent World* (New York: Harcourt, 2006).

72. Alice Miller, "The Essential Role of an Enlightened Witness in Society," https://www.alice-miller.com/en/the-essential-role-of-an-enlightened-witness-in-society/.

73. Dominick LaCapra, *Writing History, Writing Trauma* (Baltimore: Johns Hopkins University Press, 2001), 41 and, *passim*; Kanstainer, "Genealogy of a Category Mistake," 211–12.

74. Elias Canetti, *The Agony of Flies: Notes and Notations*, trans. H. F. Broch de Rothermann (New York: Farrar, Straus and Giroux, 1994).

75. Fassin and Rechtman, *The Empire of Trauma*, 10.

76. Fassin and Rechtman, *The Empire of Trauma*, 6.

77. Fassin and Rechtman, *The Empire of Trauma*, 6.

78. Fassin and Rechtman, *The Empire of Trauma*, 10.

79. Fassin and Rechtman, *The Empire of Trauma*, 10.

80. André Malraux, *Man's Estate*, trans. Alastair MacDonald (London, Metheun: 1948).

81. Vincenzo Di Nicola, *A Stranger in the Family*.

82. Vincenzo Di Nicola, *Letters to a Young Therapist*.

83. Alain Badiou, *Calme Bloc Ici-Bas* (Paris: P.O.L., 1997), 383 (my translation).

84. Primo Levi, *The Truce*, 23.

85. Agamben and Badiou address the names attributed to the destruction of European Jews. Agamben criticizes the word Holocaust (*Remnants of Auschwitz*, 28–31), Badiou the term *Shoah*. Celan referred to this series as "that which occurred." I share Raul Hilberg's concern about names and numbers: They gloss over individual suffering, augmented by the sequential traumatization and impacts of each life, multiplied by all those who share or witness that suffering. Aggregating such suffering by names or numbers, where the multitude becomes one (for example, *a* genocide, *the* Holocaust), runs counter to a philosophy of the multiple.

86. Jean-François Lyotard, "Discussions, or Phrasing 'After Auschwitz,'" in *The Lyotard Reader*, ed. Andrew Benjamin (Oxford, U.K.: Blackwell, 1989), 360–92; 363.

87. Lyotard, "Discussions, or Phrasing 'After Auschwitz.'"

88. Lyotard cites Adorno's *Negative Dialectics*; Lyotard, "Discussions, or Phrasing 'After Auschwitz,'" 363.

89. Lyotard, "Discussions, or Phrasing 'After Auschwitz,'" 363.

90. Ludwig Wittgenstein, *Culture and Value*, ed. G. H. von Wright, trans. Peter Winch (Chicago: University of Chicago Press, 1980), 80.

91. "The French philosopher Jean-François Lyotard surmised that the shock of the Holocaust was so great it destroyed the very instruments by which it could have been measured. But the aftershocks *are* measurable: we are deep into the process of creating new instruments to record and express what happened. The instruments themselves, the means of expression are now, as it were, born of trauma."—Geoffrey H. Hartmann, *The Longest Shadow: In the Aftermath of the Holocaust* (Bloomington: Indiana University Press, 2002), 1.

92. Hartmann, *The Longest Shadow*, 364.

93. This elaboration of trauma as a rhetorical configuration emerged from conversations with Thomas Zummer, European Graduate School, August 2009. Aristotle, *On Rhetoric: A Theory of Civic Discourse*, trans. George A. Kennedy (Oxford: Oxford University Press, 1991), 224.

94. J. F. Lake Williams, *An Historical Account of Invention and Discoveries in those Arts and Sciences, which are of Utility or Ornament to Man*, vol 1 (London: T. and J. Allamn, 1820), 161.

95. Thomas Zummer, "Arrestments: Corporeality and Mediation," in *Stitch & Split: Selves and Territories in Science Fiction*, curated by Constant vzw (2006), 1–13; 2. Available at http://www.scribd.com/doc/19719356/16zummer.

96. Zummer, "Arrestment," 2–3 (emphasis in original). With his gloss on Narcissus, Zummer grasped the arrestment that rupture instills. Ovid's Nar-

cissus says, "Possession dispossessed me." Blanchot's gloss is significant: Ovid forgets that Narcissus does not recognize himself. Narcissus's dispossession in Ovid occurs as a kind of Freudian insight or aftersight, a *disruptive reflection*, whereas in the myth Narcissus's rupture comes first as a non-recognition of self. See: Maurice Blanchot, *The Writing of the Disaster*, trans. Ann Smock (Lincoln: University of Nebraska Press, 1995), 125–28.

97. Pier Paolo Pasolini, *Teorema* (Milano: Garzanti, 1968), 104 (emphasis in original, my translation).

98. Giorgio Agamben, *Infancy and History*.

99. I am saying *a capacity* rather than *the capacity for experience*; such capacity is in several registers, which may be recovered, recuperated, repaired, restored, or restituted separately or collectively, and/or it is possible that individuals may acquire new capacities for such operations and for the expression of their experiences.

100. Vincenzo Di Nicola, "States of Exception, States of Dissociation," 149–62.

101. Primo Levi, *The Truce*; Giorgio Agamben, *Remnants of Auschwitz: The Witness and the Archive*, trans. Daniel Heller-Roazen (New York: Zone Books, 1999).

102. Levi, *The Truce*. Levi reports on the child Hurbinek, born in Auschwitz, whose paltry life is represented in these few repeated syllables belonging to no known language.

103. Giorgio Agamben, "'I Am Sure that You Are More Pessimistic than I Am . . .': An Interview with Giorgio Agamben," trans. Jason Smith, *Rethinking Marxism* 16, no. 2 (2004): 115–24; 116.

104. Robert Jay Lifton, "Witness to an Extreme Century," 165th Annual Meeting of the American Psychiatric Association, Philadelphia, Pa. (May 2012).

105. Terrence Handscomb, *Sinthôme: Mutant Automata in an Ill-founded World* (PhD diss, European Graduate School, 2011), ii.

106. Primo Levi, *The Truce* (1965); Giorgio Agamben, *Remnants of Auschwitz: The Witness and the Archive*, trans. by Daniel Heller-Roazen (New York: Zone Books, 1999).

107. Vincenzo Di Nicola, "States of Exception, States of Dissociation."

108. Samuel Beckett, cited in Stanley Cavell, *Must We Mean What We Say?* (Cambridge, U.K.: Cambridge University Press, 1976), 161.

109. Eugene Ionesco, *Fragments of a Journal*, trans. Jean Stewart (London: Faber and Faber, 1968).

110. Theodor W. Adorno, *Aesthetic Theory*, trans. Christian Lenhardt, ed. Gretel Adorno and Rolf Tiedemann (London: Routledge and Kegan Paul, 1984).

111. Giorgio Agamben, *The Open; Man and Animal*, trans. Kevin Attell (Stanford: Stanford University Press, 2004).

112. Stanislaw Lem, *The Investigation*, trans. Adele Milch (New York: Avon Books, 1974), 179. In this metaphysical police procedural, Lem attributes cause without agency, existence without consciousness.

Phenomenological-Contextualism All the Way Down: An Existential and Ethical Perspective on Emotional Trauma

Robert D. Stolorow

Since the mid-1970s, my closest collaborator, George Atwood, and I have been absorbed in the project of rethinking psychoanalysis as a form of phenomenological inquiry.[1] This rethinking has proven to be essential to the development of my psychoanalytic understanding and therapeutic approach to emotional trauma—a subject with which I have been preoccupied for the last three of these four decades. In the present chapter, I show how a phenomenological perspective can illuminate two of trauma's essential features—its context-embeddedness and existential significance—along with the impact of trauma on the experience of time. I emphasize the implications of these formulations for the proper therapeutic comportment toward trauma and, more generally, for an ethics of human finitude.

Phenomenological Contextualism

Intersubjective-systems theory, the name we eventually gave our psychoanalytic perspective, is a *phenomenological contextualism*. It is phenomenological in that it investigates and illuminates worlds of emotional experience and the structures that organize them. It is contextual in that it holds that such

structures take form, both developmentally and in the therapeutic situation, in constitutive relational or intersubjective contexts. Developmentally,
recurring patterns of intersubjective transaction within the developmental system give rise to principles (thematic patterns, meaning-structures,
cognitive-affective schemas) that unconsciously organize subsequent emotional and relational experiences. Such organizing principles are unconscious, not in the sense of being repressed, but in being *prereflective*; they
ordinarily do not enter the domain of reflective self-awareness. These in-
tersubjectively derived, prereflective organizing principles are the basic
building blocks of personality development, and their totality constitutes
one's character. Psychoanalytic therapy is a dialogical method for bringing
this prereflective organizing activity into reflective self-awareness, particularly as it shows up within the therapeutic relationship.

Trauma's Context-Embeddedness

Early contexts of emotional trauma are a particularly important source of
prereflective organizing principles. Nowhere is the context-dependence of
emotional life more vividly exemplified than in the phenomenon of emotional trauma. The explication of trauma's context-dependence was fore-
shadowed in a sentence that my late wife, Daphne (Dede), composed in our
early joint article: "The tendency for [painful] affective experiences to create a disorganized (i.e., traumatic) self-state is seen to originate from [. . .]
faulty [affect] attunement, with a lack of mutual sharing and acceptance of
affect states."[2] However, it was not until the aftermath of Dede's death in
February 1991, when I experienced first-hand what I later came to call "the
unbearable embeddedness of being," that I turned my attention to trauma's
context-embeddedness.[3] The result was my chapter on emotional trauma
in *Contexts of Being*, the book that Atwood and I outlined the summer after
Dede died.[4]

I claimed in that chapter that emotional trauma is an experience of unendurable emotional pain, and further, that the unbearability of emotional
suffering cannot be explained solely, or even primarily, on the basis of the
intensity of the painful feelings evoked by an injurious event. Painful emotional states become unbearable when they cannot find a context of emotional understanding—what I came to call a "relational home"—in which
they can be shared and held. Severe emotional pain that has to be experienced alone becomes lastingly traumatic and usually succumbs to some
form of emotional numbing. In contrast, painful feelings that are held in a
context of human understanding can gradually become more bearable.

Drawing on the work of Balint, Ferenczi, Kohut, Krystal, and Winnicott,[5] I contended that developmental trauma, in particular, must not be viewed as an instinctual flooding of an ill-equipped mental apparatus, as Freud[6] would have it. Rather, developmental trauma was grasped as originating within a formative intersubjective context whose central feature is malattunement to painful affect—a breakdown of the child–caregiver interaffective system, leading to the child's loss of affect-integrating capacity and thereby to an unbearable, overwhelmed, disorganized state. Painful or frightening affect becomes traumatic when the attunement that the child needs to assist in its tolerance and integration is profoundly absent. Such claims hold, *pari passu*, for adult-onset trauma as well.[7] Finding a relational home for the pain of a traumatic loss may be particularly difficult. When Dede died, the person whom I would have longed to share in and hold my overwhelming grief was, of course, the very same person who was gone.

From the claim that developmental trauma is constituted in an intersubjective context wherein severe emotional pain cannot find a relational home in which it can be held, it follows that injurious childhood experiences in and of themselves need not be traumatic (or at least not lastingly so) or pathogenic, provided that they occur within a responsive milieu. *Pain is not pathology*. It is the absence of adequate attunement to the child's painful emotional reactions that renders them unendurable and thus a source of traumatic states and psychopathology. This conceptualization holds both for discrete, dramatic traumatic events and the more subtle "cumulative traumas" that occur continually throughout childhood.[8]

One consequence of developmental trauma, relationally conceived, is that affect states take on enduring, crushing meanings (prereflective organizing activity). From recurring experiences of malattunement, the child acquires the unconscious conviction that unmet developmental yearnings and reactive painful feeling states are manifestations of a loathsome defect or of an inherent inner badness. A defensive self-ideal is often established, representing a self-image purified of the offending affect states that were perceived to be unwelcome or damaging to caregivers. Living up to this affectively purified ideal becomes a central requirement for maintaining harmonious ties to others and for upholding self-esteem. Thereafter, the emergence of prohibited affect is experienced as a failure to embody the required ideal, an exposure of the underlying essential defectiveness or badness, and is accompanied by feelings of isolation, shame, and self-loathing. In psychoanalytic therapy, qualities or activities of the therapist that lend themselves to being interpreted according to such unconscious meanings of affect confirm the patient's expectations that emerging feeling states will be met with disgust, disdain, disinterest, alarm, hostility, withdrawal, exploitation, and the like, or will damage the therapist and destroy the therapeutic bond. Such transference expectations, unwittingly confirmed by the therapist, are a powerful source of resistance to the experience and articulation of affect. Intractable repetitive transferences and resistances can be grasped, from this perspective, as rigidly stable states of the patient–therapist system, in which the meanings of the therapist's stance have become tightly coordinated with the patient's grim expectations and fears, thereby exposing the patient repeatedly to threats of retraumatization. The focus on affect and its meanings contextualizes both transference and resistance, and it is essential for the progress of therapy that such expectations and fears be carefully and repeatedly investigated.

A second consequence of developmental trauma is a severe constriction and narrowing of the horizons of emotional experiencing so as to exclude whatever feels unacceptable, intolerable, or too dangerous in particular intersubjective contexts.[9] When a child's emotional experiences are consistently not responded to or are actively rejected, the child perceives that aspects of his or her affective life are intolerable to the caregiver. These regions of the child's emotional world must then be sacrificed in order to safeguard the needed tie. Repression occurs here as a kind of negative organizing principle, always embedded in ongoing intersubjective contexts, determining which configurations of affective experience are not to be allowed to come into full being. For example, when the act of linguistically articulating an affective experience is perceived to threaten an indispensable tie, repression can be achieved by preventing the continuation of the process of encoding that experience in language. In such instances, repression keeps affect nameless.

Clinical Vignette

The following clinical vignette (a fictionalized composite) illustrates many of the ideas developed in this section.

A young woman who had been repeatedly sexually abused by her father when she was a child began therapy with a female trainee whom I was supervising. Early in the treatment, whenever the patient began to remember and describe the sexual abuse, or to recount analogously invasive experiences in her current life, she would display emotional reactions that consisted of two distinctive parts, both of which seemed entirely bodily. One was a trembling in her arms and upper torso, which sometimes escalated into violent shaking. The other was an intense flushing of her face. On these occasions, my supervisee was quite alarmed by her patient's shaking and was concerned to find some way to calm her.

I had a hunch that the shaking was a bodily manifestation of a traumatized state and that the flushing was a somatic form of the patient's shame about exposing this state to her therapist, and I suggested to my supervisee that she focus her inquiries on the flushing rather than the shaking. As a result of this shift in focus, the patient began to speak about how she believed her therapist viewed her when she was trembling or shaking: Surely her analyst must be regarding her with disdain, seeing her as a damaged mess of a human being. As this belief was repeatedly disconfirmed by her therapist's responding with attunement and understanding rather than contempt, both the flushing and the shaking diminished in intensity. The traumatized states actually underwent a process of transformation from being exclusively bodily states into ones in which the bodily sensations came to be united with words. Instead of only shaking, the patient began to speak about her terror of annihilating intrusion.

The one and only time the patient had attempted to speak to her mother about the sexual abuse, her mother shamed her severely, declaring her to be a wicked little girl for making up such lies about her father. Thereafter, the patient did not tell any other human being about her trauma until she revealed it to her therapist, and both the flushing of her face and the restriction of her experience of terror to its nameless bodily component were heir to her mother's shaming. Only with a shift in her perception of her therapist from one in which her therapist was potentially or secretly shaming to one in which she was accepting and understanding could the patient's emotional experience of her traumatized states shift from an exclusively bodily form to an experience that could be felt and *named* as terror. Through such naming within the therapeutic context, the painful states gradually became more bearable.

The foregoing clinical vignette shows that the finding of a relational home that facilitates developmental transformation of traumatic affect can be a difficult task requiring a good deal of hermeneutic specificity. Any attempt by the therapist simply to name the affect showing up in the patient's bodily states would have been ineffective. The therapeutic context of emotional understanding needed first and foremost to include an illumination of the *dangers* of such naming—that it could evoke severe shaming by the therapist as it had by the patient's mother. Only when the danger of being shamed was understood and mitigated by the therapist's emotional attunement could the terrorized states be named as such.

The Phenomenology of Trauma

I turn now to a phenomenological description of traumatized states, as I myself have experienced them. When the book *Contexts of Being* was first published, an initial batch of copies was sent hot-off-the-press to the display table at a conference where I was a panelist.[10] I picked up a copy and looked around excitedly for my late wife, Dede, who would be so pleased and happy to see it. She was, of course, nowhere to be found, having died some 20 months earlier. I had awakened the morning of February 23, 1991, to find her lying dead across our bed, four weeks after her metastatic cancer had been diagnosed. Spinning around to show her my book and finding her gone instantly transported me back to that devastating moment in which I woke up and found her dead and my world was shattered, and I was once again consumed with horror and sorrow.[11]

There was a dinner at that conference for all the panelists, many of whom were my old and good friends and close colleagues. Yet, as I looked around the ballroom, they all seemed like strange and alien beings to me. Or more accurately, *I* seemed like a strange and alien being—not of this world. The others seemed so vitalized, engaged with one another in a lively manner. I, in contrast, felt deadened and broken, a shell of the man I had once been. An unbridgeable gulf seemed to open up, separating me forever from my friends and colleagues. They could never even begin to fathom my experience, I thought to myself, because we now lived in altogether different worlds.

Over the course of six years following that painful occasion, I tried to understand and conceptualize the dreadful sense of estrangement and isolation that seems to me to be inherent to the experience of emotional trauma. I became aware that this sense of alienation and aloneness appears as a common theme in the trauma literature, and I was able to hear about it from many of my patients who had experienced severe traumatization.[12] One such young man, who had suffered multiple losses of beloved family members during his childhood and adulthood, told me that the world was divided into two groups—the normals and the traumatized ones. There was no possibility, he said, for a normal ever to grasp the experience of a traumatized one.

I eventually found an explanation for this estrangement in what I called *the absolutisms of everyday life*.[13] When a person says to a friend, "I'll see you later," or a parent says to a child at bedtime, "I'll see you in the morning," these are statements, like delusions, whose validity is not open for discussion. Such absolutisms are the basis for a kind of naive realism and optimism that allow one to function in the world, experienced as stable, predictable, and safe. It is in the essence of emotional trauma that it shatters these absolutisms, a catastrophic loss of innocence that permanently alters one's sense of being-in-the-world. Massive deconstruction of the absolutisms of everyday life exposes the inescapable contingency of existence on a universe that is chaotic and unpredictable and in which no safety or continuity of being can be assured. Trauma thereby exposes "the unbearable embeddedness of being."[14] As a result, the traumatized person cannot help but perceive aspects of existence that lie well outside the absolutized horizons of normal everydayness. It is in this sense that the worlds of traumatized persons are felt to be fundamentally incommensurable with those of others, the deep chasm in which an anguished sense of estrangement and solitude takes form.

Trauma's Existential Significance

Once George Atwood and I had embarked upon our project of rethinking psychoanalysis as a form of phenomenological inquiry, a focus on the mutually enriching interface of psychoanalysis and continental phenomenology became inescapable, and I began studying phenomenological philosophy, sometimes voraciously. In 2000, I formed a leaderless philosophical study group in which we devoted a year to a close reading of Heidegger's magnum opus, *Being and Time*.[15] When I read the passages therein devoted to his existential analysis of *Angst*, I nearly fell off my chair! Both Heidegger's phenomenological description and ontological account of *Angst* bore a remarkable resemblance to what I had written about the phenomenology and meaning of emotional trauma two years earlier. Thus, Heidegger's existential philosophy—in particular, his existential analysis of *Angst*—provided me with extraordinary philosophical tools for grasping the existential significance of emotional trauma. It was this latter discovery that motivated me to begin doctoral studies in philosophy and to write a dissertation and two books on Heidegger, trauma, and what I came to call *post-Cartesian psychoanalysis*.[16]

Like Freud, Heidegger made a sharp distinction between fear and anxiety.[17] Whereas, according to Heidegger, that in the face of which one fears is a definite "entity within-the-world," that in the face of which one is anxious is "completely indefinite" and turns out to be "Being-in-the-world as such."[18] The indefiniteness of anxiety "tells us that entities within-the-world are not 'relevant' at all [. . .]. [The world] collapses into itself [and] has the character of completely lacking significance."[19] Heidegger made clear that it is the significance of the average everyday world, the world as constituted by the public interpretedness of the "they" (*das Man*), whose collapse is disclosed in anxiety. Furthermore, insofar as the "utter insignificance" of the everyday world is disclosed in anxiety, anxiety includes a feeling of uncanniness, in the sense of "not-being-at-home."[20] In anxiety, the experience of "Being-at-home" in one's "everyday familiarity" with the publicly interpreted world collapses, and "Being-in enters into the existential 'mode' of [. . .] 'uncanniness.'"[21]

In Heidegger's ontological account of anxiety, the central features of its phenomenology—the collapse of everyday significance and the resulting feeling of uncanniness—are claimed to be grounded in what he called *authentic* (nonevasively owned) *Being-toward-death*. Existentially, death is not simply an event that has not yet occurred or that happens to others, as *das Man* would have it. Rather, it is a distinctive possibility that is constitutive of our existence—of our intelligibility to ourselves in our futurity and our finitude. It is "the possibility of the impossibility of any existence at all," which, because it is both certain and indefinite as to its when, always impends as a constant threat, robbing us of the tranquilizing illusions that characterize our absorption in the everyday world, nullifying its significance for us.[22] The appearance of anxiety indicates that the fundamental defensive purpose (fleeing) of average everydayness has failed and that authentic Being-toward-death has broken through the evasions that conceal it. Torn from the sheltering illusions of *das Man*, we feel uncanny—no longer safely at home.

I have contended that emotional trauma produces an affective state whose features bear a close similarity to the central elements in Heidegger's existential interpretation of anxiety and that it accomplishes this by plunging the traumatized person into a form of authentic Being-toward-death.[23] Trauma shatters the illusions of everyday life that evade and cover up the finitude, contingency, and embeddedness of our existence and the indefiniteness of its certain extinction. Such shattering exposes what had been heretofore concealed, thereby plunging the traumatized person into a form of authentic Being-toward-death and into the anxiety—the loss of significance, the uncanniness—through which authentic Being-toward-death is disclosed. Trauma, like death, individualizes us, in a manner that invariably manifests in an excruciating sense of singularity and solitude.

The particular form of authentic Being-toward-death that crystallized in the wake of the trauma of Dede's death I characterize as a *Being-toward-loss*. Loss of loved ones constantly impends for me as a certain, indefinite, and ever-present possibility, in terms of which I now always understand myself and my world. My own experience of traumatic loss and its aftermath was a source of motivation for my efforts to relationalize Heidegger's conception of finitude by claiming that authentic Being-toward-death always entails owning up, not only to one's own finitude, but also to the finitude of all those we love. Hence, authentic Being-toward-death always includes Being-toward-loss as a central constituent. Just as, existentially, we are "always dying already," so too are we always already grieving.[24] Death and loss are existentially equiprimordial. Existential anxiety anticipates both death and loss.

Support for my claim about the equiprimordiality of death and loss can be found in the work of Derrida, who contended that every friendship is structured from its beginning, *a priori*, by the possibility that one of the two friends will die first and that the surviving friend will be left to mourn: "To have a friend, to look at him, to follow him with your eyes, [. . .] is to know in a more intense way, already injured, [. . .] that one of the two of you will inevitably see the other die."[25] Finitude and the possibility of mourning are constitutive of every friendship.

Dissociation, Finitude, and Traumatic Temporality

In the course of my investigations of the phenomenology and existential meaning of emotional trauma, I have conceptualized dissociation as the keeping apart of incommensurable emotional worlds, and I have rethought the phenomenon of dissociation in terms of the devastating impact of emotional trauma on our experience of temporality.[26] Dissociation, I contend, is traumatic temporality, and traumatic temporality is the condition for the possibility of the defensive use of dissociation.

A patient of mine with a long, painful history of traumatic violations, shocks, and losses arrived at her session in a profoundly fragmented state.[27] Shortly before, she had seen her psychopharmacologist for a twenty-minute interview. In an apparent attempt to update her files, this psychiatrist had required the patient to recount her entire history of traumatization, with no attention given to the emotional impact of this recounting. The patient explained to me that with the retelling of each traumatic episode, a piece of herself broke off and relocated at the time and place of the original trauma. By the time she reached my office, she said, she was completely dispersed along the time dimension of her crushing life history. Upon hearing this, I spoke just three words: "Trauma destroys time." The patient's eyes grew wide; she smiled and said, "I just came together again."

I use the term *portkey*, which I borrowed from Harry Potter, to capture the profound impact of emotional trauma on our experience of time.[28] Harry was a severely traumatized little boy, nearly killed by his parents' murderer and left in the care of a family that mistreated him cruelly. He arose from the ashes of devastating trauma as a wizard in possession of wondrous magical powers, and yet never free from the original trauma, always under threat by his parents' murderer. As a wizard, he encountered *portkeys*—objects that transported him instantly to other places, obliterating the duration ordinarily required for travel from one location to another.[29] Portkeys to trauma return one again and again to an experience of traumatization.[30] As shown dramatically in the foregoing paragraph, the experience of such portkeys fractures, and can even obliterate, one's sense of unitary selfhood, of being-in-time.

Trauma devastatingly disrupts the ordinary, average-everyday linearity and "ecstatical unity of temporality," the sense of "stretching-along" from the past to an open future.[31] Experiences of emotional trauma become freeze-framed into an eternal present in which one remains forever trapped, or to which one is condemned to be perpetually returned through the portkeys supplied by life's slings and arrows. In the region of trauma all duration or stretching along collapses, past becomes present, and future loses all meaning other than endless repetition. In this sense it is trauma, not, as Freud would have it, the unconscious, that is timeless.[32]

Because trauma so profoundly modifies the universal or shared structure of temporality, the traumatized person quite literally lives in another kind of reality, an experiential world felt to be incommensurable with those of others. This felt incommensurability, in turn, contributes to the sense of alienation and estrangement from other human beings that typically haunts the traumatized person. Torn from the communal fabric of being-in-time, trauma remains insulated from human dialogue.

The endless recurrence of emotional trauma is ensured by the finitude of our existence and the finitude of all those with whom we are deeply connected. Authentic temporality, insofar as it owns up to human finitude, is traumatic temporality. "Trauma recovery" is an oxymoron—human finitude with its traumatizing impact is not an illness from which one can recover. "Recovery" is a misnomer for the constitution of an expanded emotional world that coexists alongside the absence of the one that has been shattered by trauma. The expanded world and the absent shattered world may be more or less integrated or dissociated, depending on the degree to which the unbearable emotional pain evoked by the traumatic shattering has become integrated or remains dissociated defensively, which depends in turn on the extent to which such pain found a relational home[33] in which it could be held. This is the essential fracturing at the heart of traumatic temporality. Dissociation just is traumatic temporality.

Therapeutic Implications: Emotional Dwelling

How can a therapeutic relationship be constituted wherein the therapist can serve as a relational home for unbearable emotional pain and existential vulnerability? Recently, I have been moving toward a more active, relationally engaged form of therapeutic comportment that I call "emotional dwelling."[34] In dwelling, one does not merely seek empathically to understand the other's emotional pain from the other's perspective. One does that, but much more. In dwelling, one leans into the other's emotional pain and participates in it, perhaps with aid of one's own analogous experiences of pain. I have found that this active, engaged, participatory comportment is especially important in the therapeutic approach to emotional trauma. The language that one uses to address another's experience of emotional trauma meets the trauma head-on, articulating the unbearable and the unendurable, saying the unsayable, unmitigated by any efforts to soothe, comfort, encourage, or reassure—such efforts invariably being experienced by the other as a shunning or turning away from his or her traumatized state.

Let me give an example of emotional dwelling and the sort of language it employs from my own personal life. In the immediate aftermath of my late wife Dede's death, my soul brother, George Atwood, was the only person among my friends and family members who was capable of dwelling with me in the magnitude of my emotional devastation. He said, in his inimitable way, "You are a destroyed human being. You are on a train to nowhere." George lost his mother when he was eight years old, and I think his dwelling in and integrating his own experience of traumatic loss enabled him to be an understanding home for mine. He knew that offering me encouraging platitudes would be a form of emotional distancing that would just create a wall between us.

If we are to be an understanding relational home for a traumatized person, we must tolerate, even draw upon, our own existential vulnerabilities so that we can dwell unflinchingly with his or her unbearable and recurring emotional pain. When we dwell with others' unendurable pain, their shattered emotional worlds are enabled to shine with a kind of sacredness that calls forth an understanding and caring engagement within which traumatized states can be gradually transformed into bearable and nameable painful feelings.

Toward an Ethics of Finitude

What is it in our existential structure that makes the offering and the finding of a relational home for emotional trauma possible? I have contended
that just as finitude and vulnerability to death and loss are fundamental to
our existential constitution,[35] so too is it constitutive of our existence that
we meet each other as "brothers and sisters in the same dark night," deeply
connected with one another in virtue of our *common* finitude.[36] Thus, although the possibility of emotional trauma is ever present, so too is the
possibility of forming bonds of deep emotional attunement within which
devastating emotional pain can be held, rendered more tolerable, and, hope-
fully, eventually integrated. Our existential kinship-in-the-same-darkness
is the condition for the possibility both of the profound contextuality of
emotional trauma and of the mutative power of human understanding.

I suggest, as does Vogel, that owning up to our existential kinship-in-
finitude has significant ethical implications insofar as it motivates us, or
even obligates us, to care about and for our brothers' and sisters' existential
vulnerability and emotional pain.[37] Imagine a society in which the obligation to provide a relational home for the emotional pain that is inherent
to the traumatizing impact of our finitude has become a shared ethical
principle. In such a society, human beings would be much more capable of
living in their existential vulnerability, anxiety, and grief, rather than having to revert to the defensive, destructive evasions of them so lamentably
characteristic of human history. In such a societal context, a new form of
identity would become possible, based on owning rather than covering up
our existential vulnerability. Vulnerability that finds a hospitable relational
home could be seamlessly and constitutively integrated into whom we experience ourselves as being. A new form of human solidarity would also
become possible, rooted not in shared grandiose and destructive ideological illusion, but in shared recognition and respect for our common human
finitude. If we can help one another bear the darkness rather than evade it,
perhaps one day we will be able to see the light—as finite human beings,
finitely bonded to one another.

Concluding Remarks: Phenomenological
Contextualism All the Way Down

George Atwood and I have sought to refashion psychoanalysis as a phenomenological contextualism that investigates and illuminates worlds of
emotional experience, the structures prereflectively organizing them, and

the intersubjective contexts in which these structures take form. Such re-fashioning, in turn, has led us inexorably to a deconstructive critique of psychoanalytic metapsychologies.[38] We have concluded that, in postulating ultimate realities and universal truths, psychoanalytic metapsychologies are actually a form of metaphysics, and we have elaborated upon a claim first introduced by Wilhelm Dilthey that metaphysics represents an illusory flight from the tragedy of human finitude.[39] Metaphysics transforms the unbearable fragility and transience of all things human into an enduring, permanent, changeless reality, an illusory world of eternal truths.

For me, the account of emotional trauma summarized here represents the culmination of Atwood's and my project of phenomenologizing psychoanalysis. It can be asked, Doesn't a phenomenological-contextual account of trauma have to be grounded in something more fundamental, some form of solid bedrock—in other words, in a metaphysical entity? In an Age of Scientism, the metaphysical impulse typically turns to neuroscience in search of such grounding entities.

Atwood and I previously described an encounter with someone making a claim that neuroscience has much to offer the clinician in regards to the understanding of trauma and its biological aftermath.[40] It was said that severe trauma affects the brain, permanently altering pathways of excitation and inhibition in the neurological substrate. The trauma victim, in consequence, is someone whose central nervous system will never respond in the same way again. The idea was presented in a sober tone, as if definitive evidence for this rather depressing conclusion had been discovered, and as if sharp limits to the clinical efficacy of psychoanalytic therapy had accordingly been established. What if this idea, which has become widely popular, has no actual empirical foundation and is more a neurological (that is, metaphysical) fantasy than a scientific hypothesis?

The image of irreversible structural and functional alterations of the brain reifies an experience that is central in the phenomenology of emotional trauma—that of being changed essentially and forever. When the subjective sense of a profound and everlasting change is converted into an imagined material modification of neural tissues by redescribing it in the language of neuro-talk, the terror of that sense is encapsulated.

Psychiatry's bible, *The Diagnostic and Statistical Manual* (*DSM*), is an especially rich repository of metaphysical illusion. The *DSM* is a pseudo-scientific manual for diagnosing sick Cartesian isolated minds, "thinking things." As such, it completely overlooks the exquisite context sensitivity and radical context dependence of human emotional life. Against Descartes and his legacy, the *DSM*, Atwood, and I have contended that all forms of emotional disturbance are constituted in a context of human interrelatedness.[41]

Yet even phenomenological psychopathologists continue to look to the *DSM* as a source of decontextualized psychiatric entities. A good example is Matthew Ratcliffe's book on the phenomenology of depression, which presents an analysis of the unity of existential hopelessness that is quite elegant and valuable.[42] But he presents this analysis as a phenomenological account of "experiences of depression," defining the latter according to categories of the *DSM*. Ratcliffe elaborates a phenomenological account of existential hopelessness that invites exploration and appreciation of its context-embeddedness, but encases it in an objectifying psychiatric diagnostic language that negates this very embeddedness!

There are striking similarities among Ratcliffe's characterization of existential hopelessness, Heidegger's phenomenological description of anxiety, and my own rendering of the phenomenology of emotional trauma. All three phenomenologies entail loss of significance of the everyday world. The similarities are not surprising because experiences of severe emotional trauma are the very contexts, concealed by Ratcliffe's adoption of a decontextualizing psychiatric language, in which both feelings of existential hopelessness and the emotional disturbances objectified by the *DSM* take form.

Metaphysical entities—neurological, psychiatric, and otherwise—cover up devastating contexts, replacing the tragic finitude and transience of human life with a reassuring picture of encapsulated, substantialized, and enduring realities. A perspective on emotional trauma that is phenomenological-contextual all the way down, by contrast, embraces the unbearable vulnerability and context-dependence of human existence. Such an embrace lies at the heart of an ethics of finitude and the comportment of emotional dwelling that is its condition of possibility.

NOTES

1. For a chronicling of the historical unfolding of this project, see "Legacies of the Golden Age: A Memoir of a Collaboration," in George E. Atwood and Robert D. Stolorow, *Structures of Subjectivity: Explorations in Psychoanalytic Phenomenology and Contextualism*, 2nd ed. (London and New York: Routledge, 2014).

2. Daphne D. Socarides and Robert D. Stolorow, "Affects and Self-objects," *The Annual of Psychoanalysis* 12/13 (1984/85).

3. Robert D. Stolorow and George E. Atwood, *Contexts of Being: The*

Intersubjective Foundations of Psychological Life (Hillsdale, N.J.: Analytic Press, 1992).

4. Atwood and Stolorow, *Contexts of Being*.

5. Michael Balint, "Trauma and Object Relationship," *International Journal of Psychoanalysis* 50 (1969); Sandor Ferenczi, "Confusion of Tongues Between Adults and the Child," in *Final Contributions to the Problems and Methods of Psycho-Analysis* (London: Hogarth Press, 1933); Heinz Kohut, *The Analysis of the Self* (Madison, Conn.: International Universities Press, 1971); Henry Krystal, *Integration and Self-Healing: Affect, Trauma, Alexithymia* (Hillsdale, N.J.: Analytic Press, 1988); Donald W. Winnicott, *Through Paediatrics to Psycho-Analysis* (New York: Basic Books, 1975).

6. Sigmund Freud, "Inhibitions, Symptoms and Anxiety," in *The Standard Edition of the Complete Psychological Works of Sigmund Freud, Volume XX (1925–1926): An Autobiographical Study, Inhibitions, Symptoms and Anxiety, The Question of Lay Analysis and Other Works*, trans. and ed. James Strachey (London: Hogarth Press, 1959).

7. Russell B. Carr, "Combat and Human Existence: Toward an Intersubjective Approach to Combat Related PTSD," *Psychoanalytic Psychology* 28 (2011).

8. Masud Khan, "The Concept of Cumulative Trauma," in *The Privacy of the Self* (Madison, Conn.: International Universities Press, 1974).

9. See Chapter 3 in Robert D. Stolorow, George E. Atwood, and Donna M. Orange, *Worlds of Experience: Interweaving Philosophical and Clinical Dimensions in Psychoanalysis* (New York: Basic Books, 2002).

10. Stolorow and Atwood, *Contexts of Being*.

11. Borrowing a term from Harry Potter, I call such experiences *portkeys* to trauma. See Robert D. Stolorow, *Trauma and Human Existence: Autobiographical, Psychoanalytic, and Philosophical Reflections* (New York: Routledge, 2007); Robert D. Stolorow, *World, Affectivity, Trauma: Heidegger and Post-Cartesian Psychoanalysis* (New York: Routledge, 2011).

12. For example, see Judith Herman, *Trauma and Recovery* (New York: Basic Books, 1992).

13. Robert D. Stolorow, "The Phenomenology of Trauma and the Absolutisms of Everyday Life: A Personal Journey," *Psychoanalytic Psychology* 16 (1999): 467.

14. Stolorow and Atwood, *Contexts of Being*, 22.

15. Martin Heidegger, *Being and Time*, trans. John Macquarrie and Edward Robinson (New York: Harper & Row, 1962).

16. See Stolorow, *Trauma and Human Existence*; Stolorow, *World, Affectivity, Trauma*.

17. Freud, "Inhibitions, Symptoms and Anxiety."

18. Heidegger, *Being and Time*, 231, 231, 230.

19. Heidegger, *Being and Time*, 231.

20. Heidegger, *Being and Time*, 231, 233.

21. Heidegger, *Being and Time*, 233. See also the description of my traumatized state in the second paragraph of the section "The Phenomenology of Trauma."

22. Heidegger, *Being and Time*, 307.

23. See Stolorow, *Trauma and Human Existence*; Stolorow, *World, Affectivity, Trauma*.

24. Heidegger, *Being and Time*, 298.

25. Jacques Derrida, *The Work of Mourning*, trans. Pascale-Anne Brault and Michael Naas (Chicago: University of Chicago Press 2001), 107.

26. By *temporality*, I mean the lived experience of time.

27. This patient is discussed in Stolorow, *Trauma and Human Existence*.

28. J. K. Rowling, *Harry Potter and the Goblet of Fire* (New York: Scholastic Press, 2000).

29. My wife, Dr. Julia Schwartz, first brought this imagery of portkeys to my attention as a metaphor that captures the impact of trauma on the experience of temporality.

30. See the first paragraph of the section, "The Phenomenology of Trauma," for a vivid personal example of such a portkey.

31. Heidegger, *Being and Time*, 416, 426.

32. Sigmund Freud. "The Unconscious," in *The Standard Edition of the Complete Psychological Works of Sigmund Freud, Volume XIV (1914–1916): On the History of the Psycho-Analytic Movement, Papers on Metapsychology, and Other Works*, trans. and ed. James Strachey (London: Hogarth Press, 1957).

33. In authentic existing, such a relational home is also itself recognized as finite.

34. See Robert D. Stolorow, "Undergoing the Situation: Emotional Dwelling Is More than Empathic Understanding," *International Journal of Psychoanalytic Self Psychology* 9 (2014); George E. Atwood and Robert D. Stolorow, "Walking the Tightrope of Emotional Dwelling," *Psychoanalytic Dialogues* 26 (2016).

35. See Stolorow, *Trauma and Human Existence*; Stolorow, *World, Affectivity, Trauma*.

36. Lawrence Vogel, *The Fragile "We": Ethical Implications of Heidegger's "Being and Time"* (Evanston, Ill.: Northwestern University Press, 1994), 97.

37. Vogel, *The Fragile "We."*

38. See Chapter 8 in George E. Atwood and Robert D. Stolorow, *Structures of Subjectivity: Explorations in Psychoanalytic Phenomenology and Contextualism*, 2nd ed. (London and New York: Routledge, 2014).

39. Wilhelm Dilthey, *Selected Works: Volume 3: The Formation of the Historical World in the Human Sciences* (Princeton: Princeton University Press, 2002).

40. Robert D. Stolorow and George E. Atwood, "Deconstructing 'The Self' of Self Psychology," *International Journal of Psychoanalytic Self Psychology* 7 (2012).

41. Atwood and Stolorow, *Structures of Subjectivity*.

42. Matthew Ratcliffe, *Experiences of Depression: A Study in Phenomenology* (Oxford: Oxford University Press, 2015).

CHAPTER 3

Traumatized by Transcendence:
My Other's Keeper

Donna Orange

One need not be aware of it to be suffering from psychological trauma. Several years ago, having encountered a disturbing error message on my computer, I called technical support. The competent helper, whose accent I recognized as coming from India, managed in a half-hour or so to solve my problem. During a pause, when I asked where he was located, he named an area of southern India. "Were you close to the tsunami?" I asked. "Oh yes, but we are all safe here, and all my family too, some of whom were much more exposed. Thank you for asking." Then he began to repeat, almost singsong style, "It was so unexpected. We didn't expect it. It was so unexpected. We didn't expect it." We returned to our task, but as soon as there was another pause, the refrain returned. "It was so unexpected. We didn't expect it. Thank you for your concern. Thank you for asking," and so on. Even when our task was successfully completed, it was difficult to end the call.

This incident[1] illustrates several aspects of the phenomenology of traumatic experience, familiar to all clinicians and humanitarian workers: the destruction of temporality, the violation of expectancy, emotional freezing, the need for witnessing, the selective disorganization of experience, and mourning. In this chapter, I explore links between trauma in the other, traumatism in the responder, and transcendence, arguing that a radical ethics dislocates ordinary notions of transcendence, finding it upended. The needs of the destitute precede the comforts of the affluent, and of the churches and philosophies where transcendence has been thought to reside.

Trauma—whether natural disaster, human violence, or unexpected loss —destroys our normal sense of time.[2] We lose the feeling that "I'll see you tomorrow" (*hasta la vista, arrivederci*) makes any sense. Organizing our lives toward a future, our own or that of those we love, loses sense. We feel dazed, disoriented, and lost. Trauma often destroys memory, both for the traumatic experience itself, or for the life before and around it.

Psychological trauma, familiar to every clinician but, as we know from clinical experience, not always to those who suffer its paralyzing effects, invites, even demands, interdisciplinary reflection. Integral to its worst effects, isolation makes trauma intractable. Recognition, witness, holding, finding what Stolorow calls "siblings in the same darkness"—all these mitigate trauma, if they never cure it.

Increasingly, both psychoanalysts[3] and political theorists[4] argue that background conditions matter, for good or for ill. Anna Ornstein claims that Holocaust survivors who came from stable, good-enough families had much better physical and mental health after the massacre than those whose early lives had been precarious or worse.[5] Henry Shue believes that background injustices like settler colonialism and chattel slavery matter as we try now to adapt to climate change and impose obligations for reparative justice on those of us who live as beneficiaries of such injustices, even if we did not personally commit them.[6] My own recent work suggests that unconscious inheritance of such injustice blinds us "whites" to the effects of our carbon-and-methane affluence on the world's poorest people, mostly darker-skinned.[7]

My own question here, indebted to the radical post-Shoah ethical thinking of Emmanuel Levinas and to others inspired by him, concerns what he called "le traumatisme."[8] This strange-sounding word refers to the effect that others' suffering, their hunger, their desperation ought to have on me, a potential ethical subject. Responding, non-indifferent to the other's need—for a small courtesy or for the last crust of bread "snatched from my mouth"—traumatized, taken hostage in a pre-original, anarchical responsibility, I am my other's keeper, the answer to Cain's insolent question. This ethical sensibility, relational and radical, Judith Butler formulates:

> Levinas talks about "persecution" as the primary relation to the other,
> and this usually alarms relational psychoanalysts, and understandably
> so. But what he means by this is that we are not given any choice at
> the beginning about what will impress itself upon us, or about how
> that impression will be registered and translated. These are domains of
> radical impressionability and receptivity that are prior to all choice and
> deliberation.[9]

She goes on to say that these unchosen domains of sensibility, the always already, we might say, are neither yours nor mine, not possessions, but rather ways of being in the hands of the others, as we are from birth. We might comment that Western individualism, especially in its recent form as neoliberalist economics and politics, deludes us into forgetting the vulnerability into which we are all born.

As 60 million refugees in a single year seek shelter from hunger produced by desertification, from wars arguably brought on by the poor seeing now what the rich have and keep behind their gated walls, as images of the dead from trying to escape war and poverty flood our media, indifference seems less and less possible. What if the misery we see on our televisions results from our trade policies, from our carbon-and-methane profligacy, from the refusal of education and contraception to hundreds of millions of the world's women? And yet, once we actually link the others' suffering with our carbon-happy lifestyle, how do we sustain our sense of responsibility? Am I my other's keeper?

Transcendence as Domination and Privilege

Let us consider two different uses of the word "transcendence." To traumatized, shattered, devastated people, "transcendence" might well sound empty. It could smack of "resilience" studies, placing the responsibility for hunger, torture, rape, homelessness, and their effects on the hapless sufferer. In Western cultures of egoistic individualism, idealizing self-sufficiency, exhortations to get over it, to move on, to find transcendent meaning in one's suffering, fill the self-help literature. Appeals to such transcendence may even perpetuate the political and theological systems causing the suffering the underclass and outsiders are supposed to transcend. Let us pause for a moment over the origins of this viewpoint, as our rapidly worsening climate crisis, feeding the wars and the flood of refugees, may start here.

We Westerners inherit an outsized share of the guilt and responsibility for the climate change currently traumatizing our bothers and sisters in the global south. Whatever we may think of China now, we in the West set the industrialization-at-all-costs pattern they have followed. As Stephen M. Gardiner writes, "the USA is responsible for 29 percent of global emissions since the onset of the industrial revolutions (from 1850 to 2003), and the nations of the EU 26 percent; by contrast China and India are responsible for 8 percent and 2 percent respectively."[10] To understand what has gone so wrong in our relation to the earth, including our indifference to its most destitute people, we must first briefly revisit the roots of the scientific rationalism and political individualism emergent in seventeenth- and eighteenth-century Europe. These became founding ideals in the United States.

In the modern period, beginning with Descartes and Galileo, as many have observed, the human became solitary mental substance, divorced from body and material nature.[11] In the thinking of Hobbes and Locke, this creature of mathematical reason became the political individual, negotiating social contracts to avoid the wars inherent in the state of nature but ultimately concerned only with his own life, liberty, and property (the view Dostoevsky called egoism). The deist god of this period had created and designed this world but did not interfere in its operation, except to bless the work of the colonizers and slave-traders. Scientific rationality, eclipsing all that Wilhelm Dilthey would later call the *Geisteswissenschaften* (humanities), ruled, creating technology and efficiency, destroying the earth in the turn to fossil fuels, destroying indigenous peoples seen as less rational.

Few have noticed the monism of scientific rationalism. It claims that only one thing counts, excluding the irreplaceable value of the individual human, the truth of the arts of poetry and music, the beauty of our common home, earth.[12]

Pragmatist William James articulated an alternative to the monistic presumptions of many philosophers, Western and Eastern alike. Calling his view pluralism, illustrating it best, I believe, in *The Varieties of Religious Experience*, James showed how rich and variegated is our access to whatever we feel and believe transcends us.[13] His New England forebears, Thoreau and Emerson, had already brought "transcendentalism" to the United States, where they taught living close to the earth and rejected the enslaving of other human beings. An insistent chorus of minority voices has always rejected the monism of dominating scientific rationalism.

So although monism (it all comes down to the same thing) and egoism (it all comes out best if we care only for ourselves) have predominated in the so-called developed world, combining to form what Adriaan Peperzak calls "egocentric monism," we have other possibilities.[14] Dialogic thinkers like Plato and Hans-Georg Gadamer, pluralists like James, and ethical thinkers show that the West can value multiple voices, whose prophetic call evokes a transcendence other than "moving on" after shattering trauma.[15] Such pseudo-transcendence, however, has both roots and fruits, devastating fruits, in western monisms with their correlative insistence on knowing. So we must look back again, if not to the Greek origins of this entrenched preference, at least to its ultimate idealizing in Hegel.

Assuming the essential oneness of all things, Western monism firmly adopts knowing or cognition as the exclusive—or at least primary—route or form of access to this one total reality. Hegel, probably the most capable practitioner of this approach, proclaimed: "What human beings strive for in general is cognition of the world; we strive to appropriate it and to conquer it. To this end the world must be crushed as it were; i.e. it must be made ideal."[16] Merold Westphal, to whom I am indebted for drawing my attention to these stunning words, comments that Hegel "let the cat out of the bag" about his totalizing intentions.[17] A different cat interests me here. Hegel tells us that our passion for knowing the world prepares us to treat the earth as our possession, "appropriate it," to dominate it (and its indigenous peoples?), to "conquer it," and to crush it in the service of making it ideal, that is, a mental product. Not only Genesis, probably misunderstood, but also Enlightenment rationalism taught us to dominate by knowing, to crush, not to take care.

While a passion for knowing[18] may serve humanistic, ecological, and transcendent purposes—curing disease, alerting us to climate dangers, connecting us to others geographically distant and culturally strange to us —cognition as master rather than servant destroys, appropriating, dominating, and conquering, just as Hegel wrote. It destroys the hermeneutic space where understanding emerges, where creativity flourishes, where indigenous cultures live.[19] But individual, irreplaceable human beings must not be crushed.[20] Hegemonic, all-dominating, scientific reason evokes Pascal's thought: "My place in the sun begins the destruction of the earth" (*C'est là ma place au soleil. Voilà le commencement et l'image de l'usurpation de toute la terre*).[21]

Pascal clearly links possessiveness to the destruction of the earth. In turn, such domination and destruction (*Laudato Si*) traumatizes the people who call this earth their home, like those South Pacific islanders being displaced by rising sea levels. Perhaps a clear-headed look at the climate crisis will require us to rethink our culture's deeply embedded assumptions about private property, consumption, and their associated "rights." Those dispossessed by injustice may challenge our preconceptions about what we deserve. The other who commands me, always already, to respond to her precarity challenges my unexamined, even unconscious sense of what lives are valuable, or as Butler likes to say, grievable.[22] As we will see when we come to radical transcendence, the other traumatizes me by her transcendence of my categories, of my egoistic narcissism, of my self-enclosed entitlement and possessiveness. She stands above me in her need. She upends the order of importance. But first we must consider a set of meanings from a different language game, more closely related to the monism we have been considering.

As a theological term, *transcendence* contrasts with *immanence*, associated with the "heresy" of pantheism, especially in the philosophy of Spinoza. No wonder this first of modern thinkers to call his philosophy "ethics" needed to live in hiding. Pantheists found god everywhere, in everything. The earth and all its peoples were holy. No, said the theists, believers in the transcendent deity, you have denied the creator God who provides for His creation, and you deserve to die. So philosophers and scientists became very careful to separate their published works from their private thinking. Once again, transcendence became a name for dominance, totalizing, torture, even burning at the stake.

The deists, among them Locke, Jefferson, and other U.S. founders, claimed that God, like a good watchmaker, originally designed our earth but then left it to run on its own. Whether God continues to tinker now and then with His creation, they were unsure. Deism allowed for appealing to a deity when convenient—"all men are created equal," "in God we trust"—but inventing the deity's meaning according to convenience as well, as in the slave trade's and settler colonialism's racial superiority presumptions. So we inherited a constitution that presumed both human equality, and sub-human status for blacks, indigenous people, and women.

Ironically, the greatest challenge to this fundamental inconsistency, gradually recognized in the case of slavery by Abraham Lincoln, came through a group of immanentists who called themselves Transcendentalists. Somewhat confusingly, their name arose from their insistence that spirit transcended its substratum, material yet immanently suffused with spirit. Everything and everyone was full of spirit.[23] Unlike their Puritan forebears, the New England Transcendentalists made no appeal to a transcendent deity. Instead, with Thoreau and Emerson among them, they led the abolitionist challenge to the religious people who called on a "transcendent" divinity to justify slavery and westward expansion into what they regarded with earlier popes as *Terra Nullius*, land where nobody lived.[24] The people there did not count as human. The settlers and their government understood expansionism as the will of a transcendent God. In the words of Puritan John Winthrop (1588–1649) often quoted by Ronald Reagan to justify U.S. dominance,

> We shall find that the God of Israel is among us, when tens of us shall be able to resist a thousand of our enemies, when he shall make us a praise and a glory, that men shall say of succeeding plantations: the lord make it like New England, for we must consider that we shall be as a City upon a Hill, the eyes of all people upon us.[25]

Clearly an ethical transcendence cannot be this kind of privileged transcendence, historically justifying slavery and settler colonialism, even now tolerating or justifying the domination of women, excluded from education, genitally mutilated, refused control over reproduction, shunned from leadership in many religions. The beauty of churches and mosques, the inspiration of music, all this remains insufficient. Those who do not protect the Jews may not sing Gregorian chant, Dietrich Bonhoeffer wrote in the 1930s. Something else is needed to meet the call of the traumatized other, allowing ourselves to feel our vulnerability to others' suffering. Transcendence that privileges some over others forgets the spirit, present in most of the world's religious and spiritual traditions, prioritizing the abject. Blessed are the poor.

Radical Transcendence

In his magnum opus, *Otherwise than Being, or Beyond Essence*, Levinas wrote of a *traumatisme assourdissante*, a deafening traumatism.[26] He seems to have meant the "persecution" of the always already responsible me by the suffering of the other, taking me hostage, leaving me no escape, except that of substitution. As I find myself in the place of the other in her or his precarity, trauma becomes my lot, too, in non-indifference.[27] The one affected—perhaps a psychotherapist, or any humanitarian worker—by the other's hunger, by the other's tortured devastation, by the other's homelessness, either allows the trauma to spread and infect one (traumatism), or turns away, without "the frail courage to look into our eyes," as Primo Levi wrote after Auschwitz.[28]

Levinas also wrote of useless and useful suffering.[29] Suffering in itself, he thought, is absurd, for nothing, pure evil. Theodicies—justifying a providential god, who allows evil and permits extreme human suffering in the service of greater goods—he saw as pure blasphemy. Legitimate heir of

Ivan Karamazov, he supported Nietzsche's call for "the death of a certain god."[30] And yet, for Levinas, suffering had another story to tell:

> Is not the evil of suffering—extreme passivity, abandonment, helpless-
> ness, and solitude—also the unassumable [the unbearable], whence
> the possibility of a half opening that a moan, a cry, a groan or a sigh
> slips through—the original call for aid, for curative help, help from the
> other me whose alterity, whose exteriority promises salvation? [. . .] For
> pure suffering, which is intrinsically senseless and condemned to itself
> with no way out, a beyond appears in the form of the interhuman.[31]

Here we find pure suffering, or evil, met by the possibility of useful suffering or traumatism, suffering taken on in the service of the suffering other.
Noting that perhaps this clarity could come only at the end of the century
through which he had lived, a century of "the worst," in Derrida's expression, Levinas distinguished:

> There is a radical difference between the suffering in the other, where it
> is unforgivable to me, solicits me and calls me, and suffering in me, my
> own experience of suffering, whose constitutional or congenital useless-
> ness can take on a meaning, the only one of which suffering is capable,
> in becoming suffering for the suffering (inexorable though it may be) of
> someone else.[32]

The other's suffering, absurd and evil, must become intolerable to me,
pre-primordially responsible for the other. So traumatism, the useful or
usable suffering of the one taken hostage by the other's suffering, becomes
the route to non-blasphemous transcendence. In "Transcendence and
Height,"[33] as in *Totality and Infinity*, we learn that in the ethical relation,
always radically asymmetrical, the other transcends me utterly, in a "curva-
ture of intersubjective space."[34] The other always precedes me, transcends
me. My place in the sun has become a tent with flaps open on all sides to
welcome the refugee, the widow, the orphan, and the stranger.

This transcendence can have nothing to do with religious or political
dominance, erasing the faces and voices of women, of people of color, of
LGBT people, of refugees, seeing them as members of groups, quotas, or
categories, that is, forgetting their irreplaceable humanity, their transcendent value. The miserable ones stand above me, demanding that I look
into their eyes, finding there the only available traces of any transcendent
infinite. Here is the only holy. All the rest is incantation.

How does one traumatized by transcendence look? She cannot bear in-
differently the useless suffering of the other. She may help the struggling

mother with the stroller up the subway stairs, or the senior who cannot reach what he needs in the supermarket. He may give years of life in the poorest countries to build schools where girls are welcome and protected. He may give his last crust of bread so that a child could live after Auschwitz. The examples, from simple to heroic, share an absence of self-preoccupation. They are not about me, but for the other, almost in spite of me. Non-masochistic, they have nothing to do with wanting to suffer, but with a willingness to suffer for the other's sake, replacing the self-centered ego. As a therapeutic attitude, I have called this transcendence emotional availability, less oriented to what the analyst or therapist actively does or says, less concerned with technique, rather more emptied out to be affected by the other, called out by the other's need.[35] Risky, as Chris Jaenicke clearly shows, this attitude finds me drawn inexorably into the other's traumatized suffering, non-indifferent.[36] Clinical wisdom then consists in understanding how to respond. Non-response, emotional distancing, ethical indifference, these repeat the original murders for which our patients consult us in the first place.

Many examples of what Levinas called *sainteté* (holiness), unexpected goodness, response to the other, occur without much notice.[37] A neighbor in my suburban New Jersey town recently overheard a German couple in the local pharmacy as they were refused desperately needed medication because they had no American identification. He followed them to the door of the store where he found them in tears, told them to wait, and bought them the medication. He regarded the strangers as his neighbors, and took the trouble. Granted, all the people involved in this story have white skin, and spoke good-enough English, but I see similar occurrences in New York among people who do not share language or skin color almost every day. I believe we need to notice, to remember, to reassure ourselves continually that the ethical life is real and therefore possible.

In another recent example, my 77-year-old brother-in-law needed a risky cancer surgery in a southern city, hit by a record-breaking ice and snowstorm. This city does not have a single snowplow. His famous surgeon called early that morning to say his office would be closed and he could do the surgery early. We, however, were isolated on a hill several miles away and had no way to reach the hospital. No problem, said this surgeon, he was from the north, had a four-wheel drive, and would come to pick us up. He did, carried out the successful surgery, and also offered to drive my husband and me home whenever we were ready. When I thanked him, he said simply, "I couldn't let him worry any longer about this surgery."

Simple and unpretentious, ethical transcendence often hides its traumatism. The very simplicity of these stories carries their ethical sincerity; embedding them in classical ethical theories would destroy the appeal to radical ethical transcendence and interruption of the self-centered life. The very directness, the matter-of-factness, indicates the holiness involved. Whatever the surgeon, the neighbor in the drugstore, the subway passenger, had been doing, something, that is, someone's distress, stopped her or him in their tracks. The only question was how to help, not whether. The other's suffering commands me utterly.[38] For us in the affluent world, the question is how to feel this urgency. Judith Butler often writes of her concern that our media preoccupies us with ourselves, filling our minds with triviality, obscuring the trauma of precarity.[39] According to my thesis, the traumas of others—especially at this moment of climate emergency—must traumatize us (traumatism), if we and they are to be transformed by their transcendence over us. Paradoxically, our useful and usable suffering, responding to the absurd suffering, hunger, and torture of others, takes on the trace of transcendence.

Conclusion

Theories of transcendence, including philosophical egoism, theological hierarchies, therapeutic views of cure and resiliency, can create and reinforce systemic power structures, engendering trauma and destruction for the earth's most vulnerable people. They justify whatever oppressive measures they take, when they can see them, by appealing to some allegedly transcendent good: markets, traditional interpretations of scriptures or constitutions, racial purity, ego autonomy, and mentalization. This kind of transcendence means becoming more rational, that is, not like people of color, like poets, like indigenous peoples who live close to the earth, especially not like those who flee in terror from war and famine.

Radical transcendence inverts this disordered and destructive domination, placing the self at the bottom, in service to the other, in a state of traumatism, unable to sleep comfortably when others are starving. The suffering other's face carries the trace of the infinite, as the Transcendentalists who opposed slavery saw. After the death of a certain god (the god of false transcendence), I must be traumatized by the trauma of the other in a radical transcendence toward non-indifference.

NOTES

1. Also reported in my recent *Nourishing the Inner Life of Clinicians and Humanitarians: The Ethical Turn in Psychoanalysis* (London: Routledge, 2016).

2. Robert D. Stolorow, *Trauma and Human Existence: Autobiographical, Psychoanalytic, and Philosophical Reflections* (New York: Analytic Press, 2007).

3. Anna Ornstein, "Survival and Recovery: Psychoanalytic Reflections," in *Progress Self Psychology, Volume 19*, ed. Mark J. Gehrie (Hillsdale, N.J.: Analytic Press, 2003).

4. Henry Shue, *Climate Justice: Vulnerability and Protection* (Oxford: Oxford University Press, 2014).

5. Ornstein, "Survival and Recovery."

6. Shue, *Climate Justice.*

7. Donna Orange, *Climate Crisis, Psychoanalysis, and Radical Ethics* (London: Routledge, 2017). Ta-Nehisi Coates, *Between the World and Me* (New York: Spiegel and Grau, 2015).

8. Emmanuel Levinas, *Collected Philosophical Papers* (Dordrecht, The Netherlands: Martinus Nijhoff, 1987), 75.

9. Judith Butler and Athena Athanasiou, *Dispossession: The Performative in the Political* (Malden, Mass.: Polity, 2013), 95.

10. Stephen Gardiner, "Climate Justice," in *The Oxford Handbook of Climate Change and Society*, ed. John S. Dryzek, Richard B. Norgaard, and David Schlosberg (Oxford: Oxford University Press, 2011), 315.

11. Charles Taylor, *Sources of the Self: The Making of the Modern Identity* (Cambridge: Harvard University Press, 1989).

12. Hans-Georg Gadamer and Richard E. Palmer, *The Gadamer Reader: A Bouquet of the Later Writings* (Evanston, Ill.: Northwestern University Press, 2007).

13. William James, *The Varieties of Religious Experience: A Study in Human Nature* (New York: Longmans, Green, and Co., 1902); William James, *A Pluralistic Universe* (Cambridge: Harvard University Press, 1977).

14. Adrian T. Peperzak, *To the Other: An Introduction to the Philosophy of Emmanuel Levinas* (West Lafayette, Ind.: Purdue University Press, 1993), 19. The new encyclical criticizes this monism under another rubric: "When human beings place themselves at the centre, they give absolute priority to immediate convenience and all else becomes relative. Hence we should not be surprised to find, in conjunction with the omnipresent technocratic paradigm and the cult of unlimited human power, the rise of a relativism which sees everything as irrelevant unless it serves one's own immediate interests" (Laudato Si, #122). Psychoanalysts call this attitude infantile; it wants what it wants and wants it now.

15. Plato, J. M. Cooper, and D. S. Hutchinson, *Complete Works* (Indianapolis: Hackett Publishing, 1997); Gadamer, *The Gadamer Reader*; Hans-Georg Gadamer, *Truth and Method*, 2nd ed., trans. Joel Weinsheimer and Donald G. Marshall (New York: Continuum, 1975); James, *A Pluralistic Universe*; Emmanuel Levinas, *Otherwise than Being or Beyond Essence*, trans. Alphonso Lingis (Pittsburgh: Duquesne University Press, 1998).

16. Hegel, G. W. F., *The Encyclopaedia Logic, with the Zusätze: Part I of the Encyclopaedia of Philosophical Sciences with the Zusätze*, trans. T. F. Geraets, W. A. Suchting, and H. S. Harris (Indianapolis: Hackett, 1991), 42, Addition 2.

17. Merold Westphal, "Levinas and the 'Logic' of Solidarity," *Graduate Faculty Philosophy Journal 20* (1998): 297–319.

18. Some would argue that knowing always totalizes and dominates, that when it seems peaceful, we actually find meeting, responding, nonreductionistic inquiry based on pluralistic and perspectival assumptions. See Martin Buber, *I and Thou*, trans. Walter A. Kaufmann (New York: Scribner, 1970); Emmanuel Levinas, *Totality and Infinity*, trans. Alphonso Lingis (Pittsburgh: Duquesne University Press, 1969).

19. Gunter Figal, *Objectivity: The Hermeneutical and Philosophy*, trans. Theodore D. George (Albany, N.Y.: SUNY Press, 2010).

20. Levinas, *Totality and Infinity*.

21. Blaise Pascal, *Pensées and Other Writings*, trans. Honor Levi (Oxford: Oxford University Press, 2008), 295.

22. Judith Butler, *Precarious Life: The Powers of Mourning and Violence* (New York: Verso, 2004).

23. Shelton H. Smith, Robert T. Handy, and Lefferts A. Loetscher, *American Christianity: An Historical Interpretation with Representative Documents* (New York: Scribner, 1960).

24. Eduardo Galeano, *Open Veins of Latin America: Five Centuries of the Pillage of a Continent*, trans. Cedric Belfrage (New York: Monthly Review Press, 1973).

25. John Winthrop, "City on a Hill," in *Collections of the Massachusetts Historical Society 7*, no. 3 (1838).

26. Levinas, *Otherwise than Being*.

27. Butler, *Precarious Life*.

28. Levi, Primo. *The Drowned and the Saved*, trans. Raymond Rosenthal (New York: Vintage International, 1989).

29. Emmanuel Levinas, "Useless Suffering," in *The Provocation of Levinas*, ed. Robert Bernasconi and David Wood, trans. Richard Cohen (London: Routledge, 1988).

30. Levinas, *Otherwise than Being*, 185; Jill Stauffer and Bettina Bergo

(eds.), *Nietzsche and Levinas: "After the Death of a Certain God"* (New York: Columbia University Press, 2009).

31. Levinas, "Useless Suffering," 138.

32. Levinas, "Useless Suffering," 159.

33. Emmanuel Levinas, Adrian T. Peperzak, Simon Critchley, and Robert Bernasconi, R., eds., *Emmanuel Levinas: Basic Philosophical Writings* (Bloomington: Indiana University Press, 1996).

34. Levinas, *Totality and Infinity*, 291.

35. Donna Orange, *Emotional Understanding: Explorations in Psychoanalytic Epistemology* (New York: Guilford Press), 1995.

36. Chris Jaenicke, *The Risk of Relatedness: Intersubjectivity Theory in Clinical Practice* (Lanham: Jason Aronson, 2008); Chris Jaenicke, *Change in Psychoanalysis: An Analyst's Reflections on the Therapeutic Relationship* (New York: Routledge, 2011).

37. This example comes from Orange, *Nourishing the Inner Life of Clinicians and Humanitarians*.

38. See Philip P. Hallie, *Lest Innocent Blood Be Shed: The Story of the Village of Le Chambon, and How Goodness Happened There*, 1st ed. (New York: Harper & Row, 1979). The story of Chambon, where ordinary French people, never considering themselves heroic, risked their lives to save Jews during World War II, also illustrates this ethical sincerity. Asked why she had done this, one villager responded: "Someone had to." Levinas never forgot that French nuns hid his wife and daughter while he was in captivity for nearly five years.

39. Butler, *Precarious Live*; Butler, *Dispossession*.

CHAPTER 4

Evil, Trauma, and the Building of Absences

Eric Boynton

To suffer a disaster is to lose one's star (dis-astrum), to
be cut loose from one's lucky or guiding light.

—JOHN D. CAPUTO[1]

In 1945, in one of her first essays following the end of the war in Europe, Hannah Arendt wrote that "the problem of evil will be the fundamental question of postwar intellectual life."[2] In many ways, she was prescient. In recent years, the concept of evil and traumatic suffering has reemerged as significant tropes in common parlance, in political discourse,[3] and in the work of philosophers, as well as political scientists, psychologists, and cultural critics.[4] Phenomena with a lingering enigmatic quality, evil and trauma have been "re-discovered" as a highly suggestive phenomena today.

The resurgence of the concept of evil, in particular, ought to strike moderns, especially modern philosophers, as an oddity, because it remains a theologically laden term for wrong-doing involving the illusion of dark forces. The problem of evil, in modernity, has become putatively demystified. Evil is a problem, it seems, only in so far as we remain obsessed with a worn-out intellectual horizon that understands evil as deeply contrary to the cosmic order. By tying the problem of evil to an all-too-human cause, the problem not only dissolves, but evil itself becomes an anachronism, a term for wrongdoing in a sacramental universe that in an age of enlightenment can be mitigated. For people for whom there is no such religion or god, there is no problem that needs to be solved. And there is no need to maintain in pious humility that there is no solution because the "ought not be" uttered in response to evil no longer stands in relation to the order generated by power and goodness; it merely stands in relation to the vicious capacity of humans.

Yet against this "naturalizing" task arises a second set of issues, especially after the Second World War. Some philosophers have argued that despite our desperate attempts at comprehending the atrocities of the last century, we are ultimately unable to reconcile ourselves to these contemporary occurrences of evil. Evil's source once again appears too deep, its orbit too wide. These events are simply too big to be processed or defeated by argument. The very attempt to comprehend the evil of the Holocaust, in particular, it is argued, is not only impossible but obscene and a gross betrayal of the magnitude and horror of the suffering.[5] Jean-François Lyotard, for one, asks one to "suppose that an earthquake destroys not only lives, buildings, and objects but also the instruments used to measure earthquakes," suggesting that an inability to measure the event and the lack of quantifiable evidence is the only testament to the great seismic force of an event like the Holocaust.[6] But this is not simply a statement regarding the terrible suffering that evil deeds can occasion; Lyotard wants to underscore an inability to adequately conceive of the magnitude and intensity of evil. In the face of the excessive character of evil, in Hannah Arendt's words, "we actually have nothing to fall back on in order to understand a phenomenon that nevertheless confronts us with its overpowering reality and breaks down all standards we know."[7] For Arendt, all usual and historical moral systems are rendered obsolete. So, long after the problem of evil as transcendent of thought and management was set aside, long after the death of the Being that necessitated such an evil was proclaimed, recent events have revived its transcendence.[8]

This inability to understand evil—particularly through straightforward psychological therapeutic techniques—appears in recent considerations of trauma. Echoing a certain philosophical reckoning of our genocidal age, the disaster or transcendence of trauma calls into question the promise of intelligibility: "'Trauma gives rise to no concept or, if I may, 'trauma' is not a concept. It is not even right to say that trauma challenges conceptualization, as if somehow the proper response to it is to think better. In the register of the metapsychology, the fact of trauma is that we will never be able to think well enough. In the realm of ethics and politics, that means that we are always too late in the face of trauma."[9]

Psychological considerations that seek to operationalize the suffering response in order to respond to and mitigate harm must come to terms with the condition of psychic trauma that oddly enough demands the postponement of such knowledge. For Cathy Caruth, "Traumatic experience, beyond the psychological dimension of suffering it involves, suggests a certain paradox: that the most direct seeing of a violent event may occur as an absolute inability to know it; that immediacy, paradoxically, may take the form of belatedness."[10] Once again knowledge arrives "too late"—the "experience" of trauma upon consideration appears as an original absence and/or a repetitive haunting.[11] Within a certain strain of trauma theory, the inability to give adequate testimony to trauma calls into question reductive readings of trauma and highlights the ideological character of certain medical, psychiatric, or even historical reductions of trauma built on the promise of intelligibility.[12]

In so far as recent trauma theory has distinguished trauma by its non-assimilable character and emphasized a tensive dynamic between the phenomenon's immanence and transcendence, traumatology participates in this renewed philosophical consideration of evil and suffering in our genocidal age. An isomorphism exists between the two, in that both are claimed by the odd ethical demand to understand and respond to horror that yet remains beyond comprehension. In her seminal 1995 volume, *Trauma: Explorations in Memory*, Caruth begins in the middle of this ethical double-bind: "But the study and treatment of trauma continue to face a crucial problem at the heart of this unique phenomenon: The problem of how to help relieve suffering, and how to understand the nature of this suffering, without eliminating the force and truth of the reality that trauma survivors quite often try and transmit to us."[13] The social sciences, in this regard, engage philosophical aporia that gesture at an enigmatic limit and uniquely disturb any attempt to gain access to what exceeds comprehension.[14]

Although betraying assumptions that for most contemporary thinkers are long out of fashion, evil and traumatic suffering generate an intellectually irresistible promise of allowing privileged access to murky yet potent revelations about who we are as moral beings. Evil and traumatic suffering's resurgence, then, might be particularly relevant in highlighting lacunae in predominant tendencies of modern thought, specifically in our moral or therapeutic vocabulary. Evil continues to be invoked in response to atrocities such as genocide, combat, and torture because "the secular mind-set has at its disposal no name for this type of injury."[15] The problem or challenge of evil and suffering for philosophy might provide a vector of inquiry into historical trauma and its commemoration in particular.

Yet exactly how evil remains a "problem" in the contemporary world is not always clear for many politicians, political scientists, psychologists, and philosophers who employ the word, ripped from its theological moorings. Arendt, for one, does not wish to reassert the traditional analytic problem involving the question of the reconcilability of evil and God. She declared that "the way God had been thought of for thousands of years is no longer convincing [. . .] not that the old questions which are coeval with the appearance of men on earth have become 'meaningless,' but that the way they were framed and answered has lost plausibility."[16] How then does this theological problem, that has come to be narrowly defined, find broad relevance for addressing the challenges of traumatic suffering in our genocidal age?

Paul Ricoeur opens his short yet seminal essay, "Evil, a Challenge for Philosophy and Theology," by asking whether a certain traditional approach to the "problem of evil" doesn't, in fact, obscure the "challenge" evil poses. "Do we find an invitation to think less about the problem or a provocation to think more, or to think differently about it?"[17] Approaching the problem from a broadly epistemological stance (concerned with logical coherence, economic justice, ontological intelligibility, or systematic totalization) covers over the voice of traumatic testimony and erases the "challenge" by formulating the challenge as "problem" so that any successful attempt to think the challenge means that the "success of the system is its failure."[18] Alternatively, opening up prospects of thinking more or differently about the "challenge" of the phenomena of evil and trauma may require other fundamental perspectives: failure, absence, loss, horror, and disaster[19] instead of coherence and intelligibility (the latter beholden to the traditional efforts of theodicy).[20]

Levinas, for one, offers a trajectory for thinking the contemporary challenge, developing an ethical response to evil that involves a distinctive understanding of the asymmetrical, nonreciprocal responsibility to and for the other. Levinas's ethics respond directly to concrete suffering. In the horror of evil, one is infinitely responsible to and for the other, whose useless suffering solicits one to suffer for the "suffering of someone else. It is this attention to the suffering of the other that, through the cruelties of our century (despite these cruelties, because of these cruelties) can be affirmed as the very nexus of human subjectivity, to the point of being raised to the level of supreme ethical principle."[21]

In this chapter, I examine the challenge of the commemoration of historical trauma and atrocity by considering the counter-monuments proposed and completed by the German installation artist, Horst Hoheisel.

I do so in an attempt to adopt the fundamental approach to evil from the perspective of absence and thereby attend to the failure of therapeutic techniques regarding an ignored demographic in a field such as trauma studies: the dead.[22]

Among the hundreds of submissions for a German national memorial to the murdered Jews of Europe, Hoheisel's design embodies impossible questions at the heart of Germany's memorial process, which finds peculiar elucidation in Levinas's reflection on evil. Already well-known for what Hoheisel calls "negative-form" monuments in Kassel, Germany, he "proposed a simple, if provocative, antisolution to the memorial competition in Berlin: Blow up the Brandenburg Tor, grind its stone into dust, sprinkle the remains over the memorial site, and then cover the entire memorial area with granite plates. How better to remember a destroyed people than by a destroyed monument?"[23] In Hoheisel's work, the murdered Jews of Europe are to be memorialized by a double absence: the absence of the Brandenburg Gate and the absence of statuary or other construction on the memorial site.[24]

Passivity of Suffering

Peculiar to the challenge evil generates for philosophy is the suffering of vulnerable bodies. This suffering resists conceptual grasp, at least initially, and thwarts a definitive resolution regarding its enigmatic showing in so far as the vulnerable body is always susceptible to its surprising claim in each and every future occasion. In this way, evil appears as a surd within the philosophical tradition in large measure due to the bodily concreteness of the suffering response. One is constituted, in the grips of evil, as irrepressibly passive. Evil is undergone; it produces an experience to which one submits—an odd experience that can only be considered secondarily. Evil challenges the philosopher to make sense of what remains persistently inscrutable, in so far as one's conceptual capacities always arrive too late.

The experience of bodily pain and suffering is not merely constituted by its "content," but more fundamentally the foreclosure of retreat: "In suffering there is an absence of all refuge [. . .] it is made up of the impossibility of fleeing or retreating. The whole acuity of suffering lies in this impossibility of retreat."[25] The experience of being overwhelmed or enchained by physical suffering reveals a radical passivity. Whereas intelligibility and comprehension are inscribed within the possibility of grasping or seeing, this impossibility of suffering is defined by exposure: Pain touches us, but we do not touch back. Levinas describes the experience of pain and suffering as a "state of purity" insofar as pain is not grasped by thought or by any other active gesture, but rather signifies through the passivity of agony. The passivity of exposure is the impossibility of grasping, the impossibility of intelligibility, signified in physical pain.

Levinas returns to the "experience" of pain in his brief essay, "Useless Suffering," acknowledging that suffering is similar to other sensations insofar that it belongs to consciousness as "psychological content." Levinas, however, exposes a contradiction within the psychological content of suffering that is "in-spite-of-consciousness," a "contradiction qua sensation." For Levinas, suffering is unassumable by consciousness not simply because of intensity, a "quantitative 'too much.'" Quantitative excess alone would not call into question the fundamental structures of immanence. Rather, suffering is unassumable precisely because it is not grasped by consciousness; consciousness recoils from the pain of suffering: "The denial, the refusal of meaning, thrusting itself forward as a sensible quality: that is, in the guise of 'experienced' content, the way in which, within a consciousness, the unbearable is precisely not borne, the manner of this not-being-borne; which paradoxically, is itself a sensation or a datum."[26] This limit is not a result of repression due to an excessive intensity of sensation, but rather suffering signifies the exposure to something unavailable: "It is not only the consciousness of rejection or a symptom of rejection, but this rejection itself: a backward consciousness, 'operating' not as 'grasp' but as revulsion."[27]

This inscrutability qua unbearableness is not easily ignored. Evil occasions horror in the face of what ought not be. The "absence of all refuge" demands a response, in the traditional sense, because the intelligibility and goodness of the world is at stake. For Emil Cioran, "all suffering is an abyss," infiltrating the body, disrupting the sense of self, and shattering the contours of a world. Cioran maintains that "suffering separates and dissociates; like a centrifugal force it pulls you away from the center of life, the hub of the universe where all things tend toward unity."[28] Evil is an alienating force. It liquidates or ruptures habits of moral trust and foments categorical uncertainty, generating in the one who undergoes evil a fervent desire to restore closure to a disrupted world. As Nietzsche maintains, suffering as such is not so much the problem as is its deeply unsettling senselessness or essential unjustifiabililty.[29] Evil surprises; it causes shock and horror, for although it can be thematized (if only as inscrutable), it cannot be prepared for. Cioran continues: "You never suspected what lay hidden in yourself and in your world, you were living contentedly at the periphery of things, when suddenly those feelings of suffering take hold of you and transport you into a region of infinite complexity, where your subjectivity tosses about in a maelstrom."[30] The world that once made sense, what was whole and unified, in traumatic suffering is undone.

The passivity of suffering, linked to the recent analyses of trauma, provides an alternative approach to evil. In the midst of violent and massively destructive events generated by human action, the passivity of suffering resists the dominant approach, which fixates on evil as action that embodies the egregious use of malevolent will-to-power.[31] Such a willful rendering of the "problem" of evil imagines that issues of good and evil can be adequately adjudicated within the moral sphere and scrutinized within a juridical setting in a way that evil simply becomes bad behavior on steroids. To be sure, the question of wrongdoing constitutes a large part of the historical discussion of evil. Yet, in the traditions of the West, a strange experience of passivity persists even at the heart of evildoing, turning culprits into victims by the very act that makes them guilty. The evildoer, although responsible, also suffers by succumbing or being "seduced by overwhelming powers and consequently belongs to a history of evil always already there for everyone,"[32] gesturing toward the phenomenon of "perpetrator trauma" only recently discussed in trauma theory.[33]

End of Theodicy

The passivity of suffering forms the basis of Levinas's attempt to evoke the "excessive" or "transcendent" character of evil. Not simply a statement regarding the unendurable and terrible suffering evil deeds can occasion, Levinas wants to underscore the inability to adequately conceive the magnitude and intensity of evil. For Levinas, "Evil is not only the non-integratable, it is also the non-integratableness of the non-integratable."[34] The Shoah, paradigmatically, is an event that escapes comprehension or representation. The sheer scale of destruction, the explicit desire of the perpetrators that there be no traces of their crimes, and the immense horror of its methods are just some of the features that resist comprehension.

For Levinas, reflection on the Holocaust drags theodicy, broadly conceived, to its ruin, rupturing any confidence that there might be a coherent way of making sense of the event, be it historical, ontological, founded on a conception of the good, or on the idea of a present and accessible God.[35] Echoing Arendt's assessment, all such totalities of previous philosophy and theology have been swept away in a shift so radical that it demands to be described with images of the death of God or of apocalypse. The desperate attempt to comprehend "two world wars, the totalitarianism of right and left, Hitlerism and Stalinism, Hiroshima, the Gulag, and the genocides of Auschwitz and Cambodia" propels Levinas to think beyond traditional theodical approaches to evil.[36] Levinas considers that "the most revolutionary fact of our twentieth-century consciousness [is] the destruction of all balance between Western thought's explicit and implicit theodicy and the forms that suffering and its evil are taking on in the very unfolding of this century."[37] This destruction, for Levinas, is "an event in Sacred History." In our age, then, the persistence of theodicies and moral systems held in force by the promise of a "happy end" or a coherent plan of the whole must now be seen as empty or dangerous in so far as they seek to maintain totalities.[38] Indeed, evil, during the Holocaust, found a moral context not only tolerant of its presence but at times a stimulant for its mission. "For an ethical sensibility, confirming, in the inhumanity of our time, its opposition to this inhumanity, the justification of our neighbor's pain is certainly the source of all immorality."[39]

Levinas found it necessary, then, to think the possibility of responsibility anew—uncovering a basis for an ethics "after Auschwitz" capable of measuring evil's excess in order to overcome an ethical nihilism opened by that excess. Specifically in his essay "Useless Suffering," the space is cleared for an ethics that "doesn't work" insofar as the suffering other is not subsumed as a function of the plan of the whole. Levinas sees the concern for grounding action in a *knowledge* of the Good governed by the demand for coherence and intelligibility as a profound flaw in Western tradition born of a predominant tendency to "subordinate unworthiness to failure, [and] moral generosity itself to the necessities of objective thought."[40]

Yet if the only adequate response to evil is one that is commensurate with its transcendence, for a figure such as Derrida, then, we are forced to judge as "vain and without pertinence any judgmental apparatus still homogeneous with the space within which the conditions of the Holocaust grew, any interpretation drawing on philosophical, moral, sociological, psychological concepts."[41] We are left with an intolerable position in relation to evil. If evil is experienced as a site where thought encounters its limits, then an event like the Holocaust becomes singularly awesome, a monstrous but also a sublime occasion before which we stand silent. Because the terror of the Holocaust has become absolute, by virtue of its excess, it cannot be said or represented. As unspeakable trauma, all modes of narrative representation and discourse are rejected.

While evil is excessive, incapable of being adequately comprehended or properly engaged by an ethical system, *nevertheless* there persists the demand that we respond ethically to what resists our cognition. This "nevertheless" is embedded in phenomenology of pain and suffering when the inscrutability of suffering's pure passivity is "experienced" as recoil, revulsion, or unbearableness. In fact, for a figure such as Maurice Blanchot, we are presented with an inescapable tension between our obligation and inability to respond: "And how, in fact, can one accept not to know? We read books on Auschwitz. The wish of all in the camps, the last wish: know what has happened, do not forget, and at the same time never will you know."[42] But where does this impossible demand issue?[43] It cannot be heard if it remains absolutely separated from language in the consolation of absolutes, as if the Holocaust were "an uninterpretable manifestation of divine violence."[44]

Commemoration of Historical Trauma

Artistic engagement with the Shoah often bears the weight of this aporetic search for an appropriate medium of memory to embody the ethical response. Such efforts tarry at the edge of an inescapable tension between our obligation to remember and our inability to represent. For Lyotard, artistic expression can at best explore its own limitations: "What art can do is bear witness not to the sublime, but to this aporia of art and to its pain. It does not say the unsayable, but says that it cannot say it."[45] This problem of bearing witness to absence has been, for a thinker like Gérard Wajcman, the fundamental challenge for twentieth-century artists. He recognizes the refusal to replace absence by presence across artistic attempts to bear witness and instead insists that lack must surge in the visible.[46]

At the register of the "challenge" of evil, commemorating the disaster of historical trauma must engage memory without the intelligibility of the monumental. How might we offer testament to the excess of that historical trauma? How is it possible to memorialize the immemorial? It seems we must find a way to let our silence speak, calling attention to our inability to respond through an absence of commemoration, in order that silence not compound the evil. By way of giving "substance" to a memorial commensurate with the excessiveness of the event it intends to commemorate, I turn to the counter-monuments of Hoheisel that express the "nevertheless" that stands between the inability to conceive evil and the demand to respond ethically to the horrors of the Holocaust.

Hoheisel's counter-monuments are painfully self-conscious memorial spaces conceived to challenge the very idea of the monument itself. His work asks whether the monument is more an impediment to public

memory or an incitement, and whether the traditionally didactic function of the monument displaces the past it would have us contemplate. Do
monumental memorial projects become "an invitation to think less about
the problem" of historical trauma? How can such a site instead become "a
provocation to think more, or to think differently about it?"

Hoheisel gained notoriety when the city of Kassel invited him to construct a "negative-form" monument to mark what had once been the Aschrott Fountain in Kassel's City Hall Square. Originally this had been a
12-meter high, neogothic pyramid fountain, surrounded by a reflecting
pool set in the main town square, in front of City Hall, in 1908. It was
designed by the City Hall architect, Karl Roth, and funded by a Jewish
entrepreneur from Kassel, Sigmund Aschrott. But as a gift from a Jew to
the city, it was condemned by the Nazis as the "Jews' Fountain" and so de-
molished during one April night in 1939 by Nazi activists, its pieces carted
away by city work crews over the next few days. Within weeks, all but the
sandstone base had been cleared away, leaving only a great, empty basin in
the center of the square. Two years later, the first transport of 463 Jews left
Kassel, followed in the next year by another 3000.[47]

In 1943, the city filled in the fountain's basin with soil and planted it
over in flowers; local burghers then dubbed it "Aschrott's Grave." During
the growing prosperity of the 1960s, the town turned "Aschrott's Grave"
back into a fountain, without the pyramid. At that time, only a few city-
dwellers might recall the fountain's existence. In response to this kind of
fading memory, the Society for the Rescue of Historical Monuments proposed in 1984 that some form of the fountain and its history be restored.[48]
On being awarded the project, Hoheisel described both the concept and
form underlying this negative-form monument, he writes:

> I have designed the new fountain as a mirror image of the old one,
> sunk beneath the old place in order to rescue the history of this place
> as a wound and as an open question, to penetrate the consciousness of
> the Kassel citizens so that such things never happen again. That's why
> I rebuilt the fountain sculpture as a hollow concrete from after the
> old plans [. . .]. The pyramid will be turned into a funnel into whose
> darkness water runs down. [. . .] A hole emerges which deep down
> in the water creates an image reflecting back the entire shape of the
> fountain. [. . .] And there perhaps we will encounter feelings of loss, of
> a disturbed place, of lost form.[49]

Hoheisel decided that neither a preservation of its remnants nor its mere
reconstruction would do. For Hoheisel, even a fragment was a decorative

lie, offensive. Not only would a self-congratulatory attempt to make things right again—to set the event into a larger plan of the whole—"betray an irreparable violence, but the artist feared that a reconstructed fountain would only encourage the public to forget what had happened to the original."[50] Instead the pyramid fountain was turned into a funnel into whose darkness water runs down.

The negative space of the inverted pyramid as an absent monument constitutes its phantom shape in the ground, giving testament to an absence. On a visit to City Hall Square in Kassel, none of this is immediately evident. Where there had been an almost forgotten fountain, there is now a bronze tablet with the fountain's image and an inscription detailing what had been there and why it was lost. Entering the square, the water fills narrow canals before rushing into a great underground hollow. The sound of gushing water suggests the depth of an otherwise invisible memorial, an inverted palimpsest that demands the visitor's reflection where memory is not uplifted in a fountain.

Hoheisel's commemoration prepares for a patient approach to the "horror of evil" that, Levinas maintains, "reveals—or is already—my association with the Good."[51] Here, the irredeemable, immemorial, and "unjustifiable suffering" utterly lost to history "opens suffering to the ethical perspective of the inter-human."[52] Hoheisel's site might become an occasion where "the suffering of the other [. . .] solicits me and calls me."[53]

Levinas rethinks the possibility of responsibility "beyond" the "closed dimensions sketched by the judgments of the intellect."[54] In the irretrievable loss of useless suffering, Levinas uncovers a basis for ethics "after Auschwitz," one capable of "measuring" evil's excess. It cannot therefore "be concluded that after Auschwitz there is no longer a moral law, as if the moral or ethical law were impossible, without promise" of a coherent system to make sense of ethical action.[55] The problem of suffering may well require the radical response of denying coherence or commemoration in monumental form. The excess of evil, its malignancy that resists integration, might then surge so "that this evil might touch me, as if, from the first [. . .]. *Does not the Good break through there, in evil* [. . .]? A Good that is not pleasant, which commands and prescribes. [. . .] No failure could release me from this responsibility for the suffering of the other man."[56]

In 1995, Hoheisel submitted a proposal to the competition for Berlin's Memorial to the Murdered Jews of Europe. The proposal consisted of first blowing up the Brandenburg Gate and then grinding up the remains and scattering the resulting dust on the site set aside for the construction of the memorial. The dust would then be covered over by blocks of granite. In

Hoheisel's work, the murdered Jews of Europe are to be memorialized by a double absence: the absence of the Brandenburg Gate and the absence of statuary or other construction on the memorial site.[57]

Hoheisel's memorial to the murdered Jews of Europe, in response to the impossibility of re-presenting the excessive evil of the Shoah, confronts head-on the tension of the "nevertheless" described by Blanchot and others. For Hoheisel, a memorial to the murdered Jews of Europe must bring to presence that which is essentially absent. Hoheisel deploys absence and loss as means of memorialization. No new thing is built to replace the lost gate, or serve as a symbol for the lost Jews. In drawing our attention to the sheer absence of Jewish life in Europe, Hoheisel's anti-monument calls to "presence" the excessive character of that evil. In acknowledging loss itself, the monument must be absent itself. No thing can be offered as substitution.

Hoheisel's hyperbolic proposal hollows out the task of commemoration—to make the problem of commemorating historical trauma impossible in order that its challenge become unavoidable as an ethical solicitation. For those who have learned to expect the gate, its absence would leap up, consuming the perspective of the viewer. The "memorial" is only effective as a monument when it is experienced as essentially empty. The monument in its presentation of an absence engages the ethical in a movement toward the other as other. Absence motivates a response to the horror of traumatic suffering, "through the cruelties of our century (despite these cruelties, because of these cruelties) [. . .] to the point of being raised to the level of supreme ethical principle."[58]

While presences, monuments, and intelligible therapeutic techniques might be passively absorbed, "well-constructed" absences demand a response. The absence that cannot make itself known must always be signaled as absence in order that it might constitute an ethical response to that which evokes it.[59] In a sense, our ethical response is only embodied insofar as we persistently develop ways to "hold open" a clearing that allows us to listen for what cannot be heard, a persistence that commemorates the immemorial. Hoheisel's proposal reminds us that the empty space left by the murdered Jews of Europe must be cultivated and that a substantial memorial by its very presence would actually participate in silencing the command to remember. In these terms, any effort to be in contact with an excess amounts to an attempt to delay the filling of that vacant place, to hold open the space made by loss, absence, or death. Only the absence of gate and monument can allude to the absence of the murdered Jews. It is through the memorial's double absences that we commemorate and main-tain the third, absolute absence.

NOTES

1. John Caputo, *Against Ethics: Contributions to a Poetics of Obligation with Constant Reference to Deconstruction* (Bloomington: Indiana University Press, 1993), 6.

2. Hannah Arendt, "Nightmare and Flight," *Partisan Review* 12 (1945): 259–60.

3. See, for instance, President George W. Bush, "State of the Union Address, January 29, 2002," at http://www.whitehouse.gov/news/release/2002/01/20020129-11html.

4. See, for instance, Richard J. Bernstein, *Radical Evil: a Philosophical Interrogation* (Cambridge: Polity Press, 2002); Peter Dews, *The Idea of Evil* (Massachusetts: Blackwell Publishing, 2008); Jennifer Geddes, *Evil After Postmodernism* (London: Taylor and Francis Group, 2001); Ruth W. Grant, *Naming Evil, Judging Evil* (Chicago: University of Chicago Press, 2006); María Pía Lara, *Rethinking Evil: Contemporary Perspectives* (Berkeley: University of California Press, 2001); Martin Beck Matustík, *Radical Evil and the Scarcity of Hope: Postsecular Meditations* (Bloomington: Indiana University Press, 2008); Susan Neiman, *Evil in Modern Thought: An Alternative History of Philosophy* (Princeton: Princeton University Press, 2002); Alan Schrift, *Modernity and the Problem of Evil* (Bloomington: Indiana University Press, 2005); Robin May Schott, *Feminist Philosophy and the Problem of Evil* (Bloomington: Indiana University Press, 2007); Kristen Brown Golden and Bettina G. Bergo, eds., *The Trauma Controversy* (Albany, N.Y.: SUNY Press, 2009); Robert Stolorow, *Trauma and Human Existence* (New York: Routledge, 2007).

5. Claude Lanzmann, for one, condemns what he calls the "obscenity of understanding": "This is what I called the obscenity of the project of under-standing—and more than this, it is not only obscenity, it is real cowardice, because this idea of being able to engender harmoniously, if I may say so again, this violence, is just an absurd dream of non-violence. It is a way of escaping; it is a way not to face the horror. And this escape has become now a fashion, more and more" (Claude Lanzmann, "The Obscenity of Under-standing: An Evening with Claude Lanzmann," in *Trauma: Explorations in Memory*, ed. Cathy Caruth (Baltimore: Johns Hopkins University Press, 1995), 207.

6. Jean-François Lyotard, *The Differend: Phrases in Dispute*, trans. Georges Van Den Abbeele (Minneapolis: University of Minnesota Press, 1988), 56.

7. Hannah Arendt, *The Origins of Totalitarianism* (New York: Harcourt Brace Jovanovich, 1968), 459.

8. Emmanuel Levinas, "Transcendence and Evil," in *Of God Who Comes to Mind*, ed. and trans. Bettina Bergo (Stanford: Stanford University Press, 1998).

9. Gregg Horowitz, "A Late Adventure of the Feelings," in *The Trauma Controversy*, ed. Kristen Brown Golden and Bettina G. Bergo (Albany, N.Y.: SUNY Press, 2009, 40.

10. Cathy Caruth, *Unclaimed Experience: Trauma, Narrative, and History* (Baltimore: Johns Hopkins Press, 1996), 91–92.

11. See Maurice Blanchot, *Writing of the Disaster* (Lincoln: University of Nebraska Press, 1995), 82. Maurice Blanchot, meditating on the impossibility of knowing or understanding the event(s) of the Shoah, expresses it thus: "The disaster, unexperienced. It is what escapes the very possibility of experience—it is the limit of writing. This must be repeated: the disaster de-scribes. Which does not mean that the disaster, as the force of writing, is excluded from it, is beyond the pale of writing or extratextual."

12. See Thomas Trezise, "Unspeakable," *The Yale Journal of Criticism* 4, no. 1 (2001): 41. "Clearly the verbal representability of the facts suffices, in and of itself, to disprove the claim that the Holocaust is absolutely unspeakable. But since verbal representation does not pertain to facts alone, their representability does not suffice to disprove absolutely the claim that the Holocaust is unspeakable."

13. Caruth, *Trauma: Explorations in Memory*, vii.

14. For a few representative texts see: Nancy R. Goodman and Marilyn B. Meyers, eds.,, *The Power of Witnessing: Reflections, Reverberations, and Traces of the Holocaust* (New York: Taylor & Francis, 2012) and Shoshana Felman and Dori Laub, *Testimony: Crises of Witnessing in Literature, Psychoanalysis, and History* (New York: Taylor and Francis, 1992). Clinical psychology, broadly defined as the integration of science, theory, and practice to understand, predict, and alleviate maladjustment, disability, and discomfort as well as to promote human adaptation, adjustment, and personal development, must somehow incorporate that which resists comprehension even as it promises intelligibility. This definition of clinical psychology is taken from the Clinical Psychology Division (12) of the American Psychological Association: http://www.apa.org/divisions/div12/aboutcp.html.

15. Martin Matustik, *Radical Evil and the Scarcity of Hope* (Bloomington: Indiana University Press, 2008), 24.

16. Hannah Arendt, *The Life of the Mind: Thinking* (New York: Harcourt Brace Jovanovich, 1971), 10.

17. Paul Ricoeur, "Evil, a Challenge to Philosophy and Theology," in *Figuring the Sacred* (Minneapolis: Fortress Press, 1995), 249.

18. Ricoeur, "Evil, a Challenge to Philosophy and Theology," 257. For Ricoeur, "after the catastrophes and sufferings beyond number of our century, the dissociation that [this approach] brings about between consolation and reconciliation has become, at the very least, a source of great perplexity."

19. A disaster "refers to an unrecoverable loss. Disasters are events of surpassing or irretrievable loss. By irretrievable loss I mean wasting life, something that cannot be repaired, recompensed, redeemed. A disaster is a loss that cannot be led back into a gain [. . .]. The disaster belongs to an economy or excessive cost, for which there is no compensating return. The disaster is an utter wasting, a sheer loss" (Caputo, *Against Ethics*, 29). Such a perspective resonates with Levinas's "useless suffering" and Simone Weil's "affliction."

20. The problem of evil remains linked to traumatic disasters, even in our so-called secular age, as human suffering continues to call into question our understanding of the world. "The problem of evil can be expressed in theological or secular terms, but it is fundamentally a problem about the intelligibility of the world as a whole" (Susan Neiman, *Evil in Modern Thought* [Princeton, New Jersey: Princeton University Press: 2004], 7–8). In my estimation, the novelty of obscure approaches to the "challenge" of evil from philosophers such as Ricoeur, Levinas, Agamben, Derrida, Blanchot, Edith Wyschogrod (my late mentor), and a certain reading of Arendt have yet to penetrate the consideration of the traditional problem of evil.

21. Emmanuel Levinas, "Useless Suffering," in *The Provocation of Levinas*, ed. Robert Bernasconi and David Wood (London: Routledge, 1988), 94.

22. "A language of rebirth that hurries into the future without paying homage to these ghosts from the past serves neither truth nor the spirits of the dead—who cannot speak for themselves" (Lawrence Langer, *Versions of Survival: The Holocaust and the Human Spirit* [Albany, N.Y.: SUNY Press, 1982], 15).

23. Young, *At Memory's Edge* (New Haven: Yale University Press, 2000), 90.

24. My descriptions of Hoheisel's projects are indebted to the work of James Young (James E. Young, *At Memory's Edge* [New Haven: Yale University Press, 2000] and James E. Young, *The Texture of Memory: Holocaust Memorials and Meaning* [New Haven: Yale University Press, 1993]).

25. Emmanuel Levinas, "Suffering and Death," in *The Levinas Reader*, ed. Sean Hand (Oxford: Blackwell, 1989), 40.

26. Levinas, "Useless Suffering," 91–92.

27. Levinas, "Useless Suffering," 91.

28. E. M. Cioran, *On the Heights of Despair* (Chicago: University of Chicago Press, 1992), 55 and 109.

29. "What truly enrages people about suffering is not the suffering itself, but the meaninglessness of suffering," Friedrich Nietzsche, *The Genealogy of Morals* (New York: Random House, 1967), Book 2, aphorism 7.

30. Nietzsche, *Genealogy of Morals*, 109.

31. "All evil," Emmanuel Levinas maintains, "refers to suffering" rather than evil being the cause of suffering. "The evil of pain, the harm itself, is the explosion and the most profound articulation of absurdity" (Levinas, "Useless Suffering," 157).

32. Ricoeur, "Evil, a Challenge to Philosophy and Theology," 250.

33. See the chapter by Ronald Eyerman in this volume. Broadly speaking, the approach to evil and suffering under discussion describes how the problem of evil extends beyond the confines of traditional ethical categories, complicating efforts to mitigate the harm evil occasions, determine and punish evil-doers, and offer any explanatory response to mass atrocity (see my essay, "The Transcendence and Banality of Evil," in *I More than Others: Responses to Evil and Suffering*, ed. Eric Severson [Cambridge: Cambridge Publishing, 2010]). Evil as a non-moral trope has long been the purview of theology; see, for example, Dietrich Bonhoeffer, *Ethics* (New York: Macmillan, 1955), specifically Chapter 4, "The Love of God and the Decay of the World."

34. Levinas, "Transcendence and Evil," 128.

35. "By under-estimating its temptation one could, in any case, misunderstand the profundity of the empire which theodicy exerts over humankind [. . .]. It has been, at least up to the trials of the twentieth century, a component of the self-consciousness of European humanity. It persisted in watered-down form at the core of atheist progressivism, which was confident, none the less, in the efficacy of the Good which is immanent to being, called to visible triumph by the simple play of the natural and historical laws of injustice, war, misery and illness." Levinas, "Useless Suffering," 161.

36. Levinas, "Useless Suffering," 162.

37. Levinas, "Useless Suffering," 161.

38. The Italian philosopher Giorgio Agamben (inspired by Arendt's analysis, that we can and must judge, so as to condemn and redeem the past) elaborates on this theme of justifying evil through legal means rooted in humanism and ethical systems, describing the Nuremberg trials and the hanging of Eichmann as responsible "for the conceptual confusion that [. . .] has made it impossible to think through Auschwitz," spreading "the idea that the problem had been overcome, judgment had been passed" (Giorgio Agamben, *Remnants of Auschwitz* [New York: Zone Books, 2002], 19). For Agamben, the law and ethical systems did not exhaust the problem, but rather the "very

problem was so enormous as to call into question law itself, dragging it to its ruin," reflecting "the powerlessness of men, who continue to cry 'may that never happen again!' when it is clear by that 'that' is, by now, everywhere" (*Remnants of Auschwitz*, 20). For Agamben, there is a real danger that when treating evil from the guiding light of coherence and intelligibility that this activity is caught up in a blindness to the challenge of the event.

39. Levinas, "Useless Suffering," 65–66.

40. Emmanuel Levinas, *Totality and Infinity*, trans. Alphonso Lingis (Pittsburgh: Duquesne University Press, 1969), 83.

41. Jacques Derrida, "Force of Law: The 'Mystical Foundation of Authority,'" in *Deconstruction and the Possibility of Justice*, ed. Drucilla Cornell, Michel Rosenfeld, and David Gray Carlson, trans. Mary Quaintance (New York: Routledge, 1992), 60.

42. Maurice Blanchot, *Writing of the Disaster*, trans. Ann Smock (Lincoln: University of Nebraska Press, 1995), 82. The bind held fast by evil's transcendence means that I am compelled to respond, yet I am unable to respond by reason of that very transcendence. Without the ability to comprehend the evil that confronts me, I am not able to decide how to respond to its manifestations because any response must respond to some-thing, and this is exactly what is lacking. The decision to respond in some particular way necessarily forgets or covers over the excess of evil that compels me to respond in the first place. This issue appears in Dostoevsky's, *The Brother's Karamazov*, when for Ivan Karamazov, any particular ethical response to suffering must be underwritten through a justification of the very suffering in question that makes sense of the scandal of unjustified suffering that first inspired and now simultaneously undermines the ethical response.

43. For Levinas, the challenge of evil must be approached from an ethical perspective rather than an ontological one to avoid either falling into reductive forms of speaking or allowing ourselves only silence. Levinas offers a "non-rhetorical" reading of Job 38: 4–7 in his essay "Transcendence et Mal," locating a "secret indication" that bends the question from the myopia of the ontological to the opening of ethical responsibility for the suffering of the world. Instead of reading God as putting Job in his place as a creature unable to fathom the complexities and depth of the created order, Levinas (taking up Ricoeur's invitation) thinks more and differently about the challenge of evil. "What about the question, 'Where wast thou when I laid the foundations of the earth?' in Chapter 38, verse 4, at the beginning of the discourse attributed to God, which recalls to Job his absence at the hour of Creation? Does this question address only the impudence of a creature who allows himself to judge the Creator? Does this expound only a theodicy, wherein the economy of a harmonious and knowingly arranged totality only harbors evil for the

limited gaze of a part of this whole? Can one not hear in this 'Where were you?' a statement of deficiency that cannot have meaning unless the humanity of man is fraternally bound up with creation, that is, responsible for that which has been neither his I nor his work?" (Emmanuel Levinas, "Transcendence and Evil," 133).

44. Derrida, "Force of Law," 62. The claim that trauma imposes no limits to the promise of intelligibility is as untenable as the claim that trauma is a horror beyond understanding—such a "cheap mystification" invariably already rests on a particular understanding of trauma. In *Remnants of Auschwitz: the Witness and the Archive*, Agamben suggests: "Some want to understand too much and too quickly; they have explanations for everything. Others refuse to understand; they only offer cheap mystifications. The only way forward lies in investigating the space between these two options" (13).

45. Jean-Francoise Lyotard, *Heidegger and "The Jews,"* trans. Andreas Michel and Mark Roberts (Minneapolis: University of Minnesota Press, 1990), 47.

46. Gérard Wajcman, *L'object du siècle* (Paris: Verdier, 1998). Judith Butler argues that what must be sought is an expression that maintains a hospitality to what exceeds and de-centers the privilege of that which appears. "The critical image [. . .] must not only fail to capture its referent, but also show this failing" (Judith Butler, *Precarious Life: The Powers of Mourning and Violence* [New York: Verso, 2004], 146). The critical image, representation, or concept is to be turned on itself, betraying its own inadequacy when faced by a disturbance that radically breaks with the structures of intelligibility. By showing this failing, this signification bears the trace of the excess of what it signifies.

47. Young, *The Texture of Memory*, 43.
48. Young, *The Texture of Memory*, 43.
49. Hoheisel quoted in Young, *The Texture of Memory*, 43, 45, 46.
50. Young, *The Texture of Memory*, 43.
51. Levinas, "Transcendence and Evil," 131.
52. Levinas, "Useless Suffering," 94.
53. Levinas, "Useless Suffering," 94.
54. Levinas, "Transcendence and Evil," 133.
55. Levinas, *The Provocation of Levinas*, 176.
56. Levinas, "Transcendence and Evil," 133–34.
57. Young, *At Memory's Edge*, 90.
58. Levinas, "Useless Suffering," 94.
59. Commemorative acts, insofar as they aim at fulfillment of the imperative to remember, must aim at sustaining grief in the face of loss. They must interrupt an eternally premature completion of our mourning. It has

been suggested that Hoheisel's proposal was intended precisely to defer the completion of any monument. For James Young: "Hoheisel's proposed destruction of the Brandenburg Gate simultaneously participates in the competition for a national Holocaust memorial, even as its radicalism precludes the possibility of its execution. At least part of its polemic is directed against actually building any winning design, against ever finishing the monument at all. Here Hoheisel seems to suggest that surest engagement with Holocaust memory in Germany may actually lie in its perpetual irresolution, that only an unfinished memorial process can guarantee the life of memory. Better a thousand years of Holocaust memorial competitions in Germany than any single 'final solution' to Germany's memorial problem" (Young, *At Memory's Edge*, 92). Hoheisel's project was indeed rejected but continues to inspire debate and paved the way for an exhibition of variations of the removal idea with an exhibition at the Berlin Jewish Museum in April-June, 2003. By submitting a proposal too radical to win, Hoheisel takes the stand that the process of decision has priority over the finality of representation. In this sense, the monument is itself the proposal. What if the contest itself was established with an indefinite time frame, such that any commission would be continually deferred? Would the excessive evil that places on us the demand to commemorate the Holocaust gain persistence through, in this case, the absence of any intention to construct an actual monument?

CHAPTER 5

The Unsettling of Perception:
Levinas and the Anarchic Trauma

Eric Severson

Emerging from the darkness of his prison, the hero of Plato's famous "Allegory of the Cave" does more than just wince at the glare. The allegory itself has, across the ages, provided a steady introduction to the philosophy of education. The story has been retold often enough that the sharper edges of the fable are softened, as is often the case with familiar tales. The images are vivid, of people chained to chairs with heads blocked and forced to look only forward. Like a *Clockwork Orange* nightmare,[1] the inhabitants of Socrates's "cavernous cell down under the ground" are in a position of forced passivity.[2] They are hostages to an experiment, even as their controlled environment prevents them from seeing their plight; their bonds are as familiar as their own bodies. Socrates has set out, at this point in *The Republic*, to articulate the nature of learning, of education, and he is presenting us with a dark portrait of the uneducated. To find oneself uneducated is a passive event, a situation to which one awakens in the world. Socrates is concerned with how one responds to the uneducated cave into which we are all originally thrown. The process of enlightenment, παιδεία (education), is as violent and traumatic as the original experiment.

This chapter begins with a reflection on Platonic education and points to the role of trauma in the dynamics of learning. Utilizing the works of Martin Heidegger and Emmanuel Levinas, I explore the function of trauma in education. By connecting trauma to the underappreciated role of time, Levinas opens up fresh avenues for thinking about how larger scale traumatic experience can be better understood and treated. This investigation seeks a better understanding of perception, with a particular eye on that which trauma interrupts and disturbs in the process of perceiving. Ultimately, I will argue that both perception and trauma are best understood according to the evasive concept of time. Traumatic experiences unsettle the way universal "clock" time synchronizes lives and perceptions. Levinas suggests that synchronous time is secondary to a more primordial, "anarchic" understanding of time. There is, I will come to suggest, a similarity between the unsettling of time in trauma and Levinas's notion of anarchic time. This similarity may be helpful for our understanding of both trauma and time. Clinicians might also find helpful application for Levinas's innovative ways of thinking about time and trauma.

There is, obviously, something daunting and perhaps paradoxical about pointing toward any "understanding" of trauma. Traumatic experience often undermines and destabilizes the fabric that holds together memory, emotion, history, and even language itself. Philosophy and psychology must speak of trauma and address the operations and impact of traumatic experience. Is trauma merely the symptom of a broken system? Does treating trauma simply require finding the fractured piece of this system and mending it? Such oversimplified understandings of trauma are both misguided and dangerous. Any work on the meaning and impact of trauma is undermined by the fact that trauma often indicates an unraveling of the infrastructure of thinking itself. Any sort of phenomenological reduction that might allow us to look with clarity at trauma requires some kind of critical distance. Yet trauma is often too proximate and confounding for typical phenomenological analysis. Trauma undermines the mechanisms of philosophy, of phenomenology. If philosophy might be of some service to psychology on the question of trauma, it must labor in a field where the tools of philosophical research are themselves in question. And, if Levinas is right about trauma, we may learn much about perception from the way it breaks down through traumatization.

Trauma in the Cave

Education, for the Greeks, is both more and less than the accumulation of knowledge. In *The Republic*, Socrates argues that education is not about the memorization of facts nor does it concern the accumulation of abstracted truths. Neither is education about the capacity of people to master new concepts.[3] The question of education points, instead, to the ability of a person to adapt one's way of living and understanding to match one's abode. The virtue of παιδεία points to a division in the nature of truth. The first problem, then, of the people who are chained to the floor of the cavern, is not that they are captives, nor even that they are ignorant of their situation. Socrates points to an ignorance of a different order, or a way of being-in-the-world that is poorly suited for the environment. To move toward παιδεία and away from its counterpart ἀπαίδευτος (untrained, ignorant, uneducated), the chained person does not necessarily need to *learn* anything. Education is not, first of all, about learning but about *turning*. To simply suspect the reality of the shadows on the wall is already a movement toward παιδεία.

Socrates clearly has little confidence that the inhabitants of the cave might find themselves turned toward the light. They have been so thoroughly positioned away from the light, and toward the shadows, that the idea of another reality is utterly foreign and frightening. It is important to underscore the jarring nature of the solution to the problem of ἀπαίδευτος (un-education) in Socrates's parable. The key is a kind of transition between abodes, and the transition is only enacted by way of a forceful and violent traumatization of the one who is being educated. Socrates introduces Book VII, and the famous allegory, with the words, "here's a situation which you can use as an analogy for the human condition—for our education or lack of it."[4] The transition between ἀπαίδευτος and παιδεία is the very point of the story. The first man who is freed from the chains must be "forced" into his conversion. He is "dragged forcibly away" up the "rough, steep slope" toward the cave entrance, and the painful and blinding light. The liberated man is then "pulled" into the sunlight and made to experience "pain and distress."[5] The order of salvation, for the imprisoned person, begins with trauma. He is forced up the sacred slopes toward the truth, and Socrates makes it clear that a person makes that ascent not just passively, but under active resistance and protest. The liberated man goes up the slope kicking and screaming.

Socrates also pauses the tale to interrogate Glaucon about the dynamics of language and culture experienced by the inhabitants of the cave. The captives have developed a certain competition and social structure, based on the capacity of each "prisoner" to identify the shadows, the forms they take, and the order in which they might appear. An odd cultural game arose, in their confined space, in which they developed a social hierarchy based on the skills of shadow identification. When the enlightened man eventually returned to speak to his comrades about their plight, he had no choice but to rejoin their language, their vernacular, their game. Though he no longer coveted their "honors" or envied "the people who had status and power there."[6] Yet to speak to them, he would have to rejoin their language-game. Otherwise, his words about the fresh, bright abode above remain gibberish. Worse yet, if the liberated man attempted to become a liberator, unbinding the prisoners and pushing them up toward the light, Socrates expects they would mob him: "And, wouldn't they—if they could—grab hold of anyone who tried to set them free and take them up there, and kill him?"[7]

To think with Plato about education, the movement between the realms of ignorance and enlightenment, is to come face to face with trauma. The transition is perhaps best understood as a conversion. The most strident challenge presented by the Allegory of the Cave is directed at educators. For the daunting job of the educator is to press students toward the light without becoming too alien for comprehension. The educator must somehow speak the language of shadows but point toward a jarring, traumatic transition toward an unfamiliar world. The educator risks her life, presenting ideas that are incompatible with the misleading world of shadows and simulations. We should remember, in reading this parable, that Plato has not forgotten the price that Socrates would one day pay for his earnest efforts to educate. Socrates was, as these words portend, seized, tried, and executed by people concerned that his teaching was a corrupting influence.

In the *Theaetetus*, Plato has Socrates compare himself to a "midwife" for knowledge, and suggests that he has nothing to impart to his students but can only bring to light what others already know. He watches "over the labor of their souls, not their bodies."[8] Like a midwife helping a woman give birth, Socrates can only guide and care for the process whereby illusions are converted into truth. Heidegger points to this transition as a process in which "the phenomenal first becomes unhidden and accessible."[9] In the famous midwifery passage in the *Theaetetus*, Socrates frets about being "bitten" in the process of laboring the truth into reality. "Do you know, people have often before now got into such a state with me as to be literally ready to bite when I take away some nonsense or other from them."[10] The allegories for education, both the cave and the labor room, clearly involve at least small-scale, if not large-scale, trauma. Socrates concludes the *Theaetetus* with the ominous announcement that he is headed to court to face an indictment.

Heidegger, Unconcealed Truth, and Liberation

Martin Heidegger's fascinating essay "Plato's Doctrine of Truth" explores the dynamics of the transition between these two abodes. The first abode, the subterranean cavern, is characterized by captivity. The second abode, far above, is the realm of "actual liberation."[11] Heidegger outlines the transitional stages between the two realms, and highlights the nature of freedom in Plato's doctrine of truth. The key, for Heidegger, is in the "steadiness with which one turns toward what manifests itself in its outward appearance and is in this manifesting the most unhidden."[12] The key, echoing Heidegger's prescription for Dasein's posture best expressed in *Being and Time*, is resoluteness. The one who turns resolutely toward the light, and toward the unhiddenness of the real, is oriented toward the truth. Heidegger is aware that the transition is jarring, that the movement between ἀπαίδευτος and παιδεία is full of pain and distress. But the key to a successful transition is resolve. The suffering associated with the encounter with the unconcealed truth is palpable and cause for even violent reluctance. The hostage is freed by his or her resolve and steady turn toward the truth, the truth not as facts or data but as "the ability to know one's way about in what is present as the unhidden and permanent as the present."[13] For our purposes here, it is important to point out that Heidegger sides with Plato in at least one regard: The one who knows the truth has been set free. This freedom is liberation from both the trauma that beset the unlearned mind and from the illusions that kept the captive addicted to the shadows even after the chains were loosed.

Heidegger's treatment of Plato's cave, which first appeared in 1947, does not reflect on the question of "time," despite his resounding critique of time in Plato's philosophy printed decades before in *Being and Time*. Nonetheless, one can detect in the essay "Plato's Doctrine of Truth" a movement away from time as synchronization. The prisoners of the cavern, after all, live only according to a time they receive in passivity. The shadows come and go across the wall at the bidding of others; the shadows move the collection of prisoners through time like shipmates on a boat. They experience time together, and the very idea that they might be wrong drives them to the kind of scapegoat violence outlined by René Girard.[14] The mob cannot tolerate the idea that they are capable of living outside of the "being" and "time" offered by the shadows and the cave. If they were to manage to kill their former comrade, as Plato suspects they'd endeavor to do, his blood would further seal their resolve and provide communal relief.

In *Being and Time*, Heidegger advocates a "resolve" similar to the kind needed by anyone who would emerge from the subterranean world of deception. The rugged and difficult ascent is a solitary one, for Heidegger, for the "they" that composed the cavern community have plenty of reasons to resist liberation. For Heidegger, it is not just the truth of being that lays concealed by shadows and by *das Man* (the they-self). These forces conspire to conceal, perhaps more importantly, the nature of *time*. Dasein's resolution toward the freedom of the open-air is a rejection of the bland progression of world-time. The time embraced by Dasein is ecstatic, projective, and wrenched free of the eternal progression of instants that characterized time according to Plato and Aristotle. It is crucial to point out, however, that liberation for Heidegger is a resolved movement toward the future. Dasein's liberation is unto a future that is unique to the liberated one, a projection into an ecstatic future that is liberation from the deception of the shadows and the synchronized time of the "they." Strangely, Heidegger makes no reference to the problem of Dasein's temporality in his essay on Plato's "Allegory of the Cave."

Levinas and Trauma

In his occasional references to Plato's allegory, Levinas provides an intriguing alternative to the liberation proposed by Plato and Heidegger. For Levinas, both freedom and education move backwards. Images, like the ones that appear on the wall of the cavern, bear a particular relation to being and to the being-in-the-world of those who take in the shadows and shapes. Levinas provides an analysis of images in the essay *Reality and Its Shadow*, an early essay (1948) that engages in a phenomenology of sight, art, and images.[15] This essay is often overlooked, or maligned, in part due to its scathing critique of aesthetics. But the essay is less about art than it is about perception itself. What is at stake in his evaluation of art is not aesthetics, at least not chiefly so. Levinas uses images, statues, novels, and paintings to explore epistemology, and ultimately education. The situation he poses in *Reality and Its Shadow* sets the stage for his ultimate turn toward the word "trauma" to describe the encounter with the other person. In this early essay, Levinas has begun to construct a philosophy of *sensation* in which there is a constant and pre-reflective temptation toward self-deception and insularity. Like Plato, Levinas suspects that the shadows deceive, that visual appearances mislead. For Levinas, Plato's enlightenment does little to unravel the phenomenology of perception, especially the unnoticed conversion of sensation (sight) into perception and understanding. Even outside the cave there is a phenomenology of perception that continues to undermine liberation as Levinas conceives it. The "Allegory of the Cave" may narrate freedom, but this is not true liberation.

The images on the wall of Plato's cave deceive in more than one way. They fail to be real, to be "true," in part because they are mere reflections of the real. Of particular importance to Socrates is the way the images shift and move and change. Yet for Levinas, the most misleading aspect of the shadows is that they mesmerize, both in the cave and outside of it. The world outside the cave is deemed "real," for the man who is liberated from the cave sees the things that cast the shadows. But the entire allegory presumes that clearer sight delivers a closer relation to the truth. The unconcealment of truth is a sharpening of optics.[16] In the light of day, under the all-revealing beams of sunlight, some of the shapes turn out to be remarkably similar to their shadows. On this point, Plato's allegory refuses a kind of Gnosticism, which might consider the shadows to be patently false and perhaps intentionally misleading.[17] The shadows are only inaccurate, in this allegory, because they are incomplete. They unconceal the truth, but they do so in shimmering and evasive shades. All of this indicates that the problem of perception, for the uneducated, is about improved optics. The mechanism of perception, the appropriation of sensation, is unchallenged. To put it more precisely, Plato does not account for the conversion of what Levinas calls "pure sensation" into perception. To forecast the importance of this conversion for an investigation about trauma: It is in the wake of trauma that this instantaneous and often pre-reflective conversion sometimes breaks down.

Levinas wishes to challenge this mechanism, to explore the possibility that even when the light of day makes the shapes clearer and clearer a deeper layer of deception remains. Both the enchained prisoner and (violently) liberated man remain unaware of their allegiance to a static metaphysics of presence. Their assumption is that the truth about the objects they see can be known through keen and unencumbered appropriation of that object by the senses. But as Levinas points out in his evaluation of art, that which is appropriated in this way turns into a kind of frozen statue; what is lost in this phenomenology of perception is *time*, and the rich contextualization of the world by its historicity. The "truth" about the objects observed is lifted out of the lived world in which they are encountered. Socrates is careful to explain that the entire "world of sight" is to be thought of as a prison house. Only the ascent of the soul out of this cavern will lead to education, and this ascent is toward the "intelligible realm."[18] The vision of the soul, once attended to, is clearer and brighter and keener than visual sight. Yet intellectual perception continues to utilize the same methodology, appropriating with the mind in the same manner as the eyes.

The images, along with the ideas toward which they point, turn out to be what Levinas calls "plastic."[19] Extracted from the event, the existential experience in which they are encountered, perceived objects are frozen like statues and handled in the mind in the manner of other objects. This happens, as Levinas points out, almost instantaneously and pre-reflectively. An undetected and pervasive "simultaneity of truth and image" is precisely what is interrupted by trauma.[20] The manifestations of trauma are far too diverse for any generalized account, but perhaps Levinas has pointed to that which makes trauma traumatizing. Trauma exposes the fragile synthesis between experience and its appropriation. This matter needs to be addressed more delicately than Levinas's own treatment of the concept of trauma. He will eventually propose that trauma is not entirely negative and that trauma offers salvation in an unsettling sense. The trauma that saves is not like Plato's violent and forceful educator, who drags the student kicking and screaming toward the true light. For Levinas, the trauma of the other person is simply the discovery that even in the act of perception the isolated interiority of the self has been inhabited by the needs of the other person.

What is disturbed in trauma is, at least sometimes, the very mechanism by which senses are translated into thoughts and memories. A person who has been traumatized may recoil from unfamiliar people or situations, or react negatively to sights, sounds, smells, touches, and tastes that might have been appropriated without issue before the trauma occurred. Trauma impacts the mechanisms of perception, interrupting a process that is often so seamless and simultaneous that we do not notice it happening. Those who experience trauma, studies increasingly reveal, may experience biological changes in their brains that make reversing these changes in perception exceedingly difficult.[21] When Levinas turns to the term "trauma," he does so in order to elucidate the radical change in our phenomenology of perception required to attend to the suffering of the other person. By interrupting cognition, trauma demonstrates the otherwise undetectable conversion of sensation into understanding. In this regard, as I will further outline shortly, trauma plays a positive and even salvific role in the encounter with the other person. However, and this cannot be stated too emphatically: *Levinas does not mean that actual traumatic experiences are necessarily positive, helpful, or useful events.* Levinas wishes instead to call the encounter with the other person an "ordination" toward the face of the other. This calling, or ordering, is not a tinkering with the native structures of the self.

It reorders the very mode and method of perception, and, as such, the encounter with the other is the encounter with that which is utterly foreign, "a trauma."[22] Yet by this Levinas does not intend to articulate a sweeping phenomenology of trauma, or to suggest that the encounter with the other person is traumatic in all of the ways that people are traumatized. As he puts it: "The one affected by the other is an anarchic trauma, or an inspiration of the one by the other, and not a causality striking mechanically a matter subject to it's energy."[23] Levinas uses this word to indicate the incompatibility of the encounter with the other person with native, natural structures of knowing and perceiving with being. The other traumatizes not by any action, but by being incompatible with the ego's very systems of comprehension.[24]

In his last major work, *Otherwise than Being, Or Beyond Essence,* Levinas suggests that the whole infrastructure of sensation and perception is shaken by the encounter with the other person. The other person is not encountered like another shadow that undergoes gradual elucidation. Her suffering appears in the world of perception as that which cannot be appropriated, that which cannot be categorized or synchronized with anything internal to Plato's intellectual world of the soul. The suffering of the other interrupts the seamless translation of sensation into perception, the movement between the sight and the appropriation of what has been seen. The suffering of the other person can be *sensed*, but it cannot be appropriated. And this fissure occurs not *outside* of the one who encounters the suffering, but quite internally. The machinery that I use to sense and appropriate reality is disturbed, to its core. I cannot, as I encounter the suffering of the other, find concepts, forms, or intellectual visions that would somehow make her suffering familiar. In the face of the other, particularly the suffering other, I discover that the cognitive process that allows me to operate in the world as been interrupted and called into question. Levinas calls this "a trauma" because such an interruption parallels the interruption of sensation and perception in other forms of trauma. The appearance of the other person moves between me and myself, into that undetected gap between sensation and perception.

Primordial Trauma

When Levinas questions the abstraction of art, and perceived images, from the raw experience of alterity, he is continuing a line of inquiry that begins with Heidegger. Heidegger strains, as Levinas summarizes, to "bring Being out of the oblivion in which it is said to have fallen in metaphysics and in onto-theology."[25] Being falls into oblivion when the analysis of the world, and the things in it, forgets the all-important question of what it means for things to *be*. This is true of the way all things have being, for Heidegger, but acutely problematic for human beings and their unique mode of being. Heidegger calls human there-being *Dasein*, and underscores the importance of investigating and embracing both the world into which Dasein has been thrown and the uniqueness of Dasein's future. Though titled *Being and Time*, the volume mostly focuses on the forgetfulness of being. There is a promise offered, in the early pages of *Being and Time*, to take up the way philosophy has forgotten about the experience of time and temporality. However, the project is never directly fulfilled. The result has led commentators to call *Being and Time* "that astonishing torso."[26] Such accusations are perhaps misguided because Heidegger's ongoing interest in language demonstrates a sophisticated rethinking of temporality. Furthermore, Heidegger's suggests even within *Being and Time* an analysis of Dasein's situatedness that relies on a rethinking of time according to the uniqueness of Dasein's thrownness and resolute movement into an ecstatic future.

Nevertheless, as he reflects on the "Allegory of the Cave," Heidegger is clearly not interested in a new analysis of the temporality of the drama that unfolds in the cavern. Though this scene calls for a consideration of time and temporality, Heidegger's reconsideration of Plato's doctrine of truth does not provide any direct analysis of time. Yet time is crucial in the traumatic education of the prisoner in Plato's cave. Heidegger focuses instead on the forgetfulness of the truth of being, a problem that Dasein must overcome by a resolute and determined reorientation of Dasein's there-being. This is particularly important in terms of the future, the "own-most" future into which Dasein must project its unique possibilities. Heidegger deftly overlays this dynamic onto the allegory of the cave:

> And just as one's own eye must reorient itself slowly and steadily,
> whether to the brightness or to the darkness so also must the soul with
> patience and with a relevant series of steps, get used to being in the
> realm of the beings to which it is exposed. Such a process of orientation
> still demands that the soul on the whole, in the basic direction of its
> striving, be turned around in relation to everything in front of it, just
> as the eye too can only then look about correctly and in every direction
> when the body on the whole has previously occupied the corresponding
> position.[27]

It is worth noting that Heidegger's liberated person, Dasein, is no longer liberated by trauma, as we found to be the case in the tale as it is told by

Socrates. In fact, education for Heidegger is necessarily about resolute de-
cisions to reevaluate what it means for Dasein to be, and what it means for
Dasein to interact with the world into which it finds itself thrown.[28] The
world "to which it is exposed" opens an opportunity for earnest and resolute evaluation and reorientation. But it is clear that for Heidegger these
moves are not made *for* Dasein in passivity. The transition from ἀπαίδευτος
to παιδεία, from uneducated aimlessness to appropriate situatedness in the
world, is a "slow and steady" reorientation toward a way of being that is appropriate for the world as it has become less concealed.[29] Notably, Dasein's
education is an active endeavor, and incremental.

The "Allegory of a Cave" is, we must not forget, simply an allegory and
like all metaphors it fails at some point. Yet it seems compelling to wonder
where the trauma has gone, in both the commentary on the story provided
by Socrates himself and the extended commentary by Heidegger. In the
analysis of the cave allegory, Heidegger and Plato, whatever their differences on the question of the ontological status of being and beings, say
nothing about the problem of *time*. The progression of education, for Plato
and Heidegger, is a movement toward truth that leaves intact the phenomenology of perception. The eyes can be fooled, in more than one way, but
as clarity increases a universal situation emerges. The key is to move with
resolve toward the light, toward the unconcealed truth. Levinas critiques
this common movement, calling it a movement toward "the possibility of
synchrony."[30] For Levinas, true education is not about the forceful or resolute turning toward the truth, but a discovery of the anarchic trauma that
has stirred the learner from before the onset of awareness or the beginning
of perception. This is a trauma-before-trauma.

This common, universal framework for the human situation, for education, forgets something that trauma makes us aware of: the delicate relation between raw sensation and perception. Levinas insists that a "secret
diachrony" lies undetected in the seamless and immediate relation between
our senses and our appropriation of that which they deliver. The best way
to speak of this undetected slippage is by suggesting that we have defaulted
to a metaphysics of presence, and neglected the possibility that there is a
stoppage of time that takes place as we appropriate that which we see.

In his analysis of art, Levinas calls this moment a "stoppage of time,"
for as we gather and analyze images in cognition we freeze them in place.
Art presents life in its abstraction, no matter how realistic it aims to be.
There is a temporal assumption that reigns in Plato's metaphysical account
of truth: All truth exists in the universal, eternal, everlasting "now." Hei-

degger understands that there is a problem with this configuration, and calls into question the forgetfulness of philosophy on the question of time. He nonetheless provides a configuration of Dasein's situation as the universal problem of ἀπαίδευτος. Levinas works out an alternative philosophy of time, an alternative that is simultaneously Heideggerian and very much otherwise than anything that appears in Heidegger.[31]

When Levinas calls the encounter with the other person a "trauma," he is pointing to the fracturing of the undetected synthesis whereby the self gathers in the experience of being in the world. This trauma, for Levinas, is always an event that has already happened; it occurs as an exposure to something that has already taken place, "an anarchic trauma."[32] This strange sort of trauma is for Levinas not the damaging encounter within the forces of the world, but something that is always before, always older than the field of being. The other person has already interrupted and called into question the mode of appropriation that is presumed by Plato and Heidegger. The encounter with the other person is a gift, in this regard, for in each suffering face there is reminder that the plastic image of the face cannot be stored like other images. Levinas likens this trauma to an "inspiration," for it is the mode by which one discovers that the other person has breathed life into the insularity of the self.[33] To appropriate the suffering of the other, as another experience in the world, is inhumane. Humanity, conversely, is sustained by way of responsibility, whereby the ego stops struggling to dis-own the suffering of the other. The event of this exposure, this trauma, is anarchic; it precedes and upends the organizational structures of cognition. Like physical and psychological trauma, the very composure of what it means to be a human being is called into question.

Levinas suggests a kind of hard break between being and its "otherwise." His goal is to attend to that which is not contaminated by being, but which judges and interrupts the machinations of being. Levinasian trauma is the awakening to this otherwise, the opening of being to that which is beyond its essence. The "otherwise than being" traumatizes being because it is not contaminated by it, because it is utterly foreign to beings their manner of being-there. Trauma is that which divides us from our being-there, that which interrupts the seamlessness of existence. Because the trauma has always been there, each encounter with the other person is a lifeline, a reminder that to be truly human is be attuned to the failure of the other person to fall without remainder into the field of being.

To flip the tables on the phenomenology of sight, Levinas appeals instead to listening and to hearing. Unlike the visual field, sound leaves us more acutely aware of the slippage between sensation and perceptive appropriation. Words carry tremendous ambiguity, and they reach our ears in passivity because others have sent them. For Heidegger and Plato, truth is found with increasing and incrementally clearer vision, and with more acute resolve as one gazes at the objects. But because this mode of perception is active and resolute, it misses that which has already happened in the passivity that precedes all activity. This elusive event-before-time is evident in trauma, not as violence but as in-spiration. The voice of the other, which Levinas equates at times to the voice of God, reaches from otherwise than being, from outside of synchrony, from beyond the contamination of any "essence." Rather than urge a more rigorous optics, a better mechanism of perception, Levinas presses for better listening. Levinas harkens for a saying that is always older than what is said, for the way a word calls into question the very construction of truth.

Some tentative reflections are in order regarding the relationship between these ideas and the delicate matter of treating people who have experienced psychological trauma. For starters, it is important to question an approach to trauma that focuses on repairing or rebuilding a fractured psyche. If Levinas is right about the need for an inspiration, or awakening, to the already-fractured composition of human perception, then a "repaired" trauma might very well leave a person even more isolated or insulated from the life-giving encounter with the other person. People seeking treatment for trauma might be able to identify with the invasion of the space between sensation and perception. This space has been violently invaded by calamity or cruelty, but the answer may not be to build thicker walls to keep others away from the lag-time in which synchrony breaks down. This gap between sensation and perception is exposed by *both* unhealthy trauma and the Levinasian trauma-as-inspiration. Those who treat the traumatized must delicately avoid guiding people away from their pain but into a place of isolation.

To make a more constructive suggestion, future research and exploration is needed to untangle the similarities and differences between psychological trauma and the positive Levinasian traumatization. For Levinas, the holy trauma of the other person is an epiphany, an awakening to a new way of listening and perceiving. People who have experienced trauma often report a profound and painful sensitivity, of the eyes, of the ears, and especially emotions. Further work must be done to explore how people can emerge from the ravages of psychological trauma without turning away entirely from the deeply human practices of listening, awareness, and sensitivity.

NOTES

1. Stanley Kubrick and Anthony Burgess, *A Clockwork Orange* (Los Angeles: Warner Bros, 1971). The film, in one of its more disturbing moments, depicts a man with his eyes held open and body pointed forcibly at a movie screen.

2. Plato, *Republic*, trans. Robin Waterfield (New York: Oxford University Press, 1993), 240.

3. Jonathan Leer, "Inside and Outside the *Republic*," in *Plato's Republic: Critical Essays*, ed. Richard Kraut (Lanham, Maryland: Rowman & Littlefield, 1997), 89: "Socrates argues that education is not, as the sophists think, a matter of putting knowledge into a psyche, but rather more like turning the eye from the dark world (world of becoming) to the light (world of realities)."

4. Plato, *Republic*, 240.

5. Plato, *Republic*, 242.

6. Plato, *Republic*, 243.

7. Plato, *Republic*, 243.

8. Plato, *The Theaetetus of Plato*, trans. M. J. Levett (Indianapolis: Hackett Publishing, 1990), 270.

9. Martin Heidegger, "Plato's Doctrine of Truth," in *Philosophy of the Twentieth Century: An Anthology*, vol. 3, ed. William Barrett and Henry D. Aiken (New York: Random House, 1962), 259.

10. Plato, *The Theaetetus of Plato*, 271.

11. Heidegger, "Plato's Doctrine of Truth," 259.

12. Heidegger, "Plato's Doctrine of Truth," 259.

13. Heidegger, "Plato's Doctrine of Truth," 268.

14. René Girard, *The Scapegoat*, trans. Yvonne Frecceru (Baltimore: Johns Hopkins University Press, 1986).

15. Emmanuel Levinas, "Reality and Its Shadow," in *Collected Philosophical Papers*, trans. Alphonso Lingis (Dordrecht, Netherlands: Martinus Nijhoff, 1987).

16. Gnosticism draws deeply from Plato's work, but the differences between Gnosticism and Platonism are stark. Plato's "Allegory of the Cave" is often used to demonstrate the differences. Stephan Hoeller writes: "Prisoners held in the cave, being unable to see outside, mistake shadows on the wall of the cave to be reality. The light that is the source of the shadows, however, is the true reality. The Gnostics hold that humans have the potential to turn away from the shadows on the wall permanently and commune with reality directly. This is the basis for an important point: The created world, including a major portion of the human mind, is seen as evil by the Gnostic primarily because it distracts consciousness away from knowledge of the Divine." The deception of the shadows, for Gnostics, is *evil*, and not just an unfortu-

nate confusion, covering, or obfuscation of the truth. Stephan A. Hoeller, *Gnosticism: New Light on the Ancient Tradition of Inner* (Wheaton, Ill.: Quest Books, 2002), 15.

17. For instance, when Plato's famous cosmology is presented in his dialogue "Timaeus," the one who shapes matter is called the *demiurge* and considered to be good. For Gnostics, on the other hand, the demiurge is a maleficent deceiver and intentionally arranged material things to mislead and confuse. See Andrew Philip Smith, *A Dictionary of Gnosticism* (Wheaton, Ill.: Quest Books, 2009), 69 and 198.

18. Plato, *The Republic*, 244. Socrates suggests that "if you think of the upward journey and the sight of things up on the surface of the earth as the mind's ascent to the intelligible realm, you won't be wrong—at least, I don't think you'd be wrong, and it's my impression that you want to hear."

19. Levinas writes: "To say that an image is an idol is to affirm that every image is in the last analysis plastic, and that every artwork is in the end a statue—a stoppage of time, or rather its delay behind itself. But we must show in what sense it stops or delays, and in what sense a statue's existing is a semblance of the existing of being." Levinas, "Reality and Its Shadow," 137–38.

20. Levinas, "Reality and Its Shadow," 136.

21. There is debate, among psychologists and neuroscientists, regarding the biological and psychological impact of trauma. However, there is significant consensus that traumatic experiences bring about significant biological and cognitive changes. See Jennifer J. Vasterling and Kevin Brailey, "Neuropsychological Findings in Adults with PTSD," in *Neuropsychology of PTSD: Biological, Cognitive, and Clinical Perspectives* (New York: Guilford Press, 2005).

22. Levinas writes: "What is exceptional in this way of being signaled is that I am ordered toward the face of the other. In this order which is an ordination the non-presence of the infinite is not only a figure of negative theology. All the negative attributes which state what is beyond essence become positive in responsibility, a response answering to a non-thematizable provocation and thus a non-vocation, a trauma." Levinas, *Otherwise than Being or Beyond Essence*, trans. Alphonso Lingis (Pittsburgh: Duquesne University Press, 1998), 11–12.

23. Levinas, *Otherwise than Being*, 123.

24. Levinas certainly cannot be accused of living a life immune to actual traumatic events; his brothers and parents were gunned down by a Nazi firing squad, and he spent the majority of World War II laboring in Nazi *stalag*. Solomon Malka, *Emmanuel Levinas: His Life and Legacy* (Pittsburgh: Duquesne University Press, 2006), 80. It is in the volume *Otherwise than Being, Or Beyond Essence* that Levinas elaborates most extensively on the con-

cept of trauma, and that book is dedicated to "the memory of those who were closest among the six million assassinated by the National Socialists, and of the millions on millions of all confessions and all nations, victims of the same hatred of the other man, the same anti-semitism." Levinas, *Otherwise than Being*, dedication.

25. Levinas, *Otherwise than Being*, xliii.

26. Herbert Spiegelberg, *The Phenomenological Movement: A Historical Introduction*, 3rd rev. ed. (Dordrecht, The Netherlands: Kluwer Academic, 1994), 360. See also, Theodore Kisiel, *The Genesis of Heidegger's "Being and Time"* (Berkeley: University of California Press, 1993), 1. Kisiel credits Spiegelberg for detecting the "absence of the projected second half" of *Being and Time*.

27. Heidegger, "Plato's Doctrine of Truth," 256.

28. Heidegger writes, "Resolute, Dasein has brought itself back out of falling prey in order to be all the more authentically 'there' for the disclosed situation in the 'Moment' ["Augenblick"]." Heidegger, *Being and Time*, trans. Joan Stambaugh (Albany: SUNY Press, 2010), 313.

29. Heidegger, "Plato's Doctrine of Truth," 256.

30. Levinas, *Otherwise than Being*, 156.

31. Writes Levinas, in his introduction to *Existence and Existents*: "If, at the beginning, our reflections were to a large degree inspired—for their notion of ontology and the relationship that man has with being—by the philosophy of Martin Heidegger, they are driven by a profound need to leave the climate of that philosophy, and by the conviction that we could not leave it for a philosophy qualified as pre-Heideggerian." Levinas, *Existence and Existents* (1947), trans. Alphonso Lingis (Pittsburgh: Duquesne University Press, 2001), 4.

32. Levinas, *Otherwise than Being*, 156.

33. Levinas, *Otherwise than Being*, 156.

PART II

Social and Political Analyses
of Traumatic Experience

CHAPTER 6

The Artful Politics of Trauma: Rancière's Critique of Lyotard

Tina Chanter

This essay orbits around two events of trauma that have profoundly shaped both philosophy and the public imagination, even as it questions the extent to which these two events have been allowed to eclipse other traumas. On the one hand, there is the Holocaust, with which a sizeable chunk of what goes under the name of continental philosophy has concerned itself in the shape of memorializing and mourning. On the other hand, there is 9/11 and the chain reaction it set off, from the "war on terror" to the refugee crisis in Europe. Among the effects that have spun off from what has been dubbed the "war on terror" is the difficulty, if not impossibility, of isolating a zone in which trauma has not had an impact, as if trauma has become uncontainable, contagious. Trauma, it seems, is the new normal: We are all living in a culture of trauma. We have created the conditions in which it is increasingly difficult not to be a victim of trauma in some way or other. If you are not a victim of war, you might be a veteran soldier suffering from post-traumatic stress disorder; if you are not a veteran, you might be married to one, a friend or a child of someone so affected, and so on, *ad infinitum*. The so-called war on terror seems to have created conditions under which it is increasingly difficult to isolate zones of life that are not, in some way or other, war zones. The corollary is that trauma appears to be capable of staining everything. Even if we do not subscribe to the view that we are all traumatized by birth, an era has been inaugurated in which the generalized malaise of trauma seems to have affected many of us in some capacity.

It used to be the case that there were two ways of understanding trauma. There was trauma that can be clinically diagnosed, traced back to a specific event in life, perhaps in childhood, perhaps the death of a loved one, the effect of rape or some other physical/psychic violation, whether or not caused, directly or indirectly, by war. Then there was another account of trauma that describes the condition of being born too early, which relates closely to Jacques Lacan's understanding of the premature birth of the infant, a prematurity that confers upon the human condition a dependency on the other, and haunts us all.[1] Rancière invokes such a distinction when he differentiates between the scenarios on which the films of Hitchcock and Lang draw, where "reactivating a buried childhood memory worked to save the violent or the sick" from that which he refers to as the "psychoanalytical fiction" (*AD* 113, 149).[2] In the latter, childhood trauma "has become the trauma of being born, the simple misfortune that befalls every human being for being an animal too early" (*AD* 113, 149). It is this latter notion that serves as a model for Jean-François Lyotard's conception of dependency, and which informs his aesthetics of the sublime.[3] Lyotard refers to an "intolerable suffering" that is "interminable because the dispossession of the subject, its subjection to a heteronomy, is constitutive for it. What there is of the *infans* in it [. . .] is irreducible" (*I* 33). We are seized by the other in a way that has not "first been plotted conceptually" (*I* 111). In understanding this quasi-Levinasian sense of alterity, Lyotard draws on the formlessness of Kant's sublime, which he lines up with Freud's primary repression, and with Lacan's notion of "the Thing," while associating secondary repression with the aesthetics of the beautiful. Rancière will call into question Lyotard's privileging of Kant's sublime over his aesthetics of the beautiful, and by implication also thereby associate not only the sublime with the formless, but also the beautiful.

For Rancière an encounter with beauty can undo the concatenation of form with the active shaping of the artist, and matter with the passivity of that which merely receives a form imposed upon it after the fact, as if the relation between form and matter were preconceived, such that the artist shapes passive matter according to a fully formed intellectual idea. Crucially, Rancière shows how aesthetic judgment is bound up with the imposition of form upon matter as conceived in the classical and representative regimes, an imposition itself bound up with social distinctions that cannot be divorced from judgments about what counts as art, judgments that are entangled with political judgments. For Rancière, what is at stake in the genius of the artist as Kant conceives it is a matter of an artistic intention that is beset by an unwilling or unconscious imperative, a will that is not merely active, but also passive, a willing that is also an unwilling, an activity that is also just as much a passivity, a consciousness that is at the same time unconscious, a knowledge that is also an ignorance. By corollary, beauty is perceived not through anything that can be anticipated, but precisely in a moment that is as unpredictable as it is unformed. Thus, for Rancière, Oedipus—understood through the spectrum of a Kantian understanding of artistic genius, Kant's aesthetic idea, and Schelling's theorization of art as uniting the unconscious and the conscious (see *AD* 5, 14)—becomes the modern hero, emblematic of the aesthetic regime. Kant's aesthetic idea harbors radical potential because it is a site of play with regard to form, a play that mixes up and reformulates the relation between subjects and objects inasmuch as it repudiates the canons that supported classical conceptions of the mastery of form over matter, activity over passivity, and voluntary, subjective intention imposed on an inert world.

We might extend Rancière's critique of Lyotard, the contours of which I expand below, to suggest that we are living in an epoch in which it is becoming increasingly impossible to distinguish between the specificity of a trauma provoked by an isolatable event and a cultural malaise that informs every aspect of our lives. It is as if we are becoming habituated to living in a traumatized culture. The never-ending war on terror has inaugurated a situation in which preventative war seems justified in principle. The more there is war, the more there is trauma, and the more we are traumatized, the more we find cause to wage war on those who are seen as in danger of traumatizing us further, or on those whose traumatization of others would appear, in this new and paradoxical normalization of trauma, to require our intervention. Trauma—and its management—has become an instrument of power, has entered into the lexicon of business, politics, and even war as usual. Vulnerability to trauma, understood both in terms of its likelihood and in terms of the capacity to mitigate its effects, plays a structuring role in the politics of disadvantage, whether or not the trauma in question derives from the war on terror or from some more specific isolatable event (bullying, the death of a loved one, a violent psychic or physical assault, for example). At some point in our lives, unless we die unusually early, all of us will be likely to be subjected to some such trauma, be it the bereavement of a loved one, or some other cause. Given this, irrespective of the weight we accord to Lacan's specific prematurity of birth, it seems more vital than ever to elaborate analyses that allow us to reflect meaningfully on the politics that make various populations and sectors of populations more or less vulnerable to exposure to trauma. It is crucial not to allow political distinctions to dissipate into vague ethical gestures, which fail to respect the causes of trauma or to distinguish between the dramatically divergent levels of psychic and material resources available to those who are equipped differentially with regard to how well they can negotiate the effects of trauma.

In what follows, I approach the question of trauma from within the perspective of the relationship between art and politics. Specifically, I aim to elaborate Rancière's dissensual view of art and politics. In doing so, my effort is directed toward clarifying what is at stake in Rancière's rejection of the ethical turn he sees as characteristic of Lyotard's thinking. In explicating Rancière's critique of Lyotard, we will see how Rancière situates Lyotard in relation to some other key figures to have considered the politics of aesthetics, and thereby clarify Rancière's own conception of the relation between art and politics. Central to the distance Rancière takes on Lyotard is the divergence between their readings of Kant's aesthetics. Lyotard anchors his reading in an appropriation of the Kantian sublime, although in Rancière's view he inverts some of its key points.

Rancière's Critique of Lyotard

In Lyotard's aesthetics of the sublime, art inscribes the shock of the *aistheton*, the function of which is to register the debt to the law of the Other.[4] In ascribing to art the function of a sensible inscription of the shock of the Other, Lyotard seeks at the same time to memorialize the Holocaust, the intent of which, as Rancière reads him, was to exterminate those who attested to the immemorial and unmasterable dependency on the law of the Other. By attributing to art the function of recalling the trauma of the Holocaust, Rancière understands Lyotard to subordinate art to the interests of a particular community, thereby evacuating its collective emancipatory potential. In contrast, Rancière locates dissensus, a notion that is essential to his understanding of the operation of both art and politics, not in Kant's analytic of the sublime, but in his analytic of the beautiful.[5] For Rancière, Lyotard erases the political promise Rancière sees in the free play of Kant's aesthetics, a promise Rancière finds articulated in Schiller's understanding of the statue *Juno Ludovisi*.

Rancière lines up Lyotard in the company of Badiou, Bourdieu, and Adorno, who, notwithstanding their differences, all stand accused of attempting in one way or another to safeguard the purity of art, either from the compromises to which commodification is supposed to subject it, or from what they allege to be the illusions of aesthetics. Art is thereby cast as in need of rescuing from a "perverse" (*AD* 2, 10) philosophical aesthetics by those discontent with that which is cast as the speculative illusions of idealist aesthetics, which these thinkers denounce as confused (see *AD* 4, 12). The discontent with aesthetics stems from a disillusionment on the one hand with "the 'anything goes' aspect of art" and on the other hand from the suspicion that aesthetics has "misled us with its fallacious promises of the philosophical absolute and social revolution" (*AD* 14, 25).

Rancière, for his part, recasts what these thinkers denounce as the confusion of aesthetics as "the very knot by which thoughts, practices and affects are instituted and assigned a territory or a 'specific' object"(*AD* 4, 12). For Rancière, Lyotard's stance of attempting to purify art of the confusion to which he alleges aesthetics subjects it is a way of "undoing the alliance between artistic radicality and political radicality" that Rancière understands to go by the name of aesthetics (*AD* 21, 34). For Rancière, the paradox of the aesthetic regime is that it promises precisely the elimination of art's autonomous existence insofar as it holds art to be the promise of its realization as a form of life. As "the becoming-life of art" the end it "ascribes to art is to construct new forms of life in common, and hence to eliminate itself as a separate reality" (*AD* 44, 62). At the same time, it carries the danger of turning into a form of totalitarianism. In Rancière's view, it is in response to such a threat that thinkers such as Adorno and Lyotard have rejected "engaged art," not in order to embrace a view that conforms to the idea of "art for art's sake" (*AD* 43, 62) but to endorse a view of art as political insofar as it maintains a status radically distinct from that of "objects of consumption" (*AD* 96, 129). Yet in doing so, Rancière thinks they risk isolating art from politics, in enclosing "the political promise of aesthetic experience in art's very separation, in the resistance of its form to every transformation into a form of life" (*AD* 44, 62).

In Rancière's view, the tension between politics and art must be preserved; to dissolve it would tip the balance one way or another, such that either art insists on a disengaged purity, or it dissolves itself into the political. Rancière's aim is not to "defend" aesthetics but to contribute to clarifying what aesthetics means. Rancière understands the regime of aesthetics as a "regime of the functioning of art and a matrix of discourse, a form for identifying the specificity of art and a redistribution of the relations between the forms of sensory experience" (*AD* 14, 25–26). Specifying his intention, Rancière says that he wants to "show how aesthetics, as a regime for identifying art, carries a [. . .] metapolitics" (AD 14–15, 26).

At stake for Rancière is "not merely to understand the meaning" of aesthetics but more particularly to clarify a further confusion, one that "the critique of aesthetics fosters" (*AD* 15, 26). This is the confusion into which he believes Lyotard falls in burying "art's operations along with political practices underneath the indistinctness of ethics" (*AD* 15, 26). Rancière identifies the ethics of indistinction that he sees as characteristic of Lyotard with the rhetoric of infinite justice that informs the "war on terror." In both cases Rancière claims that there has been a dissolution of the "distinction between fact and law, between what is and what ought to be" (*AD* 109, 145). Rancière's critique is aimed not only at Lyotard's politics, but also at his critique of aesthetics. In his championing an art of the unpresentable, Rancière suggests that Lyotard's unpresentable comes to occupy "the same place in aesthetic reflection that terror does on the political plane" (*AD* 123, 162). To understand this claim, to see what Rancière finds disturbing in what he construes as Lyotard's dissolution not only of the distinction between the is and the ought but also of "the specificity of political and artistic practices" (AD 109, 145) in favor of an ethics of indistinction, we will need to map the contours of Rancière's critique by articulating the difference between Lyotard's and Rancière's appropriation of Kantian aesthetics, and the significance this has for their respective views of politics and art.

Lyotard's Ethical Turn

Let me first sketch in more detail how Rancière aligns Lyotard's aesthetics of the sublime with a vision of art that endorses the claims of a specific community at the expense of embracing collective emancipation.[6] Rancière faults what he sees as Lyotard's ethical turn, which he characterizes as an ethics of indistinction, and which Rancière thinks not only eradicates that which is specific to the practices of art and politics, but in doing so evacuates the kernel of dissensus that Rancière takes to define radical politics and art. Rancière problematizes Lyotard's view by aligning it with the appeal to infinite justice that followed 9/11. In this scenario, trauma takes on the name of terror (*AD* 114, 150). While acknowledging that terror "unquestionably designates a reality of crime and horror that nobody can afford to ignore," Rancière excavates the way in which it also became a term "that throws things into a state of indistinction" (*AD* 114, 151). The term "terror" came to identify not only the "shock" of terrorist events, but also the "fear" of similar future events. The language of the "war against terror" links terrorist attacks "to the intimate angst that can inhabit each one of us" (*AD* 114, 151), which calls for a "preventative justice" that has no end, and which "places itself above the rule of law" (*AD* 114, 151). As a result, "War against terror and infinite justice [. . .] fall into a state of indistinction" (*AD* 114, 151). The "endless war on terror" becomes "a way of dealing with a trauma elevated to the status of a civilizational phenomenon" (*AD* 117, 155). It is a war undertaken on "humanitarian" grounds, a war that established itself on the "international stage" as the "right to intervene" (*AD* 116, 154).

Rancière traces the way in which "the absolute right of the victim" (*AD* 116, 154), on the basis of which "humanitarian" intervention is justified, was elevated above all other rights. The right of the victim came to replace human rights, or "the right of right" (*AD* 116, 154). Because the right of the victim was specific to those who "were unable to exercise" rights for themselves (*AD* 117, 155), victim rights were, in effect, transferred to those who took it upon themselves to exercise these rights on behalf of the absolute victim in the form of "humanitarian right/interference" (*AD* 117, 155). Thus, "Infinite justice [. . .] takes on its 'humanist' shape as the necessary violence required to exorcise trauma [. . .] to maintain the order of community" (*AD* 113, 150). Thinkers such as Burke, Marx, and Arendt have pointed out that the "bare apolitical human has no rights" and claimed that to have such rights "one needs to be 'other' than a mere 'human'" (*AD* 118, 156)—one has to be the citizen of a state.

The trouble is that in a world of endless terror that apparently requires a scenario called infinite justice, in which preventative war is condoned, there will be a never-ending production of subjects in war zones, who will be effectively denied their capacity to assert their rights. In this situation, there is a perpetuation of the ubiquity of trauma, while at the same time, politics and ethics articulate themselves on a plane in which the administration and judgment of what counts as trauma has become the business of the brokers of war. It is a war for hearts and minds as much as it is a war of bodies and death, and as such the very meaning of recognition—not just who is recognized by whom, but who sets the terms of what recognition means—is up for grabs.

In this time of humanitarian consensus, Lyotard understands the "inhumanity of human rights violations" to be the result of misrecognition (*AD* 119, 157). What is misrecognized is the "inhuman," which is "the part of ourselves over which we have no control," variously understood as "childhood dependency, the law of the unconscious, or the relation of obedience to an absolute Other" (*AD* 119, 157). It is the "radical dependency of the human on an absolutely other which cannot be mastered. The 'right of the other,' then, is the right to bear witness to our subjection to the law of the Other" (*AD* 119, 157), and this is precisely what Lyotard believes the Nazi genocide attempted to master in exterminating "the very people whose vocation is to bear witness to the necessary dependency on the law of the Other" (*AD* 119, 157).

The ethical turn Rancière takes Lyotard to have accomplished is one in which the "political community" is "transformed into an *ethical* community" (*AD* 115, 153). In a political community, Rancière understands those who are excluded to be "conflictual actor[s]" (*AD* 116, 153), who include themselves as "supplementary political subject[s], carrying a right not yet recognized or witnessing an injustice in the existing state of right" (*AD* 116, 153). By contrast, in the ethical community, the excluded are understood to have "accidentally" fallen "outside the great equality of all" and find themselves relegated to the status of those in need of "humanitarian" aid, as "the sick, the retarded or the forsaken to whom the community must extend a hand in order to re-establish the 'social bond'" (*AD* 116, 153). Or else the excluded are those who threaten us as "alien" and who must suffer "absolute rejection" (116, 153–54)—a scenario Rancière sees played out in Lars von Trier's *Dogville*.[7]

Having surveyed the grounds on which Rancière distances himself from Lyotard's politics, in order to gain a more precise grasp of Rancière's objection to Lyotard's view of art, we need to understand first exactly how Rancière situates Lyotard in relation to the aesthetic regime, and second why Rancière takes Lyotard to undercut the political promise of Kant's aesthetics. The strategy Rancière adopts in his critique of Lyotard is to develop a contrast between two tendencies he understands to embody opposing aspects of the "paradoxical sensorium" (*AD* 11, 22) of the aesthetic regime. Rancière takes Schiller's understanding of *Juno Ludovisi* as paradigmatic of the way the aesthetic regime breaks with the representative regime. He sees Schiller's account of this statue of a Greek divinity as embodying both traits that the "two great politics" (*AD* 43–44, 62) of the aesthetic regime separate out into contrary responses to the distribution of the sensible that constitutes the aesthetic regime. It is the "sublime strike of the pictorial line" (*AD* 3, 12) manifested, for example, in the art of Barnett Newman and understood as a politics of "resistant form" (*AD* 44, 62) that Rancière associates with Lyotard.[8] At the other extreme, Rancière situates the politics of "relational art" (*AD* 21, 34), or that which he also refers to as the "modest art" he sees as championed by curators and artists, the politics of art "becoming-life" (*AD* 44, 62). Sublime art tries to purify itself from any "compromise" with commercialization (*AD* 42–43, 61) and in doing so ends up enclosing itself in an avoidance of "all forms of political intervention" (*AD* 40, 58). Relational art, on the other hand, ends up making itself political at the cost of "eliminating itself as art" (*AD* 40, 58), that is, eliminating art "as a separate reality" (*AD* 44, 62) in its effort to transform art into a form of life. How, then, does Rancière relate these two opposing politics to Schiller's account of *Juno Ludovisi*?

Schiller *on* Juno Ludovisi

Schiller understands *Juno Ludovisi* as exemplary of the free play and free appearance of Kant's aesthetic idea. Whereas in the representative regime, art was defined according to its "technical perfection," in the aesthetic regime it is defined in terms of "a specific form of sensory apprehension" (*AD* 29, 44), one that is "heterogeneous to the ordinary forms of sensory experience" (*AD* 30, 45). The latter are embedded in a series of dualities characteristic of an "order of domination" that Rancière construes as ultimately resting on "a difference between two humanities" (*AD* 32, 47). In the representative regime, this domination takes shape in form's active rule over passive matter and in the governance of intelligence or understanding over sensibility, whereas in the aesthetic regime "inventive activity and sensible emotion encounter one another 'freely'" (*AD* 13, 24).

Rancière casts Lyotard's aesthetics of the sublime as responding to the "radical unavailability" (*AD* 34, 51) of *Juno Ludovisi*, its inaccessibility to thought. The idleness of the goddess is the site of a withdrawal. She encloses herself, withdraws into indifference, unnamable to any means/ends model of finality or action, remaining foreign to all desire. This strangeness or withdrawal is precisely what confers on the statue its heterogeneous sense, which in Lyotard, however, is made to testify to the "irremediable dependency" (*AD* 42, 61) in relation to the other, which in turn is cashed out in terms of the "ethical task of bearing witness" (*AD* 43, 62). Understood as such, art withdraws itself from any implication in a form of life. "In such a politics, form asserts its politicity by distinguishing itself from every form of intervention into the mundane world" (*AD* 39–40, 57).

By contrast, relational art would see in *Juno Ludovisi* the promise of a life to come in which there is no separation between "everyday life, art, politics and religion" (*AD* 35, 52). It is precisely because this statue was not created

as art but as an expression of culture in which there was as yet no separation between the spheres of politics, religion, and art that it can promise a
future community to come, a form of life in which art eliminates itself as
having a separate existence from the form of life for which it calls.

We are now in a position to understand why for Rancière the aesthetic
regime is "linked to the promise of an art that would be no more than an
art or would no longer be art" (*AD* 14, 26). Rancière situates Lyotard's aesthetics of sublime art and relational art as two divergent responses to the
"political promise" that Schiller attaches to the statue of the *Juno Ludovisi*,
and which Rancière sees as an expression of the "distribution of the sensible" with which he identifies the aesthetic regime. The statue holds promise in the first place "because it is art, because it is the object of a specific
experience and thereby institutes a specific, separate common space; on
the other [hand], it is a promise of community because it is not art, because
[. . .] it expresses [. . .] a way of life which has no experience of separation
into specific realms of experience" (*AD* 35, 52). In Lyotard's interpretation, art retreats from the promise of collective emancipation in order to
retain its purity in endorsing the claims of a specific community, whereas
in relational art it risks eliminating itself by merging with politics in its
very call for a new form of life.

The Role of Kant's Aesthetics for Rancière and Lyotard

Having clarified the way in which Rancière positions Lyotard with regard
to the aesthetic regime, let's now refine this understanding by developing
the sense in which Kant plays a different role for Rancière than he does for
Lyotard. An organizing motif of Rancière's discussion is the way in which
he locates the decisive operation of dissensus in Kant's analytic of the beautiful, without having to turn to the analytic of the sublime, to which many
recent aesthetic interventions, including Lyotard's, have returned.[9] Key to
understanding Rancière's own focus on the beautiful, rather than the sublime, is the way in which he sees Kant's free play, read through the lens of
Schiller, as breaking with the order of domination he construes as having
governed the representative regime.

In the aesthetic regime, the social distribution of roles is no longer lined
up with human nature in such a way as to adhere to the norm of mimetic
legislation, whereby the rules of art ordain that there is a class of people
whom art concerns, and a class of people to whom it is of no concern (see
AD 12, 23). The free play that is the hallmark of Kant's aesthetic idea,
in which there is a dual suspension of the "conceptual determination" by

cognition or understanding and of "the law of sensation which demands an object of desire" (*AD* 97, 130–31), disrupts the distribution of the sensible that is orchestrated by the legislation of two separate classes of humans. Read through Schiller, Kant's aesthetic common sense "challenges the distribution of the sensible that enforces" (*AD* 98, 132) the distance of these two classes, and it does so by a "neutralization of the very forms by which power is exercised" (*AD* 99, 133). What is at stake here, Rancière insists, is a "new revolution," one of "forms of sensory existence, instead of a simple upheaval of forms of state" (*AD* 99, 133).

Let's proceed more slowly in order to unpack this, by reviewing the constraints Rancière understands to have defined the representative regime, in order to comprehend the way in which aesthetic free play in Kant and Schiller breaks with the hierarchical order of representation. In the aesthetics that Kant inaugurates, "there is a break with the hierarchical order that had defined which subjects and forms of expression were deemed worthy of inclusion in the domain of art" (*AD* 10, 20), says Rancière. Stendhal stands, for Rancière, as exemplary of this break. The worth of art is no longer calibrated in terms of the dignity it establishes for itself in celebrating those deemed worthy of its representation, in which its forms of expression are bound up with the dignity of gods and goddesses or kings and queens. In Stendhal, for example, the most ordinary and apparently insignificant noises and sights become worthy of the artist's attention, the mundane minutiae of everyday experience become the material of art. Art is born of the "pure contingency" (*AD* 12, 22) that the "proximate" world presents.

For Rancière, Stendhal "testifies to an aesthetic regime in which the distinction between those things that belong to art and those that belong to ordinary life is blurred" (*AD* 5, 13). By evoking in his autobiographical *Vie de Henry Brulard* (1835) "the first—insignificant—noises that marked him as a child: ringing church bells, a water pump, a neighbour's flute" (*AD* 4, 13), Rancière understands Stendhal to be testifying to "the ruin of the old canons that set art objects apart from those of ordinary life" (*AD* 5, 14). Rancière claims that in "the neighbour's flute and the water pump which shape the soul of an artist" (*AD* 8, 17), *poiesis* (as "a way of doing") and *aesthesis* ("a way of being that is affected by it") are no longer mediated by mimetic legislation (see *AD* 7, 16); rather, they stand in a relation of immediacy with one another. Yet their relation to one another is premised on "the very gap of their ground" (*AD* 8, 17). That is, it is premised on the loss of the "human nature" that underwrote or guaranteed the mimetic legislation of the representative regime, or else it is premised on "a humanity to come" (*AD* 8, 17), a community that has not yet arrived but for which the art in question calls.

In the aesthetic regime, the function of art is no longer to celebrate dignitaries, but to see the extraordinary in the ordinary, in the flotsam and jetsam of everyday life, in a fleeting instance, to capture the beauty that is to be found in that which might have heretofore been judged to be a trivial existence. When Hegel finds beauty in the "genre scenes of Netherlandish [*sic*] painting or Murillo's little beggars" (*AD* 5, 14), Rancière takes his "philosophical revalorization" of Dutch genre painting, "following its public and commercial promotion," to signal "the beginning of [a] slow erosion of the figurative subject [. . .] that pushes the subject into the background of the picture, to make appear, in its place, the gesture of the painter and the manifestation of pictorial matter" (*AD* 9, 18). It is matter that comes to the fore in Lyotard's understanding of the *aistheton*, but matter fused with a particular approach to form, in Rancière's understanding, namely a form bound to the expression of a specific community, the Jewish community.

The break with the hierarchical forms of the representative regime that confined the subject of art to highly circumscribed arenas, to the pomp and circumstance of the lives of the rich and powerful, effects a rupture of the "norm of adequation" (*AD* 12, 22) that pertained "between *poiesis* and *aesthesis*" (*AD* 10, 20), established under the auspices of the mimetic, representative regime. This norm correlated an "active faculty" with a "receptive faculty" (*AD* 12, 22), a faculty of active intelligence responsible for imposing the appropriate form on passive matter, thereby evoking the appropriate emotional sensibility in an audience that could be molded to feel whatever was necessary to support the hierarchical order of things. In the representative regime, "artworks were tied to celebrating worldly dignities, and the dignity of their forms were attached to the dignity of their subjects and different sensible faculties attributed to those situated in different places" (*AD* 12, 23).

The aesthetic regime disrupts this arrangement, causing "disorder" such that "artworks no longer refer to those who commissioned them, to those whose image they established and grandeur they celebrated. Artworks henceforth relate to the 'genius' of peoples and present themselves, at least in principle, to the gaze of anyone at all" (*AD* 13, 24). In the aesthetic regime, "human nature and social nature cease to be mutual guarantees" and there is no longer "any hierarchy of active intelligence over sensible passivity. This gap separating nature from itself is the site of an unprecedented equality" (*AD* 13, 24). The transition from the representative to the aesthetic regime thus lies not only in the subject matter depicted, but also in the shifting contours of those to whom art became available to view. A major development that facilitates this shift is the institution of the museum, which severs "paintings and sculptures [. . .] from their functions of religious illustration and of decorating seigniorial and monarchic grandeurs" (*AD* 8, 18). Henceforth, an "undifferentiated public" comes "to replace the designated addressees of representative works" (*AD* 9, 18).[10]

When a worker stops his work, glancing up to admire the view, he takes the time he does not have *qua* worker, to enjoy a scene that is not his *qua* worker to enjoy, and he thereby disrupts the distribution of the sensible that confines his body to a certain place that the representative order designates as neither the place of art, nor that of aesthetics, but the place of the worker.[11] Hence Rancière says that the "categories of appearance, play and work are the proper categories of the distribution of the sensible" (*AD* 31, 47). There is a redistribution of the sensible in the disruption of an order in which certain humans are destined for the roles of rulers and leaders, while others are destined to be those who serve, providing the necessities of life that free their employers to pursue art and politics.

Having explicated how for Rancière the aesthetic regime breaks with the order of domination in the representative regime, let's now specify how this plays out in Rancière's critique of Lyotard. Rancière suggests that Lyotard is influenced by Adorno in allocating to art the task of "constituting a specific sensible world, separate from that governed by the law of the market" (*AD* 96, 130). For Lyotard however, the alienation to which art must testify "no longer concerns capitalist separation of pleasure and enjoyment, but is the simple destiny of dependency proper to the human animal" (*AD* 96, 130). To bear witness to this dependency becomes the task of the avant-garde for Lyotard, the project in which he enlists Kant's aesthetics. In order to understand Rancière's argument, I am going to briefly review Rancière's account of Kant's analytic of the sublime, his understanding of Kant on the beautiful, and his understanding of how Lyotard fuses elements of both the sublime and the beautiful in his notion of the *aistheton*.

For Rancière, Kant's sublime concerns a failure of imagination that results in the revelation of reason's legislative power in the domain of morality. The sublime "translates the incapacity of the imagination to grasp the monument [a pyramid, for example, or a monumental mountain or wild ocean] as a totality. Imagination's incapacity to present a totality to reason, analogous with its feeling of powerlessness before the wild forces of nature, takes us from the domain of aesthetics to that of morality" (*AD* 89, 120).

When confronted with a pyramid or a wild ocean, "imagination [. . .] reveals itself to be powerless to master the form, or the exceptional nature, of the sensible power with which it is confronted" (AD 92–93, 125). Imagination finds itself unable to provide that which might have been expected of it. As "'the greatest faculty of sense'" the imagination thus "betrays its powerlessness to give sensible form to the Ideas of reason" (*AD* 93, 125). Thus, it "proves the power of reason twice over" (*AD* 93, 125). First, it is unable to live up to reason's demand that it "provide the representation of the whole." Second, experiencing this failure or the "incapacity" of imagination, understood as the subject's faculty of sense, attests to the presence of the "unlimited faculty" of reason (*AD* 93, 125). Imagination is "thrown into disarray," which opens first onto the "autonomy of the aesthetic free play of the faculties" and then in turn to "a superior autonomy: the autonomy of legislative reason in the supersensible order of morality" (*AD* 93, 125). Thus, for Kant, the failure of imagination "brings forth the autonomous law of the legislative mind" (*AD* 93, 126).

If in the experience of the sublime, imagination's failure proves reason's autonomy, the key feature of Kant's account of the beautiful for Rancière is that "form is characterized by its unavailability" (*AD* 91, 123). In the experience of beauty, there is no "conceptual form imposing its unity on the diversity of sensation" (*AD* 91). Rather, the beautiful is "neither an object of knowledge, subordinating sensation to the law of the understanding, nor an object of desire, subordinating reason to the anarchy of sensations" (*AD* 91, 123). This "unavailability" of form makes way for "a new form of autonomy" in the "free play of the faculties" (*AD* 91, 123).[12] Rancière emphasizes the double suspension of negation that characterizes aesthetic experience for both Kant and Schiller, in which experience is "subject neither to the law of understanding, which requires conceptual determination, nor the law of sensation which demands an object of desire" (*AD* 97, 130–31). Rancière understands this double negation as a suspension not only of the law of understanding and that of sensation but also as a suspension of the "power relation that usually structures the experience of the knowing, acting and desiring subject" (*AD* 97, 131).

As we have seen previously, Rancière understands the representative regime as marked by the active imposition of what is taken to be an appropriate form on passive matter, which he understands as "a form of domination" (*AD* 97, 131) because what counts as appropriate is determined by mimetic laws of art ensconced in forms of power and privilege. These laws not only dictate what and who should be represented, by whom and for whom, but in doing so they also define a distribution of social functions and roles, which they assign to human nature. As we have also seen, there are those whom art concerns, and there are those it should not concern; the latter are to be kept in their place according to a social distribution of the sensible underwritten by a division of human nature into two classes. The class that actively imposes form on matter conceived as passive is the class that orchestrates, arranges, and authorizes sensible experience. The relation of form and matter participates in the distribution of forms of visibility and audibility, of ways of making and doing, dividing humanity into two classes. It is for this reason that Rancière claims that the relation between Kant's faculties in aesthetic experience as "the 'free agreement' between understanding and imagination is already a disagreement or dissensus" (*AD* 97, 131). It breaks with the order of domination, and it does so not merely by blurring the social hierarchy, but also by interrupting and rearranging the forms of sensibility. Read through Schiller, as Rancière understands it, "aesthetic common sense [. . .] is a dissensual common sense. It does not remain content with bringing distant classes together. It challenges the distribution of the sensible that enforces their distance" (*AD* 98, 132). Hence for Rancière, the "dissensual common sense of aesthetic experience is [. . .] opposed to the consensus of traditional order" (*AD* 98, 132). The agreement of imagination and understanding is already disagreement: "Dissensus, i.e. the rupture of a certain agreement between thought and the sensible already lies at the core of aesthetic agreement and repose" (*AD* 98, 131–32). Thus, in Rancière's view, the agreement between Kantian faculties "in aesthetic experience is not the harmony of form and matter that Lyotard claims," but rather it is precisely a "break with this [. . .] agreement" (*AD* 97, 131).[13]

For Rancière, one does not have to turn to Kant's account of the sublime in order "to discern a disagreement between thought and the sensible" (*AD* 97, 131). Reading Kant's understanding of the beautiful through Schiller's response to *Juno Ludovisi*, Rancière sees it as already involving the "double bind of attraction and repulsion" (*AD* 97, 131). It has a "charm that attracts us and a respect that makes us recoil" (*AD* 98, 131). For Schiller, the "statue's free appearance [. . .] draws us in with its charm and keeps us at a distance through the sheer majesty of its self-sufficiency. This movement of contrary forces puts us in a state of utter repose and one of supreme agitation" (*AD* 98, 131).[14] The statue of *Juno Ludovisi* both attracts us and repels us because it "manifests the character of divinity which is also [. . .] that of humanity in its fullness: She does not work she plays. She neither yields nor resists. She is as free of the ties of commandment as she is of those of obedience" (*AD* 98, 132). As such, the statue "stands in contrast to the state that governs human societies and puts each person in his place by separating those who command from those who obey, men of leisure from working men, men of refined culture from those of simple nature" (*AD* 98, 132). It is, claims Rancière, this "identity between agreement and disagreement" that enables "Schiller to confer on the 'aesthetic state' a political signification over and above the simple promise of social mediation implied by Kantian common sense, which hoped to unite the elite's sense of refinement with ordinary people's natural simplicity" (*AD* 98, 132).[15] Aesthetic sense is dissensual precisely because, divorced from the conceptual hierarchy whereby form subordinates matter, and from the social hierarchy whereby "separate classes have distinct senses" (*AD* 13, 23), the beauty of *Juno Ludovisi* is available to "anyone at all" (*AD* 13, 24). As the site of aesthetic play and the appearance of the beautiful, *Juno Ludovisi* is "the refutation within the sensible" of the "opposition between intelligent form and sensible matter which, properly speaking, is a difference between two humanities" (*AD* 31, 46).

Having specified how Rancière reads Kant on the sublime and the beautiful, we are now ready to see how Lyotard draws on both analytics in elaborating "sensuous matter in its very alterity" (*AD* 90, 122). While he privileges the sublime, Lyotard also draws on Kant's analytic of the beautiful in rendering sensuous alterity. He "accords it two essential traits," first "*pure difference*" (*AD* 90, 122). Lyotard claims the unavailability of form that Kant explores in the analytic of the beautiful for the pure difference of timbre and nuance. The singularity of timbre and nuance cannot be understood as the "play of differences and determinations that govern musical composition or the harmony of colours" (*AD* 91, 122). Rather, the "material event" of timbre or nuance, which Lyotard names with the paradoxical term "immaterial materiality" (*AD* 91, 122), is the unavailability of form. Their difference is "not determined by any set of conceptual determinations" (*AD* 90, 122). The second characteristic of matter Lyotard draws from Kant's analytic of the sublime. It is the "event of a passion" (*AD* 92, 124) that is common not only to timbre and nuance but also to "'the grain of a skin, or a piece of wood, the fragrance of an aroma, the savour of a secretion, or a piece of flesh'" (*AD* 92, 123; *I* 141). The event of passion that unsettles the mind, or, like the effect of the sublime on imagination, throws it into "disarray," is conserved only as "the feeling—anguish and jubilation—of an obscure debt" (*AD* 92, 124). For Lyotard, the *aistheton* is thus "two things in one. It is both pure materiality and a sign. [. . .] The musical timbre or the nuance of colour play the role Kant reserved for the pyramid and the wild ocean. They signal the mind's incapacity to grasp hold of an object" (*AD* 92, 124–25). But Kant's logic is inverted for Lyotard, for whom it is not the free play of the faculties that is at stake but rather, "subordination to the *aistheton*" that "signifies subordination to the law of alterity" (*AD* 94, 126).

For Rancière, by contrast, far from signifying subordination, Kantian aesthetic experience points to a "new form of sensible community" (*AD* 104, 140). If Schiller releases the emancipatory potential of Kant for politics, Rancière reads Lyotard as closing it down, converting it into its opposite, into "a sign of dependency" (*AD* 105, 140). In Lyotard, "Aesthetic experience becomes that of enslaved human mind, the mind enslaved to the sensory, but also, and above all, enslaved, on account of this sensory dependency, to the law of the Other" (*AD* 104, 140). Wary of the emancipatory dream turning into a form of totalitarianism, into the "barbarism of Nazi and soviet camps, or to the soft totalitarianism of the world of commercial culture and communication" (*AD* 105, 141), Lyotard understands the sublime "as a 'sacrificial' pronouncement of ethical dependency with respect to the immemorial law of Other; or the disaster that is born of forgetting disaster" (*AD* 105, 140–41). As in Adorno, art is "still a form of resistance" but this resistance, as Rancière sees it, takes on another meaning in Lyotard, namely the reinscription of the "subjugation to the law of the Other [. . .] that does us violence, or indulgence to the law of *self* that leads to an enslavement by commercial culture. Either the law of Moses or that of McDonald's" (*AD* 105, 141).

For Rancière, Lyotard takes up the Kantian notion of the sublime but in doing so he eliminates the political promise that Rancière takes to be inherent in Kant's aesthetics. Rather than the promise of an "unprecedented equality" (*AD* 13, 24) to which Rancière, who reads Kant's aesthetics through Schiller, takes the free play of Kant's aesthetics to point, Lyotard substitutes a submission to the law of the other. Rather than construing in art a freedom that looks to a utopian future, to the revolution to come, Lyotard sees the task of the avant-garde as that of testifying to the catastrophe of the past that he understands as synonymous with the Nazi project of exterminating the Jews. The art of the unpresentable thus becomes an art of endless mourning in the form of interminable bearing witness to past suffering. Lyotard no longer looks to the future, to the revolution to come, but to the past, to the catastrophe that is inassimilable by representation, to the holocaust. That is, the trauma that has been signified as the trauma to end all traumas—a Eurocentric view that has been rightly upbraided for its repression of the traumatic past of slavery and colonialism, the effects of which do not fail to echo all around us.

Concluding Reflections

We are living in an era that might be characterized as a culture of trauma, one in which it is becoming increasingly difficult to isolate trauma from the everyday experience of life for many of us. The more war becomes the norm, the harder it is to distinguish isolated occurrences of trauma from a broader culture in which trauma is less the exception than the rule. The combined effects of austerity cuts and the entrepreneurial model of capitalist success have generated high levels of stress for many workers on a daily level. Constant reorganization of institutions by high-level management, often involving ostensibly cost-saving measures that result in centralization in response to government mandates, leads to high levels of job insecurity, low levels of job satisfaction, disaffection and alienation of workers. Stress is induced through living and working in data-driven environments in which more time seems to be spent in assessing and reporting on work achieved than in effectively performing the work itself. Workers in many public and service sectors (such as education, health and welfare services) have borne the brunt of austerity cuts for many years, and have been subject to the stress of crisis management, living under the threat of their jobs at the same time as being held responsible for managing the consequences of dwindling resources for the populations they are trying to serve.

Despite the fact that it is increasingly difficult to find anyone who has not been affected by trauma, it remains important to respect the specificity of trauma in each individual case. It also remains important to acknowledge that there are significant differences in the ready availability of resources to address the effects of trauma depending on whether one enjoys relatively affluent and privileged means, or if the socio-economic situation already marks populations as vulnerable. The thresholds of expectation and therefore the thresholds of anxiety inducing patterns differ markedly in countries that remain relatively affluent in relation to those that are less affluent. Basic levels of healthcare, basic opportunities for education, and basic availability of food are dramatically divergent.

In a culture in which we are all increasingly liable to be exposed to some sort of trauma, it is not only important to acknowledge that resources for dealing with trauma are distributed variously across populations both nationally and internationally, but also that the likelihood of exposure to trauma has itself entered into the apparatus of power. The administration of trauma has taken shape as the war on terror and the politics of austerity, in which those who wield power do so by distancing themselves from its traumatizing effects, whether through the use of drones in war or the anonymity of managing centralized bureaucracies.

If we follow Rancière's thinking, politics and art as different forms of distributions of the sensible can create situations of dissensus, in which that which was previously invisible becomes visible, what remained inaudible as pure animal noise is converted into language that can be heard, and what was previously unsayable is translated into discourse. Perceptual grids of temporality and spatiality are dislocated as previously unintelligible sounds, and become audible and legible as meaningful signs. In dissensual politics, rather than being granted rights by benefactors who set themselves up as humanitarian, those who have been routinely excluded from humanity as political beings who do not count find ways of enacting and demanding their rights as human. Such demands would include establishing the right to access basic healthcare and education, and the freedom of artistic expression—none of which are possible in a situation of warfare, and all of which, as it happens, help to mitigate the effects of trauma that inevitably accompanies war. Ongoing war creates populations whose vulnerability makes it all but impossible for people to find ways to make their voices heard, to count as fully human, political beings. It perpetuates situations in which there is a divide between those who speak for others and those who lack the means, authority, and confidence to speak for themselves.[16]

In the preceding discussion, my effort has been to affirm Rancière's insistence that the tension characterizing the fragile alliance between art and politics is one that needs to be kept alive, even as the political promise of art cannot be guaranteed. To eliminate this tension is to risk either the elimination of art itself "as a separate reality" by transforming it into "a form of life" (*AD* 36, 53), or the enclosure of art from engagement in politics as resistant form, which, in Lyotard, as Rancière reads him, becomes a form of ethical memorialization of a specific community. Either the promise of emancipation is fulfilled by revoking the suspension that defines aesthetics (see *AD* 39, 57), or both art and politics are put at the service of an ethics geared to promoting the traumatized past of a particular community at the expense of others. Yet trauma is not something that lends itself easily to being reified, quantified, or compared. This is precisely why the traumas to which Europe has been exposed should not be allowed to morally trump every other trauma. What is allowed to count as trauma is bound up with whose voices are heard as contributing to legitimate discourse, with whose voices establish themselves as capable of recognition as properly human, which itself is decided through dissensual politics. Rancière remains critical of the metapolitics characteristic of the aesthetic regime, which he sees

Lyotard's aesthetics of the sublime as playing out in the politics of resistant form. This is because Rancière understands it as overcoming dissensus in the name of the ethical commemoration of a specific community, and in doing so, eliding the difference between art and politics. The indeterminacy of politics and art, and thus the political negotiability of the boundary separating them on which Rancière insists, does not prevent him from insisting that there must be some kind of distinction between them. The precise location and character of this distinction will, however, depend upon conditions internal to a given society, politics, and historicity, none of which are static, and which, like the distinction between politics and art itself, are thus open to challenge, reconfiguration, and negotiation.

NOTES

1. Lacan's formulation is the *"specific prematurity of birth* in man," "The mirror stage as formative of the function of the I" in *Écrits: A Selection*, trans. Alan Sheridan (Bristol: Tavistock Publications, 1977), 4.

2. Jacques Rancière, *Aesthetics and Its Discontents*, trans. Steven Corcoran (Malden, Mass.: Polity, 2009); Jacques Rancière, *Malaise dan l'esthétique* (Paris: Galilée, 2004). Subsequent references to this text are parenthetically noted as *AD*, with pagination referring to the English translation and the original French in that order.

3. Jean-François Lyotard, *The Inhuman*, trans. Geoffrey Bennington and Rachel Bowlby (Stanford: Stanford University Press, 1991). Subsequent references to this text are parenthetically noted as *I*, with pagination referring to the English translation.

4. Rancière quotes Lyotard citing reasons' "inability to 'approach matter,' in other words to be able to master the sensible event of a dependency. What sublime experience teaches us is this: 'the soul comes into existence dependent on the sensible, thus violated, humiliated. The aesthetic condition is enslavement to the *aistheton*'" (*AD* 93, 125, quoted from Lyotard's *Postmodern Fables*, 243–44). Rancière adds that for Lyotard, who both follows and reinvents Kant, the "sensory experience of the sublime is the sign of something else" (*AD* 93, 125). The *aistheton* is also the imposition of the law of the Other. "With Kant, the imagination's failure brings forth the autonomous law of the legislative mind. With Lyotard, the logic is strictly inverted: subordination to the *aistheton* signifies subordination to the law of alterity. Sensory passion is the experience of a 'debt.' Ethical experience is that of a subordination without appeal to the law of an Other. It manifests thought's servitude with regard to a power internal and anterior to the mind that it strives in vain to master" (*AD* 93–94, 125). Whereas for Kant the inability of imagination to provide sensory form for the sublime testifies to the strength

and fortitude of reason, whose compensatory facility offers a resource on which to fall back, it is the law of alterity that asserts itself for Lyotard in the face of imagination's incapacity. Subordination to the Other proves itself anterior to thought.

5. Immanuel Kant, *Critique of the Power of Judgement*, trans. Paul Guyer and Eric Matthews (Cambridge, U.K.: Cambridge University Press, 2000).

6. Lyotard employs a notion of dissensus that is close to Rancière's own notion of dissensus. See Lyotard, *The Differend: Phrases in Dispute*, trans. Georges Van Den Abbeele (Minneapolis: University of Minnesota Press, 1988). When it comes to his aesthetics of the sublime, however, Rancière criticizes him for evacuating the polemical edge of dissensus.

7. Lars von Trier, *Dogville*. Santa Monica: Lions Gate Entertainment, 2003.

8. Rancière also associates Adorno and Mallarmé with the politics of resistant form.

9. Among many other critics see Gregg M. Horowitz, *Sustaining Loss: Art and Mournful Life* (Stanford: Stanford University Press, 2001).

10. I think that, in fact, the public is not as undifferentiated as Rancière suggests, but that is a topic for another essay.

11. See Rancière, "The Paradoxes of Political Art, in *Dissensus: on Politics and Aesthetics*," trans. Steven Corcoran (London: Continuum, 2011), 140.

12. I take it that the new form autonomy to which Rancière refers is that born of the free play of the faculties of understanding and imagination.

13. See also *AD* 90, 122.

14. Rancière refers to Friedrich Schiller, *On the Aesthetic Education of Man*, trans. Elizabeth M. Wilkinson and L. A. Willoughby (Oxford: Clarendon Press, 2005), who, in a passage that some readers might find reminiscent of Kant's concept of the sublime, says, referring to Juno Ludovisi that "even as we abandon ourselves in ecstasy to her heavenly grace, her celestial self-sufficiency makes us recoil in terror" (109).

15. Rancière refers to James Meredith Creed's translation of Kant's *Critique of Judgment*, 183.

16. Rancière makes the point that it is not a lack of understanding that prevents those who are dominated from alleviating their domination, but rather it is a matter of confidence. "The dominated" says Rancière "do not remain in subordination because they misunderstand the existing state of affairs but because they lack the confidence in their capacity to transform it" (*AD* 45, 65).

CHAPTER 7

Black Embodied Wounds and the Traumatic Impact of the White Imaginary

George Yancy

Anxiety entered my body. Somewhere in the unknown
the white threat was hovering near again.
—RICHARD WRIGHT[1]

Violence is always and necessarily about wounds—
the physical harm which is often permanent—even
when this is only implied or threatened.
—ROBERTA CULBERTSON[2]

The body implies mortality, vulnerability, agency: the
skin and the flesh expose us to the gaze of others, but
also to touch, and to violence, and bodies put us at risk of
becoming the agency and instrument of all these as well.
—JUDITH BUTLER[3]

Because I critically engage forms of racialized trauma within this chapter,
I began with the preceding epigraphs to telescope what I see as a necessary
precondition for any discussion about racialized trauma, which, etymologically, means a form of wounding, hurting, or defeating. That precondition
is sociality, the reality of being embodied with others, along with a background of a shared intelligibility. The phenomenon of trauma presupposes
the reality of being exposed, open. Belief in a metaphysics of self-enclosure,
atomic subjectivity, bodily edges, in a world of white anti-Black racism is
not only false, but unethical. It is false because we are fundamentally social
ontologically *relational* beings. More philosophically robust, my claim is
that when it comes to living within structures of white anti-Black racism,
bodies have no edges. This presupposes a radical rethinking of a relational
ontology where the body does not terminate at some fictive corporeal edge
or has a clear outside limit. Instead, we are always already contiguous—
etymologically, "touching upon." It is unethical because the philosophical problematics encompassed by such a metaphysics not only mock the
lived experience of Black bodies but falsify the integrity and veracity of
their *lived* experiences. Within the context of a relational ontology, despite

the contemporary social reality of a de facto racially segregated North America, racialized bodies are always already "touching" through a socially shared skin. Within this context, the power of the white gaze functions as a species of touch. The power of the white gaze, then, presupposes collectively shared, even if not collectively endorsed, social and historical semiotics that have deep *material* implications. In other words, the white gaze constitutes a site of a vector that is not restricted to the surface of the skin qua matter.[4] The white gaze and the white imaginary are inextricably linked to broader, interlocking semiotic, sonic, sociohistorical vectors of materiality that bind us and that have a profound impact upon us from a distance regardless of whether or not we are the perpetrators of the white gaze or its recipients. On this score, the white gaze can be theorized as haptic in its impact.

The importance here is to conceptualize trauma within the context of a shared *symbolic world*, a world whose meanings are both explicit and implicit, whose meanings can impact us and undo us in violent and harrowing ways. Racialization within a shared symbolic world, one predicated upon a constitutive anti-Black ethos, is thoroughly this-worldly; it is a world in which any discussion of Black embodied wounds through the traumatic impact of the white gaze and imaginary takes as its point of departure the reality of the mundane, the quotidian, the muck and mire of a racist social integument or social skin through which anti-Black encounters are suffered. So, I actively resist the seduction of any form of abstract discourse that loses sight of the concrete expressions of trauma or wounding that human beings undergo—the funkiness and horror of broken bodies, burned flesh, troubled affect, and scarred psyches. My objective, therefore, is to conceptualize an ontology of trauma or wounding that *does not* leave existence or the weight of shared history by the wayside.

Given the pervasive and enduring legacy of anti-Black racism within the context of North America—though, here, we can also talk about how the Black body has come to function as a global trope of the monstrous, the damned and the wretched—the Black body has come to bear the marks of violence from a lived space within which to be Black is a *relational* phenomenon that presupposes whiteness as a site of bloodlust, terror, bad faith, narcissism, privilege, hegemony, and power. Hence, my discussion of Black-embodied wounds or wounding presupposes sociogeny.[5] My point of embarkation begins with the somatic gravitas of the visceral and affective dimensions of trauma; it begins within the socio-historical space of the precarious, a condition in which all of us are exposed to vulnerability. Yet within the context of an anti-Black world, one experiences both the precarious and a *racialized* precarity, which denotes forms of racialized instability with deep implications for one's social and existential welfare.

As stated previously, white gazes can touch from a distance; they are vectors or forces of influence that can hit with the force of a stick, a blow to the body that leaves its mark. Think here of the young white boy in the safety of his mother's arms saying, when he "sees" Frantz Fanon on a train in France, "Look, a Negro!"[6] The boy becomes frightened and thinks that "the nigger's going to eat [him] up."[7] This act of looking is not an inaugural event; it is an instantiation of a long and continuous history of anti-Black white racism. Fanon's body appears as an object of fear, a site of monstrosity, curiosity, dread, surprise, and disgust. In other words, this process of denigrating/assaulting the Black body is historically iterative. It neither ends nor does it begin with the visual and discursive assault on Fanon's Black body or other Black bodies. The process of Fanon's "appearing" as it does, which is a kind of "showing" or "being shown," presupposes the racial logics of white racist semiotics and white spatial distancing. Fanon is marked as the subhuman and that from which the young white child must keep his distance. Within this specific dyad, the force of white embodiment results in a form of corporeal distortion vis-à-vis Fanon's Black embodiment. The racialized transfiguration of Fanon's body is predicated upon a long history of somatic white terror. The white child's utterance functions as a warning (to other whites); it is a warning that Fanon is to be watched, his movements tracked. The white child, who fears for his life, constitutes the site of a white civilized border, as it were, beyond which Fanon mustn't cross. On this score, it is also a public warning to other Black bodies; it says that your presence is both invisible and hyper-visible to us whites. We don't see your humanity. And when we do "see" you, the appearance of something racially excessive emerges and we are filled with a sense of foreboding. After all, Fanon is not only deemed primitive with perverse gastronomic proclivities, but he is called a *nigger*, a powerful sonic racial epithet that marks the Black body, *his* Black body, as a sub-person, disposable refuse, shit. Fanon writes, "A man was expected to behave like a man. I was expected to behave like a black man—or at least like a nigger."[8]

Reflecting on his experiences on the train, and the process of having his Black body racially fixed, Fanon's writes, "What else could it be for me but an amputation, an excision, a hemorrhage that spattered my whole body with black blood?"[9] The reader will note the traumatic corporeal impact that Fanon describes and the corporeal tropes that he deploys to communicate the impact. He undergoes a process of amputation, which is a process of cutting, an excision, which is a process of removal or erasure, and a hemorrhage, which is a form of breaking. While it is true that Fanon doesn't literally bleed to death on the train, and his body isn't literally cut into pieces, there is, from the perspective of Fanon's *erlebnis*, or lived experience of his encounter with the white gaze, a process in which his "corporeal schema crumbled, its place taken by a racial epidermal schema."[10] Yet, given the embodied trauma experienced by Fanon, the "literal" is troubled.

Theorizing the concept of materiality beyond matter as a bounded surface, I argue that Fanon, through the panoptic power of the white gaze, undergoes a process of distorted *affective* corporeal intensity, which is communicated across a shared racial integument. Fanon experiences an embodied trauma through the racial fixity of his embodiment; he becomes a racialized *object*, one that bears the weight of the materialization of white mythos. The racist materialization of the white gaze marks his body, though not simply as a surface upon which a racial marking is inscribed. The white gaze and the utterance materially impact the integrity of Fanon's embodied orientation, his being-in-the-world, which is already entangled within the material power and logic of whiteness. The white gaze results in a *lived embodied* forlornness, experienced and lived as an appendage to cope with—a thing. Fanon says that he "wanted to come lithe and young into a world that was ours and to help to build it together."[11] He goes on to say, "I shouted a greeting to the world and the world slashed away my joy. I was told to stay within bounds, to go back where I belonged."[12] To have one's joy *slashed* is to undergo an intense embodied experience. The slash, the cut, is an actual separation, a loss. The point here is that the white gaze easily reaches across or through (not beyond) a racialized spatiality and touches the other precisely because it is *not* an empty space; it is a racially saturated social skin that always already connects Fanon's body vis-à-vis the white child and other whites on the train. It is a connection that truncates not only Fanon's Black body, but his aspirations, his imaginative capacity. Richard Wright, as stated in one of the opening epigraphs, comments on the white threat that was hovering near. In the train, the white gazes, hover near; they linger. Fanon writes, "I am being dissected under white eyes, the only real eyes."[13] Fanon doesn't undergo a nightmare from which he awaits to awaken; rather, to be embodied as Black within an anti-Black world *is* the lived nightmare. Indeed, his body undergoes a process of a social ontological *lived* amputation. He *lives* fragmented. His body no longer moves through space lithely or with effortless grace. He no longer moves through the world with implicit knowledge (as when he reached for a pack of cigarettes or a box of matches), but now calculates, is now "battered down by tom-toms, cannibalism, intellectual deficiency, fetishism, racial defects, slave-ships."[14] Fanon has been uprooted from a *familiar* mode of being-in-the-world. He says that he "progresses by crawling."[15] Notice that Fanon moves slowly; he references crawling, which implies a kind of spatial reduction. There is a major embodied relocation. Once standing, he now crawls. There is a fissure in Fanon's spatial movement and social engagement. His self-narrative not only describes what is occurring to his embodiment, but also the net result of what has happened. In short, Fanon has been traumatized. Kyeong Hwangbo argues that undergoing trauma is a profoundly "liminal experience of radical deracination and calamity."[16] She says that it "brings about a violent rupture of the order on both the personal and the social level. It annihilates the sense of continuity in our lives and our self-narratives, bringing to the fore the contingency of our lives."[17] Of course, as Black, the contingency of Fanon's life, and how it is brought to the fore, involves a doubling through not only the fact that all life is contingent, but through the violence of white normative assumptions projected upon Fanon's being that destabilize and traumatize his embodiment.

What Fanon describes is a powerful manifestation of somatic trauma. To shout a greeting to the world is a joyful act; an embodied affective act. To be told to go back where he belonged is to undergo a process of being stopped, policed, and violently rendered marginal. Such a process of policing has a material impact. As Sara Ahmed writes, "For bodies that are not extended by the skin of the social, bodily movement is not so easy. Such bodies are stopped, where the stopping is an action that creates its own impressions. Who are you? Why are you here? What are you doing?"[18] Each of these instances of interrogation, for Ahmed, is a kind of stopping device. The idea here is that one is "stopped by being asked the question, just as asking the question requires that you be stopped."[19] Ahmed proposes here nothing less than the rethinking of phenomenology's emphasis upon moving through space lithely. She writes, "A phenomenology of 'being stopped' might take us in a different direction than one that begins with motility, with a body that 'can do' by flowing into space."[20] Interpellation, then, is by no means inconsequential in an anti-Black world. The hail impacts the Black body through the skin of the social. The hail is the site of a social ontological and sonic material vector. The NYPD's racial profiling practice of stop-and-frisk disproportionately targets both Black and Brown bodies, a racial hailing that no doubt stresses and traumatizes hundreds of thousands of innocent people, especially as many of those individuals have been stopped at least more than once. Imagine the impact on one's body integrity to undergo stop-and-frisk based upon "reasonable suspicion" where the "reasonableness" is governed by a racial and racist logic that has already constructed certain bodies as "criminals" and "urban savages." And then imagine what it is like to live one's body as always already *stopped.*

To add to Ahmed's suggestion to begin with a phenomenology of being stopped, I would emphasize that a phenomenology of traumatization in virtue of being specifically Black in an anti-Black world (which does not exclude other bodies of color) can also take us in a different direction, one that theorizes specific forms of Black trauma that for whites don't occur. Within the context of a white normatively structured world, there is no *racialized* radical deracination and calamity for whites. It is this absence, for whites, of a *racialized* traumatic and dehumanizing deracination that also speaks to the absence of forms of white racialized grieving that helps us to understand the limits of white empathy and the ways in which these absences are underwritten by an unspoken philosophical anthropological norm that guarantees that white lives *really* matter. That unspoken white norm also frames the experience that Audre Lorde remembers in terms of the disgust and hatred directed toward her, as a young Black girl, by a white woman seated on the AA subway train to Harlem. As she sat next to the white woman, Lorde remembers this woman pulling her coat away from Lorde's snowsuit. The white woman is staring at the young Lorde. She writes, "Her mouth twitches as she stares and then her gaze drops down, pulling mine with it."[21] Lorde talks about how she thought that perhaps there was a disgusting insect that the woman was trying to avoid. This "thing" that has created such a visceral repugnance on the part of the white woman "must be something very bad from the way she's looking."[22] Yet, it was Lorde who was the perceived vermin. She writes, "When I look up the woman is still staring at me, her nose holes and eyes huge. And suddenly I realize there is nothing crawling up the seat between us; it is me she doesn't want her coat to touch."[23] This experience leaves Lorde with the impression that she has done something wrong—that *she is embodied as wrong.* Lorde came too close to the "purity" of white embodiment, to white "scared" occupied space. As a result, her Black body underwent a powerful manifestation of white perceptual violence, a racialized regulatory surveillance. The white woman's disgust communicates: As an embodied "contaminant," you are too close.

Similarly, for Fanon, it is also a problem of proximity and the occlusion of his lived mobility that constitutes a site of wounding, a site of the traumatic. He inhabits a zone of being an ontological problem, a racial excess that *must* be policed no matter the cost to his life and Black lives, more generally. W. E. B. Du Bois says that whites, though hesitant to ask, pose this question: "How does it feel to be a problem?"[24] While he answers seldom a word, perhaps part of the answer to that question is that it feels as if Black embodied existence is in a constant and unrelenting state of trauma. Or, perhaps, as Claudia Rankine notes, "the condition of Black life is one of mourning."[25] Both can be true, as trauma and mourning are mutually implicative. For example, recently, a white police officer walked into a store where I was buying some food and I remember feeling this powerful sense of wanting to flee, of feeling as if the rules and laws that are designed to govern our (white) society didn't apply to me. I could move "too quickly," placing my hand into my pocket to pay for my food, and my life would end just like that. The white police officer would explain how he felt threatened and had "reasonable" suspicion. Yet I would be dead. In short, as Rankine has suggested, because he, as a white man, can't police his own imagination, my life, and the lives of other Black men/boys are being taken.[26] Within the store, I experienced a profound sense of fear, an embodied sense of immanent death. On other occasions, in different social spaces, while standing next to other white police officers, I have felt the shadow of death bearing upon my body. There is a palpable sense of having my body shattered by a bullet fired from their guns. Given the sheer magnitude of unarmed Black bodies killed, especially Black men and boys, by white police officers and their proxies, the feeling of wanting to flee for my life, that sense of overwhelming angst, is underwritten by the contemporary expression and the historical reality of white gratuitous violence against Black people. The intense affect felt in the presence of that white police officer is *not* a case of paranoia, but based upon historically grounded fear of whiteness as a site of terror. That terror, or the historical promise of that terror, is enough to flood one's senses with dread, to impact one's sense of bodily safety, one's sense of possessing certain "inalienable" rights in virtue of being human.

"Man, I almost blew you away!" Those were the terrifying words of a white police officer—one of those who policed black bodies in low income areas in North Philadelphia in the late 1970s—who caught sight of me carrying the new telescope my mother had just purchased for me. "I thought you had a weapon," he said. The words made me tremble and pause; I felt the sort of bodily stress, trauma, and deep existential anguish that no teenager should have to endure. This officer had already inherited those poisonous assumptions and bodily perceptual practices that constitute the white gaze. He had already come to "see" the black male body (*my Black body*) as "different," "deviant," "ersatz." He failed to conceive, or perhaps could not conceive, that a black teenage boy living in the Richard Allen Project Homes for very low income families would own a telescope and enjoy looking at the moons of Jupiter and the rings of Saturn. A black boy carrying a telescope wasn't conceivable—unless he had stolen it—given the white racist horizons within which my black body was policed as "dangerous" and "inferior." To the white officer, I was something fictional. My telescope, for him, was a weapon. In retrospect, I can see the headlines: "Black Boy Shot and Killed While Searching the Cosmos."[27] When I reflect on that moment as an adult, I mourn the possible death of a younger me. It is frightening to know that one's life can be taken in the blink of an eye and at such a young age. Then again, it is even more frightening, the affective gravitas even more intense, to know that being Black was the problem, that to be Black in North America is to be deemed disposable and worthless; that it is my fate to *make peace with a traumatized existence,* a life of mourning. Being within the same space as the white police officer in the store, and within the space of the one who "saw" a gun, I experience my life, my Black body, as foregrounded vis-à-vis the background of white fabricated fear and white self-alienation. Because white people *need* me to be the criminal, the nigger, I am doomed by either playing the role or denouncing the myth. In either case, my life can be taken away with white impunity. That is the lived and remembered trauma that I sit with: "Man, I almost blew you away!" It is the "almost" that brings actual death into closer proximity.

Reflecting on his youth and his early experiences of white people, Wright observed that it "was as though I was continuously reacting to the threat of some natural force whose hostile behavior could not be predicted."[28] Wright adds that he "had already become as conditioned to their [white's] existence as though [he] had been the victim of a thousand lynchings."[29] Wrights use of the term "lynching" speaks to the actual spectacle violence of blunt traumas and bloody amputations and how such violence was used to send the chilling message to Black bodies that this could be you, that is, any Black person. Think of the thousands of lynched Black bodies. Think of the gore, the massive traumas that were both physical and psychological. Think of the traumatized embodied immobility that resulted from hearing about the realities of flayed and burned Black flesh; think of the impact on Black people who desired to dream, to come lithe into the world. Think of Claude Neal who, in 1934 in Florida, was castrated and had his genitals stuffed into his mouth and was forced to say that he liked them. Think of the amputation of his fingers, of his toes. Think of Sam Hose who, in 1988 in Georgia, was mutilated, tied to a tree and burned alive.

Think about how the skin on his face was removed. And think of Mary Turner, also in Georgia, a Black teenager who was eight months pregnant and lynched. Mary was tied up by her ankles and burned alive while having her baby cut from her abdomen. The baby hit the ground only to have its life stomped out of it by a white man. This is only a fragment of the brutal history visited upon Black bodies in North America. Yet the disposability, the trauma experienced by Black bodies, continues—Trayvon Martin, Jordan Davis, Renisha McBride, Eric Garner, Walter Scott, Sandra Bland, Laquan McDonald, Eric Harris, Levar Jones, Tamir Rice, John Crawford, Aiyana Stanley-Jones, Michael Brown, Rekia Boyd, Samuel DuBose, Freddie Gray, and so many others.

There are important gender differences to be acknowledged, theorized, and never forgotten when it comes to racialized forms of trauma suffered by Black women. Yet Black bodies share the trauma of trying *to be* in a world in which their existence is already negated, nullified; perhaps they are already dead, where existing within a white racist anti-Black world is like *waiting* one's turn to die, where the bell tolls for Black bodies in ways that leave white bodies unscathed, where Black bodies constitute a kind of "unreality" from the incipiency of Black life. Judith Butler writes, "If violence is done against those who are unreal, then, from the perspective of violence, it fails to injure or negate those lives since those lives are already negated."[30] Yet there is a strange paradox here as those lives already negated remain vibrant. Butler notes, "But they have a strange way of remaining animated and so must be negated again (and again)."[31] On this score, Black bodies can't be mourned and occupy the status of a kind of walking dead "because they are always already lost or, rather, never 'were,' and they must be killed, since they seem to live on, stubbornly, in this state of deadness."[32] For Butler, then, "Violence renews itself in the face of the apparent inexhaustibility of its object. The derealization of the 'Other' means that it is neither alive nor dead, but interminably spectral."[33] To conclude, deploying Butler's concepts, though inflected through the lens of the traumatized Black body, the endless white perverse paranoia that imagines Black people as the monstrous, the primitive, the nigger, justifies itself endlessly to wage endless white terror, and impose endless trauma, on a recursive fictional Black body that it can't live without.

Black bodies in North America endured racialized forms of traumatic life, ones replete with moments of invisibility and unreality. These moments translate into embodied wounds caused by white violence in the form of white privilege, institutional racism, white racist micro-aggressions, silences, gazes, gestures. And violence, as Roberta Culbertson makes clear in one of the opening epigraphs, is always and necessarily about wounds even when this is only implied or threatened. The violence in the utterance "Man, I almost blew you away!" is certainly threatened. And the implied horrific dimensions of the violence are there: dead black body, multiple shot wounds, flesh torn apart, and blood on the walls. Yet "Man, I almost blew you away!" is itself a part of the violence; it wounded and continues to wound after so many years. For the white police officer, I was unreal; Blacks don't own telescopes. The sonic memory, what did happen, and what could have happened, induces anxiety, embodied disquietude. But that is the dismal and unfortunate logic of trauma; it metastasizes, touching other aspects of one's affective and embodied life, spreading like a cancer; it continues to haunt. It haunts as if, to repeat Wright, one has been the victim of a thousand lynchings. This process of haunting, the lingering traumatic experience, while its implications are not fully comprehended at the moment of the traumatic occurrence, is indicative of Lorde's experience on the train with respect to the white woman's aversion to her Blackness. She writes, "Something's going on here I do not understand, but I will never forget it. Her eyes. The flared nostrils. The hate."[34]

So there seem to be aspects of the traumatic experience endured by Lorde that are, at the time experienced, not entirely understood. This doesn't rule out that one actually undergoes or experiences trauma at such moments. After all, Lorde says, "I don't like to remember the cancellation and hatred, heavy as my wished-for death, seen in the eyes of so many white people from the time I could see."[35] Think here of the cumulative impact of white gazes that attempt to cancel Lorde's being. Think of the hatred. Think of those whites who, through their gazes, wish for the death of Lorde. It is understandable why she would not want to remember such traumatic experiences. Yet not wanting to remember presupposes that there is something there to remember: a powerful and painful affective disorientation, a blunt cancellation. On this score, it appears that there are aspects of trauma that may not emerge all at once. There seem to be aspects or profiles of the traumatic experience that are linked to temporality, waiting, as it were, to be discerned or perhaps concealing themselves in other forms—self-doubt, self-hatred, negative body perceptions, sweats in the night.

Returning to Fanon, the white gaze is by no means benign, but tears at Fanon's body, reducing it to that which is a product of white racist mythopoesis. As is the case with the white police officer in whose distorted gaze I possessed a "gun," the white gaze is an act of violence and necessarily leaves its wounds. Similarly, Fanon, for all intents and purposes, became the "cannibal." The white child is not simply a victim of white racist historical myth-making, but perpetuates that history through the utterance, "Look, a Negro!" The illocutionary expression is the reproduction of white racist history. Fanon writes that he "already knew that there were legends, stories, history."[36] In short, Fanon is not simply confronted by a white racist imago, but he is also confronted by a cumulative *temporality* that does violence to his *presence*. The white child resides, as it were, in the past, in those racist legends, stories, and history. Fanon is in the present. So, there is a clash of temporalities. It is not Fanon who is the primitive, who is literally stuck in the past. Rather, it is the child's white gaze, and perhaps his entire sensorial comportment vis-à-vis Fanon's Black body, that is structured by a false history created by whites for whites that is not coeval.[37] Then again, given the power and pervasiveness of the white gaze, Fanon might be said to inhabit the past, the present, and the future. After all, he is daily subjected to, assaulted by, a fixed monstrous image of himself, a kind of "eternal" racialized archetype.

Baldwin writes, "People who imagine that history flatters them (as it does, indeed, since they wrote it) are impaled on their history like a butterfly on a pin and become incapable of seeing or changing themselves, or the world."[38] Baldwin further writes, "The great force of history comes from the fact that we carry it within us, are unconsciously controlled by it in many ways, and history is literally *present* in all that we do."[39] The white child's gaze is his frame of reference. The performance of *his* white gaze and the utterance that hails Fanon are *doubled* forces of influence that assail his body.[40] To assail means to attack, to beat, to overwhelm. So, despite the white child's "innocence," the constitution of his identity as white is dialectically linked to Fanon's Black body as a problem, as one deserving of forms of corporeal violence that are never too excessive. Yet, the child is left afraid of a myth, not Fanon. The child is afraid of a specter created by white people themselves. And it is "the fact that one has been reduced to the dark shadow of the other, and that one's existence can be reified into a despised object by the other's judging gaze brings about dire, traumatic psychic consequences."[41] Indeed, Fanon is left dehumanized, demoralized, and traumatized. In short, the child's "innocence" does not deflect the blow. His gaze and his utterance function as blunt objects wielded at Fanon. Fanon notes, "My body was given back to me sprawled out, distorted, recolored, clad in mourning in that white winter day."[42] The description of "clad in mourning" suggests an attire worn by one who has survived the death of a loved one. One grieves the death. But it is precisely Fanon who has suffered trauma and abjection, who has undergone a kind of death though the white gaze. Yet because of the impact of the trauma, Fanon would rather disappear. He writes, "I slip into corners, and my long antennae pick up the catch-phrases strewn over the surface of things— nigger underwear smells of nigger—nigger teeth are white—nigger feet are big—the nigger's barrel chest—I slip into corners, I remain silent, I strive for anonymity, for invisibility. Look, I will accept the lot, as long as no one notices me."[43] In such an abject state, Fanon flees from himself, preferring invisibility. After all, there is no apparent safety within the context of Fanon having been "laid bare."[44] It is here that "the essence of psychological trauma is the loss of faith that there is order and continuity in life. Trauma occurs when one loses the sense of having a safe place to retreat within or outside oneself to deal with frightening emotions or experiences."[45]

In late 2014, in *The New York Times* in a philosophical column called *The Stone*, I conducted a total of nineteen interviews with philosophers and public intellectuals (such as Cornel West, Anthony Appiah, Naomi Zack, Charles Mills, Judith Butler, bell hooks, Noam Chomsky, Peter Singer, Nancy Fraser, and others) on the topic of race. Following the interviews, my aim was to write a concluding article in *The Stone* summarizing some of the key points learned from the interviews. Given so much of what I perceived as the failure or denial of so many white readers to understand why race continues to matter in America, I decided to write an article in the form of a letter, something that would disarm and yet profoundly implicate white people in the perpetuation of white supremacy. So in "Dear White America," I challenged white Americans to rethink how they understand white racism and, by implication, understand questions of white racial "innocence," injustice, and complicity. The core thesis of the letter was that white Americans are racist by virtue of being privileged by the racist systemic and prejudicial forces and arrangements of America. The claim was not that white people are horrible human beings who self-consciously intend to oppress Black people. That individualist, perpetrator model fails to understand the heteronomous forces of structurally embedded and psychically opaque forms of racism. In other words, the social lives of white people are entangled within a larger socio-historical matrix that implicates them, beyond their will, in the perpetuation of racial injustice. The letter functioned as a gift, asking for a species of love in return; the kind of love that is able and prepared to endure loss, the loss of a white self. Indeed, within the letter, I use the term "gift."

However, after the publication of "Dear White America," I received hundreds of messages that were filled with despicable anti-Black vitriol.

I had not anticipated the corporeal impact. "Nigger this" and "nigger that" over hundreds of times left its mark on my body. I felt it in the form of bodily fear, isolation, a species of obsessiveness, looking over my shoulder, watching my back. There was an actual need for police presence at two of my talks. I was told that the FBI got involved. For me, the deluge of so many white racist responses, threats, felt like being in the company of that white police officer, but only magnified. I even received regular postal mail that I resisted opening in fear that it was laced with something harmful, and in fear of what might be inside. It turned out that the letters were filled with more of the same: more hatred, more white racist maliciousness. I felt that sense of loss in faith that there is predictable order, safety, and continuity.[46] Where was I to retreat? "Are you Dr. George Yancy?" I hesitated. Perhaps this is what it's like to be stopped-and-frisked. "Why?" I asked. "Didn't you write that article, 'Dear White America?'" Again, I hesitated; this time wondering if I should pretend to be someone else. I had that familiar experience of having time slow down to a crawl. I was seized by that emotion to fight or to take flight. I read as quickly as possible the white male's body language. The potential for violence was in the air. I felt in danger. "Yeah, that's me." He paused and then spoke. I could now see what appeared to be his slight shyness to speak. "I just wanted to say to you how much I enjoyed that piece that you wrote." I said, "Thanks!" We moved on.

What is important about this encounter is that the results could have been different for me, dangerously so. And the fact that I had to worry about this was part of the problem. The reality of the matter is that tons of white responses to "Dear White America" had taken its toll on my body, my sense of continuity, my sense of safety. This was not paranoia, though. The reality of white racism was/is there. As a Black person, that deep corporeal feeling of being the object of white terror, the history of white terror, hit me hard. This is why it was so palpable. As I write this chapter, I just checked my university inbox, and though it has been roughly five months since the publication of that article, I read: "George Yancy. You are a disgrace to the human race! You are BLACK TRASH!" In short, the trauma continues. Indeed, immediately after I was interviewed by Brad Evans,[47] where I explored some of the pain linked to actual messages sent to me or written about me, a swarm of white racist vitriol began again on another white supremacist website: "So I'm betting this is total bullshit. Nobody sent this nigger any 'hate mail.' [Others] should challenge him to produce it, and if he can't, should sue him for defamation. Dumb-ass nigger." This particular message cuts not only at the level of my being called a nigger (yet again!), but the writer challenges the honesty of my own testimony, what I know to be true. This is a case of epistemic violence. I am being accused of playing that fictional race card. There is no need for such a deck. To be Black in America means that one has already been barred from the card table. With each message that I received, I began to feel a deep sense of existential unease, the threat of some natural force that was uncontrollable. The words hit me like being confronted by raucous sounds just before a white mob dispenses extra-legal justice on the Black body. And let us be frank, Black people have been brutally lynched for doing absolutely nothing. The words (those sent to my university inbox, left on my answering machine, and that appear on white supremacist websites) are filled with lies, unjustified anger, racist hatred, insults, dehumanization, barbarism, images of brutalization, and white narcissism.

"You dumb ass living piece of shit."

"Hey Georgie boy. You're the fucking racist, asshole. You wouldn't have a job if it wasn't for affirmative action. Somebody needs to put a boot up your ass and knock your fucking head off your shoulders you stupid fucking goddamn racist son of a bitch. You fucking race bating son of a bitches. Man, you're just asking to get your fucking asses kicked. You need your fucking asses kicked. You stupid motherfucker. Quit fucking race baiting, asshole."

"Dear Nigger Professor. You are a fucking racist. You are a piece of shit destroying the youth of this country. You are neither African nor American. You are pure, 100% Nigger. You would never marry outside of your Nigger race. That's a fact. You're a fucking smug Nigger. You are uneducated with education. You are a fucking animal. Just like all Black people in the United States of America. Including that Nigger Kenyan that was born in fucking Kenya that has usurped the white house. Yes. It is called the white house for a reason because white people made this country great you fucking Nigger."

"You should go fuck yourself. Ok. Just go fuck yourself. You're racist fucking prick here. You are exactly the problem. So, why don't you and Al Sharpton and Jessie-jackoffson all get together and circle jerk and shoot your fucking nut on each other's racist faces. You got the NAACP, you've got the Black Congressional Caucus, you've got BET television. You've got every fucking thing. I don't owe you a mother fucking thing, asshole. You're the fucking racist you dick."

"Go fuck yourself, you racist pig."

"You're sick, Dude."

"Professor Yancy, Please put down the crack pipe . . . you *know* that it heightens your paranoia."

"Professor Yancy, All your studies have forced me to examine my self-image and my white racist mind. You clearly state that no matter what I think, I'm a racist. OK, cool. Thank you for clearing that up. Now I am forced to say, because you tell me I can say nothing else, FUCK YOU NIGGER! As always, the white guy."

"This ugly fucking nigger is just asking for access to more white females. In a sane world, this ugly nigger would be just beheaded ISIS style. Make America WHITE Again."

"Cunts like this aren't philosophers; they just hate white people, simple. He should fuck off to Africa if he doesn't like living in a white country."

"Yeah, we white people are such awful racists. I advise the author of this piece to feel free to leave whatever white country he's stuck in and go live in any number of nonwhite countries in the world, where, no doubt, the people are so much better. We'll even help you pack."

"The concept of there being an intellectual Negro is a joke."

"You should be fired now, you sick, racist POS."

"I'll admit to the imaginary racism you think white people are guilty of when you admit that [you're] a race card playing obamalicking insane retard. Bless your fucking heart."

"This is why I don't fuck niggers; tar-babies aren't cute at all."

"I live in a very nice Italian/Irish neighborhood. And we don't want ANY of you living near us. You are poison to a neighborhood."

"I find it pretty hypocritical that you've made your career out of bashing white people. Why don't you go for the people in the NAACP and Louis Farrakhan and Al Sharpton and Cornel West (or whatever his name is) about instilling hate in people. Shame on you."

"Dear professor, I am a white American citizen. You are the one who is the racist against white people, evidently. A professor—I bet you got it [your Ph.D.] through a mail order."

"Just can't believe they allow you to teach others. Affirmative action at its best."

"Continue spewing your hatred, your lies, your misinformation and your self-loathing, and you, your followers, and your offspring shall reap the benefits of it for generations to come."

"People pay money to get an education, instead they are subjected to assholes like you."

"This Nigger needs to have a meat hook lovingly, well, you know, time to use you own imagination!"

"This belief that niggers can even reason is blatant pseudo-intellectualism."

"You can dress a Nigger up in a suit and tie and they'll still be Niggers!"

"This coon is a philosopher in the same way Martin King was a PHD and the same way that Jesse Jackson and Al Sharpton are 'Reverends': Just another [jive] assed nigger with a new way to pimp."

What is utterly ridiculous and yet profoundly revealing about all of this white madness is that many whites will read this and blame me for it. White logic says that I am the "racist" who initiated the vitriol, the racist divisiveness. I am the "race-baiter" who uses accusatory discourse to force naïve whites into a position of accepting that they perpetuate racial injustice in a world in which racism is really quite infrequent. On this score, I'm a "race hustler" who plays the race card and thereby avoids the "reality" that Black people and people of color are to blame for their own character flaws, lack of responsibility, and the failure of possessing a personal and collective work ethic. Again, this raises the issue of epistemic violence. Not only have I and other Black people and people of color misunderstood the nonracial configuration of social life, according to this white logic, but I am also motivated to lie, to create racial tension where none really exists. However, to bear witness as a recipient of racism within the context of white oppression implies Black epistemological authority. Bearing witness is what my letter, "Dear White America," involved. Whiteness, however, is a site of bad faith; it obfuscates social reality through propagating, *inter alia*, a false paradigm that buttresses the so-called anomalous nature of white racism. Furthermore, whiteness fails or refuses to recognize such a false paradigm as false. Hence, "Dear White America" will be thrown back in my face as the ramblings of a Black fanatic who knows nothing or very little about the real workings of race in America and so therefore needs to be put in his proverbial place—"an intellectual Negro who is a joke" or "a dressed up Nigger in a suit and tie that is still just a Nigger!" This logic is *perverse* because it involves a species of *degeneracy*. In the face of so much anti-Black racism, white people avoid the truth that Black people suffer not only from quotidian acts of white racist aggression, but systemic oppression. So, despite the gravitas of angst and suffering experienced by Black people in America, white America denies the truth regarding the source of so much Black suffering. Indeed, white people even avoid recognizing the fact that there is an avoidance of the truth to begin with. Of course, such white madness will also hold me liable for asking white America to return love for a gift that is really a ruse for getting white people to wallow in guilt.

After so much unmitigated hate, I spoke with white intellectuals who had also been threatened after writing controversial articles that attempted to speak truth to power. I was able to gain a sense of comfort; I felt less alienated. What became clear to me, though, is that none of my white colleagues had experienced *racialized* trauma. The objective here is not to judge who suffered more, me or my white colleagues. Rather, it is important to recognize the specifically *white racist* hatred that I encountered; how my *Black body* was assaulted. The white bodies of my white colleagues were threatened, but not in virtue of their being white. So, for me, my Black body is further concretized at the level of the epidermis in its dehumanization. It is not just *a body*, but *the Black body*. There is a sense in which the white body, *as white*, is still spared. I had not anticipated how the onslaught of vile and racist discourse—nigger, nigger—would leave a wound; would traumatize. My physiology registered the wounds. Mood swings. Irritability. Trepidation. Disgust. Anger. Nausea. Words do things; they carry the vestiges of the bloody and brutal contexts within which they were animated. Like the word "nigger," one can visualize the scene. White faces with looks of excitement. Little white children brought to witness the spectacle; the so-called Black barbeque. In the air is the smell of burning Black flesh. The Black body torn to bits. "The nigger deserved it; he had it coming; the rapist; the Coon; the Black primitive." One can see the Black body hanging from some tree; its neck broken; its genitalia mutilated. Whites taking pictures, selling and buying parts of the "nigger's" brutalized body. Or perhaps he can't breathe, even as he screams, "I can't breathe!" But no one hears him. Perhaps his spine gets severed. Perhaps he is shot sixteen times (Laquan McDonald) or nineteen times (Amadou Diallo). According to white racist logic, they are just more "niggers." Perhaps she is but an innocent seven-year-old (Aiyana Stanley-Jones) within the "safety" of her home. But like Emmett Till, there is no place called being Black and being safe in North America for Black bodies. Perhaps playing the role of a secret agent (like Daniel Craig) is not meant for Black boys. Toy guns mysteriously become lethal in the hands of Black young men/boys. Or perhaps a young Black woman sits at a segregated counter with white spit on her face, bruises to her head and back. White mobs screaming obscenities in her face. Yet, she endures. For whites, the nigger is unwanted; she is not good enough to inhabit the "civilized" monochromatic space of whiteness. Like knocking on a door for help (Renisha McBride), her life can be taken because her Blackness is a violation of white space, white purity. Du Bois, in a speech that he delivered in Peking, China at the age of 91, sums up an important message that all too familiarly speaks to Black life in North America. He said, "In my own country for nearly a century I have been nothing but a nigger."

What if to be Black in white North America is, in fact, to be nothing more than a "nigger"? What if it is to live a life in a constant and unrelenting state of trauma? And what if, even during those snatched moments of respite, of feeling happy, joyous, one's life is like being on death row[48]—just waiting? Yet, these stories must be told. For it is in the telling that we gain a sense of coherence, if only in the moment of the telling. Remembrance can be painful; it has the potential to re-traumatize. However, to narrate the truth about one's life under white supremacy, to begin to see that one is *not* insane, that one's story is vital, is honest, that one's pain is real, has the power to *re-member*, to put the shattered pieces back together yet again. Telling such narratives is linked to countering epistemic violence. While all racialized trauma is painful and linked to a form of mourning, not all racialized trauma is a case of epistemic violence. Regarding epistemic violence, the genre of slave narratives is so incredibly important, especially as there is a phenomenological witnessing and an epistemic witnessing. In other words, there are both epistemological and phenomenological claims at stake. Even as forms of racialized trauma rupture Black identities, the power of truth couched in narratives can function to achieve greater psychic coherence, but also epistemic coherence, especially within a white supremacist society that manufactures white narratives that blame Black people for playing the victim, for being overly sensitive about forms of racism that are said not to exist. In short, according to this racist logic, Black people don't really know what it is that they claim to know about white supremacy. And in an anti-Black world that is underwritten by a species of a racist Hegelian ethos, where Black people are devoid of *Geist*, Black experience is also placed under erasure. Whites, then, function toward Black people in epistemologically and phenomenologically paternalistic ways. Not only do they *know* more about Black people than Black people know about themselves, but their embodied *experiences* are valorized as *the only* valid experiences, the "universal" experiences. Again, though, this does not mean that traumatic experiences are necessarily given all at once, as it were. There are temporal dimensions whereby profiles regarding the traumatic experience wait to be exposed and interpreted. As Black people testify, bear witness, narrate their traumatic experiences, they introduce subversive ways of countering a white philosophical anthropology that denies Black people their humanity as subjects-in-the-world. And while absolute narrative mastery is problematic, as a community of intelligibility that consists of shared experiences and shared knowledge production, Black people are able to make sense of their Black embodied wounds caused by white supremacy. And it is through being able to lay bare collectively their trauma, their wounds, that Black people assert their humanity.

NOTES

1. Richard Wright, *Black Boy*, with an introduction by Jerry W. Ward, Jr. (New York: Perennial Classics, 1993), 75.

2. Roberta Culbertson, "Embodied Memory, Transcendence, and Telling: Recounting Trauma, Re-Establishing the Self," *New Literary History* 26 (1995): 172.

3. Judith Butler, *Precarious Life: The Powers of Mourning and Violence* (New York: Verso, 2004), 26.

4. See *New Materialisms: Ontology, Agency, and Politics*, ed. Diana Coole and Samantha Frost (Durham: Duke University Press, 2010).

5. Frantz Fanon, *Black Skin, White Masks*, trans. Charles Lam Markmann (New York: Grove Press, 1967), 11.

6. Fanon, *Black Skin, White Masks*, 112.

7. Fanon, *Black Skin, White Masks*, 114.

8. Fanon, *Black Skin, White Masks*, 114.

9. Fanon, *Black Skin, White Masks*, 112.

10. Fanon, *Black Skin, White Masks*, 112.

11. Fanon, *Black Skin, White Masks*, 112–13.

12. Fanon, *Black Skin, White Masks*, 114–15.

13. Fanon, *Black Skin, White Masks*, 116.

14. Fanon, *Black Skin, White Masks*, 112.

15. Fanon, *Black Skin, White Masks*, 116.

16. See Kyeong Hwangbo, "Trauma, Narrative, and the Marginal Self in Selected Contemporary American Novels," (PhD Diss, University of Florida, 2004), 1.

17. See Hwangbo, "Trauma, Narrative, and the Marginal Self in Selected Contemporary American Novels," 1.

18. Sara Ahmed, "A Phenomenology of Whiteness," *Feminist Theory* 8, no. 2 (2007): 161.

19. Ahmed, "A Phenomenology of Whiteness," 161.

20. Ahmed, "A Phenomenology of Whiteness," 161.

21. Audre Lorde, *Sister Outsider: Essays & Speeches* (Berkeley, Calif.: Crossing Press, 1984), 147.

22. Lorde, *Sister Outsider*, 147.

23. Lorde, *Sister Outsider*, 147–48.

24. W. E. B. Du Bois, *The Souls of Black Folk* (New York: New American Library, Inc., 1982), 43.

25. Claudia Rankine, "The Condition of Black Life Is One of Mourning," *New York Times*, June 22, 2015.

26. See Claudia Rankine, "Q&A with Poet Claudia Rankine—Emerson College—Wed April 29 2015," filmed April 29, 2015, YouTube Video, Posted June 21, 2015. https://www.youtube.com/watch?v=kugvV79R_io.

27. George Yancy, "Walking While Black in the White Gaze," *New York Times Opinionator: The Stone*, September 9, 2013.

28. Wright, *Black Boy*, 74.

29. Wright, *Black Boy*, 74.

30. Judith Butler, *Precarious Life: The Powers of Mourning and Violence* (New York: Verso, 2004), 33–34.

31. Butler, *Precarious Life*, 33–34.

32. Butler, *Precarious Life*, 33–34.

33. Butler, *Precarious Life*, 33–34.

34. Lorde, *Sister Outsider*, 148.

35. Lorde, *Sister Outsider*, 147.

36. Fanon, *Black Skin, White Masks*, 112.

37. I would like to thank Lewis Gordon for this insight.

38. James Baldwin, *The Price of the Ticket: Collected Non-Fiction, 1948–1985* (New York: St. Martin's Press, 1985), 410.

39. Baldwin, *The Price of the Ticket*, 410.

40. Fanon, *Black Skin, White Masks*, 112.

41. Hwangbo, "Trauma, Narrative, and the Marginal Self in Selected Contemporary American Novels," 9–10.

42. Fanon, *Black Skin, White Masks*, 113.

43. Fanon, *Black Skin, White Masks*, 116.

44. Fanon, *Black Skin, White Masks*, 116.

45. See Hwangbo, "Trauma, Narrative, and the Marginal Self in Selected Contemporary American Novels," 19.

46. After the election of Donald Trump to president in 2016, the sense of disorder only increased for me. After all, an unabashed form of white nativism and neo-fascism would occupy the White House itself.

47. See Brad Evans and George Yancy, "The Perils of Being a Black Philosopher," *New York Times Opinionator: The Stone*, April 18, 2016.

48. I thank scholar Theo Shaw for this powerful imagery.

CHAPTER 8

Perpetrator Trauma and Collective Guilt: My Lai

Ronald Eyerman

You know our boys would never do anything like that.
—SENATOR MENDEL RIVERS, HEADING A
CONGRESSIONAL INVESTIGATION ON MY LAI[1]

I gave them a good boy and they made him a murderer.
—MOTHER OF ONE OF THE MY LAI PERPETRATORS[2]

Be wary of conferring the "glamour
of victimhood" on a mass executioner.
—PANKAJ MISHRA[3]

"At times now, I lie awake, I think of Mylai and say, *My God. Whatever inspired me to do it?* But truthfully: there was no other way. America's motto there in Vietnam is 'Win in Vietnam,' and in Mylai there was no other way to do it. America had to kill everyone there." These are the words of Lieutenant William Calley, the only United States soldier convicted of a war crime during the Vietnam War. They were recorded in 1971, soon after his military trial.[4] While Calley was the only individual convicted, there were many others involved in the systematic killing of more than five hundred Vietnamese non-combatants. The question of guilt and responsibility loomed large at Calley's trial and in the public discourse surrounding it. Was Calley alone guilty or was he merely a cog in a military machine, charged with winning a war at whatever cost by the American people?

This chapter is about trauma, guilt, and responsibility.[5] While most studies on the topic focus on individuals and victims, my prime concern is with collectives and perpetrators. I will first introduce the idea of perpetrator trauma and then relate it to collective guilt. I will then suggest that while both concepts are contested and problematic, they are nevertheless useful and important in the study of collective violence and its aftermath.

Perpetrator trauma occurs when individuals and collectives feel they have acted in ways that are contrary to deeply held moral beliefs. These beliefs are so foundational that identity and self-esteem appear shattered, a sense that gives rise to strong emotional response including feelings of guilt and remorse. In some cases, pathological symptoms can occur. With regard to individuals, perpetrator trauma is currently couched under the umbrella concept post-traumatic stress disorder (PTSD), a diagnosis that has exploded and expanded in recent years. PTSD has been applied to both victims and perpetrators, though the focus has been primarily on the former.[6] Though I make use of this notion and its psychological focus, my concern is more with collective response and responsibility rather than individual trauma and guilt. I will thus move discussion out of the psychological and into the social realm by relating individual emotional response to social and collective processes.[7]

In order to concretize these issues I will use the example of the My Lai massacre and of Lieutenant Calley and the soldiers of Charlie Company under his command. With this in mind, a foundational belief that is connected to individual identity would be the Judeo-Christian commandment, "Thou Shalt Not Kill." Given the pervasive nature of religious sentiment in the United States, American soldiers must be taught that such moral principles are situational, not universal, and that any transgression required by their profession is not only permissible but also right and just under specifiable conditions. Being a good soldier, in other words, does not always imply being a good human being.[8] Military culture rewards skillful killing; guilt feelings within this context are most likely suppressed and, should they occur, are more likely to arise afterwards, upon return to civilian life and another moral order. Once it became known, after having escaped the control of military censorship, My Lai was cause for great public debate, raising issues not only of culpability but about the Vietnam War and national identity. Though it began as a discussion about the proper behavior of soldiers in battle, My Lai invoked probing questions of guilt and responsibility at all levels, from the soldiers who actually pulled the trigger to the military and civilian political hierarchy that put them in that situation, and finally to the American public whose taxes, votes, and opinions ultimately legitimated their actions.[9]

Central to notions of guilt and responsibility is a distinction between perpetrator and victim, where an illegal or immoral act is done by the one to the other. The term "trauma" has been used to circumscribe the affect related to such acts. Victim trauma is well theorized and researched, while perpetrator trauma is less so and remains controversial.[10] A perpetrator is guilty of acting in a harmful way toward her victim. One can speak of perpetrator trauma when such an action injures the doer as well as the victim, an injury that may be moral and psychological, if not physical. A sense of guilt, arising from taking responsibility for the untoward is often contained in what is meant by trauma as it is applied to individuals. Establishing individual guilt is the aim and justification of legal systems. In the case of collective guilt, a difficulty lies in identifying, and identifying with, perpetrators, those individuals deemed responsible for the act or actions, and in establishing such identification within a wider collectivity. Giessen, for example, suggests that the German public avoided taking responsibility for the Holocaust by placing blame on a fervent group in the Nazi party who were claimed to be the perpetrators of that genocidal crime. As we will see, public response to the My Lai massacre reversed this, as many (perhaps the majority) Americans identified so closely with the perpetrators that that they could not conceive of their guilt. It was not collective guilt that motivated such identification, but a sense that they, too, could have been perpetrators. In fact, many like Calley felt the actual perpetrators to be victims, as we shall see. For both Germans confronting the Holocaust and Americans confronting the My Lai massacre, the positions of perpetrator, victim, and bystander were made relatively fluid as the trauma of war was worked through.

As a contested notion, collective guilt must be narrated, assigned, and accepted by a collectivity that is itself reconstituted in the process. I identify this discursive process as cultural trauma, where the foundations of individual and collective identity are brought up for public reflection.[11] In order to move from individual to collective responsibility, a coherent and compelling case must be put forward declaring that members of a collectivity (whose identity and boundaries are established in the process) bear responsibility for the actions of its members. Should this be successful, it would imply that "Germans" accept responsibility for the mass killings known as the Holocaust and that "Americans" feel responsible (and perhaps guilty) for what was done "in their name" in Vietnam. Such an argument does not require that all Germans or Americans agree, but that the possibility of collective guilt has been articulated, assessed, assigned, and accepted either by a significant number and/or by authoritative representatives who act in their name. Such representative figures may, for example, issue an official apology though not all members of the collective agree or accept responsibility.

The Incident

In March 1968, in response to the Tet-Offensive begun a few months earlier in which all major cities and military installations in South Vietnam
came under attack, American soldiers engaged in a "search and destroy"
mission moved through a series of small hamlets in the coastal area of
central Vietnam killing hundreds of unarmed Vietnamese, most of them
women, children, and elderly. It was a planned and sanctioned operation
that aimed at killing combatants in an area known to be sympathetic to
the enemy. The entire region had for this reason been designated a "free-
fire zone," meaning that every living being, including livestock, was to be
treated as suspect and a target. The soldiers were told to expect heavy resistance and that local villagers would have gone to market and thus not
be present when their helicopters set down. This intelligence proved to
be false on both counts, yet the soldiers began firing at everything and
everyone in sight as soon as they hit the ground. There was no return fire.
The "killing began without warning"; the first victims being a woman and
a baby who fled in panic over a rice paddy as the helicopters arrived.[12] Once
begun, indiscriminate killing went on for nearly four hours. In the end
more than 500 Vietnamese lay dead, many of them piled into mass graves.
The commemorative museum at the site lists 504 victims, where "twenty-
four families were obliterated—three generations murdered, with no survivors. Among the dead were 182 women, 17 of them pregnant. One hundred seventy-three children were executed, including 56 infants."[13]

The "post-action" report filed by the field commander listed the action as a major success and commendation was awarded from the highest
command downward. However, because of the great disparity between the
large number of enemy claimed killed and the small number of weapons
captured, and an official complaint lodged by a helicopter pilot who claimed
to have observed the killing of unarmed civilians and had attempted to
stop it, an internal investigation was opened. No wrongdoing was found
and the matter dropped. This inquiry would later be called a "cover-up" by
a more independent military investigation.[14]

My Lai is now generally accepted as an atrocity and a war crime by
all sides in the conflict. Perpetrators and victims have been identified and
a military tribunal has established guilt and assigned responsibility. The
trial, which occurred as the war was ongoing, was closely followed in the
United States and around the world and the guilty verdict of Lieutenant
Calley raised great public outcry. So great was that outcry (and the political
possibilities this entailed) that the sitting president, Richard Nixon, even-

tually pardoned the guilty officer. For some, the massacre and the resulting trial became symbolic of the war itself; one recent book on the topic bears the title *The Vietnam War On Trial*.[15] At issue, among other things, was how an individual soldier could be punished for doing the duty assigned him by his organizational superiors and, ultimately, by the nation itself. In the process, questions were raised about the morality of the war, as well as about the strategies and tactics employed. In the ongoing debate those who carried out the killings, the perpetrators, would be transformed into victims.

The Aftermath: Articulating and Establishing Responsibility

As will be elaborated in the following sections, two prime narrative frameworks emerged out of the struggle to understand what happened at My Lai, and to identify who was responsible and why. Both can be characterized as tragic and redemptive, but one heroic and the other ironic. Both these narrative frames derived from long established political cultural traditions. The first, which was dominant and hegemonic at least up to the Tet Offensive, was commonly known as American exceptionalism. In this frame, the American nation was founded upon universal principles of freedom and justice and the God-given mission to rid the world of evil. Unlike other powerful nations, American wars were never self-interested or aggressive, but always guided by the aim of helping others in their desire for freedom and justice. From this perspective, the United States was in Vietnam to help the "South" Vietnamese in their struggle against an evil Communist aggressor, not only from the "North," but also from Russia and China. Though never officially declared, this war was righteous and just, one that had to be fought and won. The recently stalemated Korean Conflict provided the prism through which Vietnam was viewed, along with the fear of other nations in the region "falling like dominoes." This narrative is heroic because the nation is the protagonist in an endless struggle against evil. It became tragic because, for whatever reason given, this quest ended in defeat. For some, the defeat was only temporary, as the fall of the Soviet Union and the "end of Communism" post-1989 eventually revealed the righteousness of American intervention. In the extremes of this perspective, the American military was never a perpetrator, though some "bad apples" existed.

The second narrative frame is also tragic, not because the war was lost but because American soldiers were asked to fight an unjust war in an immoral way, turning "good boys into murderers." From this perspective, no matter that these soldiers may have had excellent training and the best intentions, they had been lied to from the very beginning about the real purposes of the war and placed into "an atrocity producing situation."[16] Several variations exist concerning the basis for such lies. For the most radical, such as those formulated by Noam Chomsky and others on the political left, the lies stemmed from imperialistic motives of conquest; other lies stemmed from wrong-headed beliefs about the nature of Communism and/or about the unified interests of China and the Soviet Union. Finally, more simply, the lies stemmed from an application of the wrong tactics in the "right" situation.[17]

The mass-media was a central medium for articulating the issue of individual and collective responsibility, as was Calley's trial and the political processes and opportunities it set in motion. The main agents in this discursive process on both sides were intellectuals in the broadest sense of that term, those who make use of various media and social forums, including newspapers, television, novels, films, theater, and artworks, to impact and mold public opinion. Various social movements provided stimulus and became vehicles in this process of argumentation and meaning making, and the worldwide anti–Vietnam War movement was a powerful stimulant and vehicle for this articulation.

There were two emotionally compelling mass-mediated interventions that helped propel My Lai into a major event after the initial attempt at containment failed. The first was a televised interview with one of the perpetrators, Paul Meadlo (whose mother is quoted in the epigraph), who tearfully confessed to murder to an astonished interviewer. During a nationally televised evening news broadcast in November 1969, reporter Mike Wallace asked Meadlo how many people he had killed at My Lai. The former soldier replied, "Well, I fired on automatic, so you can't—you just spray the area, on them and so you can't know how many you killed 'cause they were going fast. So, I might have killed ten or fifteen of them." Wallace then asked, "Men, women and children? [. . .] and babies? To which Meadlo replied "And babies."[18] The second was the publication in *Life* magazine of color photographs from the day of the mass killings.[19] These were taken by a former Army photographer who, along with a soldier/reporter from a military newspaper had been assigned to record the search and destroy operation and the progress of the American response to Tet. As public interest in the case was growing, the photographer, Ronald Haeberle, decided to make public and to sell his secretly taken photographs of the murderous events. The piles of dead Vietnamese and terrified women and children huddled together just before being shot have now become iconic images of the war, many emblazoned with Wallace's question, "And babies, too?" Haeberle was complicit in the original cover up as he helped author the false official account that appeared in the military press but was never formally charged because he, like so many of the others involved, was no longer in the military when this was all revealed.[20] The issue of whether Haeberle and others involved as bystanders and in the coverup had a moral as well as legal responsibility to speak out is one to be considered. Haeberle, who later returned to My Lai to again photograph the villagers, spoke out only when there was something to be gained.

Even as the story of what actually happened emerged, the American public was divided about its meaning and who might bear responsibility. It was now obvious that hundreds of unarmed women, children, and elderly had been killed and that the act of killing was systematic and cold-blooded. But was this a massacre and a war crime or merely a "tragic wartime occurrence," as the Secretary of the Army preferred to call it? And if it was a war crime, who was responsible? After a long investigation by a military commission, which included the pros and cons of group or individual trials, it was decided that only one person could, with some certainty, be proven responsible, Lt. William Calley.[21] From a strict legal point of view, a murder conviction required that the prosecution show that the perpetrator had "the capacity to form the intent to kill" in addition to actually carrying out the act; also, because this was a military court, only those still in service could be tried. Calley's immediate superior officer, Captain Medina, who was also present on the ground during the operation, claimed to have drawn the line at killing civilians in his pre-operation pep talk. There were conflicting accounts as to the truth of this statement, and Calley claimed to be following orders in his murderous acts. Those more superior officers circling above in helicopters and responsible for overseeing the operation were never brought to trial.[22] They were, however, investigated and charged in relation to the coverup, some of them receiving career damaging reprimands. In a thorough study of the trial, the mass coverage, and the political response, Kendrick Oliver convincingly reveals the significant pressure to individualize the killings and to convict those deemed guilty.[23] It was, he argues, in the interest of the American military and those holding political power to identify guilty individuals in order to fend off any claims to organizational or collective responsibility. The aim was to ensure that it was not military or political policy that led to the mass killing of civilians, but rather deviant individuals.

In legal matters, responsibility and guilt are adjudicated through the courts; in the case of My Lai, it was a military court that ultimately decided the fate of Calley and those under his command. In this case, individuals were the object of judgment. The situation is different with regard to collective guilt. Ashenden suggests that the "very notion of political community implies the possibility of collective guilt."[24] Political community, however, is an abstract concept that must be actualized and made real through public discourse, as well as practices such as political campaigns. Collective guilt must be articulated and attributed through various means; the collective must be named and made aware of itself. Trials can be useful in this process, as they can act as a catalyst to public reflection, where notions of guilt and responsibility can be debated and attributed in ways beyond the limits of the legal system.[25] This, for example, was the point of the Vietnam War Crimes Tribunal led by Bertrand Russell and modeled after the Nuremberg Trials, which followed World War 2. Social movements can play a similar role. In the case of the My Lai trial, the American pro- and antiwar movements and associated intellectuals articulated the idea of collective guilt and named those deemed guilty. Groups of veterans, such as those organized through the Vietnam Veterans Against War and the "rap groups," which Robert Lifton helped construct, also provided means of moving guilt from the individual to the collective level.[26] In these group sessions and in the public demonstrations that occurred at the same time, veterans might discover that the things they did and felt guilty about were actually widespread and rooted in military policy. The ongoing antiwar movement was important in providing a context for opposition and the articulation of collective guilt. All this helped lift guilt beyond the individual to the institutional level, which the wider antiwar movement then pushed even higher to include the American government and its policies.

The mass media, and popular culture in general, had their own ways of attributing responsibility, with journalists such as Seymour Hersh, David Halberstam, and Neil Sheehan writing books and articles about the chain of command in decision-making.[27] The publication of the "Pentagon Papers" by the *New York Times* and the *Washington Post* had an even more powerful impact, as it revealed a long history of deception by American politicians and policy makers as the war was still ongoing. On the other side, the pro-war movement received new life after the Calley verdict, as protesters took to the streets in support of the convicted murderer. In similar fashion to their ideological opponents, they blamed the government for placing American soldiers in what was described as a morally impossible situation. Initial mass media coverage in the United States contributed to this by portraying Calley as a "typical American boy," making it easier for

Americans to identify with him.[28] All this complicated the attribution of guilt and responsibility.

The Perpetrator as Victim

Basic to the issue of establishing responsibility at My Lai was determining how the massacre could have happened in the first place. The first and most obvious factor is that these were trained soldiers for whom killing was their profession and part of warfare. However, the deliberate killing of unarmed and unresisting people is forbidden by military protocol, even if they are known to be combatants. Those killed at My Lai were not armed, resisting, or combatants. Their killing was illegal by the principles of the Geneva Convention and the rules of engagement printed on a card that all American soldiers in Vietnam were required to carry. These rules of engagement placed responsibility on the individual soldier to refuse an illegal order. The officer giving such an order would also be subject to punishment, but the onus was on the soldier to refuse to obey and also to report an illegal order. Some at My Lai did refuse, though none of the actual perpetrators made a report. The majority did neither.

Group pressure and group dynamics have been used to explain the killing.[29] Those present described a "killing frenzy" once the first victim was murdered. The soldiers had been prepped for killing. Prior to the operation, their unit had been subject to several days of frustrating combat operations and had sustained many casualties, most involving land mines and booby traps. Nothing it seemed could be trusted in Vietnam, not even the ground one walked on. Before heading off, there had been a memorial service for those killed and Captain Medina gave an emotionally rousing pep talk in which he told the group "now is the time for revenge." The operation began early in the morning and the soldiers arrived on site fearful and anxious, huddling tightly together in their helicopters. They expected heavy resistance and streamed out firing blindly and at will. Few noticed there was no return fire. Once the first unarmed Vietnamese was killed there seemed no stopping what followed. Nearly everyone got involved in the rampage and a few in systematic rape and murder. The order, both explicit and implied, had been to "kill everything that moves." And they did.

Grossman explains atrocities, which he defines as the "close range murder of the innocent and helpless," with the aid of three processes: peer pressure, the presence of a commanding authority, and a preservation instinct. All were at play at My Lai.[30] Another, discussed by Bauman and others, is the dehumanization of the other.[31] This process began long before My Lai; American soldiers of all ranks routinely referred to the Vietnamese as "gooks," "slants" and "dinks." As interviews with the perpetrators reveal, the soldiers had little understanding of, or empathy for, those they killed, their world, and a way of life that was not theirs.[32] Under peer or group pressure, I would include and differentiate group pressure from group dynamics and cohesion. Once the killing began, nearly everyone joined in, not simply because they felt pressure to conform but because it was part of what it meant to be a member of this particular group. They were a killing machine, oiled and primed. The presence of an "order-giving authority" is undeniable and many present explained their behavior as following orders. This was a military operation and all were under orders to succeed; success had been defined as clearing and securing the area through destroying everything that might be of use to an enemy.

Imparted military culture, through basic and advanced combat training, focuses on the creation and maintenance of group cohesion, stripping away individuality and instilling group dependence. One is taught that survival depends upon cooperating with others, as well as following the commands of superiors. There is thus a mixture of horizontal solidarity and vertical obedience inculcated through basic military training and reinforced in combat operations. This was also a masculine culture, of an American sort, where norms of conformity blend with displays of prowess and bravado and where competition and cohesion are not seen as opposites but rather as intertwined. Loyalty and morality were also intertwined, where notions of right and wrong are both situational and filtered through the group. At My Lai, more traditional military codes of duty and honor interacted with contemporary American notions of masculinity, where the need to prove oneself, to be a "man," mix easily with youthful bravado.[33] The military focus on deference to authority, teamwork, and group loyalty builds upon the sporting traditions of American high schools where phrases like "revenge" and "pay back" easily resonated, especially when delivered by an officer, Captain Medina, whom everyone seemed to admire and respect.

In the context of Vietnam combat units, Charlie Company was both usual and unusual. It was usual in that it was made up of a cross-section of draftees from all parts of the country, with a range of ethnicities. It was unusual in that most of the men had been together since advanced training on Hawaii and had arrived in Vietnam together by ship. Many of those Americans who served in Vietnam arrived and departed individually by commercial airliner. This helped create a very different experience than those who served in World War II, where the average American soldier was not only older, but also arrived and left collectively by sea. This common experience reinforced the sense of collective effort and group solidarity, just as it did for Charlie Company, at least as they arrived in country. Because of the one-year rotation policy in place during the Vietnam War, the men left individually and thus missed out on what Shay identifies as the therapeutic potential of working through their "collective trauma" on the long route home.[34] In one sense, the men at My Lai were more like the soldiers who served in WWII, whose Hollywood and comic book representations they had absorbed. However, as service was limited to one-year rotations for enlisted personnel and half that for combat officers in the lower ranks, creating a "Band of Brothers" mentality was a bit more difficult, to say nothing about its impact on the skills necessary for successful combat.

In another contrast to WWII, those doing the killing at My Lai were not the "ordinary men" described by Browning in his classic study of Nazi executioners.[35] The men of Charlie Company were ordinary in the sense of being draftees, conscripted rather randomly from an American cohort. The qualifying "rather" is important in that the bias in the selection made by the Selective Service administration is well known.[36] Upon turning 18, American males were then required by law to register for the draft, but the selection of those who would actually serve (especially in combat units) depended upon a range of exemptions, which for the most part excluded those from the middle class, or with a high school education. It was largely the marginalized, those with few other options, that made up the combat units in the American Army in Vietnam. This applied to the lower ranking officers as well. Both Calley and Medina had been recruited from the enlisted ranks, hustled into Officer Training programs when the supply of more qualified others began to run dry. Calley (whom Hersh[37] rather disparagingly describes as a "junior college drop out") had been rushed into service with a minimal amount of training and he was deemed and demeaned as incompetent by those he commanded, including Medina, his immediate superior.[38] The soldiers at My Lai were thus a particular segment of "ordinary" men, those from the lower strata of American society, with very little real understanding of what they were fighting for or who their enemy was. They were also very young, the majority between the ages of 18 and 21.

A fundamental idea in understanding collective behavior is that an individual might do things in the presence of a group of significant others that he or she might not otherwise do. Researchers point to a "loss of self" in group dynamics, where in a particular context, a set of emergent, group-related norms might be more determinant than any internalized ideas about right and wrong. This appears to be the case at My Lai, where young American males thrown into an unknown and terrifying environment, where newly induced norms of group behavior and an order-giving hierarchy were their main points of reference. As many combat soldiers have repeated, there was no right or wrong in Vietnam, only survival, which was largely group dependent. This led to some bizarre behavior, such as the lunch break in the midst of the killing and sharing cookies with some young survivors who emerged out of hiding as the soldiers ate.[39]

From this perspective, the murderous actions at My Lai are not that surprising. In fact, what is surprising is that such incidents did not happen more often, something which has been argued continuously since.[40] If group dynamics help explain the killing, group pressure helps us understand the coverup. No one spoke out about the obvious and illegal killing of unarmed and unresisting villagers. Whether or not one also believed them to be civilians did not matter; this should have been reported according to American military regulations. When the first investigation was carried out soon after the incident, no one spoke up; this, of course, includes those who refused to kill. Two factors help explain this; the first is the fact that all were implicated, whether or not they had killed. Speaking out would have been self-incriminating at the very least. Secondly, there was real pressure to be silent. Anyone speaking out would be subject not only to negative reactions but also to the direct threat of violence. Death by "friendly-fire" was not uncommon in Vietnam.

From Individual to Collective Responsibility

While it may be clear who actually pulled the trigger at My Lai, it is less clear who bears full responsibility for what happened.[41] As discussed previously, it is possible to describe the men of Charlie Company as themselves victims and to place responsibility for their acts higher up the chain. This was a viewpoint articulated not only by soldiers but also by activists and intellectuals within the antiwar movement and, after Calley's conviction, by some on the other side of the issue as well. With the distance of time, this understanding has become a common theme in contemporary analyses of the incident.[42] As discussed, the men of Charlie Company have been described as victims of America's class and racial divide and of the selective service administration, which actualized this divide and sent the poor and working class into combat. I have analyzed how their training and that of those who led them may have been problematic. More abstractly, as young

American men, I have shown how they have been described as victims of an ideology-driven socialization process where schools, religious institutions, and popular culture instilled heroic notions of war and the warrior, while at the same time demonizing enemies. Higher up the chain of responsibility, these men, and the rest of the American public, were said to be led into a war on false premises by politicians and their advisors.[43] Once at war, heavily armed and licensed to kill, they were given little understanding of those they were fighting beyond ideological indoctrination and dehumanizing stereotypes. The rules of engagement cards, one of the things they carried, to use Tim O'Brien's famous phrase, informed them that they were guests in Vietnam and ordered them to act accordingly.[44] Up until the Tet Offensive, this may have made some sense to those in rear areas who interacted in superficial ways with those Vietnamese who cleaned their rooms, washed their clothes, and satisfied their sexual appetites, but after Tet, every Vietnamese became suspect. In the "free fire zones," American soldiers were not guests; they were warriors who determined who was to live and die.

Afterwards, some expressed regret even as felt they were doing exactly what they had been trained and told to do. Upon returning to civilian life and another moral code, some were remorseful. This included Calley, who in 2009 said "there is not a day that goes by that I do not feel remorse."[45] Most of those who consented to media interviews, including Calley, pushed blame up the chain of command. Some exhibited perpetrator trauma, such that, as Belknap reports, "In the wake of the My Lai massacre, what had once been the 'best company in Hawaii' seemed to be falling apart. The men were in bad shape, both mentally and physically. They were often ill." Such a reaction could of course stem from fear of being found out and of possible punishment.[46] It could, however, also stem from the shame and guilt from doing something obviously wrong. An indication can be found in an exchange between Paul Meadlo and Calley the day following the massacre, after Meadlo lost a foot to a land mine. As he was being evacuated by medical helicopter, Meadlo yelled at the lieutenant, "Why did you do it? Why did you do it? This is God's punishment to me, Calley, but you'll get yours! God will punish you, Calley."[47] This was the exception, however; most chose silence.[48]

Only after returning to the United States was the silence broken. It began with individual feelings of remorse and the encouragement of the antiwar movement, feeding then into the wider public discourse about the meaning of the Vietnam War.[49] Along with the "rap groups" and the Winter Soldier hearings, the movement provided a context in which individual guilt could be made collective. There were calls to make such unofficial expressions of collective guilt more authoritative, with some in the mass media calling upon the U.S. Congress or some other official body to initiate formal war crimes hearings.[50] Chants calling President Nixon and his security advisor Henry Kissinger "war criminals" became a common part of demonstrations. There were even veterans who publicly asked to be arrested for their "war crimes."[51] However, Nixon's program of Vietnamization (which allowed the withdrawal of American combat troops while at the same escalating the bombing and Vietnamese casualties) and then the Watergate Hearings turned public attention to other matters and the momentum disappeared. What has not disappeared is the impact of images of My Lai that continue to haunt American memory.

Collective Guilt Versus Shame

Rape and warfare have always been coupled. Women were traditionally considered legitimate spoils of war and raping women identified with one's enemy is a common tactic of degradation and humiliation. There have been counterforces, including the introduction of aristocratic moral codes, and later, the professionalism of warfare, which condemns rape as well as the killing of civilians. To the extent that such codes were present on the American side during the Vietnam War, shifting responsibility from the individual to the collective and up the chain of command would seem less possible with regard to rape than killing non-combatants. While commanders are ultimately responsibility for the conduct of those under their command, it is expected that individual soldiers know and follow norms of proper behavior with regard to women. Thus, an unspoken side of the My Lai massacre is the number of rapes and sexual assaults that occurred alongside the killings. One of the most well-known of Ronald Haeberle's photographs shows a clutch of Vietnamese women and children in agony just before being shot. To the right is a young woman buttoning her blouse as she holds a young child on her arm. From official testimony we know that the woman had just been sexually assaulted and the anguished face of the older woman next to her comes from the attempt to stop the assault. This woman is being clasped from behind by another young woman presumably also so threatened. In a few seconds, they will all be dead, executed in cold blood. There is no photograph of the assault, as there are none of the actual killing, only of agony and fear in the moment of execution.

There are other documented incidents like this at My Lai, including gang rape. This aspect of the massacre is seldom mentioned, and except for recent feminist inspired interventions would remain so.[52] At Calley's trial, focus was on killing, not rape. War rape cannot be easily legitimated by reference to the fog of war and has never been an accepted part of the American understanding of correct military behavior. Soldiers are trained to kill, but they are not trained to rape. The group dynamics of rape are different from those of murder. For one, there are usually no weapons involved, as they must be put down while bodily contact is made. Rape is very personal, an act of power and domination that is thoroughly gender infused; this is not necessarily the case in mass murder. While group pressure and aggressive displays of masculinity may be an accepted part of male-dominated military culture, public confession of rape seems less acceptable and more stigmatized than killing innocents. Rape is more shameful, harder to talk about and to collectivize. As moral as well as psychological injury, its affect is devastating: "Psychological injuries to the surviving rape victims are often lifelong. Likewise the soldier inflicts lifelong injuries on himself when he makes rape or rape-murder part of his war."[53] Shay notes that rapes and rape victims have never been counted as civilian war casualties. They are part of the shame of war, a world apart from the killings. Shame falls upon the individual and the collective, both the soldier and the military organization represented are tainted.

Feelings of shame are bound up with how others see us and thus with self-esteem. Guilt is tied to actions, to what has been done and can be relieved by taking responsibility, acknowledging, and confessing. Shame is harder to relieve and often involves aggressive acting-out. If rape is more shameful than killing it follows that it would be more difficult to acknowledge and its impact on the individual deep and long standing. Tied to how others see us, shame is linked with honor and respect.[54] In the context of My Lai and the prevailing military culture, gaining respect was easily connected to displays of masculinity, which in that context could be revealed through aggressive acts in which killing and even rape might be included. As Singer puts it, "In the field, a soldier must live up to the expectations of the men he fights alongside of, even if that means committing atrocities, or he will feel ashamed."[55] Rape however would be more shameful should it be exposed outside the confines of this culture. Though rape might be formally condemned and punishable by reigning military law, it was condoned, even encouraged within the group culture at My Lai and in Vietnam generally. Soldiers egged each other on and there was great pressure to participate. It would have been shameful not to. Such behavior was very situational and restricted, seldom spoken of, certainly not written home about, and of course, never photographed. To do so would have exposed the group to the wider moral eye. Like the murder of civilians, it was condemned by organizational rules, but yet silently accepted as part of the nastiness of war. While the murder of women and children could possibly be legitimated by a predisposed public as those who supported Calley demonstrated, legitimating war-rape would be much more difficult. This means identification with the perpetrator of rape is not as easily assumed as was apparently possible with those who committed murder.[56] For the perpetrator of rape, guilt would almost certainly be individual not collective.

The idea that there is a causal link running from the actions perpetrated by soldiers up the organizational chain of command all the way to the common citizen depends not only on making such a connection clear and apparent but also on the recognition of the humanity of the victim. It is not only the tendency to individualize that must be countered but also the tendency to dehumanize the "enemy." Taking responsibility, whether individual or collective, means acknowledging the humanity of the victim. This requires countering organizational dehumanization processes, both military and civilian. In the case of My Lai and the American Vietnam War, such responsibility would require seeing the Vietnamese as complicated human beings, as victims and bystanders as well as perpetrators. It would also mean seeing American soldiers, and up the entire chain of command, in similar fashion.[57]

Perpetrator trauma results from moral injury, which requires humanizing the victim, where one recognizes that one has acted immorally toward another human being. Sherman defines moral injury as "experiences of serious inner conflict arising from what one takes to be grievous moral transgressions that can overwhelm one's sense of goodness and humanity."[58] Such feelings can arise from (real or apparent) transgressive commissions (and omissions) perpetrated by oneself or others; they can also arise from "bearing witness to the intense human suffering and detritus that is a part of the grotesquerie of war and its aftermath."[59] Similarly, Weaver speaks of "perpetrator-induced trauma" in her discussion of rape during the Vietnam War.[60] Such trauma can be thought of here as cultural in the sense that the foundations upon which identity rest have been exposed and shattered. One can speak of perpetrator trauma as individual and collective in the same way as one can speak about guilt and responsibility, where the logic of development would follow a similar path. A war may cause moral injury to individual soldiers, to the military institutions that train and deploy them, and to the nation, which legitimated the entire process.

The killings at My Lai were of a traditional sort. They were hands-on and the enemy was dehumanized and lumped, literally, into a faceless mass.

It was the unintended consequence of Haeberle's photographs to put a face on the victims and, at the same time, transform the soldiers into perpetrators. The photographs, as Oliver insightfully points out, "replicate the gaze of the killers" without disclosing their agency.[61] At the time of their killing, no attempt was made to distinguish non-combatants and no prisoners were taken. Still, there was ambiguity of the sort that insurgent warfare makes possible. Present also was the possibility of shifting responsibility up the ladder, even for those who clearly felt they were doing wrong. For others though, any feelings of wrong-doing would come later, usually after they had left the organizational culture and formal control of the military. This time lapse is not the "latency period" one finds in psychoanalytic notions of trauma; it has more to do with moving from one moral universe to another. Shay speaks of modern warfare as a form of "captivity" that generates "a profound gulf between the combatants and the community left behind.[62] Accordingly, the veteran carries the "taint of the killer" when re-entering society. Any such stigmatization and feelings of alienation would be only intensified by negative reactions to the war itself. As is well documented, returning Vietnam veterans were not hailed as heroes, and were often branded "baby-killers," as were those, like President Lyndon Johnson, deemed responsible for their acts. The uniform was not proudly worn upon return, but was more often discarded as soon as possible. The transition from one moral universe to another was thus clear and often dramatic.

Conclusion

Let's return to the quotation from Lt. Calley, which opened our discussion. Apparently willing to accept the guilty verdict weighed against his person, Calley placed ultimate responsibility for what he had done with the American nation. "America," he said, wanted to win in Vietnam and to do so had to "kill everyone there." On the one hand, this is a familiar ploy, shifting responsibility up a chain of command, as was done at his trial. What is uncommon, however, is its abstractness. Accepting it would mean viewing the nation as protagonist, a collective actor with intentions and, therefore, responsibility. This is exactly the idea proclaimed in the narrative of American exceptionalism, one into which Calley and his generation were indoctrinated. Like many Americans caught up in the Vietnam War, Calley understood his actions through this narrative frame. America had a mission in Vietnam and sent him there to realize it. He was serving his country, an arm of its collective will.

As opposed to other forms of explanation, such as that offered by Grossman[63] and Collins,[64] which emphasize group and situation dynamics, I have called attention to the stories we are told and tell ourselves in understanding what happened at My Lai, in particular, and the Vietnam War generally. Such scripted frameworks, or social imaginaries, provide actors with means to understand a situation, as well as prescriptions regarding how to act with regard to it. This is not to exclude these other accounts, but rather incorporate them within a wider framework of interpretation.

Taking this into account, we can ask whether Calley and the men of Charlie Company are the only ones responsible for the killings at My Lai. Those in the wider American public who identified with Calley clearly thought not. Responsibility, in their view, was collective, not merely because of the nation's presumed mission but also because they could imagine themselves in the same position doing the same thing. And given the existence of the draft and the selective service system, they could very well have been. Given such responsibility, was the collective then also guilty and, if so, in what sense? One could further complicate the matter by asking which collective as there were several to blame, including the military and those elected and civilian officials who designed and organized the war. Before considering such claims, we should first of all distinguish juridical guilt, such as that determined by the military court, from responsibility and emotional guilt. Juridical or legal guilt refers to action and commission, emotional guilt to feelings that may or may not follow from such actions. Responsibility, on the other hand, is a wider concept referring to agents and agencies that can be held accountable for the acts or actions of others.[65] With regard to juridical guilt, we should ask who is guilty of what; further, what is the purpose of such judgment; and finally, what are we meant to do with it? Calley was found guilty by a military court of mass murder and later may have felt remorse, but who bore responsibility?

The aim and purpose of the court's judgment was to establish guilt and punishment for an illegal act, a war crime. Another purpose, clearly unspoken in this judgment, was to exonerate the institution of which Calley was part, namely that American military, of any responsibility. The claim that the military and other state institutions might bear some responsibility was never seriously addressed at the trial but was articulated through the antiwar movement and by various commentators in the mass media. As noted, this has become a theme in many subsequent accounts. Going even further, Oliver says the American people, as least that part of the collectivity that supported the war, could be said to be held responsible for what occurred at My Lai.[66] This, of course was Calley's claim as well.

What could military and political leaders and the American people be guilty of? The military could be guilty of designing strategies and tactics that set the conditions in which Calley's acts were carried out.[67] This is a claim strongly made by Lifton.[68] The same could be said for the civilian leaders charged with creating the policies that put the military in motion. One could also hold accountable those institutions and individuals who created and disseminated the ideologies in which these policies were couched, but here, however, we would more likely be speaking of responsibility rather than guilt.[69] And the American public could be held responsible for endorsing all of the above, including Calley's actions. Alternatively, the public could be charged with indifference, the shirking of all responsibility or, more willfully, of shifting it up the chain of command.[70] Within these collectivities, the positions of victim, perpetrator and bystander might be fluid. However, given all the media attention to the war and Calley's trial, American citizens could hardly claim ignorance. The Vietnam War polarized American society and the visibility and the omnipresence of opposing sides forced spectators in the United States to take a stand.

What would be the arena in which such judgment could be made and what would be its purpose? Many have asked about the "lessons of Vietnam" and this has become one way to couch the issue. For the military, such questioning led to internal reform and reorganization. The American Army was near collapse as troops were being withdrawn from Vietnam in the early 1970s, with morale and trust in leadership at a dangerous low. This was one "lesson" that the military took onboard, which can be construed as recognition of responsibility, if not guilt. As for political institutions, President Nixon oversaw the replacement of the draft by a presumably more reliable professional army, and his Vietnamization policy, which turned over full responsibility for the conduct of the war to the South Vietnamese, was recognition that the war could no longer be won. Prior to that, the war had taken its toll on Lyndon Johnson, who did not run for re-election in 1968 as it was thought he certainly would, and his Democratic successor, the inheritor of his Vietnam policies, was defeated by a Republican who campaigned on ending the war and reuniting the country around an "honorable peace." More directly, former Secretary of Defense Robert McNamara, one of the chief architects of the war, came close to apologizing for his "mistakes" with regard to its "tragedy." In his memoir, McNamara wrote, "We were wrong, terribly wrong. We owe it to future generations to explain why."[71] McNamara acknowledged responsibility and felt remorse, if not guilt, for his ill-placed beliefs and policies.[72] Members of Congress, that branch of the American government most responsive to the public, called for war crimes investigations and set budgetary limits on funding the war. In direct response to the actions of the executive branch, Congress passed the War Powers Act of 1973, limiting the ability of any president to send troops into conflict zones without oversight and prior approval. In these responses, one can detect the trauma of the perpetrator, with stages of denial (from soldiers who wondered how we could win every battle and still call it defeat), to shifting of blame and responsibility (from military and political leaders who claimed it was the media and the politicians who lost the war), to hurtful retribution (from political leaders and the general public who denied recognition and refuge to those Vietnamese who were allies). These, more than the so-called Vietnam Syndrome, are indicators of the American trauma in Vietnam.

The individuals who perpetrated the Mai Ly atrocity could claim victimhood with regard to the military and political forces that placed them in that "atrocity producing" situation. This position was not an easily available stance for the public. While deception and manipulation were clearly involved in convincing Americans of the war's necessity, the public bore ultimate responsibility for the war. The claim to public accountability and responsibility is fundamental to the American idea of democracy.[73] As the basis upon which legitimate political action rests, the American people, or at least that segment that votes and pays taxes, bear responsibility for what is done in their name. As Young defines it "the imperative of political responsibility consists in watching these institutions, monitoring their effects to make sure that they are not grossly harmful, and maintaining organized public spaces where such watching and monitoring can occur and citizens can speak publicly and support one another in their efforts to prevent suffering."[74] Claiming to be a victim or merely a bystander would be hard to sustain given the recorded surveys of support for the war. A vast majority of Americans expressed strong support for the war until after the Tet Offensive, after which that support increasingly turned into open criticism. Recognizing the notion of collective responsibility and guilt as something more than empty rhetoric, the conservative political scientist Guenter Lewy was moved to ask in 1979, four years after the war had ended, "Is American Guilt Justified?"[75] While Lewy's answer would be "No," the pervasive sense of guilt was, to him, apparent: "The impact of the war on American society was highly damaging [. . .] it has left the country with a tremendous sense of guilt, not only because, in the eyes of many, the entire enterprise was flawed, the war was criminal and immoral."[76] That such questions could even be raised in a public forum, especially by someone supportive of the war, is indicative of the depth of the moral issues the war raised in the American consciousness.

Defeat may have been the key factor in opening the possibility for such questioning beyond the bounds of the antiwar movement and its support- ers. The humiliation of defeat, represented so spectacularly in the images of the last days of Saigon and the hasty withdrawal of the last Americans and some of their Vietnamese allies, brought the issue of guilt and respon- sibility into everyone's home. Defeat not only affected political and mili- tary organizations but it forced its way into the collective conscience as it threatened the myth of American exceptionalism. A deep sense of betrayal permeated the country, emerging from the war after all the rhetoric about its importance and the tales of easy victory, feelings that were intensified by the ongoing Watergate Hearings. The growing distrust in government and in American institutions generally resonated for a time with narratives of collective guilt. Those Vietnamese who allied themselves with the United States and who came to identify with the new nation of South Vietnam felt betrayed by the American government and Richard Nixon in particu- lar.[77] Many Americans, including some of those who fought the war, felt betrayed by their military and political leaders. Some military leaders, such as General Westmoreland, felt betrayed by politicians and policy makers, by the mass media and the antiwar movement. Such feelings encouraged shifting of responsibility, from oneself and one's group or organization to more abstract others; with no settled center, collective responsibility be- came difficult to establish. In the end, no one knew whom to blame, except those who fought. Responsibility was attributed to this collectivity, and individually experienced feelings of guilt were alleviated.[78]

Coda

The Tet Offensive changed the way the American press and then the Amer- ican public viewed the war.[79] As the possibility of defeat became clearer, death and destruction were suddenly visible in a way that they had not been. Despite attempts by the military command, most especially by William Westmoreland, to counter this new awareness by rhetorically propounding the idea of American victory, a shift was already underway in media re- porting and more importantly in public opinion. When Westmoreland and Johnson lost control of the discourse, "negotiated settlement" and "honor- able withdrawal" became the bywords in official circles, with the unthink- able defeat looming at the edges of consciousness. This helped create the possibility of My Lai and enhanced its impact. What had been occurring all along, the potentially meaningless death of American soldiers and their part in killing of Vietnamese civilians were now within the frame, the register of the visible. The shift in discourse also impacted what Oliver identifies as the "moral coordinates" of the war.[80] Could the death of American soldiers and Vietnamese civilians be so easily justified with the stakes so drastically changed? Could the ultimate sacrifice be justified in the absence of victory? Who was willing to die to ensure an honorable withdrawal? The effect was to make soldiers more reluctant and at the same time more brutal. The idea of helping others and of being an invited guest aiding an ally evaporated; for the individual combat soldier, it was now more than ever a question of raw survival. This added to the anger and frustration, the sense of being captive in an impossible and morally ambiguous situation.

Could My Lai have happened, that is, been reported, pre-Tet? Would it have been visible within the discourse of victory? Probably not, as we now know about other such incidents, though on a lesser scale.[81] My Lai was seen only because it had been photographed, and these images were released when the public was more or less ready to view them. My Lai occurred because the perpetrators were out of the military and its culture of silence and group solidarity. It entered public consciousness because American citizens had been prepared by the growing antiwar movement, which helped shatter the hegemony of the victory discourse. Tet created My Lai and raised the spectra of defeat. With the changed "moral coordinates," My Lai became visible and along with it, the understanding that American soldiers could be perpetrators. All of which added force to claims of collective guilt.

NOTES

1. Michel R. Belknap, *The Vietnam War on Trial: The My Lai Massacre and the Court-Martial of Lieutenant Calley* (Lawrence: University Press of Kansas, 2002), 138.

2. Seymour M. Hersh, *My Lai 4: A Report on the Massacre and Its Aftermath* (New York: Random House, 1970), 181.

3. Pankaj Mishra, "James Baldwin Denounced Richard Wright's 'Native Son' as a 'Protest Novel.' Was He Right?" *New York Times Sunday Book Review*, February 24, 2015.

4. Kendrick Oliver, *The My Lai Massacre in American History and Memory* (Manchester: Manchester University Press, 2006), 117.

5. The classic text on this distinction is Hannah Arendt, *Responsibility and Judgment* (New York: Random House, 2003). For her, "Guilt, unlike

responsibility, always singles out; it is strictly personal. It refers to an act, not to intentions or potentialities" (147). One can be responsible but not guilty, however, for what was done by others. In proscribing the conditions of collective responsibility, Arendt writes, "I must be held responsible for something I have not done, and the reason for my responsibility must be my membership in a group (a collective) which no voluntary act of mine can dissolve" (149). See also, Iris Marion Young, *Responsibility for Justice* (New York: Oxford University Press, 2011). Marion Young amends and extends this distinction, as does Larry May in *After War Ends: A Philosophical Perspective* (New York: Cambridge University Press, 2012). May discusses My Lai and the Calley trial as well.

6. See Aleida Assmann, *Shadows of Trauma* (New York: Fordham University Press, 2016), 63. Assmann makes a clear distinction when speaking about the traumatic memory of perpetrators and victims. She points out, "There is no clear sense of a memory of the perpetrators that would correspond to that of the victims because perpetrators do not seek public recognition [. . .] they prefer to remain invisible. Suffering strengthens a self-image, but guilt threatens to destroy it. It is from out of this difference that a fundamental asymmetry between the memory of the victim and that of the perpetrator arises." While victims seek to distance themselves from an incident that overpowers them, perpetrators develop "a defense against guilt as a strategy for saving face . . . .Whereas the suffering of harm and injustice is deeply registered in the body and soul of the victim, the perpetrators ward off their guilt under the pressure of the social effects of shame."

7. We have no term to capture an irrational and symptomatic collective response to perpetrator trauma. Political conservatives in the United States launched the term "Vietnam syndrome" to explain what they perceived as a pathological reluctance to employ military force following the defeat in Vietnam. One could interpret the invasion of Iraq as an attempt to overcome this reluctance.

8. For an elaboration, see Karl Marlantes, *Matterhorn: A Novel* (New York: Grove Press, 2010); Karl Marlantes, *What Is It Like to Go to War?* (New York: Grove Press, 2011).

9. Oliver, *The My Lai Massacre*, 2006.

10. Bernard Giessen, "The Trauma of the Perpetrators: The Holocaust as the Traumatic Reference of German National Identity," in *Cultural Trauma and Collective Memory*, ed. Jeffrey Alexander et. al. (Berkeley: University of California Press, 2004); Volker Heins and Andreas Langenohl, "A Fire That Doesn't Burn? The Allied Bombing of Germany and the Cultural Politics of Trauma," in *Narrating Trauma: On The Impact of Collective Suffering*, ed. Ronald Eyerman et. al. (New York: Taylor & Francis, 2011); Raya Morag,

Waltzing with Bashir: Perpetrator Trauma and Cinema (New York: I. B. Tauris, 2013). The articles by Giessen and Heins and Langenohl concern Germany and Germans. Giessen's point is that Germany felt compelled to re-narrative its collective foundations post-Holocaust, ridding itself of the blood and iron rhetoric that permeated much of its founding national narrative. He considers the "memory of the perpetrators as a collective trauma" ("The Trauma of the Perpetrators," 114), where perpetrator is defined as "human subjects who, by their own decision, dehumanize other subjects and, in doing so, did not only pervert the sovereignty of the victims but challenged also their own sacredness" ("The Trauma of the Perpetrators," 114). Heins and Langenohl, on the other hand, ask why the terrible trauma wrecked on the German civilian population through Allied bombing did not evoke cultural trauma. Part of the explanation they offer lies in collective guilt, the guilt of the survivor and indirect perpetrator. Morag takes a more classical psychoanalytic approach and on that basis develops an analytic framework to distinguish perpetrator from victim trauma. Her central claim is that one can detect a paradigm shift from victim to perpetrator trauma in contemporary cinematic representations, using the case of Israeli documentary film as an example.

11. Jeffrey Alexander, et. al, eds, *Cultural Trauma and Collective Identity* (Berkeley: University of California Press, 2004); Ronald Eyerman, Jeffrey Alexander, and Elizabeth Butler Breese, eds., *Narrating Trauma: On The Impact of Collective Suffering* (New York: Taylor & Francis, 2011).

12. Seymour M. Hersh, *My Lai 4: A Report on the Massacre and Its Aftermath* (New York: Random House, 1970), 48.

13. Seymour Hersh, "The Scene of the Crime," *The New Yorker*, March 30, 2015: 57. For a newly published account of this event, which will become a definitive text, see Howard Jones, *My Lai: Vietnam, 1968, and the Descent into Darkness* (New York: Oxford University Press, 2017).

14. From the Peers Commission Report: "Within the Americal Division, at every command level from the company to the division, actions were taken or omitted which together effectively concealed from higher headquarters the events which transpired in [Task Force Barker's] operation" (cited in Belknap, *The Vietnam War on Trial*, 79).

15. Belknap, *The Vietnam War on Trial*.

16. Robert Jay Lifton, *Home from the War: Learning from Vietnam Veterans* (New York: Other Press, 2005).

17. For example, see David Halberstam, *The Best and the Brightest* (New York: Fawcett, 1993).

18. Transcript published in the *New York Times*, November 25, 1969

19. See the December 5, 1969 publication in *Life* magazine.

20. Belknap includes Haeberle amongst those responsible for the cover-up. As an assigned reporter for the military, Haeberle wrote a glowing account of the engagement in the Army newspaper and never reported the killing of civilians he witnessed. He also took two sets of photographs, black white with an Army camera, which he turned in and which presumably did not have photos of the civilian deaths, and color photos, which he took with his own camera, which he didn't turn in and which he later sold to newspapers and *Life* magazine. Haeberle has never spoken about this, or how he managed to deceive the Army and keep his photos. In later newspaper accounts, he is praised as having "exposed" My Lai to the world. He returned to Vietnam and My Lai in 2011 and appears in photographs with some survivors.

21. Mary McCarthy, *Medina* (New York: Harcourt, 1972), 13. McCarthy presents the discussion of a collective trial this way: "Before Calley was arraigned, some of the young lawyers in JAG (the Judge Advocate General's office) proposed holding a mass trial on the Nuremberg pattern, will all the suspects in the dock together, from Gen. Koster (never brought to the bar, but censured), down to Staff Sgt. Mitchell (acquitted at Fort Hood, Texas) and Sgt. Hutto (acquitted at Fort McPherson)—a clean sweep. The idea was vetoed, but it might have satisfied, at least visually, a desire for even-handed justice, avoided repetitiousness, and apportioned blame in large, small, and medium slices according to a single measure [. . .] My Lai was a single big crime, committed by many parties, with accessories before and after the fact; whether Lt. Calley was more or less guilty than Gen. Koster need not have been left to the public, in the throes of hysteria and, finally, indifference, to decide." In the end, McCarthy places ultimate responsibility on the American public: "Had public pressure been maintained, it might not have been left to the Army to decide when enough was enough. If there was a conspiracy, it was a great nationwide breathing together of left, right, and much of the middle to frustrate punishment of the guilty" (62).

22. The height at which these helicopters were placed symbolically reflected the military hierarchy, with the highest ranking officer flying at the greatest height. Orders flowed literally from "above."

23. Oliver, *The My Lai Massacre*.

24. Samantha Ashenden, "The Persistence of Collective Guilt," *Economy and Society* 43, no. 1 (2014): 58.

25. See Joachim Savelsberg and Ryan King, *American Memories* (New York: Russell Sage Foundation, 2011). Savelsberg and King show there were three different narratives describing what happened at My Lai and that the military court chose the narrowest in deciding responsibility. They first identify the military's investigation (which has become known as the Peers Report) and point to its limited timeframe and focus on individual and

organization behavior. The second account is that compiled and published
by the journalist Seymour Hersh, which they identify as broader and con-
taining "more graphic detail" than the commission report (Savelsberg and
King, *American Memories*, 39). The third and most narrow in focus is the trial
proceedings, which are entirely focused on being able to establish and prove
guilt and responsibility. One could say that all three are "true" and accurate,
but the latter is the one that has had the most impact. Their book goes on
to show how American school textbooks represent My Lai. Most do not
even mention it, but those that do follow the account given at the trial and
the guilty verdict. The trial of Adolf Eichmann has been similarly discussed
as more than just concerned with the guilt of the accused (Hannah Arendt,
Eichmann in Jerusalem: A Report on the Banality of Evil (New York: Viking
Press, 1963); Deborah Lipstadt, *The Eichmann Trial* (New York: Schocken,
2011).

26. Lifton, *Home from the War*.

27. David Halberstam, *The Unfinished Odyssey of Robert Kennedy* (New
York: Random House, 1968). Neil Sheehan, *A Bright Shining Lie: John Paul
Vann and America in Vietnam* (New York: First Vintage Books, 1989.

28. Oliver, *The My Lai Massacre*.

29. Dave Grossman, *On Killing: The Psychological Cost of Learning to Kill in
War and Society* (New York: Back Bay Books, 2009); Randall Collins, *Violence:
A Micro Sociological Theory* (Princeton: Princeton University Press, 2009).

30. Grossman, *On Killing*, 226ff.

31. Zygmunt Bauman, *Legislators and Interpreters* (New York: Polity,
1989).

32. The view that the Vietnamese were fundamentally different filtered
all the way up the chain of command (see the interview with General Westmoreland in "Hearts and Minds").

33. See Marlantes, *Matterhorn*, 100–1. Marlantes, a Vietnam veteran
platoon commander, writes eloquently about these issues. He highlights the
upside down morality at play in the logic of group combat where being "bad"
is good. On the gender dynamics involved, he writes "soldiers [. . .] are also
subtly prepared by our society from early childhood to accept this switch in
what is considered good and bad [. . .] when I was growing up, [boys] seemed
more often than girls to do so [rebel] by being bad. Girls were good. Therefore, if you were to prove you weren't a girl, then [. . .] you had to be bad [. . .]
being bad helps give many males identity as men, it fills a need for esteem."

34. Jonathan Shay, *Achilles in Vietnam: Combat Trauma and the Undoing of
Character* (New York: Scribner, 1994).

35. Christopher Browning, *Ordinary Men: Reserve Police Battalion 101 and
the Final Solution in Poland* (New York: Harper Collins, 1998).

36. Ronald Spector, *After Tet: The Bloodiest Year in Vietnam* (New York: Free Press, 1992).

37. Hersh, "The Scene of the Crime."

38. Medina was also put on trial after Calley and found not guilty, as was their superior Colonel Henderson. For a vivid description and comparison between the trials, see McCarthy, *Medina.*

39. Ron Ridenhour, "Jesus Was a Gook," in *Nobody Gets Off the Bus: The Vietnam Generation Big Book*, ed. Dan Duffy and Kalí Tal (Woodbridge: Viet Nam Generation, 1994). Ridenhour describes a macabre scene reconstructed from what he was told by two soldiers, friends of his, who had been there. They were part of a group that followed Calley's platoon into the village and had just sat down to eat a lunch of C-Rations. "Eating must have been difficult. There were dead Vietnamese everywhere. To sit down near the ditch, however, must have been a special horror. For there arose from the ditch a continual, sometimes piercing din, the wailing and thrashing of the wounded. Earlier, somewhere between 9:00 and 9:30, after Charlie Company's first sweep through the hamlet, Lt. Calley ordered his men to round up the rest of the living and bring them to the bank of the ditch at its edge. When somewhere between two hundred and three hundred people were herded into the ditch in a clump—nearly all of whom were women, children, and old men—Calley ordered his men to open fire. A few soldiers resisted, but there were plenty who did not. [. . .] By the time Mike and Billy hunkered down for lunch an hour later [. . .] the undead in the ditch had begun to cry out [. . .] After a certain point, after the pork and beans but before the peaches, Mike and Billy stood, checked their M-16s, and walked down the ditch, dividing up the survivors and finishing them off [. . .] [Mike] made the distinction between what Calley had done at the ditch and the coups de gras that he and Billy administered later. The people he and Billy polished off, Mike said, were mercy killings. Those people were going to die anyway. No need for them to suffer. How many were there? He didn't know. A dozen. Maybe two. It was hard to count."

40. Nick Turse, *Kill Anything That Moves: The Real American War in Vietnam* (New York: Picador, 2013).

41. For a detailed discussion of the difference between guilt and responsibility at My Lai, see Kurt Baier, "Guilt and Responsibility," in *Collective Responsibility*, ed. Larry May and Stacey Hoffman (Lanham: Rowan and Littlefield, 1991).

42. Belknap, *The Vietnam War on Trial*; Hersh, "The Scene of the Crime."

43. Halberstam, *The Best and the Brightest*; Daniel Ellsberg, *Secrets: A Memoir of Vietnam and the Pentagon Papers* (New York: Penguin, 2003).

44. Tim O'Brien, *The Things They Carried* (London: Flamingo, 1991).

45. William Calley, "Calley Apologizes for 1968 My Lai Massacre. Democracy Now 8/24/2009," filmed August 24, 2009, YouTube video, posted August 24, 2009, https://www.youtube.com/watch?v=LPHEva Njdhw.

46. Belknap notes that, if the latter, they needn't have worried, "their superiors had no interest in punishing them; they were bent on concealing their crimes" (*The Vietnam War on Trial*, 88). Their immediate superiors were all worried about their own careers and feared blemishing them.

47. Quoted in Belknap, *The Vietnam War on Trial*, 88.

48. In her coverage of the testimonies given by the members of Charlie Company at the trial of Captain Medina, McCarthy writes, "For the men of Charlie Company as heard at the Medina trial, conscience seemed to be chiefly an organ of self-justification. It did not tell you to refrain from an action but helped you explain what you did, afterward, when questioned. The witnesses talked about casualties inflicted upon them by the enemy as though these were atrocities [. . .] as though they themselves were *civilians*" (*Medina*, 79, emphasis in the original). She goes on: "That attitude was the precipitating cause of the massacre. When a man in uniform, with a gun, makes no distinction between himself and a civilian, he will scarcely make a distinction between the military and civilians on the other side" (79–80).

49. Those who first opened up to Ridenhour did not intend for the story to go beyond the group. As one of the My Lai soldiers put it, "We told you, but that's it. If you say anything to anybody, we'll deny it" (quoted in Christian G. Appy, *Patriots: The Vietnam War Remembered from All Sides* [New York: Penguin Group, 2003], 353).

50. Neil Sheehan, "Should We Have War Crimes Trials," *New York Times Book Review*, March 28, 1971: 1ff; Benjamin Paquet, "Is Anyone Guilty? If So, Who?" *New York Review of Books*, September 21, 1972. Newly elected California Congressman Ronald Dellums petitioned to open hearing on American war crimes in the aftermath of My Lai (see Ronald Dellums, *The Dellums Committee Hearings on War Crimes in Vietnam* (New York: Vintage, 1972). This came at the initiative of a citizens group and was modeled on the Bertrand Russell International War Crimes Tribunal. Twelve members of Congress attended these hearing and the results have been published. Their call for wider Congressional investigation went unheeded. Most of those testifying were Vietnam veterans and these hearings held in April 1971 followed the Winter Soldier hearings, which took place the previous January. Senator Mark Hatfield of Oregon asked the Senate to incorporate the testimony made at these hearings into the Congressional Record and called for formal Congressional investigation, also in April 1971.

51. Oliver, *The My Lai Massacre*, 127.

52. For example, see Gina Weaver, *Ideologies of Forgetting: Rape in the Vietnam War* (Albany, N.Y.: SUNY Press, 2010).

53. Shay, *Achilles in Vietnam*, 134.

54. James Gilligan, "Shame, Guilt, and Violence," *Social Research* 70 (2003).

55. Mel Singer, "Shame, Guilt, Self-Hatred and Remorse in the Psychotherapy of Vietnam Combat Veterans Who Committed Atrocities," *American Journal of Psychotherapy* 58 (2004): 381.

56. In a comment to a journalist, Calley said, "I may be old-fashioned but I don't approve of rape on the battlefield" (quoted in McCarthy, *Medina*, 80).

57. This process has only just begun. Vietnamese Americans have reached a stage of assimilation where representations of their experience have reached the wider culture. Two novelists, Vu Tran (2015) and Viet Thanh Nguyen (2015), are exemplars of this. "North" Vietnamese authors are barely visible at all; the one clear exception is Bao Ninh's *The Sorrow of War*.

58. Nancy Sherman, *Afterwar: Healing the Moral Wounds of Our Soldiers* (New York: Oxford, 2015), 8; see also David Wood, *What Have We Done: The Moral Injuries of Our Longest Wars* (Boston: Little, Brown and Company, 2016).

59. Sherman, *Afterwar*, 8.

60. Weaver, *Ideologies of Forgetting*, xii.

61. Oliver, *The My Lai Massacre*, 133.

62. Jonathan Shay, *Odysseus in America: Combat Trauma and the Trials of Homecoming* (New York: Scribner, 2003), 152.

63. Grossman, *On Killing*.

64. Collins, *Violence*.

65. For a nuanced discussion, see Baier, "Guilt and Responsibility."

66. Oliver, *The My Lai Massacre*, 116ff.

67. In his reflections on the possibility of applying the "Nuremberg rules" to My Lai and the Vietnam War more generally, Taylor points to the case of a Lt. Duffy who was convicted first of murder and then had the charge lessened to involuntary manslaughter because he was thought to be following unspoken military procedure when he killed a defenseless Vietnamese prisoner. Taylor writes, "The Duffy case was not the first in which the defense was based on the assertion that war crimes in Vietnam are not isolated atrocities, but are a manifestation of command policy" (*Nuremburg and Vietnam*, 163). The policy in question was that of counting bodies as a measure of success, Duffy it was claimed and then acknowledged in the punishment, was doing what he was supposed to do, that is, provide his commanders with dead bodies. His violent act was thus "involuntary," rather than cold-blooded murder, in violation of the rules of war.

68. Lifton, *Home from the War*; Turse, *Kill Anything That Moves*; see also Dellums, *The Dellums Committee Hearings*.

69. Arendt, *Responsibility and Judgment*; Young, *Responsibility for Justice*.

70. During the French war in Algeria (1954–62), a French intellectual, Jean-Marie Domenach, wrote in an article entitled "Culpabilitie collective" (Collective Guilt) after revelations of systematic torture by the French military had been revealed: "Beyond a few individuals responsible the hierarchy and who should be punished, it is the entire collectivity that bears the blame. By this I mean the entire nation, its institutions, its newspapers, its churches, all of us Frenchmen who allow 400,000 young men to sink into a war in which we search for information, to be obtained no matter what the price, and the repression of an elusive terrorist movement have led to such excesses. We French are all responsible." Cited in David Schalk, *War and the Ivory Tower* (Lincoln: University of Nebraska Press, 2005), 36–37.

71. Robert McNamara, *In Retrospect: The Tragedy and Lessons of Vietnam* (New York: Times Books, 1995).

72. In an editorial comment, *The New York Times* wrote, "Mr. McNamara must not escape the lasting moral condemnation of his countrymen [. . .] Surely he must in every quiet and prosperous moment hear the ceaseless whispers of those poor boys in the infantry, dying in tall grass, platoon by platoon, for no purpose. What he took from them cannot be repaid by prime-time apology and stale tears, three decades late" (http://www.nytimes .com/2009/07/07/us/07mcnamara.html?pagewanted=all).

73. There is significant debate concerning the extent and type of responsibility the general public has with regard to the conduct of war as carried out by their government. See Neta Crawford, *Accountability for Killing* (Oxford: Oxford University Press, 2013). Crawford offers both a comprehensive summary and extension of the various positions. The most salient from our point of view concern a distinction between political and moral responsibility and one between direct, causal responsibility and indirect responsibility. Given that the American Constitution proscribes civilian oversight in matters of war, the civilian authorities within the government have more direct responsibility for the conduct of war than the general public. Because the United States is a democratic society, the voting public does, however, carry some responsibility for how a war is conducted "in its name." How much and of what sort are points of debate among moral and political philosophers.

74. Arendt, *Responsibility and Judgment*, 88. For a discussion of how much responsibility citizens might have for the acts carried out in their name, see Janine Clark, "Collective Guilt, Collective Responsibility and the Serbs," *East European Politics and Societies* 22 (2008). Clark discusses this issue with reference to Serbs and Serbia.

75. Guenter Lewy, *America in Vietnam* (New York: Oxford University Press, 1979).

76. Lewy, *America in Vietnam*, 257. Lewy, who thought American guilt "self-inflicted," argued that the war was both justified and carried out in a legal and moral manner, even though he was critical of some of the tactics applied. Using the Nuremberg trials as his touchstone, Lewy argued that the United States had not broken international law and that American atrocities were exaggerated. As for the war's morality, he pointed out that "immoral conduct must involve immoral intentions" (258) and that this was not the case in Vietnam. The tactics employed by Americans, such as search and destroy and the use of chemical weapons, were not intended "to terrorize the civilian population," but rather were deemed essential to winning the war (258–59). This perspective is one that would be labeled "military realism" by Philip Dine in *Images of the Algerian War* (New York: Oxford University Press, 1994). In his account of the various representations by the French of the Algerian War, Dine distinguishes three guiding modes of representation: military realism, military romanticism, and liberal humanism (48ff). Military realism sees war as a situation where "bad things happen," where moral rules are naturally suspended, and where actions that might otherwise be deemed criminal are seen as "natural and normal," as McCarthy (*Medina*, 23) puts in her account of the reaction of the military court with reference to some of the policies followed during the Vietnam War. One characteristic of military realism that McCarthy identifies is "the tranquil acceptance of organized brutality" (*Medina*). Military realism, as used to describe aesthetic representations of war, is related to the legal concept of "military necessity," which was codified already in 1863 as "those measures which are indispensable for securing the ends of war, and which are lawful according to the modern law and usages of war" (cited in Telford Taylor, *Nuremburg and Vietnam* [Chicago: Quadrangle Books, 1970], 33). These issues relate to civilian oversight and the responsibility of the general public raised in the preceding footnote. Military authorities usually prefer being relatively autonomous from civilian oversight in the daily conduct of war. The latter was cause for much finger pointing in the aftermath of the Vietnam War.

77. In the early 1970s, Nixon had secretly promised full American support should the insurgency escalate as the withdrawal of American combat forces began under the policy of Vietnamization. Sincerely made or not, Watergate and growing domestic opposition made this an empty promise.

78. In his insightful book based on interviews and therapy sessions with antiwar veterans, Robert Lifton distinguishes several kinds of guilt, including what he calls "animating guilt" and the "animating relation to guilt" (Lifton, *Home from the War*; for an expert on international law, see also Richard Falk,

"American Guilt: An Interview with Richard Falk," in *The American Experience in Vietnam*, ed. Grace Sevy [Norman: University of Oklahoma Press, 1989]). Lifton's point in making these distinctions is that some forms of guilt can be inward turning and passive, a vague feeling of wrongdoing that might soon be forgotten, while others can animate action—for example, accepting responsibility for what one has done and seeking ways to right those wrongs. His prime example of animating guilt is those veterans who spoke out against the war they had fought by first acknowledging their acts and then joining the public discussion about responsibility.

79. Oliver, *The My Lai Massacre*, 26ff.

80. Oliver, *The My Lai Massacre*, 26.

81. Turse, *Kill Anything That Moves*.

CHAPTER 9

The Psychic Economy and Fetishization of Traumatic Lived Experience

Peter Capretto

> Indeed, the term "traumatic" has no other
> sense than an economic one.
> —FREUD[1]

Among the paradoxical demands facing contemporary trauma theory, the impossibility of bearing witness to the traumatic experiences of others is perhaps the most perennial. In conversation with the early contributions of Dori Laub,[2] Nannette Auerhahn,[3] and Shoshanna Felman,[4] trauma theorist Cathy Caruth describes this as "the fundamental dislocation implied by all traumatic experience that is both its testimony to the event and to the impossibility of its direct access."[5] The impossibility of adequately bearing witness to traumatic experience thus puts trauma researchers in an ethically and methodologically problematic situation, wherein failure becomes a near inevitability. Whatever the ethical hopes of trauma researchers may be, subjecting victims to further reductionism and inadequate description does not live up to the ambition.

Asking trauma researchers for purity of motivation, on the other hand, does not seem to be an appropriate demand either. It is of course true that a social philosopher or psychologist ought not relish the discovery that someone in her community recently survived a traumatic assault, which now creates an opportunity for her own research and writing. At the same time, it may be unreasonable to expect her to pay no thought to the benefits of such an encounter. This would give her proximity to an exceptional perspective on a devastating experience; she would be recognized as someone who has been close to something otherwise unimaginable. More still, witnessing to these events is crucial for furthering the study and raising awareness of marginalized suffering. So long as we are not exacerbating the suffering of others and remain committed to an ethic of care, perhaps it is not inappropriate for researchers to be excited at the opportunities afforded by even the most traumatic events befalling others.

The strange tension at the heart of this situation generates the seemingly inevitable fetishization of traumatic experience for researchers in trauma theory. While the impossibility of bearing witness demands an insatiable and infinite response to traumatic experience, the transcendent quality of this demand may also force us to lower the ethical standards we establish for a response; if we can only ever fail, then adjusting one's social and ethical ideals becomes an understandable psychological and motivational strategy.[6] Fetishizing traumatic experience thus lurks as a symptom of the impossibility of bearing witness to trauma: Because we are not able to satisfy the demand of bearing adequate witness, we substitute proximity to the lived experience of trauma as a more intellectually permissible way of encountering others. Not only does this appear like an inevitable development for a researcher's personal struggle in adequately working with trauma, but it is difficult to condemn the compassion of someone venturing into the difficult affective space of closeness with survivors.

While paying closer attention to our personal motivation may not directly alleviate traumatic violence on a broader political scale, scrutinizing the motivation behind our research may reveal crucial ethical traps facing trauma studies. Despite trauma theory's heavy engagement with psychoanalytic and phenomenological methods, it has perhaps neglected how easy it is for researchers to satisfy their impossible ethical demands by substituting something more attainable: proximity to lived experiences of trauma. This fetishization should not be confused with sadism,[7] which derives pleasure from harm inflicted with others, or scopophilia,[8] which finds satisfaction in spectating others in a voyeuristic and surreptitious way. Rather, the fetishization of traumatic experience follows the classical psychoanalytic structure of substituting an unattainable or taboo object with one that is more readily satisfied and culturally accepted. That is, the impossibility of satisfying the ethical demand of witnessing is replaced with one's proximity to a more visceral and embodied experience; yet with this proximity and apparently immediate appeal to lived experience, we lose sight, as Derrida puts it, of "our powerlessness to name in an appropriate fashion, to characterize, to think the thing in question."[9] There may be no outright way fully to avoid this fetishization. But the challenge and prospect for thinking trauma research may lie in how we comport ourselves toward this impulse in ways that minimize harm and resist the reduction and trivialization of traumatic suffering to intellectual or possibly libidinal satisfaction.

To begin this task requires an analysis not only of the structure of fetishistic disavowal as it pertains to trauma, but also of the psychoanalytic understanding of the ego's psychic economy wherein lived experiences of trauma abide. This chapter thus opens by clarifying the metaphor of psychic economy deployed by Freud, including how traumatic experience functions and disturbs this economy and its boundaries—especially if we are to understand ethics in the social context of traumatic encounter. It continues by examining how traumatic experience is fundamentally social in Freud's economy, particularly in psychic exteriority. Its analysis then turns to the phenomenological limitations of using *Erlebnis* or lived experience as a way of justifying experiential proximity as a substitute for witnessing; on this point, Martin Heidegger's critique of *Erlebnis* proves useful for explaining how appeals to lived experience merely disguise our separation from truth.

Through these psychoanalytic and phenomenological resources, this chapter argues that trauma research must develop more critical tools for scrutinizing our everyday impulses to lower the ethical standards of our relation to traumatic experience. My task is not to outline the fetishization of traumatic experience as a diagnosis of the shortcomings of contemporary trauma research in the humanities. More sympathetically and critically, the aim of this chapter is to think fetishization within an ethical framework for relationally approaching trauma that does not neglect our personal fascinations with the traumatic lived experiences of others. My most basic insight is a simple one, yet perhaps it is easy to neglect for that very reason: Trauma theorists should be mindful of what they stand to gain in their work on the traumatic experience of others, and of how easy it is for them to disavow the insufferability of vicarious trauma by instead fetishizing lived experience. This is not to discourage allies nor to shame those who have gained recognition as trauma researchers. The insight, rather, is that however perverse it may be to admit a researcher becomes genuinely excited by the traumatic experiences of others, failing to scrutinize these impulses risks turning perversity and ambition into harm.

Freud on the Psychic Economy of Traumatic Experience

A crude but important objection may be raised at the outset: What, if anything, is unique about trauma when it comes to relational ethics for researchers? Should not researchers be mindful of exploitation and perverse motives in all of their work? After all, the importance of doing no harm and being conscientious of others in one's research and practice is nothing new, even for rudimentary clinical and professional ethics. The concern over fetishization may be important, yet it would seem to apply to all interpersonal relation, not just to traumatic experience. More still, within psychoanalysis there is perhaps no greater body of literature than on countertransference, precisely because of the negative impact that pre-existing drives and attachments may have on interpersonal interpretation.[10] To borrow a Freudian metaphor, if there is a psychic economy structuring intrapersonal and interpersonal relations, it would seem it is already a highly regulated one within the scholarly community. It is true, of course, that ethical concerns over exploitation, objectification, and "speaking for" others is relevant for all social and clinical research. The difficulty, however, is that generalizing these problems into trauma research neglects some of the unique ways that traumatic experience shifts the structure of intrapsychic experience and the landscape of interpsychic social relation.

This unique structure of traumatic experience is documented well at the outset of the modern psychoanalytic movement. While Freud of course pioneered an analytical approach to clarifying psychic experience, he drew closely on the precedent of his lesser-known teacher and early phenomenological psychologist Franz Brentano. Like Freud after him, Brentano held strong suspicions for speculative work in psychology that risked conflating the discipline with the metaphysical lineage of philosophy. For Brentano, the solution for a more rigorous psychological study of experience is to accept "only mental phenomena in the sense of real states as the proper object of psychology [. . .] that psychology is the science of mental phenomena."[11] Relegating psychology to an "empirical standpoint," as Brentano put it, does not subject human experience to a reductionistic lens, but rather clarifies the focus of its methodological reach. Any analytical and experientially driven approach to the human situation, in trauma or otherwise, requires this focused attention on mental phenomena and nothing else. Contrary to the history of psychology from Aristotle to the early nineteenth century—which implicated psychology closely with the transcendental study of what it means to possess a soul—for Brentano, psychology's only chance of scientific rigor is if it diverts its attention away from such grand analyses and onto the more concrete study of mental phenomena.[12] As Brentano insists, "Psychology can and should exist nonetheless, although [. . .] it will be a psychology without a soul."[13]

It is through psychoanalysis's close attention to more quotidian and less transcendental experiences that Freud structures much of the work in his *Introductory Lectures on Psycho-Analysis*. Freud lures in his largely medical audience by anticipating a common objection to psychoanalysis, that it pays too much attention to trivial details that mainstream medicine does not even bother to study.[14] Instead of shying away from this charge, Freud takes it as a point of pride that psychoanalysis has been marginalized from other material and medical sciences, sciences wherein examining parapraxes or slips of the tongue would seem like an absurd waste of time.[15] But despite picking up the crumbs from the table of other medical disciplines, Freud holds that psychoanalysis maintains the same rigor through its attention to the conservation of psychic energy and the importance of empirical verification for its concepts.

Building from Brentano's more restrained approach to psychology, Freud saw the psychic life of mental phenomenality as fundamentally rooted in libidinal energy and a desire for the "economic" exchange of satisfaction in the pleasure principle.[16] But whereas for Brentano the concept of mental phenomenality often remains a vague and perhaps merely philosophical construct, for Freud the psychic life of mental phenomenality is fundamentally rooted in libidinal energy and a desire for the economic exchange of satisfaction in the pleasure principle. The psychic economy of the pleasure principle for Freud has obvious parallels to the classic theorem of economic subjectivity: Consumers and economic agents are "rational maximizers."[17] Though Freud will later problematize the totality of the economic perspective of psychic energy in *Beyond the Pleasure Principle*, the sense of the psychic economy has at least two enduring implications for Freud's exploration of traumatic experience in psychoanalytic theory.[18]

The first implication of Freud's theory of psychic economy is that the ego seeks out as much exposure to pleasurable psychic phenomena and stimulation as possible. This principle applies to Freud's remarks in his broader cultural analysis of *Civilization and Its Discontents* as well as the microcosmic, that "happiness, in the reduced sense in which we recognize it as possible, is a problem of the economics of the individual's libido" even when looked at from a larger societal lens.[19] This is perhaps the simpler sense of the psychic economy, which pertains to an unfixed limit of psychic return of libidinal expenditure. The resources of libidinal satisfaction and pleasure are only scarce insofar as societal forces or material resources might be vehicles for this pleasure. In this first regard, the only limit to the psychic economy is libidinal desire itself.

The second implication of Freud's theory of psychic economy pertains to the psyche's economic behavior in relation to external stimulation that may present itself not as pleasurable, but as traumatic or dangerous to the integrity of the ego. While for Freud the physical parallel of the psychic economy is not as strict as the laws of thermodynamics around equal and opposite reactions, he nonetheless insists that, for ego-integrity and the self-preservation of psychic life, there is a long-term economic tenor of the ego's reaction to threatening experiences. With traumatic neuroses in particular, "patients regularly repeat the traumatic situation in their dreams [. . .]. It is as though these patients had not finished with the traumatic situation, as though they were still faced by it as an immediate task which has not been dealt with."[20] This psychic response, the classic "repetition compulsion" that characterizes defense to trauma, allows Freud to illustrate the essential feature of the psychic economy: The ego compensates itself for depleting its own affective encounters over an extended course of time, as if to repay or replenish the debt of what has been taken from the ego's psychic sovereignty. It is for this reason, he notes, that trauma "shows us the way to what we may call an *economic* view of mental processes. Indeed, the term 'traumatic' has no other sense than an economic one."[21] When the ego experiences something that has robbed it of an essential experience of the world, in time or in quiddity, the ego adjusts its response in and through its psychic economy, trumping the more immediate desire to merely maximize pleasure with longer-term economic considerations.

At first glance, these two implications of Freud's psychic economy may appear at odds with one another. It is hard to see how the ego's compulsion to relive painful experiences does not contradict the insistence that the ego is a rational maximizer in the pleasure principle. Yet this desire to repeat is itself an economic drive to return to the ego a sense of control. The compulsion to repeat the event of trauma over and over again acts as an economic override to the ego's otherwise systematic desire for pleasure. As Freud notes in *Beyond the Pleasure Principle*, explicitly on the issue of the death drive and repetition compulsion, "These efforts [of painful repetition] might be put down to an instinct for mastery that was acting independently of whether the memory was in itself pleasurable or not."[22] Even before considering the ways that a traumatic event occurs, the mere fact of its strategic and long-term response to the attack upon its ego-integrity in trauma points to the utility of approaching the ego's psychic relations in economic terms.

One important limitation to keep in mind about Freud's psychic economy is that it is unquestionably a "weak metaphor" for understanding traumatic experience. There are indeed many structural parallels between the
language of economy—deriving from the financial exchange of capital and
commodities—and the ego's desire to maximize pleasure and to redistrib-
ute unpleasant stimulation. The metaphor has far-reaching advantages of
explaining psychic motivation and behavior, including the structures of
neurosis and defensiveness. But, the fungibility of these psychic assets or
libidinal energies involved is not as restricted or regulated as in financial
markets and economies; the flexibility of this psychic market means there
is no fixity of psychic capital that must be redistributed upon death, as if to
impose an inheritance tax. If a person were working out traumatic healing
through repetition and therapy, so as to offset and replenish a psychic debt
that has been taken from them, there would be no need or logic to settling
the psychic debts of this person after their death. The ego's logic of libidinal energy in the pleasure principle may then paint a picture of the ego as
a rational maximizer of an economy of stimulation—both in auto-arousal
and through external stimulation. Yet, for Freud, there are clear breaches
to the boundary of the psychic economy, breaches where a person's commonplace defenses and reactions are permeated by exterior forces that are
both physical and psychical in nature. That is, while it may seem that the
genesis of traumatic experience in Freud's psychic economy is fundamentally intrapsychic—emerging within the isolated individual—the ego's
psychic economy is impacted by the traumatic exteriority of dwelling in
social space.

Exteriority and Defense in Freud's Psychic Economy of Trauma

Though the exteriority of the other is, by and large, taken to be a site
of truth and revelation for many thinkers in the phenomenological tradition, Freud's understanding of the sociality of traumatic experience is
more protective and defensive than much work in the continental philosophy of religion. For figures such as Husserl,[23] Buber,[24] and Levinas,[25] a
basic challenge of their philosophical systems is how to broaden subjective
foundations of their methods, such that they might be receptive to the
prospect of external intuition or alterity. Freud's sustained interest on the
relational processes of transference and, to a lesser extent, empathy would
suggest that he holds a similar set of concerns. Yet in his later writings,
this attitude toward exterior mental and societal forces on the ego takes a
definitively more cautionary tone. In this context, Freud understands the

ego to take "as 'traumatic' any excitations from outside which are powerful enough to break through [its] protective shield," adding that "the concept of trauma necessarily implies a connection of this kind with a breach of an otherwise efficacious barrier against stimuli."[26] While some theorists have nearly venerated trauma because of its structural parallels to revelation, alterity, or the divine, for Freud the exterior threat of trauma is quite serious for the economy of the ego, and not something to trivialize in clinical or theoretical settings.[27]

Particularly in *Beyond the Pleasure Principle*, Freud uses the highly biologized language of the "cortical layer" and "membrane" of the ego's boundaries to conceptualize how trauma penetrates us.[28] That is, the ego's social relation with exteriority causes neurosis when the boundaries of its psychic economy have been compromised. In his *Introductory Lectures* as well, Freud characterizes traumatic neuroses from foreign threats not as a simple matter of unconscious repression shaping habit, but rather as a fundamental challenge to the structure of the ego's psychic economy. It is in "traumatic neuroses," Freud explains, that "we are unmistakably presented with a self-interested motive on the part of the ego, seeking for protection and advantage [. . .]. This motive tries to preserve the ego from the dangers the threat of which was the precipitating cause of the illness and it will not allow recovery to occur until a repetition of these dangers seems no longer possible or until compensation has been received for the danger that has been endured."[29] The openness of the psychic economy to exteriority and its "dangers" makes the ego fundamentally vulnerable to a fragmentation that elicits a complex series of responses.[30]

It is this fundamental vulnerability of the ego that leads Freud to develop his theory of psychic defense. While Freud's work with veterans of WWI largely propelled his writings on trauma from the mid to late 1910s and beyond, he began theorizing the relation of the psychic economy to violent externalities near the beginning of his clinical research in the early 1890s. In 1894, in an essay on "The Neuro-Psychoses of Defence," Freud was already well on his way to developing a theory of ego defensiveness in relation to trauma: "When once such a nucleus for a hysterical splitting-off has been formed at a 'traumatic moment,' it will be increased at other moments [. . .] whenever the arrival of a fresh impression of the same sort succeeds in breaking through the barrier erected by the will, in furnishing the weakened idea with fresh affect and in re-establishing for a time the associative link between the two psychical groups, until a further conversion sets up a defence."[31] Derivative of medical and neurological metaphors of psychic processes, due in part to his research role in neuro-biology and the nascence of the psychoanalytic movement at that time, Freud describes the core-like defensive response that the ego has to trauma. The biological or neurological impulse of the ego in these moments of trauma, naturally, is to defend itself from exteriority.

The reason for Freud's defensive attitude toward externality, presented empathically, transferentially, or experientially, is that if it takes on an internal locus in the psychic economy, this presents profound problems to the ego's ability to economize the effects: "Towards the outside it is shielded against stimuli, and the amounts of excitation impinging on it have only a reduced effect. Toward the inside there can be no such shield; the excitations in the deeper layers extend into the system directly and in undiminished amount, in so far as certain of their characteristics give rise to feeling in the pleasure-unpleasure series."[32] The danger or threat of the ego becomes internalized not as if one had entered a debt into one's accounts, which would simply be paid off later with interest; it is incorporated through the de-corporation or fragmentation of the ego such that its normal economic apparatuses are no longer able to respond in what might appear to be an economically sensible way. In the response of repetition compulsion in trauma, Anna Freud similarly notes that "the ego no longer remains outside, its energies diminished, its strength reduced, its attitude that of objective observation, with no active part in what is going on. It is caught up, overwhelmed, swept into action. Even though, under the domination of the repetition compulsion, it behaves wholly as an infantile ego."[33] Thus, while the death instinct may appear to be at odds with the theory of Freud's psychic economy, it is merely that the ego's instinctual inclinations override what might otherwise be an intellectual hospitality toward exteriority.[34] Repetition compulsion, along with less dissociating defenses, similarly functions as a cautionary attitude for the ego toward foreign phenomena. Whether one finds this in the hostility of resistance on the analytic situation by means of transference, or by non-clinical encounters wherein cathexes open the ego to various psychic vulnerabilities, Freud's theory of trauma is keen to note the extensive fragility of the ego in its relation to exteriority, and the subsequent need for its defensiveness.[35]

Although Freud describes trauma and its neurotic symptoms for survivors in a highly scientific and objective tone, he is at the same time reluctant to develop what might be described as a metaphysically realist account of trauma on the basis of this defensiveness. There are, for Freud, unquestionable features in trauma around the distortion of the ego's experience of time, memory, and affect because of a transgression of the boundaries of its psychic economy. But here, again, the limits of Freud's metaphors for describing the economic and social character of trauma come into view,

> We may, I think, tentatively venture to regard common traumatic neurosis as a consequence of an extensive breach being made in the protective shield against stimuli. This would seem to reinstate the old, naive theory of shock, in apparent contrast to the later and psychologically more ambitious theory which attributes aetiological importance not to the effects of mechanical violence but to fright and the threat to life. These opposing views are not, however, irreconcilable; nor is the psycho-analytic view of the traumatic neurosis identical with the shock theory in its crudest form. The latter regards the essence of the shock as being the direct damage to the molecular structure or even the histological structure of the elements of the nervous system; whereas what *we* seek to understand are the effects produced on the organ of the mind by the breach in the shield against stimuli and by the problems that follow its train.[36]

Complications, though not "irreconcilable" ones, arise with Freud's economic and biological metaphors around trauma's relational response. Many variables, both biological and psychological, influence the mind's susceptibility to trauma. Among them, Freud notes the social psychological structure of strong attachment is often a "decisive factor in determining the outcome" of a traumatic experience.[37] Hypercathexis—the heightened unconscious attachment energy of the ego to other libidinal objects—proves to be a significant determinant of how it is that the psychic economy of the ego will respond to trauma. That is, having an external network of connections or attachments will assist the ego in its defense to trauma. The vulnerability that comes with the openness of the psychic economy also affords other unconscious vehicles for defense.

Though arcane in its use of metaphors, Freud's theories of the psychic economy of trauma and the defensiveness of the ego provide a framework for approaching the vulnerable sociality of another ego within the precarious site of traumatic experience. While the force of the pleasure principle and the economic metaphor of the ego establishes a baseline for everyday defensiveness, the symptomatic response of repetition compulsion in traumatic neuroses reveals the tragic social character trauma: The prospect for affective and libidinal cathexis with another person—an analysand, analyst, or a relational self object more generally—is both a vehicle for traumatic experience and the defense against it.[38] What is to be gleaned from the drastic defensive responses of the ego is not that it is universally opposed to social existence or what might occur from outside the interiority of the drives.[39] Far from attesting to the isolationism of the ego, for Freud the defensiveness of the ego merely testifies to the logic of the psychic economy, which is both internally regulated and externally influenced.[40] Defensiveness ultimately concerns the management of pleasure and displeasure within the ego. However, the ego is not merely subject to its own doings, but also to those with whom it relationally attaches.

The Phenomenological Problem of Lived Experience in Trauma Theory

Freud's ambulation between biological and relational descriptions of trauma indicates he is not as much of a methodological purist as might immediately meet the eye, perhaps falling short of the restrictive methodological boundaries precedented by Brentano. The revelation of the prospective violence and trauma that exteriority or foreign mental phenomenality may have upon the ego thus poses a problem to those desiring a constructive theory of exteriority and other minds from Freud. For the well-intending researcher who cautiously approaches and witnesses to the traumatic experience of another, it is difficult to discern whether Freud's methodological ambivalence is an asset or liability for attempts to ethically respond to the traumatic experience of others. The basic theoretical structure of the psychic economy of trauma may offer a helpful social heuristic, but it may also lead to an inherently reductionistic theory of experience in trauma.

It is for this reason that more humanistically inclined research within the social sciences has prioritized the "lived experience" of others as a primary mode of engaging trauma in a vicarious yet rigorous way.[41] To speak generically of "experience" without specifying its empirical or lived character runs the risk of glossing over the worlded and embodied site of experience's occurrence. While "experience," or *Erfahrung* in the German philosophical tradition, stresses the more scientifically empirical quality of experience, Gadamer explains that *Erlebnis*, or lived experience, is a paradoxical term that articulates the extremes of the individual's temporal occurrence.[42] *Erlebnis* describes "both the immediacy, which precedes all interpretation, reworking, and communication, and merely offers a starting point for interpretation—material to be shaped—and its discovered yield, its lasting result."[43] Gadamer's temporal distinction of *Erlebnis* from *Erfahrung* militates against the idea that experience is something to be divorced from the act of living itself. The occurrence of *Erlebnis* underscores the individual's immediate engagement with the world; the concept of lived experience gives greater substance and credence to experience within research settings, such that it resists simplistic critiques of personalism and subjectivism. The term *Erleben* points to experience that is "still alive when something happens," and thus "suggests the immediacy with which something real is grasped."[44] In part borrowed from his mentor Martin Heidegger, Gadamer's contention is that when experience is deployed merely as a vehicle for *episteme*, experience becomes disconnected from its origin in worlded experience.

Certain moments in the phenomenological tradition, particularly in Husserl and early Heidegger, maintain a soft form of solipsism where the phenomenological richness of lived experience is sufficient for its own narrow analysis. Specifically for Husserl, the invocation of a "transcendental solipsistic science" signifies the irreducibility of the content of transcendental experience, and the complete refusal of any and all attempts to translate what is present in the phenomenological *epoché* into any public discourse.[45] Despite numerous attempts to develop a theory of exteriority on the basis of the phenomenological reduction, Husserl repeatedly encounters the inability to export lived experience into an intersubjective space without subsuming the other into the purview of the transcendental ego: "The only conceivable manner in which others can have for me the sense and status of existent others, thus and so determined, consists in their being constituted *in me* as others."[46] In this strategy, the boundary of lived experience is never transgressed, and is instead acknowledged as impenetrable.

For Heidegger, experience is already a loaded term derived from this particular vision of Enlightenment subjectivity. Responding critically to the post-Cartesian and even Husserlian metaphysical tradition of the human subject emerging from the *ego cogito*, Heidegger rejects the definition of the human being on the interpretive basis qua *animal rationale*, which roots itself in a classical understanding of the subject as animated or spirited in and through experience.[47] In his struggle to spiral outside of the Western tradition in his fundamental ontology, Heidegger's posture toward "experience" (*Erlebnis*) is one of respect and critical refinement, especially in his early writings.[48] To think the question of being in a new way, he stresses the importance of separating ontic interpretations of the "who" of the human being from a vulgar or chronological sense of temporality: "The who is answered in terms of the I itself, the 'subject,' the 'self.' The who is what maintains itself as an identity throughout changes in behavior and experiences, and in this way relates itself to this multiplicity."[49] Heidegger's take on lived experience is thus problematized by the fact that experience has been inscribed in a particular, hyper-rationalized vision of the ego as *animal rationale*. He contends that phenomenality does not merely sketch our existence upon a continuum of "vulgar" or chronological time. Particularly critiquing Bergson's concept of *durée*, but also the work of Dilthey, Husserl, and Scheler on "philosophy of life,"[50] Heidegger notes that insofar as they have tendencies toward a "philosophical anthropology" and "personalism," visions of Dasein that reduce its existential occurrence to experience "no longer ask the question about the '*being* of the person.'"[51] In these instances, we mistake gaining more temporal data about lived experience for an actual understanding of the meaning of being.

What is deceptive about this critique of researching lived experience, however, is that it far from diminishes Heidegger's appreciation of experience for the task of thinking; it does not diminish the value of experience for Heidegger in his understanding of subjectivity, but has precisely the opposite effect. Heidegger's concern for the misuses and misconstruals of experience for Dasein suggests that there is a need for the retrieval of a more originary approach to the experience of being. It forces him to locate a mode of asking the question of being that tends to phenomena as phenomena, "the self-showing in itself" of the worldliness of the world, and not as the "*vulgar* concept of phenomenon" as in Kant, as that which is structured by the autonomous ego.[52] The very articulation of the subject and its relation to the world in terms of its thereness, its there-being or Dasein, testifies to the fact that, if there is to be an *ekstasis*, a transcendence, or a standing out in what was once the subject, it will not be through the reification of its concepts, but rather through the prioritization of what is most one's own: the experience of being-in-the-world.[53] On this point, literary theorist Hans Ulrich Gumbrecht affirms the assertion that lived experience is akin to irreducible "moments of intensity," suggesting that in the context of Heidegger's discourse, the possibility of *ektasis* may lie within lived experience.[54] More specifically, Gumbrecht highlights the ambiguous appropriation of religious lived experience that might serve as a heuristic to the challenge faced in translating one's experiential being in a public way.[55]

Particularly in his *Contributions to Philosophy (Of the Event)*, Heidegger takes aim at those forms of philosophical discourse that claim to venerate experience, yet ensnare Dasein in a repetitious methodology of *Seynsvergessenheit*, or the forgetting of Beyng. Heidegger respects and operates within the domain of phenomenological thereness,[56] but his criticism is that by rushing to inscribe the phenomenological within the category of *Erlebnis*, thinkers "count as actually 'being' [. . .] only what is or can be the object of lived experience."[57] Philosophies that use *Erlebnis* as a special insight into human experience—vicariously or otherwise—can only ever indulge in machinations that distract from a phenomenological attunement toward being. What is only present as a theoretical object is taken as constitutive of its ontological constitution.

The problem of prioritizing lived experience as a means for researching the human situation is that it ultimately purports to hold phenomenology's interests in mind, but insidiously conceals Dasein from the questions necessary to encounter the event of truth, revelation, and what he describes in the *Contributions* as "the last god."[58] Specifically with the concept of experience, the derivation of an anthropology of Dasein qua *animal rationale* on the basis of "lived experience" is the perfect storm for the illusion of progress and the forgetting of beyng.[59] Heidegger bemoans this at length,

> Whether anthropology is dressed in an enlightened/moral, psychological/natural-scientific, human-scientific/personalistic, Christian, or political/ethnic coiffure is a matter of utter indifference for the decisive question, i.e., for the question of whether the modern era is grasped as an end and another beginning is sought, or whether the decline that has been in effect since Plato is perpetuated and insisted on, which ultimately can still happen only through the conviction that one's lack of any presentiment is in fact an overcoming of the tradition [. . .]. Just as at the time of neo-Kantianism, however, the current history of the age did not recognize the still quite considerable learning and careful work that was done, so today's age of "lived experience" will make even less of a fuss with respect to this boring and commonplace mock-up of its own superficiality.[60]

What Heidegger identifies here is a daunting challenge to studies of traumatic experience in phenomenology and the continental philosophy of religion. It is true that the dangerous depths of Heidegger's conservatism bleed out from these private writings, but his challenge of superficiality touches precisely upon the recurrent issue of appropriation. Though Heidegger is critical of the tradition from which the concept of *Erlebnis* emerges, there is no question that he desires a methodological discourse that can remain captivated by the primordial question of beyng that is rooted in Dasein's originary thrown experience of being-in-the-world. Uprooting "mysticism" for concernful evaluation, under the guise of valuing its richness, has the same effect as presenting a real "lived experience" with any number of technological garbs—theological or otherwise.

Whereas Heidegger's philosophy in the existential analytic was one of spiraling and excavating being as Dasein's temporal horizon toward death, in the *Contributions* Heidegger contends that beyng is only ever to be approached in "the absconding of the gods in the gods' farthest withdrawal."[61] The potential moment of truth's occurrence absconds from the weak attempts of anthropology, "newspaper science," and numerous forms of liberalism—both in the classical individualist and the multicultural sense—that elevate the particularity of an individual in a public way to change the dynamics of voice and influence.[62] The special danger is that in nominally protecting "lived experience," one all the more deceptively conceals the fact that we have lost what it is we were after: the experience wherein the occurrence of truth might come to pass. For trauma studies to believe it has what it does not in its exposition of traumatic experience only further entrenches us in the banality of increasingly greater degrees of machination and despair than we know.

Conclusion: Naming the Fetishization of Traumatic Lived Experience

The implications of Freud's psychic economy and Heidegger's critique of lived experience for trauma theorists are complex, particularly in what they imply about trauma researchers' comportment toward the traumatic lived experience of others. For Freud, the fragility of the ego's psychic economy and its prospect of trauma provide a different sense of how psychology is broadly to understand social relation.[63] Whether one attributes this feature of Freud's thinking to positivism, medical materialism, Darwinism, or the like, the general attitude of defense in the psychic economy is in great contrast to much philosophical discourse of the twentieth century on exteriority. Despite the shortcomings of conventional psychoanalytic practice within clinical settings, what Freud succeeds in revealing is the essentially social dimension of traumatic experience. Though limited, the Freudian metaphor of the psychic economy illustrates a fundamental feature of trauma's sociality: It is not that trauma is merely a social construct; rather, traumatic experience devastates us precisely because it confounds the social structures[64] and "assumptive world"[65] through which we process and understand ourselves.

Lived experience, or *Erlebnis*, has been used by social researchers as a way to investigate traumatic experience, both interiorly and exteriorly, without reducing traumatic encounter to data-driven testimony and empty forms of empirical observation. Yet Heidegger reveals that deferring to lived experience as a way to understand anthropology through a phenomenological lens ultimately backfires. Prioritizing a closeness to human lived experience ignores what it means to be situated and attuned to a world wherein trauma rupture occurs and wherein the "last gods" might appear. In tandem, Freud and Heidegger demand a socio-psychic-economic examination of traumatic experience that also resists trauma's conceptualization in terms of lived experience—even when approached charitably in hopes of truly understanding its occurrence.

It would be an overstatement, however, to suggest that Freud's and Heidegger's contributions mean proximity to another's experience in moments of trauma is unimportant. The original concern for the trauma researcher remains crucial still: The failure of witnessing traumatic experience in a psychic economy or through vicarious engagement with lived experience does not mean one is not called to witness. Blending resources in psychoanalysis, phenomenology, and trauma theory, Kelly Oliver thus describes the social and expressive challenge of witnessing to traumatic experience, "The heart of the paradox is that oppression and subordination are experiences that attempt to objectify the subject and mutilate or annihilate subjectivity, that is, your sense of yourself, especially your sense of yourself as an agent."[66] In the wake of traumatic experience and the specific threat of annihilation, the survivor is deficient in their communication and understanding; both their individual and social understanding is alienated from their own experience. If anything, Freud and Heidegger seem only to entrench trauma theory more fully into the quagmire of the impossibility of witnessing, both demanding a response and immediately revealing the paucity of our relational and phenomenological engagement with traumatic experience.

Strategies for navigating the double bind of witnessing differ across these psychoanalytic and phenomenological perspectives, particularly around the sense of agency one has in the analysis of bringing about understanding and unconcealment. Despite his efforts to pursue the absconding gods of metaphysics in his *Beiträge*, for Heidegger the concept of *Gelassenheit* or releasement becomes the crucial way of approaching the event of being in his later works; here, activity and passivity are bridged through a middle voice that does not pursue nor simply wait for the last god, but prepares the way for its coming event.[67] In a clinical setting, psychoanalytic literature points to countertransference as a perennial tool for understanding how one's personal attachment history affects the relational dynamic in therapy. One of the greatest sources of harm done by researchers and clinicians is to re-enact prior attachments and unfulfilled desires on those whom we aim to help in moments of crisis. This is why psychoanalytic training requires therapists to undergo analysis themselves: Psychoanalysis has a keen appreciation of our unconscious tendencies to render others vehicles for our personal satisfaction. For those in trauma theory bridging resources in the philosophy of religion and the social sciences, the psychoanalytic perspective may seem to have an advantage of offering a clearer intrapsychic method for examining one's proclivity to harm others in their times of need.

Yet even from a purely clinical and practitioner-based scenario, research from trauma clinicians such as Judith Herman[68] and Lyn Layton[69] make a clear case that the task of witnessing it assumes a level of stability and equanimity in psychoanalysis that is generally not afforded in traumatic scenarios. The sort of sustained reflection required by psychoanalysis is not possible in a war zone or when tending to a friend after assault. In short, the urgency of witnessing to traumatic experience does not afford the luxury of the couch.

As work in post-Heideggerian phenomenological ethics has argued, to admit the impossibility of witnessing is to put oneself in a situation where absolving oneself from transgressions against the other in trauma is besides the point. Resisting alienation from one's own lived experience involves a more radical gesture toward this other, from whom I am alienated in my witnessing. What it means to be proximate to an other, in the Levinasian sense, is to invert the structure of the economy wherein I allegedly understand this other better simply because I am close to it, affectively and spatially. It is a situation wherein "[t]he right of the human is here, in this straightforwardness of exposition, of commandment and assignation, a right more ancient than all conferment of dignity and every merit. The proximity of the neighbor—the peace of proximity—is the responsibility of the ego for an other, the impossibility of letting the other alone faced with the mystery of death."[70] The challenge of witnessing already presumes that there is an urgency to respond, which cannot be ignored in clinical and proximate settings. It is one thing if one is preparing the way for an understanding of the meaning of beyng; it is another if one prepares the way for an ethic of caring for an other in a moment of acute need in the wake of a traumatic encounter.

The impossibility of witnessing the traumatic experience of the other thus recurs in a rather insufferable way for the theorist and researcher trying to respond ethically to the events that confound any coherent framework for understanding trauma's broken worlds. In this sense, the failure to witness adequately to the other in their time of trauma risks being a failure of theological imagination as well. As Freud points out, these wounding encounters pose a threat to one's cultural and religious sense of purpose, one that demands a transcendent and fetishizing projection if the ego is to maintain any equanimity in its psychic economy:

> If a man is unfortunate it means that he is no longer loved by this high-est power; and, threatened by such a loss of love, he once more bows to the parental representative in his super-ego—a representative whom, in his days of good fortune, he was ready to neglect. This becomes es-pecially clear where Fate is looked upon in the strictly religious sense of being nothing else than an expression of the Divine Will. The people of Israel had believed themselves to be the favourite child of God, and when the great Father caused misfortune after misfortune to rain down upon this people of his, they were never shaken in their belief in his relationship to them or questioned his power or righteousness. Instead, they produced the prophets, who held up their sinfulness before them; and out of their sense of guilt they created the over-strict command-ments of their priestly religion. It is remarkable how differently a primitive man behaves. If he has met with a misfortune, he does not throw the blame on himself but on his fetish, which has obviously not done its duty, and he gives it a thrashing instead of punishing himself.[71]

Recognizing the proclivity to fetishize traumatic experience is to appre-ciate how natural it is for us to displace our desire in seemingly impos-sible situations. In its most direct and classical form, the need to fetishize emerges when "a piece of reality which was undoubtedly important [is] disavowed by the ego," particularly when the religious and cultural norms prohibit satisfaction of the psychic economy and its drives.[72] So laden with a pejorative tone, it is easy to neglect that the characteristic experience of the fetishist is suffering,[73] which, according to Freud, is symptomatic of the anxieties that emerge from "the trauma of birth" itself.[74] The need to disavow one's unsatisfied desires in experience and the "creation of the fetish [is] due to an intention to destroy the evidence of the possibility of castration" and the profound lack that accompanies it.[75] As such, the fetish is both a placeholder for the divine and for our repressed desires. The impossibility of satisfying this desire is the flipside of the impossibil-ity of witnessing: The other makes a demand that cannot be satisfied, and rather than seeing this traumatic moment as revelatory of acute injustice, we disavow the insufferable quality of the experience and turn it into a site to be honored.

For philosophers, theologians, and social theorists to take the impos-sibility of witnessing seriously, for us to take proximity to the neighbor seriously, will require sustained attention to the recurring possibility of the fetishization of the traumatic experience of others. In an important way, this lens extends the warnings of Freud and Heidegger only for this specific task of witnessing trauma. Yet insofar as psychoanalytic and phenomenological resources continually reinscribe the impossibility of adequately witnessing to others, it will be important to find within these methods strategies for resisting the impulse to lower our ethical standards in the face of impossibility. That is, analyzing the seemingly perverse quality of fetishism in social relation offers a more concrete way of striving toward the infinite response demanded by traumatic lived experience.[76] Negotiating the fragile boundaries of our psychic economy and the futile machinations of lived experience means trauma theorists must be vigilant in accounting for the moments we displace the traumatic lived experience of the other with a tolerable surrogate.

NOTES

1. Sigmund Freud, *Introductory Lectures on Psycho-Analysis*, trans. and ed. James Strachey (New York: Norton, 1966), 340–41.

2. Dori Laub, "Bearing Witness, or the Vicissitudes of Listening," in *Testimony: Crises of Witnessing in Literature, Psychoanalysis and History*, ed. Shoshana Felman and Dori Laub (New York: Routledge, 1992).

3. Dori Laub and Nanette C. Auerhahn, "Failed Empathy: A Central Theme in the Survivor's Holocaust Experience," *Psychoanalytic Psychology* 6 (1989).

4. Shoshana Felman, "The Return of the Voice: Claude Lanzmann's *Shoah*," in *Testimony: Crises of Witnessing in Literature, Psychoanalysis and History*, ed. Shoshana Felman and Dori Laub (New York: Routledge, 1992), 224.

5. Cathy Caruth, *Trauma: Explorations in Memory* (Baltimore: Johns Hopkins University Press), 9.

6. For an empirical assessment of this trend in comparative social performance, see Todd Rogers and Avi Feller, "Discouraged by Peer Excellence: Exposure to Exemplary Peer Performance Causes Quitting," *Psychological Science* 27 (2016).

7. For a classically psychoanalytic perspective on sadism, see Sigmund Freud's description of "Sadism and Masochism" in *The Standard Edition of the Complete Psychological Works of Sigmund Freud, Volume VII (1901–1905): A Case of Hysteria, Three Essays on Sexuality and Other Works*, trans. and ed. James Strachey (London: Hogarth, 1953).

8. For a clear synopsis of scopophilia as a psychoanalytic framework for understanding visual pleasure and voyeuristic relation, see Laura Mulvey, "Visual Pleasure and Narrative Cinema," *Screen* 16 (1975).

9. Jacques Derrida, *Philosophy in a Time of Terror: Dialogues with Jürgen Habermas and Jacques Derrida*, ed. Giovanna Borradori (Chicago: University of Chicago Press, 2003), 86–87.

10. See Jeremy Holmes, "Countertransference Before Heimann: An Historical Exploration," *Journal of the American Psychoanalytic Association* 62 (2014): 603–29.

11. Franz Brentano, *Psychology from an Empirical Standpoint*, trans. Antos C. Rancurello, D. B. Terrell, and Linda L. McAlister (New York: Routledge, 1995), 77.

12. For Aristotle, it was the second or perceptive soul in his hierarchical psychology that explained an individual's reception to perceptual experience and, subsequently, animation. Aristotle, *On the Soul*, in *The Complete Works of Aristotle: The Revised Oxford Translation, Volume 1*, ed. Jonathan Barnes, trans. J. A. Smith (Princeton: Princeton University Press, 1984), 413b1–4. Pagination refers to the standard Stephanus.

13. Brentano, *Psychology from an Empirical Standpoint*, 8.

14. See Sigmund Freud, *Introductory Lectures on Psycho-Analysis*, trans. and ed. James Strachey (New York: Norton, 1966), 10. In his 1917 preface, Freud describes the audience of this extensive work: "This volume is a faithful reproduction of the lecture which I delivered [at the University] during the two Winter Terms 1915/16 and 1916/17 before an audience of doctors and laymen of both sexes."

15. Freud wryly responds to these critiques in *Introductory Lectures on Psycho-Analysis*, 31: "I should reply: Patience, Ladies and Gentlemen! I think your criticism has gone astray. It is true that psycho-analysis cannot boast that it has never concerned itself with trivialities. On the contrary, the material for its observation is usually provided by the inconsiderable events which have been put aside by the other sciences as being too unimportant."

16. Freud, *Introductory Lectures on Psycho-Analysis*, 443. Freud writes, "We can only venture to say this much: that pleasure is *in some way* connected with the diminution, reduction or extinction of the amounts of stimulus prevailing in the mental apparatus, and that similarly unpleasure is connected with their increase [. . .]. Since in such processes related to pleasure it is a question of what happens to *quantities* of mental excitation or energy, we call considerations of this kind economic."

17. See a discussion of the "rational maximizer" theory and its reception in contemporary behavioral economics in Richard A. Posner, "Rational Choice, Behavioral Economics, and the Law," *Stanford Law Review* 50 (1997), 1551–75.

18. Sigmund Freud, *Beyond the Pleasure Principle*, trans. and ed. James Strachey (New York: Norton, 1961).

19. Sigmund Freud, *Civilization and Its Discontents*, trans. and ed. James Strachey (New York: Norton, 1961), 34.

20. Freud, *Introductory Lectures on Psycho-Analysis*, 340.

21. Freud, *Introductory Lectures on Psycho-Analysis*, 340–41. Freud continues, "We apply it to an experience which within a short period of time presents the mind with an increase of stimulus too powerful to be dealt with or worked off in the normal way, and this must result in permanent disturbances of the manner in which the energy operates."

22. Freud, *Beyond the Pleasure Principle*, 15.

23. In particular, see the fifth meditation of Edmund Husserl, *Cartesian Meditations: An Introduction to Phenomenology*, trans. Dorion Cairns (The Hague, Netherlands: Martinus Nijhoff, 1960); Edmund Husserl, *Ideas Pertaining to a Pure Phenomenology and to a Phenomenological Philosophy, Second Book*, trans R. Rojcewicz and A. Schuwer (Boston: Kluwer Academic Publishers, 2002).

24. See Martin Buber, *I and Thou*, trans. Walter A. Kaufmann (New York: Scribner, 1970).

25. See Emmanuel Levinas, *Totality and Infinity*, trans. Alphonso Lingis (Pittsburgh: Duquesne University Press, 1969).

26. Freud, *Beyond the Pleasure Principle*, 33.

27. See, for example, Greg Morgenson, *God Is a Trauma: Vicarious Religion and Soul-Making* (New York: Spring Publications, 1989).

28. Freud, *Beyond the Pleasure Principle*, 31.

29. Freud, *Introductory Lectures on Psycho-Analysis*, 474. It is important to highlight, also, that Freud's extensive work with veterans of the First World War had a lasting impact on Freud's understanding of traumatic neurosis, and what might today be called post traumatic stress disorder. In that same passage, Freud notes that this characterization of trauma applies "particularly in those brought about by the horrors of war."

30. Freud, *Introductory Lectures on Psycho-Analysis*, 498. Freud elaborates, "We next learn from these spontaneous attacks that the complex which we describe as a state of anxiety is capable of fragmentation. The total attack can be represented by a single, intensely developed symptom, by a tremor, a vertigo, by palpitation of the heart, or by dyspnea; and the general feeling by which we recognize anxiety may be absent or have become indistinct."

31. Sigmund Freud, "The Neuro-Psychoses of Defence," in *The Standard Edition of the Complete Psychological Works of Sigmund Freud, Volume III (1893-1899): Early Psycho-Analytic Publications*, trans. James Strachey (London: Hogarth, 1962), 49–50.

32. Freud, *Beyond the Pleasure Principle*, 32.

33. Anna Freud, *The Ego and the Mechanisms of Defense, Revised Edition*, trans. Cecil Baines (New York: International Universities Press, 1966), 27.

34. Freud, *Beyond the Pleasure Principle*, 47. Freud writes, "Hence arises the paradoxical situation that the living organism struggles most energetically against events (dangers, in fact) which might help it to attain its life's aim rapidly—by a kind of short-circuit. Such behavior is, however, precisely what characterizes purely instinctual as contrasted with intelligent efforts."

35. Sigmund Freud, "The Dynamics of Transference," in *The Standard Edition of the Complete Psychological Works of Sigmund Freud, Volume XII (1911–1913): The Case of Schreber, Papers on Technique and Other Works*, trans. James Strachey (London: Hogarth, 1958), 104. Freud notes the mode of resistance that transference often takes in the analytic context: "Thus transference in the analytic treatment invariably appears to us in the first instance as the strongest weapon of the resistance, and we may conclude that the intensity and persistence of the transference are an effect and an expression of the resistance. The *mechanism* of transference is, it is true, dealt with when we have traced it back to the state of readiness of the libido, which has remained in possession of infantile imagos; but the part transference plays in the treatment can only be explained if we enter into its relations with resistance."

36. Freud, *Beyond the Pleasure Principle*, 35–36.

37. Freud, *Beyond the Pleasure Principle*, 36.

38. It is worth noting that not all trauma necessarily comes from human sociality or foreign *mental* phenomena; trauma may very well ensue from a flash of lightning or other natural events which are not attributable to human sociality, intersubjective experience, or, in analytic parlance, "other minds." The more essentially social character in this context is that even a seemingly "natural evil" has essentially social consequences within a psychoanalytic theory.

39. Sigmund Freud, "Further Remarks on the Neuro-Psychoses of Defence," in *The Standard Edition of the Complete Psychological Works of Sigmund Freud, Volume III (1893–1899): Early Psycho-Analytic Publications*, trans. James Strachey (London, Hogarth, 1962), 172. Returning to the analysis of defense two years later in his essay "Further Remarks on the Neuro-Psychoses of Defense" in 1896, Freud insists, "A psychical analysis of [defense] shows that, in spite of their peculiarity, they can always be fully explained by being traced back to the obsessional memories which they are fighting against."

40. Freud also elaborates upon this economic feature of defense in *Introductory Lectures on Psycho-Analysis*, 465–66: "You will no doubt have observed that in these last discussions I have introduced a fresh factor into the structure of the aetiological chain—namely the quantity, the magnitude, of the energies concerned. We have still to take this factor into account everywhere.

A purely qualitative analysis of the aetiological determinants is not enough. Or, to put it another way, a merely *dynamic* view of these mental processes is insufficient; an *economic* line of approach is also needed."

41. Max van Manen, *Researching Lived Experience: Human Science for an Action Sensitive Pegagogy*, 2nd ed. (New York: Routledge, 2015).

42. Hans-Georg Gadamer, *Truth and Method*, 2nd ed., trans. Joel Weinsheimer and Donald G. Marshall (New York: Continuum, 1975), 54–55. Gadamer's philosophical etymology notes, "The coined word Erlebnis [. . .] expresses the criticism of Enlightenment rationalism, which, following Rousseau, emphasized the concept of life (Leben)."

43. Gadamer, *Truth and Method*, 54–55.

44. Gadamer, *Truth and Method*, 54–55.

45. Edmund Husserl, *The Paris Lectures*, trans. Peter Koestenbaum (Boston: Martinus Nijhoff, 1964), 12. This and all subsequent references refer to the original German pagination.

46. Edmund Husserl, *Cartesian Meditations*, 156. This and all subsequent references refer to the original German pagination.

47. Martin Heidegger, *Being and Time*, trans. Joan Stambaugh (Albany, N.Y.: SUNY Press, 2010), 48. This and all subsequent references refer to the original German pagination.

48. For Heidegger and Germans alike, the available distinction between *Erfahrung* and *Erlebnis* makes for a clearer way of differentiating the more colloquial description of experience (*Erfahrung*) from the technic description of the lived world of experience (*Erlebnis*).

49. Heidegger, *Being and Time*, 114.

50. Heidegger, *Being and Time*, 46.

51. Heidegger, *Being and Time*, 47.

52. Heidegger, *Being and Time*, 31.

53. Heidegger, *Being and Time*, 38. Heidegger explains that "the transcendence of the being of Da-sein is a distinctive one since in it lies the possibility and necessity of the most radical *individuation*."

54. Hans Ulrich Gumbrecht, *The Production of Presence: What Meaning Cannot Convey* (Stanford: Stanford University Press, 2004), 100.

55. Gumbrecht, *The Production of Presence*, 88. In the concept of world and its integration as an existential of Dasein—something not readily stripped of its thrown context—Gumbrecht notes, "There is a mode of world-appropriation in which, on the one hand, the presence of the world or of the other is still physically felt although, on the other hand, there is no perception of a real object that would account for this feeling. This is what we call *mysticism*."

56. The language of "immediacy" might sound better in this instance, but Heidegger repeatedly stresses that the ideal of immediacy is itself a

metaphysical desire for the *res extensa*. The idea of unfiltrated connection to the world is already constituted in *Da-sein*, there-being.

57. Martin Heidegger, *Contributions to Philosophy (Of the Event)*, trans. Richard Rojcewicz and Daniela Vallega-Neu (Bloomington: Indiana University Press, 2012), 104.

58. Heidegger, *Contributions to Philosophy*, 16ff.

59. Heidegger adopts the medieval spelling of *Seyn*, translated as "beyng" by Daniela Vallega-Neu and Richard Rojcewicz, to gesture toward a retrieval of the study of being from its first beginning in Greek thought.

60. Heidegger, *Contributions to Philosophy*, 106.

61. Heidegger, *Contributions to Philosophy*, 17.

62. Heidegger, *Contributions to Philosophy*, 121. In context, "The human sciences will expand into a comprehensive newspaper science whose scope will be gigantic and in which the current 'lived experience' will always be interpreted historiologically and, as so interpreted, will be *published* as quickly as possible and in the form most easily comprehensible to everyone."

63. Freud, *Civilization and Its Discontents*, 59. Here and elsewhere, Freud characterizes the way that cultural and societal sacrifices are made to individual psychic and libidinal commitments: "Taboos, laws and customs impose further restrictions, which affect both men and women. Not all civilizations go equally far in this; and the economic structure of the society also influences the amount of sexual freedom that remains. Here, as we already know, civilization is obeying the laws of economic necessity, since a large amount of the psychical energy which it uses for its own purposes has to be withdrawn from sexuality."

64. See, for example, Judith Butler's discussion of the social dynamics of psychic recognition in her chapter "Psychic Interceptions: Melancholy, Ambivalence, Rage" in *The Psychic Life of Power: Theories in Subjection* (Stanford: Stanford University Press, 1997).

65. See the theoretical perspective of trauma as a loss in "assumptive world" in Jeffrey Kauffmann, ed., *Loss of the Assumptive World: A Theory of Traumatic Loss* (New York: Routledge, 2002).

66. Kelly Oliver, *Witnessing: Beyond Recognition* (Minneapolis: University of Minnesota Press, 2001), 95.

67. For an extensive discussion of the phenomenological and political implications of Heidegger's work on *Gelassenheit*, see Bret W. Davis, *Heidegger and the Will: On the Way to Gelassenheit* (Evanston, Ill.: Northwestern University Press, 2007).

68. See the discussion of the steps to recovery, particularly the emphasis on securing safety, in Judith Herman, *Trauma and Recovery: The Aftermath of Violence—from Domestic Abuse to Political Terror* (New York: Basic Books, 1997).

69. See Lyn Layton, "Psychoanalysis and Politics: Historicizing Subjectivity," *Psychiatry, Mental Health and Psychoanalysis* 11 (2013). Despite a strong commitment to psychoanalysis' potential contributions to trauma recovery and a progressive politic, Layton remarks, "I do not think that the practices promoted by psychoanalysis are inherently democratic, precisely because of the way the social is dissociated from conceptualisations of subjectivity" (77).

70. Emmanuel Levinas, "Peace and Proximity," in *Emmanuel Levinas: Basic Philosophical Writings*, ed. Adriaan T. Peperzak, Simon Critchley, and Robert Bernasconi, trans. Peter Atterton and Simon Critchley (Bloomington: Indiana University Press), 167.

71. Freud, *Civilization and Its Discontents*, 88.

72. Sigmund Freud, "Fetishism," in *The Standard Edition of the Complete Psychological Works of Sigmund Freud, Volume XXI (1927–1931): The Future of an Illusion, Civilization and Its Discontents, and Other Works*, trans. and ed. James Strachey (London: Hogarth, 1961), 156.

73. Freud, "Fetishism," 152.

74. Freud, "Fetishism," 155.

75. Sigmund Freud, *An Outline of Psycho-Analysis*, trans. and ed. James Strachey (New York: Norton, 1949), 76.

76. For future research on this matter, it is important to note that what is potentially gained by understanding ourselves as fetishizers of traumatic experience also includes the risk of sublimating too much desire in this other, wherein fetishism takes on a focused pathological character. Freud describes a fetish taking on a pathological character in *Three Essays on Sexuality and Other Works*, 154: "The situation only becomes pathological when the longing for the fetish passes beyond the point of being merely a necessary condition attached to the sexual object and actually takes the place of the normal aim, and, further, when the fetish becomes detached from a particular individual and becomes the sole sexual object." It is in these scenarios that the ego develops a heightened cathexis to a surrogate object, which effectively divorces the ego from its more immediate desires.

PART III

Theological Aporia in the Aftermath of Trauma

Theopoetics of Trauma

Shelly Rambo

In remarks honoring the career and contributions of a noted Christian theologian, one panelist offers these cautionary words: Theology is in crisis. It has lost sight of its primary subject matter, which is God. He lauds the honored guest while suggesting that not only has a "golden age" of theology passed but the discipline is in peril. Naming a crisis in theology is not new, and the panelists are strongly influenced by a lineage of German theology that has its roots in Karl Barth's dramatic rejection of liberal theology and the language of "crisis" represented in Barth's statement: "On that day, theology died."[1] This theologian's words are met with some degree of recognition by those present, an auditorium filled with theologians and religious studies scholars. The guild meeting is filled with a sense of the need for academic work to speak to the current political situation, but it is this urgency that this theologian interprets as theology losing its way.

Particular assumptions about the aim and purpose of theology are embedded in this statement, but the central implication is that theologians are talking about everything else, but God had dropped out of the discourse. Theology is no longer recognizable because it is not speaking in a certain way. These declarations have a certain function and effect. This rallying cry for theology to return to its primary work is delivered within the container of a retrospective. It invokes nostalgia for a time when theologians were operating more visibly and were, in this theologian's assessment, speaking more audibly about God. The way that theologians are speaking amidst the current climate of economic, social, and political dis-ease is not God-talk—not theology.

An anniversary of great Catholic theologians prompted a similar stream of reflections, yet with different conclusions. Charles Curran reflects on the state of theology following Catholic Society of America's celebration of famous twentieth-century theologians by posing the question: "Where have all the dominant theologians gone?"[2] Curran interprets the more diffuse and pluralistic landscape of theology not as a loss to be mourned but as an occasion for celebration. Martin Marty responds to Curran's reflections, lauding his posture towards these shifts. The era of the dominant theologians has passed away, Marty says, and people are no longer turning to the forms of "theological theology" for reflections about God. Interest in the primary questions of theology has not waned, but the modern modes of theological transmission are not communicating. People are not receiving theological wisdom from the "theological theologians," as they were in the previous generation.[3] Marty reflects, "Most believers and seekers today derive theological meanings from literary, spiritual, and ethical writers. Maybe it's the old Greco-Germanic models that are changing."[4]

And yet these new models face the test of credibility within academia. "Theological theologians" know the mode, the form, in which their work will be recognized. Where will these new models come from if theological theologians keep returning to the known models? This is a different concern about the state of theology than the one named by the panelist. The repetition of a particular form of theological discourse means that theology will no longer be relevant to a broader audience. These reflections on the current state of theology imply that theological work is recognizable in one primary form.

Relevance is one concern. But the concern about form also arises when we think about theology's ability to speak to certain kinds of experiences. The rise in theological attention to trauma identifies form as a primary question for theology. And yet the struggle to recognize certain forms as theological remains. In *The Spirit of Life*, Jürgen Moltmann gestures toward theological reflections on trauma. Aiming to "break open and expand the modern concept of experience," he takes into account the sensory and the bodily, recognizing the prominence that a "Western view" has placed on cognition and reason.[5] There are some experiences that we do not master, he says.

There are events in the past that never become "past," but are continually present to us. We repress them, we work on them, we puzzle over them and interpret them, for we have to live with them. Our biographies are molded by experiences like this, experiences that affect us in this elemental way.[6]

He ascribes these experiences to biography, but they do not find a way into theology proper. They remain testimonies that are noted and even notable.

The connection between trauma and theopoetics is instinctual to those who work within either of these arenas. Experiences that defy form must be expressed in language that can account for the shattering of experience. And yet the significance for theological work more broadly has yet to be articulated. This essay explores the exigency of attending to form in theology, precisely for its capacity to speak to the heart of theological matters, namely experiences of trauma.

Theopoetics of Testimony

Studies in trauma have provided new grounds for theological attention to form. Theologian Rebecca Chopp suggested a new mode for theology in response to the growing awareness of trauma.[7] In an essay first delivered as an address in 1997, Chopp registered the impact of studies in trauma and identified key scholars in contemporary "trauma theory." Elie Wiesel named the twentieth century as the century that birthed the genre of testimony and witness. Wiesel's comments and the rise of trauma studies prompted Chopp to suggest that theology needs to take the form of a "poetics of testimony."[8] Her essay both pioneers theological work in trauma and forecasts a surge in what is identified as theopoetics.[9] In the decades following, a post-traumatic sensibility has set in, indicating that trauma is the assumed context out of which theological work is done.

Chopp presents the need for new forms of theology, given that present—modern—modes fail to hear the truths contained in testimonies. Marginalized communities, she says, are turning to the genre of testimony to speak truths about their experiences that would not be recognized within the arena of rational discourse. Rational discourse is the mode of modern theory that privileges a certain form of speaking while, Chopp says, excluding discursive practices of particular communities. Literatures of harm and exclusion express truths differently and in ways that are not recognizable as theory. The image of the courtroom guides her reflections. In the modern courtroom, reason sits as judge, and testimonies presented within this space must align with a certain way of truth-telling in order to be heard. The testimonies themselves stand in judgment: "Witnesses, testimonies, are the stuff to be judged, and the modern theorist is the judge, prosecutor, and jury."[10] Theology, conceived in terms of a modern (rational) discourse, does not access these testimonies but, much like the modern modes that it emulates, it places these testimonies on trial in the modern courtroom of truth. She writes: "Bearing witness is the realm of blooming confusion, the jarring messiness of history itself. Theory, on the other hand, is the clear-headed judge who decides the truth by ordering coherent narratives of history."[11]

And yet, she notes, Christian theologians have "increasingly attended to the poetics of testimony."[12] The impulse to do so comes from a commitment (an imperative) to hear voices often excluded in the public arena. This is theological work, they argue. But the dominant forms of modern theology do not register the forms of testimonial speech. The challenge is to bring the truths conveyed there into view in such a way that they are not only given a hearing but that they are understood as revelatory. Reason should not be the final arbiter of their truth. Instead, they must be received and heard by those who are attempting to reshape the social imaginary. Chopp is using the term "poetics" in a broad sense, as discursive practices of imagining the world in varied ways. Testimonies, as forms of speech, are messy, and while reason is useful in providing coherence and ordering, testimony "requires that it be heard in its own voice, style, and content, neither as a variation of a common experience nor a representation of that which stands on the margins, opposed by the dominant discourse."[13] She proposes a reversal of the courtroom in which testimonies determine how truth is assessed: "It is important to observe the peculiarity of these testimonies."[14]

Chopp's analysis provides a helpful commentary on the declaration of theology's demise. If the courtroom is not reversed, then the matter of theology will always exclude these truths, deeming them secondary. The judgment that theological truths lie elsewhere is reflected in Moltmann's impulse to keep certain experiences within the realm of autobiography. The challenge is not to pay attention to experiences or to deem them important, but to engage experiences with corresponding forms that *count* as theology.

The notion that the real business of theology lies elsewhere is often bound up with claims about transcendence. The modern theological courtroom is structured according to a contrast between transcendence and immanence. The assertion is that God is either beyond the universe or within it. Transcendence implies separation and distance; God is independent from creation and not determined by it. Immanence, by contrast, depicts the divine as present within the created order and intimate with it, even determined by it. The concern, from one end, is that God will be undifferentiated from the created order, thus having no power in relationship to it. From the other end, the emphasis on God's distance raises questions about God's relationship to the world and whether the material world can be affirmed or, in some versions of transcendence, is meant to be controlled. The critique of binary thinking, associated with modern theory, is that there is an implicit hierarchy operating, with transcendence as the dominant term and immanence as the implied subordinate term. The association of immanence with materiality, dependence, and earthiness has a long history. Mayra Rivera writes: "Whether the term 'transcendence' is explicitly invoked or not, the Western imaginary retains the versions of the disembodied controlling power that theism commonly associates with transcendence."[15]

And yet Chopp challenges readers to reconceive transcendence in relationship to these testimonies. Reversing the modern courtroom, she does not capitulate to the contrast. Aware that many like-minded colleagues reject conceptions of transcendence, Chopp is concerned about ceding the term. For her, transcendence lies in the transformation of testimonies from despair and survival to affirmations of life; it attests to the possibility that suffering can be transfigured: "Transcendence is a matter of the power and spirit of transfiguration."[16] Transcendence is no longer a contrasting term as it became in modern theology; it is envisioned as a "moral summons" to imagine the world differently.[17] Witnessing the testimonies will require particular attention to how language is used, as these testimonies often break and shatter when surfaced in language. Theological writing at the edges of such experiences will look different. Imagining something else in the face of what is, and even the demand to do so, is a matter of transcendence. Could this story be told another way? What forms of discourse can do that work?

Concerns about the wedding of modern theology to one particular form (rational discursive thought) are prominent in the work of Mark D. Jordan. Christian theology has lost its way, he says, by straying from the richness of its genres and by neglecting the particular rhetorical devices that can speak multiple truths: "We contemporary Christians inherit a rich library of rhetorical shapes [. . .]. Why is it then that so much of modern theology is unrhetorical or antirhetorical?"[18] Truths require accompanying forms.[19] And theology is multi-vocal. There is no single form of speech about God, as is evident in the history of Christianity, and no form can presume to capture the truth about God. In capitulating to one form of writing, perhaps by neglecting to think that form matters, theology has relinquished its ability to speak in varied modes and expressions.[20] The power of Christian speech, Jordan contends, is in its ability to foster the desire for truth and not its claim to contain it. The question theologians should be asking is how, through their speech, they can best foster that desire. To draw attention to rhetoric and to the genres of theology is not merely an aesthetic inclination; it is bound up in the subject matter of theology.

If theologians are attentive to form, they will be positioned at the sites in which language breaks and will ask which forms of discourse attest to that shattering. The implication is that an adeptness in form enables the reception of multiple truths, spoken from multiple sites. Theologians would have a certain flexibility and an ability to match particular experiences with particular forms of writing. The concern that Chopp flags is the potential, and perhaps inevitable, dismissal of experiences in the privileging of certain forms of theology. The gavel drops, and certain truths are rendered out of bounds.

The claim that theology has lost its way is declared simultaneously with what is being identified as a "new civil rights movement" calling for a reassessment of life, rights, and dignity.[21] This confirms Chopp's insight that unless transcendence is rethought in and through a poetics of testimony, the suffering of our times will remain unaddressed by the discipline of theology. This lack of address is rooted in a failure to take form seriously. And yet to take it seriously will require exercising the imagination and becoming conversant in other forms of writing. It will require some combination of "poetics, rhetoric, and hermeneutics."[22]

Writing Exercises

The professional poet guides us through an afternoon of words. She hands us copies of Allen Ginsberg's "Footnote to Howl."[23] The poem is a lyric poem with each line beginning with the word "holy." Directing us to read a line each, moving around the table, we begin: "Holy" followed by fourteen exclamatory Holy's. The poem proceeds with body parts, musical instruments, cities, and forms of transportation—each is holy. Some prompt amusement, low giggles, and others a tilt of the head. The exclamation marks dot the page, as the poet refuses to see one thing as more holy than another—the beggar or the angel, the bum or the seraphim.

We develop a rhythm, as each picks up a line, like a verbal baton pass. The language is familiar to us, as religion or theology professors, as women who have built careers on the study of holy things. It is obvious that the things listed could be deemed the opposite of holy, and the pervasiveness of his attribution sweeps across the page in order that nothing is lost or outside the reach of the holy. The power of the exercise is that something is happening to those things in the process of our collective reading. The naming of the things as holy attributes holiness to them. But, more than that, the act of reciting, of reading, is positioning us a new relationship to these things.

The "praise" poems, as she calls them, enact a posture in the writer or the reader. The language of praise and blessing is the language of worship; it is doxological. Poets like Ginsberg inhabit these liturgical forms, not to give authority to religious institutions or to place readers under the umbrella of theology, but to offend. He assumes the priestly function of transfiguring the ordinary. He turns readers to the things of the world in such a way that our perceptions are challenged.[24] The things themselves did not need to change. Instead, the collective, the readership, is brought into a different relationship to them.

This recitation spurs a writing exercise. Write about a moment just prior to a significant memory, she instructs us. Go back hours before. Write down what you see, what is around you, the sights, sounds, and smells. Leaning forward to take in our words and back to take them away, she leads us, one by one, through an editing process. As a gathered assembly, we witness what is happening to our words, what they can do. It is a graceful but vicious exercise in extraction and letting go. You do not need that, she says. Tell us what is there. Most of us, in our writing, move away from the sensory to make sense, to make meaning, of what is there. We move from description to explanation. She meets each attempt to explain with the words: Get rid of that. Just include what you observe. Any move to make meaning of what is there is in the way. Working in the mode of explanation is so familiar to us, and, yet this proficiency required for our academic careers, is unwelcome in this space.

The imposition of conceptions of the holy onto things is the realm of the religious professional but also the practice of the "theological theologian"; both attribute words to God. But to pay attention to how those words fall, to reflect on what we need them to do, is something altogether unique. In

"Reflection on the Right Use of School Studies with a View to the Love of God," Simone Weil identifies a concerning aspect of this attribution by describing an approach to knowledge built into the foundations of education, from its early stages.[25] We learn to bring what we already know to what we study and approach it as if it is something to conquer. We learn, early on, to impose our understanding on something foreign to us—to approach a problem with a view to solve it. And yet our posture toward what we do not know is not receptive; it is imposing. In Weil's depiction, there is a level of violence involved because the impulse to solve is wedded with notions of mastery and control. We already presume to know and therefore, we bring the puzzle into the arena in which it cannot speak anything new to us. Weil is convinced that unless we change the mode of learning, we will do violence. This is a critique of a mode of Western education, but it is interesting that Weil presents it within a spiritual framework. She identifies a different way in spiritual terms, presenting an alternative as a spiritual path to God. There is a theological counterpoint to this approach. The practice of attention involves a posture of radical receptivity and curiosity in the face of what is different. This practice opens us up to transformation, which she translates as the possibility of addressing affliction. This possibility of hearing the "mute cry" of affliction, often presented as an impossibility in her writings, comes only if one develops the posture of attention.[26] For Weil, attention is the opposite of imposition.

In succession, each shares her poem. The master editor appears impatient, even frustrated, but it is in service of something else, instead operating like a midwife coaching a mother in labor who resists her own breathing. She instructs, "Cross it out. Yes, literally, put a line through it." The editing process is both individual and collective. And after the edit, each of us looks at the page. The extractions still visible, the poems seem to us raw, stripped down, naked. "Read it again, without the explanation." The poem can survive, and in fact thrive, with less.

It was only after working through the poem that she proposes a title. "Before my father died," she says. "You see. His death is there in the words that did not name it as such." The deaths, losses, and celebrations (the "subject matter" of the poems) are inscribed within the poem without being stated. The experience is there without being named. Yet, if the writer starts with that line and writes the poem from the title, it would be a different poem. All of the stock expressions about death, about fathers, would have taken the texture out of the poem. The experience would no longer be there. It is by *not* writing about the experience but writing before it that distinguishes it. It does not presume immediate access but, instead, enacts a reverent pause by the exercise of indirection.

Sensing the explanatory impulse, she throws out this question: Why are the things that you observe not enough? In each case, we feel that we have to do something more, something else, to *make* a poem. Why is *what is* not enough? The connection to the previous exercise is striking. The repetition of the word 'holy' is not about making something profane holy, but about shaking off conceptions of the holy to make way for a change of perception. The language of praise and blessing is often understood as some outside authorizing, consecrating, blessing, authorizing, but, enacted in the poem, "holy" becomes a container for a transformation of perception. Turning a floodlight on our delineations—holy and unholy, sacred and profane—they could no longer hold in that space. Ginsberg's jarring antitheses prompt readers to release categories and assumptions.

We get stuck in familiar patterns of seeing the world. Poetry unsticks us. From the experience of the religion scholars gathered, it is so clear, so striking, that something like a "transcendent impulse" is operating. This is the impulse that tells us that description is insufficient on its own. This is transcendence in its most recognizable form. Transcendence is a mode at work in the Western imaginary more broadly, Rivera reminds us. It is theologically rendered but not exclusive to theology. It manifests as a sense that something more needs to be infused into the description to give it meaning. Instead, the writing exercise demands that we get rid of all of that, that we relinquish it. The authorization cannot come from outside. Instead, the exercises loosen the hold of longstanding assumptions, but they also open us to different ways of configuring life. The practice of writing can deepen attunement to the textures of life, awakening perception and wresting us from familiar grooves of thought.

Witnessing Trauma

The writing exercises suggest that exercising a posture toward life might precede any precise definitions of it. Poetics provides containers for framing that allow for the expressions of life and attest to the significance of the senses; the forms allow breathing room while also working toward precision. "Poetics seeks not so much to argue as to refigure, to reimagine and refashion the world," Chopp writes.[27] The writing exercises offer touchstones for thinking about the importance of form and how poetics might operate in witnessing to trauma.

Literary scholars responding to the phenomenon of trauma question its impact on the reading and writing of literature. Literatures of survival, testimony, and witness call into question the ability of language to refer to the real. One group of literary scholars believes that literature must rethink itself in light of the rupture of experience in trauma. Trauma "brings us to the limits of our understanding" and invites us to rethink experience itself.[28] This is not just a challenge that relates to content but to literary form and to practices of reading, writing, and interpreting literature. Aligning deconstructive readings of literary texts with clinical insights from Holocaust survivors, they represent what is now commonly identified as trauma theory.[29]

Cathy Caruth, one of the most prominent figures associated with this wave of scholarship, resists identification as a trauma theorist. This insistence addresses some of the misapplications of her "theory," but also mirrors a concern expressed here: that the theory becomes a whole enterprise unto itself that takes away from the testimonies. Instead, she insists that she is primarily a reader of texts. What concerns her is that trauma theory becomes a method imposed or imported into readings of particular literary texts and thus ceases to make what is its central contribution: to read texts for how they witness to the gaps in experience. Texts carry histories of suffering. And texts can also, through exercises of reading and writing, bear witness to those histories.

Read alongside Chopp's assessment of theology, Caruth shares concerns that theorizing can violate testimonies. One point of resonance between theology and this strain of trauma theory is what Chopp refers to as the "moral summons" coming from the site of testimony: "Testimony invokes a moral claim; it is from someone to someone about something. A decision is called for, a change in reality is required."[30] This summons is bound up in a relationship to life, and Chopp speaks of it as a reverence for life, a sanctification of it. Caruth envisions something similar to this through the literary example of Tancred and Clorinda that Freud invoked in *Beyond the Pleasure Principle*.[31] The voice, the summons from the slashed tree, is a site of debate within trauma studies, but this summons to receive, to hear, is also what makes Caruth's reflections on trauma so influential, its impact so broad. The structure of trauma as constituted by rupture, belatedness, and the awakening to what was not fully known, has implications for how we think about history, experience, and language. Traumatic experiences, when "theorized," are carried out of a very particular discourse of victim and perpetrator. It is precisely on those grounds that Caruth's work is critiqued.

Geoffrey Hartmann noted that it is the ethical intensity displayed in these readings (by Caruth, Johnson, Felman, and so on) that gives literary studies renewed purpose.[32] And yet his words of caution forecast its mixed reception. This movement of scholarship has urgency and purpose to it, calling literature out of its academic hiding place to speak about the relationship between language, history, and suffering. He notes its charged language. It raises questions about the ubiquity of trauma and whether histories of trauma can be thought together. With its wide reach and textual fervor, Hartmann detected what we might call a "theological impulse" within these readings.[33]

Trauma theory emphasizes the impossibility of speech and the collapse of representation. It underscores the negative and refused modes of reading forward, of futurity, and of promise. This, in turn, challenges religious scholars to rethink the ways in which religious logics have supported, even undergirded, such modes. Insofar as theology provides an undergirding logic for such "promissory" readings and a trajectory of life overcoming death, it often fails to attest to a more complex process of living beyond trauma.[34] The presentation of life on the other side of death, triumphantly rather than traumatically inflected, is not only incongruous with the experience of living beyond trauma; it feeds a transcendent imperative to "get over" or "get beyond" the experience.

Resisting transcendence in this familiar mode, theology attests to other ways of conceiving the relationship between death and life. The "new knowing" that arises from trauma takes the form of a language of life arising out of death. And yet, as Moltmann notes, those deaths are "continually present to us."[35] They are not overcome but, instead, live on. This Moltmanian testimony seeks an accompanying theological claim about the persistence of death in life. While it is often too messy for the courtroom, it resides in the stories of sacred scriptures or in the practices of midrash that present "life" in this more precarious state. The question of whether and where life can be found amidst the dry bones and the valley of death is posed to the prophet Ezekiel: Can these bones live?[36] Ezekiel is asked to summon the *ruah* (spirit) from the four winds. This summons calls forth life, but its form is undetermined. Life is a question posed to Ezekiel and to readers. It is posed as a question from the site of death.

Chopp's proposal to reposition theory in respect to testimonies and to develop alternative conceptions of transcendence features a different dimension of theology that bumps up against more recognizable modes of theology, as witnessed in the comments about theology's demise. The central nerve point in theology about whether experience can be authoritative and revelatory grounds for theological claims surfaces, and it is significant that Chopp does not evade it. She is aware of how the division of transcendence and immanence plays out in the modern theological courtroom. Rooting authority in experience is suspect, subjective, and messy. It requires negotiation rather than verdict. And, not surprisingly, she turns to a theology of the Spirit in order to ground the authority of such testimonies. The key, however, is to refuse to interpret God's Spirit and the human spirit along the fault lines of transcendence and immanence. As one responds to Chopp's invitation, it is tempting to simply locate "God" or "Spirit" within the testimonies. To make the experience, the testimony, authoritative (in and of itself), runs the danger of "sacralizing" testimonies. While this is a reversal of the courtroom, more is needed.

Altered ways of conceiving of transcendence insist on interpreting transcendence within, rather than apart from, the material. Transcendence is reimagined close to the surface of the skin, through a sharpened attunement the senses of touch, taste, and smell. The power of transcendence is reflected in the ways in which life is sustained and reanimated in the midst of the complexities of life, in its exigencies. Moltmann's testimony is theological insofar as it connects to longstanding discourses that receive the question of life again and again as *what is neither fully exhausted in thought nor fully realized in the visible expressions of it.* Put words to that, the poet instructs. Give it shape.

Trauma studies has revived modes of spirit that theology knows but perhaps has forgotten.[37] By capitulating to the seductions of modern transcendence, theology presumes to claim truth rather than to quest(ion) it. The discourse around witnessing trauma emphasizes the posture of "not knowing" and the counterpoint of reception as participation in the creation of new knowledge.[38] While this "not knowing" has been the subject of critique within trauma studies, the dynamics of witness evoke aspects of religious traditions that speak about the disclosure of truth and the unknown making itself known. The doctrine of revelation, an organizing category within theology, directs theological attention to truth as the disclosure of what is unknown. Yet when revelation is thought alongside the language of life as departure, as continuation, it turns back to traditions to think about death as the site of emergence. Discussions about revelation fall within the purview of "theological theologians" and this longstanding discourse about how truth discloses itself may contribute to discussions about what constitutes witness in trauma.

In her newest work, Cathy Caruth asks, "What is the nature of a life that continues beyond trauma?"[39] The turn to rethinking "life" through trauma comes at a time when life is no longer considered to be a stable or universally applicable category. The summons to sanctify and revere life assumes that theologians need merely to appeal to life. But life, operating as a negotiated term, is in need of definition.[40] In its depiction of survival, trauma theory in its various iterations, gestures toward conceptions of life that emphasize its precarity, in Judith Butler's terms, and also its radical connectivity (non-singularity).[41] The challenge is to transpose the supernaturalism of transcendence into discourses that argue for life even as it is passing away. Perhaps this is the "theological impulse" that trauma theory shares.

Conclusion

Theologians have stopped speaking about God. That is the charge laid out, and the instructions are clear: Go back to a recognizable form of theological writing and speaking! This return is presented as faithful theologizing. But perhaps theology *is* attending to its subject matter in modes that do not register outside a certain zone of authorization. To inhabit different forms and to reclaim their authorial power from the site of testimony constitute a "theo-poetics of testimony."

Writing about God might be done more effectively by writing just before the name and the concept. This does not mean that God is written out of it. Instead, God is there without being named as such. Instead, divinity is inscribed in the observations and in the attunement to what one smells, tastes, hears, and touches. This poetic instruction is present in the writings of fifth-century philosopher and Christian theologian, Pseudo-Dionysius, who provides a meditation on *how* to name what is outside of human grasp. Divine naming is not a straightforward business, he says; it is the pause before and after the name that is the fine balance of the doxo-logical. But it is Pseudo-Dionysius's lists of objects employed in the naming exercises that is often ignored—sun, star, fire, water.[42] These are the observable things. Write that, the poet whispers to us, as she leans in. Tell us more about those things, and trust that the subject matter is there. Write what you can touch. This, Jordan reminds us, is why theologians need to turn to practices of writing, not to put words on what is known, but to revivify life through the promiscuity of forms.

Theodicy has been the most recognizable modern form of theological engagement with suffering. Theodicy follows the form of argument, or defense, of the nature of God and God's control. But this exercise of making sense of suffering by defending the transcendence of God aligns with the concept of transcendence ascribed to life beyond death instead of life in the midst of it. It defends God's sovereignty and can serve, as Wendy Farley has argued in *Tragic Vision and Divine Compassion*, as a cool rationale for suffering, a theological justification of God's character but a character that lacks the capacity for relationship.[43]

Poetics, according to Chopp, is a "discursive practice" of imagining the world differently and how we can live together in it.[44] But perhaps this requires releasing what is known through simple practices of writing less and trusting that the words carry. One of the modes of poetics is release.

It is tempting to make theopoetics an arena of theology that has its own distinctive subject matter. And yet it is the writing exercises conducted by the poet that instructs us otherwise. Do not make it something more. Instead, let it stand as a mode of refusing explanation for the sake of observation. Perhaps what "theo-poets" do is observe the world by exercising a poetic mode of release, of writing just prior to the main subject, the event, the assigned topic, but also enacting the courage to write less and to focus, instead, on leaving room for the reader, the listener, to pause. Instead of being concerned with offering a full explanation, the criteria will be, in Jordan's words, whether or not they are able to stir desire for an alternative way of perceiving the world and whether their words facilitate such a transformation. The theo-poet holds a space without predetermining what happens there. In hopes that suffering will not go unheld, untouched.

NOTES

1. Protestant theologian Karl Barth was referring to a particular moment that forced him to rethink the nature of theology. Clifford Green notes that Barth's experience of witnessing his theological teachers sign onto the war policy of Kaiser Wilhelm II prompted a radical turn in Barth's theology. Green writes: "Disillusioned with the ruling theology, the question was how to speak of God," 16. Karl Barth, *Theologian of Freedom*, ed. Clifford Green, *The Making of Modern Theology* series (Minneapolis: Fortress Press, 1989).

2. Charles Curran, "Where Have All the Dominant Theologians Gone?," *National Catholic Reporter* 41, no. 14 (February 4, 2005): 16.

3. Martin Marty, "Under Many Influences," *Sightings*, February 14, 2005, https://divinity.uchicago.edu/sightings/under-many-influences-%E2%80%94-martin-e-marty.

4. Marty, "Under Many Influences."

5. Jürgen Moltmann, *The Spirit of Life: A Universal Affirmation* (Minneapolis: Fortress Press, 1992), 20.

6. Moltmann, *The Spirit of Life*, 20–21.

7. The essay is based on a talk that Chopp gave at Emory Law School in 1997. It was subsequently published in a *University of Chicago* journal, and then revised for an edited volume. Rebecca Chopp, "Theology and the Poetics of Testimony," *Criterion* (Winter 1998); *Converging on Culture: Contemporary Theologians in Dialogue with Cultural Analysis and Criticism*, ed. Sheila Davaney, Delwin Brown, and Kathryn Tanner (Oxford: Oxford University Press, 2001). Citations are taken from this edited volume.

8. Chopp, *Converging on Culture*, 56.

9. For an introduction to theopoetics, see Callid Keefe-Perry, *Way to Water: A Theopoetics Primer* (Portland, Ore.: Cascade Books, 2014).

10. Chopp, *Converging on Culture*, 60.

11. Chopp, *Converging on Culture*, 60–61.

12. Chopp, *Converging on Culture*, 57.

13. Chopp, *Converging on Culture*, 65.

14. Chopp, *Converging on Culture*, 62.

15. Mayra Rivera, *Touch of Transcendence: A Postcolonial Theology of God* (Minneapolis: Fortress Press, 2007), 5.

16. Chopp, *Converging on Culture*, 66.

17. Chopp, *Converging on Culture*, 58.

18. Mark D. Jordan, *Telling Truths in Church: Scandal, Flesh, and Christian Speech.* (Boston: Beacon Press, 2004), 100.

19. Jordan, *Telling Truths in Church*, 101. Jordan writes, "Particular forms are required for particular truths."

20. Jordan takes his readers through an exercise. Note the tone: "Imagine Christian theology as a literature of the crucified God soaked in the tears of Mary Magdalene—I mean, soaked in the tears of those who have gone looking for his missing body (John 20:11–18) [. . .]. As if I had ignored the warning signs posted along the borders separating theology from 'mere literature,'" 93. Mark D. Jordan, "Writing-Terrors: A Dialectical Lyric," *Modern Theology* 30, no. 3 (July 2014), 89–104.

21. Gene Demby, "The Birth of a New Civil Rights Movement," *Politic Magazine*, December 31, 2014, http://www.politico.com/magazine/story/2014/12/ferguson-new-civil-rights-movement-113906.

22. Chopp, *Converging on Culture*, 68.

23. Allen Ginsberg, "Footnote to Howl," http://www.poetryfoundation.org/poems-and-poets/poems/detail/54163.

24. See Richard Wilbur's, "Love Calls Us to the Things of the World," http://www.poetryfoundation.org/poems-and-poets/poems/detail/43048.

25. Simone Weil, "Reflection on the Right Use of School Studies with a View to the Love of God," *Simone Weil Reader* (New York: McKay, 1977).

26. Scholars have connected her concept of affliction to trauma. In her essay, "Human Personality," she describes the condition of affliction by appealing to the imagination of someone whose cry, if voiced, cannot be heard. "His cry is mute," *Simone Weil Reader*, 333.

27. Chopp, *Converging on Culture*, 61.

28. Cathy Caruth, *Trauma: Explorations in Memory* (Baltimore: Johns Hopkins University Press, 1995), 4.

29. A collection of essays that engages this theory, both positively and negatively, is: *The Future of Trauma Theory: Contemporary Literary and Cultural Criticism*, ed. Gert Buelens, Sam Durrant, and Robert Eaglestone (New York: Routledge, 2013).

30. Chopp, *Converging on Culture*, 63.

31. Cathy Caruth, "Introduction: The Wound and the Voice," in *Unclaimed Experience: Trauma, Narrative, and History* (Baltimore: Johns Hopkins University Press, 1996).

32. Geoffrey Hartman, "Reading, Trauma, Pedagogy," in *The Geoffrey Hartman Reader*, ed. Geoffrey Hartman and Daniel T. O'Hara (Edinburgh: Edinburgh University Press, 2004).

33. The theological represents, here, an underlying impulse toward normativity, universals, and metaphysics.

34. In relation to Christian theology, I made this case in *Spirit and Trauma: A Theology of Remaining* (Louisville, Ky.: Westminster John Knox Press, 2010). Sharon Betcher and Flora Keskgegian present similar concerns about Christian triumphalism with respect to trauma. Sharon Betcher, *Spirit and the Politics of Disablement* (Minneapolis: Fortress Press, 2007); Flora Keskgegian, *Time for Hope: Practices of Living in Today's World* (New York: Continuum, 2006).

35. Moltmann, *The Spirit of Life*, 20.

36. Ezekial 37: 1–11.

37. For more on the notion of haunting and ghosting with respect to trauma, see Toni Morrison, *Beloved* (New York: Alfred A. Knopf, 1987); Avery Gordon, *Ghostly Matters: Haunting and the Sociological Imagination* (Minneapolis: University of Minnesota Press, 2008). With respect to deconstructive thought, see Jacques Derrida, *Specters of Marx: The State of Debt, the Work of Mourning and the New International*, trans. Peggy Kamuf (New York: Routledge, 1994).

38. Shoshana Felman and Dori Laub, *Testimony: Crisis of Witnessing in Literature, Psychoanalysis, and History* (New York: Routledge, 1992). In "Bearing Witness, or the Vicissitudes of Listening," Dori Laub writes, "The emergence of the narrative which is being listened to—and heard—is, therefore, the process and the place wherein the cognizance, the 'knowing' of the event

is given birth to. The listener, therefore, is a party to the creation of knowl-edge *de novo*," 57. I am aware of the critiques of witnessing, represented in the work of Thomas Trezise, *Witnessing Witnessing: On the Reception of Holocaust Survivor Testimony*, (New York: Fordham University Press, 2013). One of his most strident critiques is the assumption of the unspeakability of testimony. See especially, pages 16–18. Even if there is not a full "unknowing," Laub's invitation to conceive of listening/witnessing as a participation in the cre-ation of something new is not foreclosed.

39. Cathy Caruth, *Literature in the Ashes of History* (Baltimore: Johns Hop-kins University Press, 2013), 7. She speaks of this in terms of a language of parting that comes from within the life drive. It is a different form of witness that is evident in the child's play of *fort/da*, which is not simply a language of the absent mother but a creative act. "To this extent, the question of creativ-ity—as a creativity arising in the context of trauma—is bound up with the question of truth," 96n13.

40. The term "biopower" is associated with the thinking of Michel Foucault, and scholars have developed it in respect to analyses of the political control that sovereign states wield over basic operations of human life.

41. Judith Butler, *Precarious Life: The Powers of Mourning and Violence* (New York: Verso Books, 2006); Veena Das, *Life and Words: Violence and the Descent into the Ordinary* (Berkeley: University of California Press, 2007).

42. Pseudo-Dionysius, "The Divine Names," in *Pseudo-Dionysius: The Complete Works*, trans. Colm Luibheid (New York: Paulist Press, 1987), 56.

43. Wendy Farley, *Tragic Vision and Divine Compassion: A Contemporary Theodicy* (Minneapolis: Fortress Press, 1990), 23.

44. Chopp, *Converging on Culture*, 57.

CHAPTER II

Body-Wise: Re-Fleshing Christian Spiritual Practice in Trauma's Wake

Marcia Mount Shoop

To what extent does it make sense to conclude that
the traumatized view of the world conveys a wisdom
that ought to be heard in its own terms?

—KAI ERIKSON[1]

Bodies Re-Member

As a constructive feminist theologian who is engaged in both academic and ecclesial conversations around the body, I often find myself cast in a liminal space between scientific acceptability and confessional orthodoxy. Both extremes can have little time or place for hybridized embodied theologies. My engagement with trauma only complicates the task of categorizing my constructive embodiment theologies. I encounter fear (and even loathing) at either side of the continuum: too personal/confessional (read Incarnational) for the scientists and too cross-contaminated for the systematic theologians.

At the same time, when one is engaging the amorphous and bewildering realities of trauma, this diffuseness of identity and categorization seems proper to the nature of the subject matter. The pressing question for this volume rests in this dynamic of ambivalence around the connection between real bodies and the theological task. What are the limits and prospects of theology, both methodologically and constructively, for engaging the embodied realities of trauma?

One obvious limitation manifests itself in the habits and dispositions of intellectual conversation itself. For us to hold space for bodies in the philosophical enterprise, we need habituations that emerge from the limits of cognition as well as those that engage bodies in their most primal created nature. To that end, I will take the unorthodox step of asking you, the reader, to invite your body into your engagement with this chapter. Take a deep breath—a really deep breath. Notice how you are sitting and give your lungs the most room you can to fill and empty. Sitting up straight can help. Let the breath come in through your nose and out through your mouth. Take three more breaths just like that: in through your nose and out through your mouth. When you inhale, feel your belly expand. When you exhale, take a few seconds to really let all the stale air out of your body.

In this simple step you took before digging into this chapter you have created a more hospitable environment in your body for many good things —relaxation, openness, calm, clarity, creativity, and connection. The efficacy of deep, intentional, attentive breathing is, you may be relieved to know, a fact proven by science and not just an anecdotally derived suggestion by a theologian interested in embodiment like me.

That science-centric ethos created by the confidence the Western world puts in the "proven" realities of embodied existence, as told to us by biology, psychology, and other quantifiable sciences, has helped to slowly erode the role of theology in both the academic conversation of the human condition and in the Christian spiritual practices of attending to human bodies, especially bodies who have been harmed. To be fair, the guild of theology played our part in that erosion. Some theologians pushed (and continue to push) science away, fearing perhaps that engagement with the hard sciences would somehow lead to the eventual erasure of God, and, *ipso facto*, of the theological task itself. Others have held tight to an obsolete dominant narrative around ontology that made many intellectuals see theology as an antique of patriarchy's hay day in Western intellectual culture. Theology must find its way to a clearer understanding of its own reason for being in the academy. Its unique capacity to engage trauma's complexity is an opportunity for that clarity to surface.

The Theological Task

Exploring the methodology and constructive limits and possibilities of theology's engagement with trauma must first gesture toward the ambivalence Western theology has had around engaging bodies themselves, traumatized or not. What is it that frightens theology about the complexity of our embodied condition, especially as this condition shows itself in trauma? Is it the harsh truths of suffering, death, and decay that are laid bare in trauma that scare Christian practitioners? This would seem an ironic twist for a faith tradition that so confidently boasts a savior who took away death's sting. Is it the potential chaos of passion or desire that scares us? The puritanical streak that runs through Western Christianity has helped to create a culture of loathing around our flesh and blood existence to be sure. But I doubt it is such moralism around bodies that is holding theology back when it comes to trauma. Perhaps it is not wanting to truly take in the danger that we can be harmed and that we can do harm with these bodies of ours. The violent capacity that we all carry is a chilling reality. And some bodies carry this truth with more brutality than others. And certain kinds of bodies carry the bulk of the weight of our vulnerability to violence. Both of these realities are, indeed, hard to look at straight on and clear eyed, especially when the still-lingering assumptions of white-male-able-bodied-heterosexual normativity continue to whisper in our theological ears.

For some, theology's most robust expression comes in the form of systems fitting together through doctrine and the loci of theological concern (God, human condition, creation, and so on). Theology becomes a tight circle of argumentation that answers its own questions about the ultimate nature of all things. For others, theology is not an exercise of our doctrinal muscle, but the provisional expression of that which cannot be totally described. In either its systematic or constructive iterations, theology is about mystery and transcendence. It engages the ineffable and seeks to gesture toward Divinity's unnamable and proximate character.

Theology is tasked with describing the contours of redemption—this loci of the theological lexicon would seem to demand nimble and responsive methodologies so that we theologians can "know it when we see it" and describe it from there. Psychology and legal theories engage trauma with fencing material—how to herd it into discernible, diagnosable, and provable markers. Theology's task is more descriptive and phenomenological. This *raison d'être* makes theology tailor-made for engaging trauma. And yet, the theological practices spawned by theology's own Western canon continue to circle mostly around some apparently normative experience of sin and selfishness that afflicts all of humanity. Theological systems still tend to offer a one-size-fits-all solution to a suggested monolithic human condition of sin—redemption through the saving death of Jesus Christ. This sin-guilt-forgiveness cycle can actually serve to retraumatize many who seek a framework for healing from trauma in the Christian faith.[2]

And so, this one-size-fits-all theological calculus to heal what ails humanity stands up poorly to the challenges trauma carries with it.

Embodied Trauma and Theological Method

I came into my own as a theologian through the portal of tragedy, of loss that could not be redeemed. And my borning cry as a theologian came when I found a way to name the inadequacy of Christian theology's linchpin of the human condition, sin, in response to my own experience of sexual violence. My experience has taught me that sexual trauma shatters any sense of safety a person used to feel. The shattered pieces penetrate the deepest parts of who we are. We are not safe in life's most intimate spaces; we are not safe in our own bodies. The truth is that trauma lifts a veil on something that is true about our condition as sentient beings—on some level we are always in peril.

Theology's job, after all, is not to diagnose, but to describe humanity's situation in rich and thick ways; not to fix, but to elicit a spark of recognition; not to pathologize, but to draw a person closer to something he/she/they can trust about who we are within a transcendent framework of meaning. If Christian theology and spiritual practice do not open themselves up to the wisdom that trauma offers us about bodies, about suffering, and about healing, then theology will have just thrown away one of its most compelling invitations to "do its thing" that exists in our world today. This theological opportunity in-forms a theological anthropology that begins in the potency of tragic suffering and has the capacity to richly describe the embodied character of redemption.[3]

Theology's methodology is called to pay attention; trauma does not allow itself to be ignored. It demands attention.[4] My own trauma in-forms my theological method. And this methodological approach is tangled up with my own unresolvable vulnerability. It is tethered to the violence of a dangerous world, a world that knows no boundaries when it comes to annihilating our innocence.[5] Much of my constructive theological work and practice has been improvisational—and deeply contextual. There are some approaches that seem to resonate across situations, but mostly embodied spiritual practice must be response-able and attentive to both the subtleties and concreteness of trauma. I have drawn from resources across disciplines, traditions, and experiences searching for body-attentiveness and the capacity to respond in ways that dignify bodies, in ways that are trustworthy.

Far from creating a way to contain trauma, theology unveils truths of our vulnerability. And Christian theology boldly claims that God, an incarnate

suffering God no less, meets us there. Christian theology's unique asset is
that suffering surfaces the true nature of God's power and love. Suffering
is not about the absence of God. Suffering is not God's punishment. It an
emblem of humanity's profound need for that which an incarnate God has
to offer. Theology does not generate safety in the face of trauma, but it can
trace the contours of life's hope of finding its stride again in trauma's wake.
Suffering does not signal God's absence, but God's choice to be "very present" with a redemptive capacity. Theology brings with it more than diagnostic tools, it brings clues about a power that seeks healing in our very
cells. This healing capacity and possibility of an Incarnational God is the
core of my constructive theological anthropology.

In order to stay connected to sentience, I learned to seek out connections that awakened the cellular connections that exist between me and
all else that exists. Doing theology is impossible for me otherwise. I must
begin with bodies and with how my own body is idiosyncratically tangled
up with all other bodies in order to find a lifeline of meaning, of hope, of
connection in this reality. The intellectualization of trauma is inadequate
to the task of addressing its true nature and fails when sought as the sole
means of healing. The created world, the sentient world, is a golden thread
of both survival and regeneration. Animals have been some of my most life-
giving, life-saving teachers and have showed me some of the subtleties that
my work as a theologian now embodies around trauma. All animals have
their ways of making a life in the midst of the constant threat of peril. All
are vulnerable with uniqueness and with shared aspiration for survival.

My life in proximity to several different kinds of animals has been theologically generative in terms of substantive embodied habituations that are
redemptive in their capacity. Even though they are the biggest of the animals I care for, my horses are the most fearful of these creatures.[6] Horses
are habitually fearful—everything is something that could potentially do
them harm, from a plastic bag blowing in the wind to a coyote hiding in
the brush in the woods. Connecting with a horse is about building trust
and cultivating confidence in these huge creatures that they are able to trust
you, they are able to trust the space, they are able to trust this moment.
But even with all the trust and training you can give a horse, there remains
the vigilance of awareness that there always lurks "out there" a trigger
that signals the activation of survival mode. For horses this is flight—they
run, fast.

Horses are intuitive enough to learn how to simultaneously trust and
remain vigilant. They are herd animals and so community brings with it
comfort enough to graze. They are prey animals and so they watch, liter-

ally out of the corner of their eyes. Horses' eyes are physiologically situated for this kind of vigilance. My horses embody an honesty I need. They show me everyday how lack of safety and life-giving trust can coexist. And cultivating trust is an embodied practice constructed from breath, body language, and a deep connection that horses intrinsically have with everything around it. Their attentiveness is at work whether we acknowledge it or not. In order to acknowledge it we must sink down into a non-cognitive mode of connection. Life is richer when there are more sources of trust, more layers of connection to cultivate. And this survival aspiration, this metrics of trust and fear are knit together with identity and context.

When it comes to theology and the sciences engaged in trauma, pathologizing embodied ways of living out of trauma can also create the illusion that somehow there is a way to steal ourselves from the vulnerability that characterizes all sentient life. This pathologizing of trauma is the heart of psychological diagnosis and practice. Bodies who are "outside the range" of normativity in white male patriarchy are, in our very selves and in our very vulnerability exacerbated by the culture itself, the irritants that disrupt "white male able-bodied, educated, Christian men."[7] For us, trauma is normal and it happens in our homes, in our bedrooms, in our most familiar relationships. The "constant threat of trauma" for certain bodies is "continuing background noise rather than an unusual event."[8]

The assumption that we should be able to secure the assurance of safety is a construct of privilege and power. My whiteness and my resources give me ways to create the assumption of safety. My privilege gives me pathways to better odds when it comes to certain hazards. And my whiteness gives me another kind of security in some situations even as my femaleness also creates insecurity in some of those same contexts. The more resources and social capital you have, the more complex your safety measures may become. The elusive quest of safety can also morph into norms and institutions and perceptions that that things like walls make us safe, locks make us safe, guns make us safe, and having more and more might, more and more power over makes us safe.

The brutality of trauma retrenches itself again when those who we are told will protect us from harm are the ones who hurt us, the ones we cannot trust. Living with the remains and the repetitiveness of trauma tells me the truth about some things even as it threatens to diminish me with the lies it tells me, too. I am never truly safe, that's true. But it is a lie that I should stop allowing myself to be vulnerable. I am permeable to harm that can be devastating, that is true. But it is a lie that I cannot find vitality in this dangerous world. All intimate connections are risky, that is true. And some are more than others. But it is a lie that I should trust no one. I have intuitions I need to pay attention to about when to feel more open and when to seek ways to protect myself, that is true. But it is a lie that I need to craft a tiny world for myself to be as safe as I can possibly be.

The truth of embodied trauma is that safety evaporates as a familiar sensation, but trust and openness do not have to disappear. They can be cultivated, they can be relearned, but the body must be the primal site of the learning. These are not simply ideas; they are visceral sensations that require cellular address. And theology must grow out of the shared reality in order to engage the human condition. Theological method requires existential engagement with the vulnerability of life, which is not the same thing as human fallenness and sin even as these dynamics may intermingle in how they live and breathe.

When Bodies Matter: Idiosyncrasy and Intricacy

In the work I do with practicing Christians, people often confide in me an almost guilty confession about how much practices such as Yoga, Reiki, massage, healing touch, and other kinds of bodywork feed and heal them. Many are conflicted about what this could mean for their Christian identity and belief. Their conflict rests in some vaguely thematic line of demarcation they believe they are supposed to observe between was is "really Christian" and what might potentially threaten their status as a "true Christian." It is as if practices that allow one to honor and attend to one's body with generosity and with love break with the self-sacrificial norms they associate with the practice of Christianity in such a way that they violate their very status as a Christian. In some cases, practices such as Yoga or Reiki have even been labeled as "dangerous" by their faith communities and a road to a godless, human-centered, self-indulgent "New Age" way of life. The fact that a deep hunger for body connection is pitted against their Christian practice is a profound distortion of Christian theology. The fact that this spiritual conflict is cultivated around Christian practice is even tragic in a faith tradition that comes from an in-the-flesh Deity, and is built from a doctrine of Incarnation.

Jesus was a flesh and bone person, with dusty feet, small intestines, fingernails, and hair follicles. And he entered the world through a birth canal, and was fed at the breast of an ordinary woman with an ordinary body. The physicality of the Christ event is breath-taking, or should I say breath-inducing. And Jesus was a put-his-hands-on-people kind of healer. He also invited us to stay connected with him, to be filled by his presence, and to wake up to who we are with something as carnal as eating bread and drinking wine.

When bodies matter, when bodies have a stake in transcendence, then both practices that engage the body and theorizing that addresses the body are characterized by idiosyncrasy and intricacy. These character traits are surfaced and enfleshed in bodies engaged in body-attentive spiritual practice. Three icons of embodied idiosyncrasy and intricacy help to enflesh the potency and possibilities of body-wise spiritual practice: engagement, epistemology, and encounter. Each icon is reflected and refracted in concrete examples of theological, spiritual, and methodological practices that engage real bodies.

Engagement

In their paper "Meaning, God, and prayer," Kevin Ladd, professor of Psychology at Indiana University, and Daniel McIntosh, professor at University of Denver, explain that traditional prayer postures elicit distinctive physiological effects.[9] For instance, "the bowing of the head results in an increased blood flow to the head. It also causes a shifting of the chin [. . .] that preferences nasal breathing." And nasal breathing cools the air that comes into our system. Cooler air in turn cools the blood supply "elevating the blood oxygen content." These physiological changes, according to Ladd and McIntosh, create conditions for better processing of information and for positive social connection. Ladd and McIntosh conclude that "bodily postures can enhance prayer-related experiences" especially among those who regularly practice these behaviors.

In further research Ladd has done on prayer, he has found that the more our senses and physicality are engaged in prayer the more meaningful the prayer becomes for practitioners. With a grant from the Templeton Foundation, Ladd researches the effects of labyrinth walking on the self-reporting of participants in terms of the meaning and impact of a prayer experience. While walking in a straight line, walking around a room, and walking a labyrinth all produced positive emotional effects for participants, the labyrinth walkers reported about the practice twice as long and with more detail than the participants who walked the other patterns. Ladd's conclusions are that "the body being engaged really does get the spiritual life moving both literally and figuratively."[10] More focused movement tends to engage more of the senses and allows practitioners to be fed "by the process itself, not simply by the outcome of the process."

Sr. Joanna Walsh fcJ, a former spiritual formation leader at Duke Divinity School in Durham, North Caroline, and a member of the Faithful Companions of Jesus, invites students, pastors, nurses, and other believers to "trust touch." She sees in her work how estranged many people are from the power of touch: "We have lost the power of touch as a part of companionship because touch has been associated almost totally with sexuality."[11]

In Sr. Walsh's hand blessing meditations, she invites participants to experience respectful, prayerful touch with the hands of another. Partners both give and receive hand blessings silently, in a time of guided meditation. The challenge is for them to be present and vulnerable, to trust touch and to both give and receive the blessing. In the debriefing sessions that follow the hand blessing practice, Sr. Walsh hears many testimonies of how surprised people are that they were able to touch and be touched in a way that was healing, non-threatening, and respectful. Walsh says, "Many surprise themselves when they are not embarrassed but instead affirmed and comforted. It is an extraordinary experience of the power of personal presence. It is not unusual to see people weeping."

Both Ladd and Walsh attend to how the level of engagement with the body directly correlates with the depth of religious/spiritual experience reported and felt by participants. The more the body is engaged, the more meaningful the experience is. Depth of meaning is reflected in a range of ways including substantive descriptive content about the experience, emotional expression, and an attribution of transcendence to the experience itself.

EPISTEMOLOGY

The efficacy of body-centered practices reveals itself in how Yoga has exploded in popularity. Yoga scratches an itch we have as human beings to be more at home in our bodies, to be integrated in who we are spiritually and physically. True to form, American society has channeled this hunger and popularity into a business opportunity. Yoga is a new reason to buy gear and join a health club. And most churches are allowing this deep, mysterious human need to be met by outsourcing to the market place what Jesus invited us to embrace—the image of God in us, the healing power of Divinity's proximity to us, the both/and way that the Holy Spirit moves and breathes in the world.

Yoga is increasingly being used in mental health research and practice. And the findings are clear. Patients in a study of psychiatric inpatients in a New Hampshire hospital experienced consistent improvements in the five negative emotion factors of the Profile of Mood States (POMS) survey.[12] This particular study indicates that regardless of gender or diagnosis (participants included people with mood disorders such as bipolar disorder and major depression, and psychotic disorders such as schizophrenia as well as other diagnoses), patients consistently reported statistically significant improvements in five areas: tension-anxiety, depression-dejection, anger-hostility, fatigue-inertia, and confusion-bewilderment.

This study shows us in quantifiable terms that Yoga, the integrating of breath and movement, has consistent, palpable healing effects. Other studies have shown that people who do Yoga in the general population also report all kinds of positive benefits. The body is a source of knowledge, an epistemology treasure chest of wisdom that is efficacious in ways that are consistent across many different needs and contexts.

I have seen how such body-derived knowledge and information creates the conditions for beloved community to emerge and the wisdom of embodied regeneration to surface. This is where spiritual embodied practices are born—in the womb of beloved community, where the gestating realities of new life are the single-minded goal of the system. In the lovely symmetry of provision that emerges in beloved community, bodies can show us the way back to ourselves, to each other, and to a wisdom that has legs to move and live in many contexts. In the Wandering Home Retreats that I help lead with Wendy Farley and Maggie Kulyk, the generative capacity of pop-up beloved communities is undeniable.

Wandering Home is a retreat, described to potential participants this way:

> Coming home to a place where we are nourished, where we are understood, known, and accepted is a gift all of us need to experience and yearn to feel. Our "One-ing" with Divinity/Christ/Spirit is the promised sensation of such a homecoming. And yet we live everyday in the midst of estrangement, misunderstanding, hunger, and harm. Sometimes we are left wanting, wounded, and excluded from the very places and spaces that profess to be a place of welcome. Wandering Home is a place to bring your hunger, your vision, your practice, your whole self to encounter and reclaim, indeed to indigenize Christian community and practice in life-giving, home-coming, transforming ways.[13]

While the experience of trauma is nowhere mentioned in the description, many speak openly of trauma they carry. From sexual abuse, to severe illness, to struggles with gender identity and sexuality, to rejection from family and other forms of violence, Wandering Home mysteriously gathers in those who seek trauma healing in some form.

The retreat itself is a practice-oriented experience in which participants engage layers of embodied life. The practices used in the retreat are varied. They span from guided meditations to body prayer to artistic expression with clay, drawing, and collage to intentional wandering to small group work and silence. The body is the focal point and the community is formed around the shared aspiration to have a trustworthy place to be our true selves, wounds and all. The feedback of participants describes how something awakens, a connection is made, and self-understanding and the capacity for healing is enriched. Participants describe Wandering Home as "the strong, joyful, weighty, resilient tapestry/cord of sisterhood," "a wonderful neutral safe space for communal sharing," "very nourishing," "restorative," "refreshing and life-giving." One participant said, "I feel like I'm visible again and I have to go back and make a new way for myself to be fed and to get healthy and to find support and places of joy." Another said, "I found deep unnamed healing."

Re-fleshing Christian spiritual practice means indigenizing stretching, breathing, movement, and other embodied healing modalities to our collective Christian identity. Re-fleshing Christian spiritual practice allows these practices to be the generating force of beloved community. The community itself, in turn, generates embodied healing.

Encounter

Many of these voices, these bodies stretching into a new vitality, are coming from the bodies of the most ravaged among us: victims of violence, veterans of war, survivors of trauma. And the healing promise of our created nature, our embodied condition is emerging from these liminal spaces, these direct encounters with the sharp edges of lives altered by profound violation and harm.

Shelly Rambo, theologian and author of *Spirit and Trauma: A Theology of Remaining*, has found connection around trauma and spirituality with military chaplains. What began as a few military chaplains taking one of her classes at Boston University on trauma has turned into a revolutionary conversation between Rambo and the U.S. Military about how trauma can be addressed by those charged with the spiritual care of soldiers.

Rambo explains that many of the chaplains in her class resonated with questions about "what chaplains bring to the table that is different than clinicians" for veterans suffering from PTSD.[14] Because of the context of crisis these chaplains minister in they resonated with Rambo's exploration of trauma from a theological standpoint. And they began to find ways to name the "disconnect between faith practices and the crises they face."

Some chaplains are, with Rambo's theological partnership, exploring how their spiritual support can address the ravages of embodied trauma in ways that the military medical establishment is either not able or not willing to be. These chaplains are following an intuition that they could have unique capacity to address trauma among soldiers. They are on to something to be sure. Christian spiritual embodied practice can be enriched by what is emerging from these intuitions and responses as well.

In the course of this conversation with the military, Rambo discovered Warriors Journey Home, a "healing circle" ministry with veterans, families of veterans, and civilians who want to support the ministry (called "people of strong heart").[15] The Senior Pastor at the First Congregational Church in Tallmage, Ohio, John Schluep, and the Director of the Red Bird Center in Columbus, Ohio and Native Ceremonial Leader, Shianne Eagleheart (Haudenosaunee-Seneca), built an almost six-year partnership and a healing ministry with circles of people ritually telling their stories and hearing the stories of others who suffer from the ravages of combat. While Ms. Eagleheart is no longer involved in the circle, Pastor Schluep's work with veterans continues.

For several years, Rambo has been in conversation with Schluep, a non-combat veteran who developed a heart for veterans and their deep need for healing. He found that Christianity had little to offer in terms of healing practices. Through his partnership with Eagleheart, these healing circles started in the basement of Schluep's UCC church. With the "earth medicine" of some Native practices, such as smudging, burning sage, and the talking stick, these circles have become ritualized spaces of storytelling, multilayered reconciliation, and deep healing.

Rambo interviewed several participants in the healing circles, and she went through the trainings for those who want to support and participate in this growing ministry. She witnessed and heard about profound healing experiences. Families who were blown apart by PTSD and could find no way back to one another experienced reconciliation through the healing circle. Rambo describes her experiences with these stories and rituals as a "spiritual force of healing and connection that moves through the circle." She says, "These practices tap into a deep spiritual energy" that Mainline Christians don't even expect to feel.

When trauma survivors feel it, many desire to let that power find life in others who suffer. Many participants in the healing circles speak of their desire to help others who suffer from trauma. "War trauma doesn't have to be an ending," Rambo explains. "Instead they are channeling their trauma into a healing space." There is a compassionate connection that finds life through the sensations of embodied healing moments—and these connections seek more and more connection. It is a blessed spiritual gift—like nerve endings coming back to life and seeking renewed connection with the world of sight, sound, smell, and touch.

ENGAGEMENT, EPISTEMOLOGY, AND ENCOUNTER

Christians believe in a God who inhabits flesh. Yet our bodies have been ignored, even reviled, by that same faith tradition. Disembodied faith languishes as integrative practices gather new steam in the larger culture. Even as the institutional church is largely resisting the Incarnational symmetry between embodied practice and Christian identity, there are voices and bodies dancing around the margins of mainline practice who are feeling their way into the healing power of coming home to our Divinely created nature, to ourselves, in the flesh.

The truth is, many Christians may not know if we even believe this kind of healing force and power to be real. We are so estranged from these body-wise possibilities that we wonder if such healing can really be true. Those who live with trauma stand at a precipice where the need for the power of healing is so acute that we are forced into a re-embodied mode of navigation. Trauma elicits a strange and excruciating dance of body destruction and body wisdom. Shattered lives hang in the balance and the shards cut through relationships and communities with a destructive force. Trauma survivors know they need healing, and they know it must seep into deep cellular recesses of harm. And they know healing power when they feel it.

The brutality of violence and betrayal are no strangers to me. And neither is the wonder of regeneration in this always-pregnant world. Navigating safety and vulnerability in this dangerous and fertile world is as immediate to my days as breathing is. With one deep cleansing breath I am at once at ease on the planet and tangled up with unspeakable groans of all that breathes with me. Safety is not what fills me in the potent oxygen of our creaturely condition. It is connection that does. The poetics of dividing cells and shared realities, the meandering eruptions of delight and joy, the solace of affection and fidelity, and the startling tenacity of love stitch their way through the vulnerability that defines sentient life. This is the mystery of Incarnation, and this is where Christian spiritual practice and theology must bring their constructive spirit.

While trauma unveils both the power and the peril of embodied existence, an Incarnational faith points us toward the redemptive possibilities in all of what being flesh, bones, and blood entails. Embracing the transformative possibilities of Christianity means exploring this barren place in ourselves—where we long for connection and vitality, and where we are uncomfortable in our own skin.

Trauma surfaces the truth of our created nature; the needs and power of the body become undeniable. They will not be silenced. Those of us who have embodied trauma come to the edge of our cognition repeatedly in the tenacity of how our bodies hold memory, harm, grief, and pain. Giving the body space to breathe and move and connect and lament saves lives. These practices are the pathways back home to ourselves when so much has been lost. The truth that trauma tells us begins with how important body-centered practices are for spiritual life to be robust, life-giving, and transformative.

On Mystery and Ambiguity as Possibility and Discretion

Theology will find its most robust engagement with human life when its net is cast wide in terms of knowledge sources and methodologies. This body attentiveness does not water theology down; it engages it in the realities about which it is its purpose to describe. When bodies matter, theology can't but be engaged in contexts, lived experiences, and mystery. And the ensuing ambiguities may, indeed, continue to generate an outlier identity for theology in academic conversations that gravitate toward the quantifiable. This movement toward the quantifiable metrics of description in religious studies is a concrete limitation for the theological task, but it is not a limitation for theology's very existence. On the contrary, this limitation can help regenerate theological identities. We cannot mask the idiosyncrasies, the mysteries and the ambiguities of our subject matter as theologians. And so we need not apologize for our task or our contribution to the conversation.

Trauma does not bring with it theological limitations that have not always existed for theology, but it does carry with it wisdom for the theological task and method. And it points us toward some important markers of discretion as well as possibility for the work of theology. Theology is a poetics of humanity that has the capacity to engage dissonance, the unresolvable morass of human life, with an imagination that invites notice of a transcendent thread in human communities and connections. Our discretion comes with our willingness to be honest about the impossibility of tidying this all up. Body-wise theology and contextual spiritual practices that attend to bodies could find no other way to be. And casting theology's methodological net wide does not threaten theology's existence. On the contrary, such a wide net dissolves the dualistic biases of Western mentalities around bodies that first privileged and now have side-lined the theological task. In short, such generous engagement with other disciplines and methods allows theology to highlight the unique framework it brings to the conversation: the redemptive capacity of transcendence, and in particular the way a Christological framework infuses bodies themselves with traces of transcendence. This radical and embodied connection between human bodies and the "something more" is the heart of theology's unique identity.

This might be another good time for a deep, cleansing breath that opens you up to connection and a new vitality, and one that empties out the paralyzing tension we can feel with our own created nature, with our unresolvable vulnerability. Opening up to the capacity of bodies to regenerate out of the interdependence, idiosyncrasy, and intricacy of our created nature is a reality that constructive theology has the capacity to name and claim with great potency. The remarkable thing is that in an Incarnational faith we are invited to be present in life's trials and snares fully accompanied by a Divine source of redemption that honors the power of our bodies enough to inhabit one, too. How we indigenize this attentiveness and the practices that emerge takes seeing ourselves body-wise, too.

NOTES

1. Kai Erickson, "Notes on Trauma and Community," in *Trauma: Explorations in Memory*, ed. Cathy Caruth (Baltimore: Johns Hopkins University Press, 1995), 198.

2. Marcia W. Mount Shoop, *Let the Bones Dance: Embodiment and the Body of Christ* (Louisville: Westminster John Knox Press, 2010).

3. Wendy Farley's *Tragic Vision, Divine Compassion: A Contemporary Theodicy* (Louisville: Westminster John Knox Press, 1990) provides a template for this reframing as well as Farley's *The Wounding and Healing of Desire: Weaving Heaven and Earth* (Louisville: Westminster John Knox Press, 2005).

4. Excerpts of the following description of Incarnational theology appeared in "Safety and Vulnerability in a Dangerous and Fertile World: A Meditation on Incarnation," *Feminism and Religion* (blog), January 29, 2015,

http://feminismandreligion.com/2015/01/29/safety-and-vulnerability-in-a-dangerous-and-fertile-world-a-meditation-on-incarnation/.

5. See commentary on tragic bodies in Chapter 3 of Mount Shoop, *Let the Bones Dance*.

6. The power of horses to mediate and generate deep emotional healing is indicated in the growing use of horses in therapeutic modalities. Equine Therapy is a form of experiential therapy that involves interactions between patients and horses. Equine Therapy can be used for many kinds of therapeutic needs, including for trauma survivors, children with sensory issues, anxiety disorders, and particularly those who are on the autism spectrum.

7. Laura S. Brown, "Not Outside the Range: One Feminist Perspective on Psychic Trauma," in *Trauma: Explorations in Memory* (Baltimore: Johns Hopkins University Press, 1995), 101.

8. Brown, "Not Outside the Range," 102–3.

9. Kevin L. Ladd and Daniel N. McIntosh, "Meaning, God, and Prayer: Physical and Metaphysical Aspects of Social Support," *Mental Health, Religion, and Culture* 11, no. 1 (2008).

10. Kevin Ladd, telephone interview with author, May 2012.

11. Joanna Walsh, telephone interview with author, May 2012.

12. Roberta Lavey, Tom Sherman, Kim Mueser, Donna Osborne, Melinda Currier, and Rosemarie Wolfe, "The Effects of Yoga on Mood in Psychiatric Inpatients," *Psychiatric Rehabilitation Journal* 28, no. 4 (2005).

13. "Wandering Home: A Retreat for Women," http://marciamountshoop.com/wh2016/.

14. Shelly Rambo, telephone interview with author, May 2012.

15. For more about Warriors Journey Home, see www.warriorsjourneyhome.org.

CHAPTER 12

Trauma and Theology: Prospects and Limits in Light of the Cross

Hilary Jerome Scarsella

The discipline of Christian theology is itself a response to trauma. Without the traumatic event of Jesus's crucifixion and the rupturing belief that the one who was killed rose again from the grave, Christian theology as we know it would not have come into being. Had Jesus lived into his elder years, died unsensationally, and stayed in the ground, it is historically unlikely that his teachings would have spread with enough speed and might for those who took them up to become eventually known as a distinct and significant group. Even if the life and teachings of this imaginary, uncrucified Jesus were able to cultivate a following, any critical discipline that might have developed from its roots could bear little resemblance to that of the Christian theology we know. For, the very first task of Christian theology as it emerged in the first century CE was to speak into and out from the staggering rupture created by crucifixion and resurrection. The subsequent work of Christian theology as a discipline cannot be separated from that original challenge. To put it another way: Because Christian theology is itself a response to trauma, the investigation of trauma is the starting point of the discipline, not a secondary interest.

The task of this chapter is to discern specific prospects and limits of the study of trauma from within the discipline of Christian theology. In particular, it asks what, if anything, theology has to contribute to the interdisciplinary effort within scholarship in the humanities to comprehend trauma and support the traumatized. Answering this, however, requires attention to a second question: Does the fact that Christian theology is itself a response to a particular series of traumatic events—the crucifixion of Jesus, its repercussions for those who loved him, and the subsequent advent of resurrection—mean that theological disciplines are destined to repeat the trauma of the cross and retraumatize their objects? Or, does the intimacy between Christian theology and traumatic rupture mean that the discipline is poised to offer particularly keen insight into the nature of trauma and into methods of caring with and for the traumatized? Here, the limits of the discipline with respect to the study of trauma will come into focus such that its prospects may be judiciously discerned.

With respect to the second question, I will argue that the centrality of the cross for Christian theology functions in the discipline much the same way as a traumatic event functions in the life of an individual or community. While the fact of the cross is nearly always remembered, its traumatic nature is frequently forgotten in theological memory and narrative. Whenever the trauma of the cross is forgotten, theology is primed to repeat its harm. If, however, the event of crucifixion is theologically remembered and narrated *as traumatic*, the discipline is in a position to speak into and out from the rupture of crucifixion in ways that carry import for contemporary efforts to understand trauma and support those who survive it.

Therefore, to answer this chapter's primary question and discern particular contributions of Christian theology to the wider study of trauma, I turn to womanist, mujerista, and feminist theologians who have led the way in articulating crucifixion as traumatic rupture. These three strands of theological scholarship share commitments to using gender as a primary lens of analysis and producing work that contributes to the liberation and well-being of women and their wider communities, even as they do so differently. Feminist theologians epistemologically privilege the histories, experiences, and liberation of women broadly speaking. Though feminist theologians are now diverse culturally and intellectually, at its twentieth-century inception, feminist theological scholarship privileged white, middle class women in the United States while claiming to be representative of all women. This is a history that continues to mark the discipline even as many feminist theologians now consider it regrettable. Womanist theologians specifically privilege the experiences of black women in the United States. As a result, womanists emphasize the value of survival in addition to liberation and insist that interrogating the intersection of race, class, and gender is crucial to responsible scholarship. Mujerista theologians privilege the experiences of Latina women in the United States and, like womanists, are committed to an intersectional analysis of oppression as well as scholarship that supports the actualization of liberation and well-being for Latina/o communities.

In the anthropological work of womanist, mujerista, and feminist theologians who remember Jesus's crucifixion as traumatic, that which is described as constitutive of personhood has substantive implications for a theological understanding of trauma. Drawn to their conclusions, the anthropological visions painted by such womanist, mujerista, and feminist theologies posit trauma as a devastating yet incomplete undoing or prevention of human personhood in that trauma obstructs relation, abuses vulnerability, and yet fails to wholly eliminate possibility for remaking.[1] The relation of this conceptual claim to Christian theology's prospects for caring with and for those who are traumatized lies in the observation that theology of this sort—that is, theology that remembers and narrates crucifixion as traumatic—both is and cultivates space that constructs, preserves, and models narrative re-membrance of traumatic events in which the reality of catastrophic devastation is acknowledged alongside the possibility of remaking. Precisely because Christian theology is itself a process of giving voice to what has been traumatically silenced, theology can draw individuals and communities of faith who engage it into that process in a way that supports such individuals and communities in bringing their own silenced trauma to voice and pursuing processes of remaking after trauma.

Crucifixion, Trauma, Memory

The centrality of the crucifixion event for the development of Christian theology has been a propellant for devastating systems of violence and oppression. One need only bring to mind images of the medieval European Crusades to be convinced of the theological connection forged between the symbol of the cross, Christian triumphalism, and divinely ordained, rampant slaughter. The distinctively blocky, red cross of St. George (warrior saint) marked crusaders' coats of arms and flew high on military flags as a sign that the dominating mission of the crusaders was willed by God. Indeed, to join a crusade was to take up one's cross in obedience to Christ.[2] Attached to the armor of those bent on violently seizing land, power, and dignity from the religious other, the cross operated as a mark that justified, and therefore encouraged, all manner of terrorizing destruction.

Contemporary iterations of empire and religious intolerance are, at least in part, fueled by the centrality of crucifixion to Christian theology as well. The wars waged by the United States in the Middle East in recent decades are widely supported in the United States by a Christian theological paradigm that views U.S. Americans as God's chosen people, Muslims as an inherent threat to the reign of God, and unbridled violence as the means by which God's chosen people ought to give God glory. Similarly to the crusade mentality, demonstrating the dominance of the United States is, in this paradigm, demonstrating the power and superiority of the Christian, crucified God.

Within the United States, the image of a burning cross speaks with a clarity beyond words. The cross has been appropriated by the KKK so successfully that in their hands it functions now as a tool of terror. Analyzing the success of this appropriation, systematic theologian Stephen Ray observes, "For a given symbol to exist with some power in a given context there must be a necessary matrix of ideas and cultural assumptions in which that symbol can be made sensible."[3] While the majority of contemporary Christian theologians do not support readings of the cross that explicitly link it to the racist, lynching project of the Klan, in order for the cross to have become the symbol of the Klan in the first place the appropriation of theology into culture must have created a matrix of ideas and assumptions in which the cross could be interpreted as promoting racism and murderous executions of innocent African Americans.

These three examples—Crusades, wars waged by the United States in the Middle East, and the Ku Klux Klan—serve to exaggerate a reality that has metastasized and taken up residence throughout Western, and particularly U.S. American, cultures. Because crucifixion has been central to the development of Christian theology, and because Christian theology has been central to the development of Western cultures, the propensity of the cross to exacerbate traumatizing systems permeates Western personal, social, and political existence.

This fact, however, does not exhaust the impact of crucifixion in Christian theology or Western cultures. Christian theology has also been significantly shaped by the event of Jesus's crucifixion in ways that resist unjust violence and oppression. There is strong reason to believe that many of the earliest Christians centered their faith around an insistence on life in response to violent death, on resurrection as the divine answer that must be given to the injustice of crucifixion.[4] In the first century of Christian theological thought, women, the poor, and others largely disempowered were encouraged, at least to some meaningful extent, to come to voice.[5]

In twentieth-century theology in the Americas, both the Christian peace tradition and liberation tradition exhibited theological responses to the cross that sought to interrupt systems of traumatic harm, working instead for justice and well-being. The peace tradition, promoted largely by Anabaptist and Quaker thought and practice, has tended to regard Jesus's crucifixion as an example of God's nonviolent, sacrificial love for humanity that followers of Christ are to emulate. It encourages followers of the crucified Jesus to actively seek out the places of the world characterized by suffering—particularly, traumatic suffering fueled by political conflict—and offer loving solidarity in movements of resistance no matter the personal cost.[6] Because Jesus was willing to suffer on the cross in order to remain steadfastly committed to embodying God's just love for the persecuted and nonviolent resistance to abusive power, the cross reminds Christians of the peace tradition that they, too, are to nonviolently devote their living and dying to solidarity with the oppressed. The cross, then, becomes the center of the nonviolent ethic that organizes Christian peace communities.

The liberation movement, first led by Latin American and African American theologians, reads the cross as a violent act wielded by the hand of empire and intended to silence those beginning to resist oppressive rule. Jesus's willingness to endure violent suffering and execution is seen as an element of Jesus's determined and unwavering commitment to manifesting the love of God for the poor, the weak, and the marginalized. According to liberationists, it is the manifestation of this loving, divine solidarity that makes hope for continued life possible. Black liberation theologian James Cone makes this explicit: "A symbol of death and defeat, God turned it into a sign of liberation and new life. The cross is the most empowering symbol of God's loving solidarity with the 'least of these,' the unwanted in society who suffer daily from great injustices."[7] For Cone, the fact that God in Jesus was willing to take on the flesh of marginalization, act consistently for the cause of liberation, and experience the very worst terror imposed on the oppressed of the world means that those discarded by society are preserved as valuable by God. This solidarity that insists on the value of the oppressed abolishes ultimate despair because, as Latin American liberation theologian Jon Sobrino explains, "love becomes a possibility for this world because it is real,"[8] because love has been made real by Jesus's act of solidarity with the oppressed and all acts of human solidarity modeled on this event.

Memory of a Different Kind

Even as these contemporary movements meaningfully resist systems of traumatic harm and make strides toward empowering survival and well-being, they can be unintentionally retraumatizing as well. We see how when we turn our attention to the context of sexualized violence. Many survivors of this particular form of harm report that the only appropriate responses—the only possible responses—to the story of Jesus's crucifixion are fear, lament, or outrage. For some, the thought of Jesus's crucifixion jolts one into a visceral awareness of all it means for one's body to be dominated and one's existence to be threatened. It is an awareness that comes from beyond the intellect and requires little of the imagination. As is true of all trauma survivors, these survivors have (or, rather, *are*) bodies and psyches and souls that have come into contact with their own violent erasure. The memory, insofar as memory of absence can be called memory at all, is woven through their nervous systems, periodically bringing the traumatic past to life in the present. For many, there is no way to approach the cross without recognizing the anguish of Christ as that which they hold within. There is no way to face the cross without encountering and living the trauma of its violence in the here and now. For some, the cross triggers terror and full-blown retraumatization. For others, it summons deeply felt cries of agony, grief, and resistance.

Contemporary theologians writing about this form of violence have recognized a connection between the cross and the trauma of sexualized violence. Feminist theologian Serene Jones opens her book, *Trauma and Grace*, with a scene in which a woman named Leah, whom we are told was sexually abused by her father and raped by a supposed friend, is traumatically triggered during a communion service. Leah says,

> It happens to me sometimes. I'm listening to the pastor, thinking about God and love, when suddenly I hear or see something, and it's as if a button gets pushed inside of me. In an instant, I'm terrified; I feel like I'm going to die or get hurt very badly. My body tells me to run away, but instead, I just freeze. Last week it was the part about Jesus' blood and body. There was a flash in my head, and I couldn't tell the difference between Jesus and me, and then I saw blood everywhere, broken body parts, and I got so afraid I just disappeared.[9]

As Jones recounts the story, it was the pastor's narration of Jesus's crucifixion that brought forth Leah's traumatic memory of her own harm. Leah became unable to tell the difference between her body and the body of Jesus, and the theologically framed celebration of Jesus's crucifixion in communion became too threatening and overwhelming for Leah to endure.

In their first collaboration, *Proverbs of Ashes*, feminist theologians Rita Nakashima Brock and Rebecca Ann Parker elaborate on the ways that Christian theology in response to the cross poses a threat to women. Opening this discussion in the first chapter, Parker reflects on the role of sacrifice in this system:

> I began trying to understand why the gesture of sacrifice was so easy, so familiar to my body, so related to my sexuality, and so futile. Why did I know so well how to do it? Why did the women I knew as friends, counseled as parishioners, preached to in my congregation, know so well how to do it? I recognized that Christianity had taught me that sacrifice is the way of life. I forgot the neighbor who raped me, but I could see that when theology presents Jesus' death as God's sacrifice of his beloved child for the sake of the world, it teaches that the highest love is sacrifice. To make sacrifice or to be sacrificed is virtuous and redemptive.[10]

Because Christian theology taught Parker to value Jesus's crucifixion, sacrifice became a good in and of itself for her, regardless of whether it interrupted or exacerbated systems of traumatic violence. A theology of the cross need not affirm substitutionary atonement, however, to pose the same danger. Peace and liberation theologies that respond to the cross by 1) expressing gratitude for Jesus's willingness to endure bodily torture, 2) naming this willingness *love*, and 3) exalting this form of sacrificial love as the source of salvation and liberation, have long been challenged by theologians committed to epistemologically privileging the experiences of women[11] on the grounds that such theologies exacerbate systems of sexualized violence even as they work against violence in other forms.

Thus, the traumatic event of Jesus's crucifixion works in the discipline of Christian theology like any significant trauma works in the lives of survivors. When it is forgotten, it repeats. In the Crusades, the American wars in the Middle East, and in the hands of the Klan, while the fact of crucifixion may not have been forgotten, memory of the anguish it inflicted certainly was. When memory of the harm crucifixion caused for Jesus and those who loved him is repressed, it is no surprise that the cross surfaces and functions in the very same way it did when it was used by Rome against Jesus and his community—as a weapon of terror that destroys bodies and reinforces oppression.

The peace and liberation traditions, each in their own way, recognize the cross as horrific, but they remember the site of violent suffering as also productive. It is simultaneously a source of anguish and salvation.[12] In fact, for thinkers such as James Cone, it is because Jesus's crucifixion was so thoroughly fracturing that it also produces hope for liberation. As commonly defined by trauma studies, a trauma is a tear, a break, an emptiness. To make the event of crucifixion productive is to deny, on some level, that it is truly traumatic. Sure enough, through the memory of crucifixion as salvifically productive, the violence of the cross repeats in the lives of women and those vulnerable to sexualized violence, and likely others.

Remembering traumatic events and patterns as the terrorizing, rupturing events and patterns that they were is a necessary prerequisite to processes of remaking in which systems of violence propelled by the repetitions of repressed memory can be transformed. Womanist, mujerista, and feminist theologians have, within the discipline of Christian theology, led the way in recovering memory of crucifixion as traumatic rupture. It is thus this strand of the contemporary discipline of theology that I turn to in order to discern the insight of theology for comprehending trauma, resisting its harm, and supporting those struggling to survive and remake lives worth living. Because trauma is broadly conceived in the humanities as an undoing of selfhood, exploring theological anthropology is an entry point for contemplating trauma vis-à-vis theology.

Theological Anthropology: Womanist, Mujerista, and Feminist Perspectives

I will articulate what I see as four areas that are recognized as fundamental to humanness in contemporary womanist, mujerista, and feminist theologies: interpersonal relation; human-divine relation; the interconnection between freedom, vulnerability, and evil; and, finally, gift as a possibility for new life. While there are substantive differences in the anthropological scholarship of the womanist, mujerista, and feminist theologians I engage, my focus here is on the overlaps of their work that suggest particular ways theological anthropology impacts broader comprehension of trauma and how we know to respond.

Throughout this section, you will see that I prefer to speak of theological anthropology in terms of personhood. This emphasis is substantive and not reflective of a simple preference for one of several, arguably interchangeable, terms (for example, person, self, ego, subjectivity). The Christian theological concept of personhood stretches back to antiquity and informs the ways that contemporary theology thinks the human. John D. Zizioulas, an Orthodox theologian who interrogates this history, remarks,

> *Historically* as well as *existentially* the concept of the person is indissolu-
> bly bound up with theology. [. . .] The person both as a concept and
> as a living reality is purely the product of patristic thought. Without
> this, the deepest meaning of personhood can neither be grasped nor
> justified.[13]

As the doctrine of the Trinity was formulated, each of the three relations within the trinitarian God was ultimately described in terms of personhood: one God, three *persons*. The ancient Church needed a way to talk about the relations within God that refrained from positing them as separate, stand-alone selves and simultaneously maintained their individual uniqueness. It was in patristic thought that the term "person" was gradually transformed from its prior Greek and Roman senses (face, mask, and role) to describe an ontological entity that is simultaneously unique and constituted by rela-tion. The relation constitutive of personhood was, in turn, determined to be rooted in love, specifically, divine love.[14] Zizioulas remarks thusly,

> Outside the communion of [divine] love the person loses its unique-
> ness and becomes a being like other beings, a "thing" without absolute
> "identity" and "name," without a face. Death for a person means ceas-
> ing to love and to be loved, ceasing to be unique and unrepeatable,
> whereas life for the person means the survival of the uniqueness of its
> hypostasis which is affirmed and maintained by love.[15]

Discussing theological anthropology in terms of personhood is, in part, an exercise in intellectual transparency for me as a theologian, while it is at the same time meant to bring attention to the specifically theological dynamics of the anthropologies I engage—the relation between humanity, all parts of the cosmos, and divinity/love. The womanist, mujerista, and feminist theo-logians I converse with here are, in some sense, engaging the ancient con-cept of personhood, renegotiating its meaning for contemporary thought, and articulating its centrality for understanding humanness, which in turn funds theological analysis of that which threatens humanness with rupture.

Interpersonal Relation

It is not enough to say that human beings are relational, that we *have* re-lationships. Rather, we *are* relation. We are particular sets of relation between tissue and bone, between countless living cells, between our bodies and the earth, our bodies and other bodies, between past and present, divinity and creation. As womanist postmodern process theologian Monica Coleman puts it, "We are not discrete selves that can choose whether or not we want to relate to one another."[16] We can only be selves because we are relation. Because human beings are formed by the world and society, and because these are, in turn, formed by human beings, Coleman declares wisely, "There is nothing outside of relationship."[17]

In agreement, feminist process theologian Catherine Keller rejects all modern conceptions of selfhood that idealize independence and mastery. For Keller, humanness as relation ought to be described in terms of both change and continuity. Because the particular state of the relations that constitute us (physical, psychological, social, spiritual, and so on) is different in each new moment, Keller uses the term *self* to refer to the specific dynamics of relation that exist in the present. The self is fluid, changing, and exists newly in each moment. The *person*, then, is a collection (or relation) of selves. The person is none other than the particular process of evolving relations that we recognize as continuous over time.[18]

Wendy Farley, who is not a process theologian, affirms a critique of the common, modern conception of the human being that parallels Keller's. For Farley, we do not begin as independent selves and enter into relationships subsequently. Rather, the human subject is founded on and by obligation to the other. Persons literally come into being only in response to and in relationship with the call of the other.[19] Independent existence is not only doomed but impossible. Mujerista theologian Nancy Pineda-Madrid,[20] womanist theologian Delores Williams,[21] and numerous others motion toward a similar, though less explicit, understanding of humanness as constituted by relation in their emphasis on the degree to which social relations of race, gender, and class inform the matrix in which personhood forms.

Conceptualizing humanness in terms of personhood allows for the recognition of distinct human beings at the same time that it reveals the boundaries that mark that distinction as blurred. Here, theology finds some degree of common ground with strains of psychoanalysis and philosophy that describe subjectivity as the product of processes that negotiate, create and maintain boundaries that separate one subject from another.[22] Theologies that conceptualize humanness in terms of relation think the precarity of such boundaries in terms of its potential to both strengthen and threaten life, depending on a whole variety of social, ethical, and theological conditions. The assertion that relation comprises the core of humanness is often extended by theologians beyond the human to the cosmos and embraced as having a largely positive impact on both human and nonhuman existence even as it poses specific dangers—namely, the traumatic disintegration of subjectivity.[23]

Human-Divine Relation

Theology is unique among other disciplines in asserting one particular relationship as among those that participate in constituting personhood: the relationship between the human and the divine. Serene Jones, who engages trauma studies explicitly, is one of many theological thinkers who emphasize that humanity is accompanied by divinity. In this view, God's promise to be and remain with humanity without interruption is essential for understanding the human condition. For the traumatized, the promise of divine accompaniment means that the Spirit sustaining the life of the world "enters into the depths of their traumatic anguish" and holds the weight of their suffering with them.[24] To be human, then, is to never be alone in suffering. It is to be persistently graced with divine presence and solidarity. Such grace does not erase traumatic wounds or relieve the traumatized from suffering. Rather, it creates the possibility of post-traumatic transformation.

Coleman is among those who go a step further. For her, God is not only *with* us, but "God is *in* us, and we are *in* God."[25] She explains, "We are distinct from God—we are not God ourselves—but we are part of who and what God is, and God is part of who and what we are."[26] The God Coleman describes is one who influences creation, and as God does so, God becomes part of it. God also feels and experiences all that the world is, and in order to do so God takes creation into Godself and is influenced by it. As a result, human personhood involves both human-divine relation and the whole web of relation present within God that connects all persons and all of creation. Through human-divine relation, personhood implies and includes one's interrelation with stardust and light, salmon and maples, iron and gravity. Coleman's conception of the divine relation to humanity, like Jones's, insists that persons do not suffer alone. However, for Coleman, divinity and humanity are entangled, like breath and body. God's promise to be with us takes on an intensely intimate valence. Because God is *in* us and we are *in* God, God is substantively impacted by the suffering of the traumatized, and the traumatized can be likewise impacted by God. This opens up options for thinking and pursing person/al remaking that are not available in non-theological paradigms.

Coleman's description of humanness as radical interconnection reveals that recognizing divinity in the other and caring for others' well-being is necessary for human persons to discover divinity within themselves and achieve their own well-being. It is at this juncture that Coleman's womanist commitments meet her use of process metaphysics. Womanist theology has been a pioneer in recognizing webs of interconnection as central to human experience and personhood. Specifically, womanist theology analyzes the intersecting systems of racism, sexism, and classism that oppress many black women. The claim in process metaphysics that these oppressions arise from disordered relation, together with a womanist emphasis on community as essential to survival and well-being inform and reinforce Coleman's thinking. Her use of womanist theology positions human relation as fundamental not only to personal[27] existence, but to social and political existence as well. Thus, caring with and for the traumatized requires attention to the sociopolitical dimensions of both trauma and processes of person/al remaking.

Freedom, Vulnerability, and Evil

Womanist, mujerista, and feminist Christian theologies often speak of traumatic harm in terms of extreme suffering,[28] concerning themselves primarily with the sort of extreme suffering produced by evil and injustice.[29] Rather than explain evil as an aberration in human life, womanist, mujerista, and feminist Christian theologians tend to consider it a regular part of existence. Evil and injustice characterize the state of the world. Traumatic harm, though potentially shocking to the one who incurs it, is predictable, woven through the fabric of the cosmos, and yet contrary to divine intention. Thus, to be human is to be vulnerable.

Coleman describes evil as a consequence of freedom. Divine power is not omnipotence but the power to persuade, to lure creation toward its best possible future. Farley's understanding of God's power is similar. She conceives of God as the ultimate reality of transformative love (eros), which is definitively not the power of control.[30] For both Coleman and Farley, to be a person is to have the capacity to be persuaded by love, which entails freedom. One cannot be genuinely persuaded if one does not have the freedom to choose otherwise. In this paradigm, evil occurs, partly, when humanity chooses not to be persuaded by the divine lure that beckons toward the good. When evil is seen as a consequence of freedom, it is understood as "part of the world we are born into."[31]

Because all parts of the world are interconnected, when one person uses their freedom to refuse the lure of God/eros/the ultimately real, there are ripples. Persons and whole communities are often prevented from becoming that which God desires for them because of evil that others have created. Coleman represents the positions of many womanist, mujerista, and feminist theologians in saying that when we repeatedly use our freedom without regard for the interconnection of the world, and when we do this within systems of power and influence, we create systemic evils that produce traumatic harm.[32]

Though she does not explicitly invoke the language of *trauma*, Coleman describes what we might call traumatic suffering in terms of the way persons respond to and are impacted by particularly intense experiences of evil. When our feelings become too painful for us to bear, we block them out of our experience. When evil overwhelms us, our ability to feel the beauty around us is destroyed. In order to survive and go on with daily living, Coleman says we push our suffering to back of our consciousness.[33] However, that which is blocked out and unacknowledged continues to influence us. It shapes the way we experience the world, influences the options we have going forward and impacts the choices we make about whether or not to follow the lure of God.

The notion that evil, traumatic suffering is a consequence of human freedom is implicit in Jones's view of the world as one broken by the violence and suffering we inflict upon each other. She conceptualizes trauma in terms of disordered imagination. Imagination, for Jones, "refer[s] to the fact that as human beings we constantly engage the world through organizing stories or habits of mind, which structure our thoughts. Our imagination simply refers to the thought stories that we live with and through which we interpret the world surrounding us."[34] Disordered imagination, then, is characteristic of a person who cannot sustain images and tell stories about themselves and the world that are life giving and encourage flourishing. Disordered imagination, in the form of traumatically intrusive thoughts, memories, and images, is a particular habit of mind that obstructs well-being. For Jones, attention to the nature of traumatically disordered imagination and the kinds of events that give rise to it reveals human personhood as, again, deeply vulnerable. We are vulnerable to being harmed by others, and we are vulnerable to experiencing harm and profound loss within our own bodies and interiors.

Brokenness, injustice, evil, vulnerability—this is the state of the world as Coleman, Farley, and Jones describe it. Because persons are free, evil is possible.[35] Because we are interconnected webs of relation, we are vulnerable. Trauma grows out from the very nature of humanness.

GIFT, POSSIBILITY, NEW LIFE

In a Christian theological paradigm, this, however, is not the end of the story. Into the overwhelming hopelessness of traumatic harm gifts are offered that open new ways toward survival, person/al remaking and flourishing. I use the term "person/al remaking" intentionally. In the theological perspective on trauma I am outlining, *remaking* describes the specific task put to trauma survivors. The relation destroyed by trauma is not recoverable. The process of forging relation in order to reconstruct personhood in the aftermath of trauma is, thus, not a process of recovery but one of creation. It is a process of making something new in the place of that which has been lost.

In womanist, mujerista, and feminist theologies, the gifts given to aid survival, person/al remaking, and flourishing are described differently, but each is divinely given, or put differently: given by the power in the cosmos that enables the possibility of transformation, whatever name we want to give that power. For Jones, the gift is grace. For Farley, it is desire. Salvific presence plays the role of divine gift for Pineda-Madrid. Keller and Coleman describe God's gift to humanity as opportunity. The differences between these ways of conceptualizing God's gifts to humanity are valuable. In each case, however, divine gift reasons that the evil systems of the world that produce traumatic harm will not prevail in permanently destroying life. Being a recipient of such a divine gift is integral to human personhood.

Farley speaks of the gift of God's eros (love, desire) as that which allows for transformation in the wake of evil. Our own desire draws us toward what she calls the ultimately real (God) and allows for an interior remaking of ourselves. When we allow the eros of the ultimately real to draw our own desire into alignment with its own, we are inwardly transformed such that love, in resistance to fear, comes to characterize our ways of being in the world.[36] Insofar as love is a drive toward connection, this process is one that resists the disintegrating force of trauma and works to create possibilities for renewal even when a person has been thoroughly shattered.

Womanist theologians speak powerfully of the divine gift to humanity as that which helps black women to "make a way out of no way," to struggle for survival in the midst of oppression: "'Making a way out of no way' involves God's presentation of unforeseen possibilities; human agency, the goal of justice, survival, and quality of life; and a challenge to the existing order."[37] In Coleman's work, God assists black women in "making a way out of no way" by providing options in the midst of trauma

and systemic oppression that would not otherwise have presented themselves. It is a gift of possibility that allows persons to make choices that are
not wholly determined by the unjust or traumatic circumstances of either
past or present.[38]

Jones means something similar when she speaks of the divine gift to humanity in terms of grace. In her thinking, grace is found in God's insistence
on loving humanity even when we are broken apart. Grace is God's following through on God's promise to be with us in our suffering and never leave
us alone. The grace of God's love and presence is what creates the possibility
for abundant life to be cultivated in the wake of traumatic rupture. It makes
what ought to be impossible possible.[39] Through grace, when our worlds
have been decimated and all is lost, God offers us the possibility of a future.
"From a place beyond, grace comes toward us," and in doing so disrupts
the disordered imagination formed by traumatic memory as it "disturbs us,
traverses our boundaries, and dwells disruptively within us as it gives testimony to the previously unspoken sins/traumas that occupy us."[40] Much like
processes of post-traumatic remaking, the work of grace in us is not always
comfortable. It does, however, open the way toward transformation.

In these womanist, mujerista, and feminist Christian theologies, to
be human is to have the possibility of a future. This does not mean that
the possibility of a future, let alone a future that includes well-being and
person/al remaking, becomes reality for all persons. One look at the world
tells us that it, in fact, does not. That all persons have the *possibility* for a
future does mean that persons who are traumatized have reason to hope,
which is essential in sustaining the struggle for survival, well-being, and
person/al remaking. These womanist, mujerista, and feminist theologians[41]
join the chorus of Christian theological voices in asserting that even when
a person's future on earth is ruined by violence and injustice, the broader
systems of evil in the world that traumatize, as real and devastating as they
are, do not wield totalizing power. Their power is subverted by divine
insistence on life and resurrection as an ultimate response to terror and
crucifixion.

Conceptualizing Trauma

From this brief review, what can we learn about the nature of trauma?
What does Christian theology offer in terms of strategies for resisting
traumatic harm and offering care to those who are traumatized?

It makes a difference to conceptualize trauma as undoing the *person*. The
theological concept of personhood refuses the modern assumption that

there is something independent at one's core, something that can persist on its own even if it is profoundly influenced by and in need of its relationships with others. Conceptualized through the constructive work of the theologians I have engaged, thinking the human as person insists as well that the relation that constitutes us includes human social relation as well as relation between the human and the natural world and between the human and the divine. To speak in terms of personhood is to make the claim that, at our core, we are relation and that the relation that constitutes each individual is both particular and inclusive of all that is. We are not individuals who need relation to maintain ourselves. We are relation organized in particular ways; without it we don't exist. There is, then, no separation between the disintegration of relation and the disintegration of personhood. When trauma undoes one's ability to sustain particular relations, it does not *lead* to the disintegration of the person; it quite literally *is* the disintegration of actual parts of that person. This is an intensification of commonly held understandings of trauma.[42]

In conceptualizing trauma, theology also must take seriously the fact that vulnerability is an integral part of personhood. It is woven through our being as a consequence of both our relational nature and our freedom. Our conception of vulnerability is distorted if we think of it as a source of harm. Without vulnerability, relation and freedom would be impossible because these are mutually constitutive dynamics of personhood. Because we are vulnerable, we are free to create beauty and cultivate bonds of connection that embody and promote love. It is true, however, that vulnerability can be a *site* of harm. Because we are radically interconnected, we are impacted in ways we do not choose. Because all are free, our well-being cannot be secured.

When committed to speaking of vulnerability as a component of personhood, theology cannot conceptualize trauma as a straightforward undoing of personhood. Trauma does not undo, obstruct, or prevent vulnerability. Rather, trauma abuses human vulnerability. Trauma takes this quality of personhood that enables the beauty of freedom and relation and exploits it such that it works against its own purpose. Thus, we are led to think of trauma as an undoing or prevention of particular aspects of personhood and an abuse of others. Through an abuse of human vulnerability, trauma obstructs that which vulnerability cultivates: relation, freedom, love.

The theological perspective I am elaborating affirms alongside other disciplines that trauma is, in fact, rupture, breakage, silence, and utterly destructive.[43] It works against any attempt to trivialize the severity of traumatic harm. At the same time, it is a perspective that claims that resources

for resistance and remaking are as present and real as the event of destruction. For trauma to annihilate personhood, it is not enough for it to tear
apart one's relation to others because the relation of one's present self to
all past selves persists.[44] If this is destroyed, one's relation to the world
through social memory and history persist. If, somehow, this too is de-
molished, the relations of ligaments and bone and flesh that make up one's
body persist, and if even the relations of the body are destroyed, one's relation to the earth as a creature made of the same stuff as grass and clouds
remains. A broken body becomes earth, is transformed into a set of new
relations, and is given new forms of being. I will be the first to admit that
the persistence of some small part of relation when the vast majority has
been destroyed is not at all satisfying. This is not the kind of resistance that
can preserve the lives of the traumatized or guarantee that they will be able
to remake lives worth living post-trauma. It is, nonetheless, resistance. The
world exists in such a way that traumatic harm cannot realize its ultimate
goal. Trauma undeniably shreds a person. It cannot, however, completely
undo that person's bonds of relation. Theologically, this is described as
one manifestation of God's promise to resist evil. It functions as a concrete
reminder of God's promise to respond to crucifixion with resurrection, to
beckon forth life in the face of violent death. It is a reminder for those who
are traumatized that there is reason to hope and resist and struggle toward
survival and well-being. Such a concept is dangerous because in careless
hands it could easily be used to trivialize trauma. It is, however, only when
the severity of trauma is respected that such an observation of trauma's
limits has any potential to be useful.

The human-divine relation in persons both resists the harm of trauma
and functions to support person/al remaking. Certainly, a person's sense of
connection to the divine can be obliterated, and this does real harm to that
relation. It does not, however, completely sever the relation because God
chooses to remain with the one who suffers. In love and solidarity, God
remains with and in the one who is traumatically harmed even when that
person cannot perceive it. This means the person is never alone. When
a traumatized person cannot perceive God's presence, the fact of divine
presence functions as resistance in the same manner as the persistence of
other forms of relation. God's persistence in relation, however, becomes
concretely valuable for survivors of traumatic harm in that it offers a reliable other with whom one can begin the process of reestablishing connection in the wake of violent rupture. When a person becomes aware, or
even suspicious, of God's presence, the possibility for newly constructed
relation opens.[45]

The gifts of God to humanity are rich resources for survival and person/al remaking because they provide ground for hope. Without hope, survival is impossible. As God gifts humanity with love, grace, desire, salvation, and opportunities not wholly determined by past or present circumstance, the possibility of a way toward survival and person/al remaking not only exists but does so even if a traumatized person's own resources for survival have been entirely exhausted. In other words, survival and person/al remaking do not depend solely on the one who has been shattered or on the world around them that produced an environment of such harm to begin with. This is good news. It means, also, that there is at least one aspect of personhood that traumatic rupture cannot tear. To be a person is to be gifted with the possibility of transformation, and because this is a gift continually given, trauma cannot undo it.

We finally arrive at an understanding of trauma as that which forcefully obstructs particular aspects of personhood (relation), abuses others (vulnerability), and leaves at least one as it is intended (giftedness). For Christian theology, the destructive power of traumatic harm is overwhelming and yet not complete. The possibility of resistance and resources for survival and remaking are built into the structure of the world and into the nature of personhood itself.

Caring with and for the Traumatized

It is necessary to pause, at this point, and address a tension that has been developing. If the possibility of remaking a life worth living after traumatic rupture is given, and if the possibility goes unrealized in the lives of traumatized persons and communities, is this theological conception of trauma suggesting that unactualized possibilities of person/al remaking mark a failure primarily attributable to trauma survivors? In, effect, does this theological paradigm end up blaming the victim for slow or failed recovery? In simple form, the answer is no, absolutely not. The person or community struggling to reconstruct life does not have sole and absolute power to actualize the divine gift of possibility and such actualization is not the result of sheer will. The conditions that allow for the actualization of possibility are at least as relationally determined as personhood. The social, political, economic, and material relations of one's context have as much to do with the actualization of possibility as the fact of one's giftedness and one's exercise of will. The role of the divine, as conceptualized by several of the theologians engaged in this chapter,[46] is to provide possibility and then attract, lure, and lovingly persuade the created order, in its full complexity and interrelation, toward a future in which the possibility of renewed living for particular created beings within that order is realized. The divine, the person or community struggling to survive, ever widening concentric circles of human community and sociality, and all else that fills the cosmos play a specific role in making that which is possible actual. It is a shared process. To challenge the notion of a God who provides possibility without the guarantee of its actualization is a worthy pursuit taken up by many, but venturing into theodicy is outside the scope of this project.

Rather, let us focus on observing that this claim—that possibility for remaking is given while its actualization is not guaranteed—shapes the way theology understands and engages the task of offering support and solidarity to survivors in the struggle for person/al remaking. It leads to the theological conclusion that ethical human communities interested in caring for the relations that constitute each person, as well as the wider world, must be about the work of cultivating contexts in which the possibility of remaking can be realized in the lives of particular persons and communities who are traumatized.[47] Christian theology that remembers and narrates crucifixion as traumatic makes itself a part of that project in multiple ways. Perhaps, most immediately, it does so by both becoming and calling for space that constructs, preserves, and models narrative re-membrance of traumatic events in such a way that those traumatically silenced are themselves invited into processes of narratively forging new bonds of relation, and thus, of reconstructing their own personhood.

Trauma and narrative theorists have posited trauma as a decimation of speech and demonstrated the central role of narrative in person/al remaking.[48] Pointing to narrative as a significant feature of Christian theology's approach to caring with and for persons who are traumatized is informed by the critical work of such theorists. It is particularly appropriate for theology to affirm this work, however, because the construction and preservation of narrative in the wake of trauma has been a theological focus for millennia. Trauma and narrative theories help to explain why this practice has been central to the theological task and meaningful in the lives of the communities for whom Christian theology is developed.

Turning to narrative brings us back to the claim that the first task of Christian theology is to speak into and out from the traumatic events of crucifixion and resurrection. By this, I do not mean that the primary task of theology is to rationally explain these events or articulate a theory that could account for their impact on the community that bore them. I mean, rather, that the task of theology is to speak, period. Speech, in its very mechanics, is a particular way of relating, a particular sequence of signifiers put into relation with one another and the objects to which they point in order to produce meaning. Similarly, the components of a narrative—characters, objects, settings, timelines, gaps, actions, voice, sense, emotion—could be written in a list, and that list would not become a narrative until each part is put into a particular relation to the rest. However, language can communicate meaningfully without doing so in the form of a neat, linear, single story. Narrative, in the way I use it, need not be tidy, complete, unbroken, or composed in perfect correspondence with history. Nonetheless, an inability to construct a narrative—be it jagged or smooth—reveals an absence of relation, which in theological terms reveals a breech in personhood. When persons become traumatized and a degree of the relation that constitutes their personhood is undone, it is not simply that such persons cannot *tell* their story. They cannot, themselves, even know it. It is not there.

With regard to crucifixion, the already silencing impact of trauma was intensified by the explicit Roman expectation that communities of those crucified would never again speak of the ones put to death on the cross. As a tool for squashing movements of political rebellion, crucifixion was designed not only to kill but to annihilate every last trace of its victims in the memory of their loved ones and followers. For Christian theology to develop, then, the doubly silenced community from which it was born needed to cultivate a voice that could say something rather than nothing about the decimating horror of crucifixion and the shocking hope of resurrection. It needed to re-member the narrative components fragmented by rupture and piece them into a sequence of relation that could tell forth new life, life worth living in spite of catastrophe. Each of the four gospel accounts of Jesus's crucifixion represents this work of narrative construction.

The four Gospels model various forms of narrative that differ both from the linear, singular type we have come to expect from novels and from that typical of journalism which prioritizes historical correspondence. The four canonical Gospels tell the story of the same traumatic events—Jesus's crucifixion and resurrection—four different ways. They emphasize at least as many different truths. Some are more comprehensive, others sparse. Taken as a whole, the Gospel narratives are more like collections of small bits woven together than they are like independent, full-bodied manuscripts. They are full of gaps, starts and stops, and jumps through time and space. This is what trauma narratives are often like: partial, multiple, layered, and precarious, while at the same time, potent.

While accounts of Jesus's crucifixion gave birth to the specifically Christian discipline of theology, they are by no means the only trauma narratives preserved or constructed by the discipline. Christian theology narrates and preserves accounts of trauma constructed centuries before the crucifixion of Jesus, and in the two millennia since the Christian tradition emerged from its Jewish roots, Christian theological disciplines, particularly those that remember crucifixion as traumatic, have continued to construct and preserve narratives that bring persons and communities traumatically deprived of speech into voice.[49] Thus, the construction and preservation of narrative in the wake of trauma describes a central element of what Christian theology does now and has been doing for the span of its existence in response to the trauma experienced by its members and the surrounding world.[50] Informed by the task of speaking into and out from the rupture of crucifixion, theology adopts the construction and preservation of traumatic narrative as one of its primary strategies for encouraging survival and well-being in the wake of trauma. This is what it means to say that theology *is* space that constructs, preserves, and models narrative remembrance of traumatic events. The text itself forges and preserves bonds of relation constructed in the narratives it tells.

People are influenced by the spaces in which they dwell. Dwelling in the space framed by the trauma narratives preserved in theological texts provides a person with resources for resisting traumatic harm and pursuing processes of remaking in the wake of trauma. Thoroughly describing how is a large enough task that it deserves to be the subject of its own essay. For now, I can offer a glimpse.

By dwelling in this space, those who have not been subject to horror themselves have the opportunity to experience the deepening and strengthening of their own personhood that comes about through authentically witnessing the trauma narratives of others.[51] In the event that such persons themselves become traumatized, they have the advantage of already knowing by experience that narrative is powerfully able to create connection that strengthens personhood. Hearing and telling narratives preserved in theological texts can help persons connect with pieces of their own experience before they are ready to come to speech. A person can come to recognize parts of themselves in the story of another and can thus be gifted with words that stubbornly refuse to come on their own. Exposure to the diverse array of trauma narratives preserved in theological texts can reveal that horror befalls persons of all walks of life, that the one engaging the text is not alone. The fact that so many narratives have been preserved can communicate that trauma is common at the same time that it can reveal that the construction of narrative and the remaking of personhood in the wake of trauma is possible. The diversity of the narratives preserved can let persons know their own narratives will be particular and can encourage openness to the way one's particular circumstances will shape their own processes of remaking. The telling of these narratives in community can suggest that one's community will be important in that process.

Indeed, Christian theology of the sort that gives voice to traumatic narrative not only becomes space in which that narrative can form, but it also beckons human communities to themselves take up the practice of narrative construction in the wake of trauma. It encourages the communities for whom it is written to become deeply informed by the narratives of cross and resurrection, disruption and relation, trauma and possibility, and encourages them to bear witness to the horrors that plague the world, to listen to those struggling to find a voice, and to hear the voiceless into speech.

Because the first task of Christian theology was to create space for narrative remaking, and because this task has become central to the work of those strands of theology that narrate crucifixion as trauma, Christian theology of this sort invites those who engage it into that process with respect to their own lives. It does the work of narrative construction in its composition. It preserves trauma narratives in order that they and the bonds of relation they forge are not forgotten. Both in familiarizing those who engage it with the process of narrative construction and in asserting that trauma narratives are relevant to the lives of those who engage them, this theology encourages and nurtures persons and communities in making themselves about the work of narrative construction—work that is itself the process of remaking personhood and struggling toward the actualization of the divinely given possibility that life can be worth living even when that life has been irrevocably marked by traumatic rupture.

NOTES

1. Trauma can undo relation or prevent it from forming to begin with. Because these functions are cumbersome to outline every time the issue is articulated in this chapter, I will refer to trauma as obstructing relation, preventing relation, and undoing relation interchangeably.

2. See, for example, an account of Pope Urban II's address at the Council of Clermont given in Guibert of Nogent's "The Deeds of God through the Franks," in *Readings in World Christian History Volume 1: Earliest Christianity to 1453*, ed. John W. Coakley and Andrea Sterk (Maryknoll, N.Y.: Orbis Books, 2004).

3. Stephen Ray, "Contending for the Cross: Black Theology and the Ghosts of Modernity," *Black Theology* 8, no. 1 (2010): 54.

4. For example, see Rebecca Ann Parker and Rita Nakashima Brock, *Saving Paradise: How Christianity Traded Love of This World for Crucifixion and Empire* (Boston: Beacon Press, 2008).

5. This is suggested by early primary texts such as *The Martyrdom of Perpetua and Felicity* and *The Acts of Paul and Thecla*, in which women, in the midst of violent persecution, are depicted as authoritatively challenging Roman oppression.

6. Quintessential of this position is John Howard Yoder, *The Politics of Jesus* (Grand Rapids: Wm. B. Eerdmans Publishing, 1972).

7. James H. Cone, *The Cross and the Lynching Tree* (Maryknoll, N.Y.: Orbis Books, 2011), 156.

8. Jon Sobrino, *The Principle of Mercy: Taking the Crucified People from the Cross* (Maryknoll, N.Y.: Orbis Books, 1994), 80.

9. Serene Jones, *Trauma and Grace: Theology in a Ruptured World* (Louisville: Westminster John Knox Press, 2009), 7.

10. Rita Nakashima Brock and Rebecca Ann Parker, *Proverbs of Ashes: Violence, Redemptive Suffering, and the Search for What Saves Us* (Boston: Beacon Press, 2002), 25.

11. This is, of course, not to say that all theologians who epistemologically prioritize the experiences of women come to this conclusion. Some, such as womanists Sean Copeland and JoAnne Marie Terrell, take a more liberationist approach, and others, particularly feminist Anabaptist theologians, follow the approach to crucifixion developed in the peace traditions.

12. This is particularly true of liberation theology as represented by foundational thinkers such as Cone and Gutiérrez. Others, such as Leonardo Boff and Marcella Althaus-Reid, have moved the tradition away from reading moments of traumatic violence, the cross in particular, as producing liberation.

13. John D. Zizioulas, *Being as Communion: Studies in Personhood and the Church* (Crestwood: St. Vladimir's Seminary Press, 1985), 27.

14. For a fuller analysis of the contemporary concept of personhood in relation to the development of trinitarian thought, see John D. Zizioulas's *Being as Communion: Studies in Personhood and the Church* (Crestwood: St. Vladimir's Seminary Press, 1985).

15. Zizioulas, *Being as Communion*, 49.

16. Monica A. Coleman, *Making a Way Out of No Way: A Womanist Theology* (Minneapolis: Fortress Press, 2008), 55.

17. Coleman, *Making a Way Out of No Way*, 55.

18. Catherine Keller, *From a Broken Web: Separation, Sexism, and Self* (Boston: Beacon Press, 1986).

19. Wendy Farley, *Eros for the Other: Retaining Truth in a Pluralistic World* (University Park: Pennsylvania State University Press, 1996).

20. Nancy Pineda-Madrid, *Suffering and Salvation in Ciudad Juarez* (Minneapolis: Fortress Press, 2011).

21. Delores S. Williams, *Sisters in the Wilderness: The Challenge of Womanist God-Talk*, (Maryknoll, N.Y.: Orbis Books, 1993).

22. For example, in *Powers of Horror: An Essay on Abjection*, trans. Leon S. Roudiez, (New York: Columbia University Press, 1982), Julia Kristeva describes the process of learning to protect and control bodily orifices and excretion as a process of creating the difference between that which is oneself and that which is not.

23. While this is not true of every individual theologian, it is worth acknowledging that theological scholarship tends, broadly speaking, to be more optimistic than that of other disciplines in the humanities. This can be both an asset and a liability—an asset if it reveals critical insight missed by others or enables constructive solutions to intractable problems, and a liability if it leads to scholarship that fails to take the severity of the problems upon which it meditates seriously. Surely, theology's commitment to relieving suffering influences the discipline to treat such relief as possible and pursue it with intention.

24. Jones, *Trauma and Grace*, 52.

25. Coleman, *Making a Way Out of No Way*, 60 (emphasis added).

26. Coleman, *Making a Way Out of No Way*, 75.

27. I do not mean *personal* in the colloquial sense of interior or individual. Rather, I mean it in the theological sense of personhood.

28. Here, I do not mean to say that theologians critically define trauma as extreme suffering. Rather, most theologians, including some I engage in this chapter, have not used the broad concept of trauma as an explicit category of analysis and only recognize trauma when it presents itself in the form of unjust, extreme suffering. With a few notable exceptions (Shelly Rambo, Rita Nakashima Brock, Flora Keshgegian, Serene Jones), not many womanist, feminist, and mujerista theologians have dealt carefully with the overlap and distinctions between trauma and extreme suffering. This is a potential limitation in current theological discourse on trauma, even as theological treatment of extreme suffering is useful in trauma research.

29. Some disciplines maintain a much broader view of trauma. Theology would use different language and methods of analysis to address harm that is not extreme or not a product of evil/injustice.

30. Wendy Farley, *The Wounding and Healing of Desire: Weaving Heaven and Earth* (Louisville: Westminster John Knox Press, 2005).

31. Coleman, *Making a Way Out of No Way*, 55.

32. Coleman, *Making a Way Out of No Way*, 55.

33. Coleman, *Making a Way Out of No Way*, 58.

34. Jones, *Trauma and Grace*, 20.

35. In theology, it is tempting to read a statement like this as invoking a traditional approach to theodicy—the defense of God's benevolence and omnipotence in light of the existence of evil. While "because persons are free, evil is possible" is a statement that reflects Jones's and Coleman's theologies, greater attention to the way each scholar approaches theodicy, which cannot be sustained within the scope of this chapter, would show that both depart from the classical paradigm. As we have already seen, both Coleman and Jones think the power of God outside the patristic conceptualization of omnipotence. And neither focuses on a philosophical defense of God as the primary demand put on theology by the existence of evil. Likewise, I find classical approaches to theodicy often inadequate for contemporary discourse on trauma. For a sketch of my thought on theodicy in light of trauma, see my essay "What's Love Got to do with It: Theodicy, Trauma, and Divine Love," *The Other Journal* 25 (2015).

36. Farley, *The Wounding and Healing of Desire*.

37. Coleman, *Making a Way Out of No Way*, 93.

38. Coleman, *Making a Way Out of No Way*, 93.

39. Jones, *Trauma and Grace*, 72.

40. Jones, *Trauma and Grace*, 159. I will note, for those who might have an aversion to the term, that Jones does not mean "sins" to imply personal moral failings. It is a term used here and throughout various forms of theological scholarship to refer broadly to all that creates distance between the inhabitants of the world and the relation with the divine that sustains them. In other words, the term can include systemic oppression and traumatic harm without placing responsibility for that harm on those victimized. This is the sense in which Jones speaks of the sins/traumas that occupy us.

41. Those committed to process metaphysics are a possible and notable exception to that chorus.

42. For example, it is an intensification of the view of trauma put forward in Judith Herman's *Trauma and Recovery: The Aftermath of Violence—from Domestic Abuse to Political Terror* (New York: Basic Books, 1997).

43. In the course of the development of trauma studies in the last century, describing trauma in terms of rupture has, at times, unhelpfully limited what is recognized as trauma to those forms of trauma most commonly experienced by white societies and people of privilege—namely, a catastrophic break in an otherwise secure and meaningful experience of life. Because describing trauma as rupture can imply, first, that one's sense of self, culture, community, and meaning were vibrant and secure at some prior time,

and second, that the source of trauma is an identifiable and explosive event, generational trauma, cultural trauma, and trauma incurred in contexts of perpetually systemic oppression have not always been well served by such a definition. To responsibly speak of trauma as rupture and breakage, the terms must be conceptually extended to include the rupture of cultural meaning, a process that is likely to be linked to a broad series of events that may be explosive but may also be mundane. The sale of African human bodies in United States slave markets was both mundane and often traumatic (to those being sold) in the cultural context in which it occurred. We must understand the relationship between traumatic rupture, which may occur in parent generations or particular individuals, and the role of such rupture in preventing the formation of meaning to begin with in subsequent generations and other individuals. In other words, while trauma does have to do with rupture, our conception of trauma must not be limited to this description or to a narrow sense of the term when it is used. Stef Craps sustains a more comprehensive critique in *Postcolonial Witnessing: Trauma Out of Bounds* (New York: Palgrave Macmillan, 2012). For a resource on the relationship between the development of trauma studies and contemporary cultural theories of trauma, see Jeffrey C. Alexander's chapter "Toward a Theory of Cultural Trauma" in *Cultural Trauma and Collective Identity* (Berkeley: University of California Press, 2004).

44. I am using *self* in Katherine Keller's sense of the term: specific dynamics of relation that exist in a particular moment.

45. I go into greater detail in my essay on theodicy referenced earlier: "What's Love Got to Do with It? Theodicy, Trauma and Divine Love." Rebecca Ann Parker provides an example of this process in *Proverbs of Ashes*.

46. This is a view most explicitly articulated by process theologians such as Monica Coleman and Katherine Keller.

47. It is important to note that, for the same reason, theology of this sort also calls for the cultivation of human communities that resist unjust systems and events that bring about traumatic rupture in the first place. In its study of unjustly suffered trauma, theology seeks equally to eliminate the cause and support survivors toward person/al remaking.

48. See, for example, Judith Herman, *Trauma and Recovery*; Elaine Scarry, *The Body in Pain: The Making and Unmaking of the World* (New York: Oxford University Press, 1987); Cathy Caruth, *Unclaimed Experience: Trauma, Narrative and History* (Baltimore: Johns Hopkins University Press, 1995); Michael White and David Epston, *Narrative Means to Therapeutic Ends* (New York: Norton, 1990).

49. The practice of narrative construction is, of course, not unique to Christian theology at all, which is evidenced by the fact that many of the

trauma narratives preserved in Christian theology were constructed and first preserved in the texts of the ancient Hebrew religion and are now preserved in both Jewish and Christian theology.

50. Examples of contemporary theology taking up this task can be seen in the discussion of both liberation theology and womanist and feminist treatments of sexual violence articulated earlier in this chapter.

51. I mean *witness* in the theological sense of *bearing witness*. This does not suggest that a person is able to observe the trauma incurred by those whose narratives are preserved in the text.

The Transcendence of Trauma: Prospects for the Continental Philosophy of Religion

Mary-Jane Rubenstein

About a week before the 2016 election, in the midst of what felt like an endless discursive bombardment but now seems a serene prelude to the furious unbridling of white supremacy, sexual violence, and "Christian" nationalism in its immediate aftermath, I spent one Sunday morning—I'll admit it—in a yoga class. As I made my way through the scented candles and inspirational tank tops on the way out of the studio, a woman caught my eye and asked if I had had a good practice. I answered affirmatively and asked the same of her, to which she replied, "Yes—a lot better than I'd thought. It was hard for me to come today. I have PTSD."

Hearing such a straightforward articulation of that which presumably defies articulation, I became—quite awkwardly—speechless. Dumbstruck amid the salt lamps and the mantra bracelets. And indeed, theoretically speaking, silence might have been an appropriate response to such a saying of the unsayable. Socially, however, the situation clearly demanded that I speak; after all, the trauma in question was clearly *not* unsayable from the survivor's perspective. But neither was it simply communicable: Even after the direct revelation, I was left ignorant of the particular violence that had caused the trauma, so I had no way to translate or sympathize with it.

"PTSD" served at once as a direct and an empty signifier; upon hearing it, I suddenly knew both too much and not enough to respond, which I eventually both did and didn't do by whispering something equally direct and empty like, "Oh, I am so sorry."

"Thanks," she answered. "It's okay." But of course it wasn't.

This volume thinks collectively from and of the irreducible yet entangled duplicity of trauma studies. As Vincenzo Di Nicola argues and as many of the other contributors demonstrate, such duplicities emerge in many different forms and at many different levels: between the individual and the communal, the mimetic and the anti-mimetic, the asemic and the polysemic, the individualizing and the desubjectifying, the disordered and the tropological. And although each of these pairs could give rise to unique explorations of trauma's duplicity, this particular volume tends to assemble them under the meta-distinction between the sayable and the unsayable— in other words, between medicalized, militarized, and empirical studies of trauma on the one hand (for example, "I have PTSD") and cultural, philosophical, and psychoanalytic approaches on the other (for example, trauma as absolute rupture, as the presence of an absence, as the possibility of the impossible).

Of these two approaches to trauma, Boynton and Capretto warn that the former tends toward "reductionism," whereas the latter tends toward "obscurantism" (Introduction). Trauma studies is therefore in equal danger of obliterating and enshrining its subject matter; "*It's not even a subject,*" the philosophers will say. The medical approach risks explaining trauma away, whereas the philosophical approach risks not explaining anything at all—a pitfall all too familiar to those of us who write and read within the continental tradition. Charged as I am with the task of examining the potential relationship between trauma studies and philosophy of religion, especially in its broadly continental iterations, I will therefore focus on the clearest point of their intersection, which is to say their shared—and indeed, potentially obscurantist—focus on the unassimilable, the inadmissible, and the unthinkable.

As theorists such as Cathy Caruth, Shoshana Felman, and Dori Laub have argued, trauma can be distinguished from other forms of psychic injury by its unassimilability.[1] The reason the survivor keeps repeating the traumatic "event"—usually in the form of dreams[2]—is that trauma is not an event at all; the occurrence in question is so overwhelming that it cannot be integrated into the normal functioning of the psychic apparatus. In fact, trauma *qua* trauma disables the psychic apparatus itself, unraveling the one who undergoes it "such that [. . .] one cannot [even] speak of a traumatized subject" (Di Nicola, Chapter 1). Nor can one isolate the "moment" of trauma or narrate it chronologically. Unsettling linearity at every turn, the temporality of trauma unfolds variously as deferral (Yancy, Chapter 7), prematurity (Chanter, Chapter 6), repetition (Capretto, Chapter 9), fragmentation (Stolorow, Chapter 2), frozenness (Severson, Chapter 5), absence (Boynton, Chapter 4), and the foreclosure of futurity (Orange, Chapter 3). There is a certain fidelity, therefore, to the theoretical insistence upon the unassimilable nature of trauma. Insofar as trauma dismantles the subjectivity and temporality of the one who undergoes it, it must likewise dismantle the thought that tries to think it. To paraphrase St. Augustine, if you can comprehend it, then it is not trauma; it if is trauma, then you cannot comprehend it.[3]

Trauma's unthinkability is arguably intensified by its massive distribution and reduplication in the recursive forms of interminable wars, forced migration, unnatural disasters, neo-colonial capital, elemental toxicity, the serial execution of black Americans, and the normalization of sexual assault—not to mention the intensification of all these by means of the endless (and largely unconscious) repetitions of social, network, and cable media. As Tina Chanter suggests, a mark of this "age of trauma" is "the difficulty, if not impossibility, of isolating a zone in which trauma has not had an impact, as if trauma has become uncontainable, contagious. Trauma, it seems, is the new normal: We are all living in a culture of trauma" (Chanter, Chapter 6). On the one hand, then, this omnipresence exacerbates our inability to think trauma; after all, "we" are constituted and undone by precisely the rupture of which we are trying to give an account. On the other hand, one might argue that it is precisely trauma as the unthinkable condition of thinking's possibility that actually calls for thinking. Heideggerian being, Derridean *différance*, the Levinasian Other—all of these exceed and disrupt the metaphysical categories to which they give rise, and therefore demand most pressingly, somehow, to be thought. As Kierkegaard's Johannes Climacus attests in the *Philosophical Fragments*, "this, then, is the ultimate paradox of thought: to want to discover something that thought cannot think."[4] Or, as Derrida was fond of saying in seminar settings, "It's only the unthinkable that's worth thinking. Who would ever want to think the thinkable?" Along this line of thinking, trauma would "be" the condition of (im)possibility of late capitalism itself, which is to say, that which most compellingly calls—right now—for thinking.

There are numerous dangers, however, in simply running trauma through the post-Heideggerian machine of the impossible. The first is that it risks speaking about (purportedly unspeakable) trauma without doing anything about it, forgetting ethics in the interest of some ontology-without-ontology and recapitulating paradoxical tropes for the sake of sounding clever. The second is that such un-thinking risks eviscerating the political by configuring trauma as the global condition of being as such. If "this" is the way things "are," one might think, then things clearly cannot be otherwise; and even if they could, we are too (de)constituted by trauma to envision a concrete alternative. The third danger of configuring trauma as the universal condition of being-undone is that it evacuates the specificity and unequal distribution of trauma. For while it is in some sense true that "we" all live in a global age of trauma, it is also the case that we do not share the burden of trauma equally, and that trauma takes different (shapeless) shape along the lines of race, gender, ability, and economic status.

Unthinkability notwithstanding, then, we must find a way to think—and to think clearly. We must understand the specific policies that have led to the poisoning of communities of color in the United States and to the strategic "dumping" of "toxic waste" in what former World Bank Chief Economist Larry Summers referred to as "the LDC [lesser developed countries]."[5] We must calculate the rising sea levels that threaten island nations and low-lying continental regions, most of them inhabited by low-income, nonwhite communities. We must historicize the "stop and frisk" and "stand your ground" policies that inflict specifically racialized trauma on Black Americans, extending the execrable legacy of the "white gratuitous violence against Black people" that renders Black bodies disposable (Yancy, Chapter 7). And none of this understanding, calculating, or historicizing is possible if we rest with the notion that trauma is the universal condition of being-in-the-world, or that it is in any way *strictly* unthinkable. At the same time, if we simply integrate "trauma" into the psycho-politico-economic order, fitting it in alongside categories like "challenges," "struggles," and "collateral damage"—if trauma *simply* becomes thinkable—then we lose trauma altogether; specifically, we lose the spectrality, rupture, nonlinearity, and non-integratability that mark the traumatic as such. Unthinkability edges into irresponsibility and incoherence, whereas thinkability collapses into the normal—which is to say the nontraumatic.

In keeping with the title of the volume at hand, we might assemble these twin dangers under the phrase "the transcendence of trauma." Reading the genitive both objectively and subjectively, this locution could name either an overcoming of trauma or the resistance of trauma to any earthly logic: the transcending of trauma or trauma's transcendence. And interestingly enough, both readings run us up against insidious theologies. Objectively speaking, the transcendence of *trauma* promises not only recovery and resolution—what Shelly Rambo calls "a transcendent imperative to 'get over' or 'get beyond' the experience" (Rambo, Chapter 10)—but also explanation and even justification. As Donna Orange worries, "to traumatized, shattered, devastated people, 'transcendence' might well sound empty. It could smack of 'resilience' [. . .] egoistic individualism, idealizing self-sufficiency, exhortations to get over it, to move on, to find transcendent meaning in one's suffering" (Orange, Chapter 3). The old theological category for finding such transcendent meaning is "theodicy": the attempt to justify the goodness of God in the face of unbearable suffering. Such attempts are notoriously unsatisfying and often ethically questionable; as Kenneth Surin has argued, to claim as some "philosophical theists" do that God inflicts suffering on certain people so that others might be redeemed, or to suggest that "the screams of the innocent" are quieter from the perspective of eternity "is precisely the sign of a corrupt mind."[6] It is ethically insupportable to try to find a position from which trauma can be simply transcended.

Subjectively speaking, by contrast, the "transcendence *of* trauma" means just the opposite: Trauma cannot be transcended because it is itself transcendent. It cannot be understood or integrated because it is the incomprehensible and non-integratable itself. As Boynton demonstrates, this is the position of Emmanuel Levinas, who insisted on evil's transcendence as a means of avoiding theodicy in the wake of World War II. For Levinas, nothing could explain or account for the "magnitude and intensity of evil" enacted as the Holocaust (Boynton, Chapter 4). Rather, this absolute disaster could only be thought as the unthinkable and "unjustifiable" itself: "In the appearing of evil," Levinas writes, "there is announced [. . .] a counter-nature, a monstrosity, the disturbing and foreign in itself. *And in this sense transcendence!*"[7] Thus does Levinas prevent us from justifying, incorporating, or accommodating evil. Even as it avoids and invalidates theodicy, however, trauma's transcendence does not escape theology. To the contrary, it runs from the false comforts of philosophical theism right up the sheer rock face of the apophatic.

Insofar as it takes place as "the unbearable and unendurable [. . .] the unsayable" and the unexperienceable (Stolorow, Chapter 2), Levinasian trauma begins to look uncannily like the God of negative theology. Like the source of all things, trauma in its desubjectifying and transcendent valence exceeds "everything perceived and understood, everything perceivable and understandable, all that is not and all that is," and can only be endured, as Pseudo-Dionysius counsels his apprentice, by "an undivided and absolute abandonment of yourself and everything."[8] Levinas himself comes close to identifying the transcendence of evil with the transcendence of God, locating the "breakthrough of the Good there, where the evil suffered by the other man" demands that I attend and intervene: "Theophany. Revelation. This is the horror of the evil that addresses me."[9]

On the one hand, to call evil the site of the appearance of the Go(o)d is to interrupt any philosophical effort to understand it with the ethical imperative to respond. On the other hand, it is also to grant evil a revelatory, even divine status—"as if," Boynton quotes Derrida, "the Holocaust [or the Rwandan genocide; or the extermination and forced removal of Native Americans; or the intertwined hyperobjects[10] of global warming, capitalism, and anti-blackness] were 'an uninterpretable manifestation of divine violence'" (Boynton, Chapter 4). And here, the apophatic risks giving way to the sadistic. The unknowable, ineffable Un-ground morphs into the "batter my heart" God, the God who granted Julian "three wounds," the God who demands Isaac, the God of substitutionary atonement (read: torture) who keeps Christian women in the abusive relationships they consider their "cross to bear."[11] Again, then, "the transcendence of trauma" collides with theology at both extremes, slipping into theodicic coherence at the limits of the thinkable and masochistic "veneration" (Capretto, Chapter 9) at the limits of the unthinkable.

Likewise caught between these extremes, the subfield of philosophy of religion has been accused in recent years of being "crypto-theological," and, as such, nothing more than what Jonathan Z. Smith calls "data" for the genuinely academic study of religion.[12] As Timothy Knepper charges, "philosophy of religion is usually either a fictionalized and rarified theism or the latest critical notion of some continental philosopher," most of whose ruminations are so obscure they recede into the mists of mystical theology.[13] One could make a strong case, then, against the involvement of continental philosophy of religion (CPR) with trauma studies, likely as the latter is to seduce the former into the familiar terrain of the numinous: our cozy *mysterium tremendum*. At the same time, it is precisely CPR's attunement to subterranean theo-logics that allows it to uncover the various and covert theologies animating purportedly secular disciplines such as trauma (or indeed, religious) studies—not for the sake of vindicating any particular theology, but for the sake of seeing and *understanding* it, especially where it is least obvious. Moreover, there are strategies within this liminal (in)discipline that might contribute to the seemingly impossible task of coming to terms with trauma—a task that will involve thinking at the limits of thinking (Derrida), speaking from silence (Kierkegaard), and breaking the very logic of the language that structures oppression (Irigaray, Glissant, Rambo).

In terms of the particular double-bind animating this volume—the dual "traps of reductionism and obscurantism" (Introduction) harbored within the polyvalent *transcendence of trauma*—the continental philosophy of religion might offer Derridean "negotiation" as a place to start.[14] If it is the case that empirical and theoretical trauma—what Derrida would call the "conditional" and the "unconditional," respectively—each "falls into ruin" without the other, if it is the case that trauma without the unthinkable is annihilated and trauma without the thinkable is divinized, then thinking trauma would take shape as a constant tacking back and forth between these poles.[15] Such thinking would therefore entail the concrete work of "learning, reading, understanding, interpreting the rule, and even calculating," so that the specific and unjustly distributed contours of trauma become as clear as possible.[16] At the same time, it would require attending to the persistent unassimilability, indeed unbearability (Stolorow, Chapter 2) that makes trauma what it "is," obstructing at all turns the theodicic impulse that would assimilate trauma into the regime of the ordinary—or the simply "thinkable."

Even as it brings such strategies to bear on the question of trauma, however, CPR must also allow trauma to call *it* into question: to unsettle its coherence, trouble its boundaries, and reveal its constitutive erasures. Perhaps most pressingly, an attunement to trauma must disrupt the smooth, continental heritage that begins with Descartes and allegedly unfolds internally, dialectically, through Spinoza, Hume, Kant, Schleiermacher, Hegel, Feuerbach, Kierkegaard, Nietzsche, Heidegger, Levinas, Derrida, Deleuze, Nancy, Badiou, and Meillassoux. To be sure, it is important to interrupt this mostly white, male, and Christian lineage, as some syllabi and textbooks now do, with an emphasis upon the Jewishness of its occasional Jews, and by turning to the work of, say, Fanon, Césaire, Glissant, Irigaray, Kristeva, Butler, and Malabou. But such tactics of representational inclusion fail on their own to account for the racist and sexist logic that has formed and continues to form the continental and philosophical canon as such. If it is the case, as George Yancy argues, that "the social lives of white people are entangled within a larger socio-historical matrix that implicates them, beyond their will, in the perpetuation of racial injustice" (Yancy, Chapter 7), then the same must be said of white philosophy, as well. To come to terms with the un-category of trauma, the continental philosophy of religion will therefore have to come to terms with the collective trauma its dominant lineage has justified, encoded, and largely ignored during the long history of European imperialism.

Although there are numerous ways in which such work might be done, three interresonant approaches come immediately to mind, all of which have long been in operation among critical race, feminist, and post- and decolonial thinkers both within and around the field. The first would be to continue the admittedly insufficient project of widening the racial, sexual, and religious scope of "continental philosophy of religion" and its typically lionized figureheads. In so doing, however, it is important to read such texts not as expansions or varieties of the "core" tradition—as if to say, "and *here* is the decolonial/queer/black/ArabJewish form of continental philosophy"—but rather as entangled unveilings of the traumatic encodings that help constitute that fiercely guarded core. When, for example, Glissant uncovers the "nomadic," "rhizomatic" character of European conquest, he is not "applying" Deleuze and Guattari to the colonial situation in the Americas.[17] Rather, he is locating a colonial logic within the aspirationally anti-dominological thought *even of Deleuze and Guattari.* From this perspective, then, minoritarian philosophies do not "diversify" the canon; far more powerfully, they expose its unwitting constitution by the very exclusions, hierarchies, and tropes it allegedly deconstructs— including that of canonicity itself.

The second, interrelated, and equally obvious approach would be to continue to attend to the explicit constructions of racial hierarchies—however overt or incidental—in the *Urtexts* of the continental tradition as it reflects on religion. It should be impossible, for example, to teach or write about Hegel's critique of Spinoza's pantheism without exposing the infantilized and feminized "Indian philosophy" Hegel maps onto the teachings of the "Oriental" Jew.[18] It should be impossible to say anything about *Aufhebung* at all without acknowledging its sources both in Christian eschatology and in Hegel's racialized projection of geo-temporal "progress," which moved from an allegedly ahistorical Africa through the ancient Orient and mid-life Middle East to find its dialectical *telos* in modern Europe.[19] It should be imperative to expose, not simply the well-rehearsed anti-Semitism of the politically disastrous Heidegger, but also the persistent racism of his defender and critic Hannah Arendt, who in the very process of criticizing the European conquest of Africa re-justifies it by asserting that the inhabitants of that continent had never reached "any adequate expression of human reason or human passion [. . .] and [. . .] had developed human institutions only at a very low level."[20] The list, unfortunately, could stretch on for days—from Hume's strictly racialized "development" of human religion, to Kant's denial that Africans and Native Americans possessed the "reason" that constitutes true religion, to Julia Kristeva's more recent insistence that Europe re-discover its Christian heritage to combat the invasive force of "Allah's madmen."[21] Any continental philosophy of religion that attempts to think trauma must face up to the specifically racial trauma endorsed, enacted, and inspired by its heroic foreparents in their various constructions of religion.

Finally, philosophy of religion must learn to listen out for the more subtle signs of trauma within the very canon that gathers itself against it. In *Playing in the Dark*, Toni Morrison entreats literary scholars to attend to the "dark, abiding, signing African presence" that haunts even the whitest of American literature.[22] "Even, and especially, when American texts are not 'about' Africanist presences or characters or narrative or idiom," she argues, "the shadow hovers in implication, in sign, in line of demarcation."[23] Especially in its romanticized presentations of autonomy, individuality, property, and freedom, Morrison suggests, the American canon implicitly and neurotically constitutes itself over against the heteronomous, exchangeable, owned, and unfree black slave.[24]

Similarly, European philosophy's constant preoccupations with the same tropes are a clear function of its emergence alongside—and by means of— the European slave trade. "The inherent contradiction of human slavery had always generated dualisms in thought," writes Brion Davis, "but by the sixteenth and seventeenth centuries Europeans had arrived at the greatest dualism of all—the momentous division between an increasing devotion to liberty in Europe and an expanding mercantile system based on Negro [slave] labor in America."[25] It is therefore crucial to read these "Enlightenment" texts—and their romantic and even postmodern critic-inheritors— as constructed by means of a strategic erasure of the unthinkable Middle Passage that enabled them.[26] As Charles Mills has argued, it would not be possible to undertake a Cartesian meditation as a black man—much less a black woman. The "global doubt" that plagues Descartes is simply not available to people who are owned and oppressed, Mills explains:

> The whole point of subordinate black experience, or the general experience of oppressed groups, is that the subordinated are in no position to doubt the existence of the world and other people, especially that of their oppressors. [. . .] If your daily existence is largely defined by oppression, by *forced* intercourse with the world, it is not going to occur

to you that doubt about your oppressor's existence could in any way be
a serious or pressing philosophical problem.[27]

Not existential doubt or the *cogito* alone, but all of the founders' purportedly neutral categories—like "reason," "nature," "good," "evil," and especially "God" and "man"—are in large part the anxious productions of
European men seeking to justify their liberty, property, and dominion over
against the owned, tortured, and dislocated African and indigenous other.
They are efforts, in other words, to transcend the trauma with which they
have been complicit.

When it comes to coming to terms with trauma, then, there is a disciplinary imperative *not* to try to transcend it. To refuse to deal any longer
in the ahistorical "universals" that cover over the constitutive violence of
the European adventure, and to let trauma do the un-working it does to
individual and collective identities alike. But it is equally imperative not
to grant such untranscendable trauma the status of transcendence, which
would configure it as somehow necessary, beautiful, or worthy of silent
reverie. Neither transcendable nor transcendent, trauma must rather be
constantly negotiated—thought where it seems unthinkable, un-thought
where it seems commonplace, and ruinous of any philosophy that claims to
have nothing to do with it.

NOTES

1. Cathy Caruth, Introduction to *Trauma: Explorations in Memory*, ed.
Cathy Caruth (Baltimore: Johns Hopkins University Press, 1995); Shoshana
Felman, "Education and Crisis, or the Vicissitudes of Teaching," in *Trauma:
Explorations in Memory*, ed. Cathy Caruth (Baltimore: Johns Hopkins Uni-
versity Press, 1995); Dori Laub, "Truth and Testimony: The Process and the
Struggle," in *Trauma: Explorations in Memory*, ed. Cathy Caruth (Baltimore:
Johns Hopkins University Press, 1995).

2. Sigmund Freud, *Introductory Lectures on Psycho-Analysis*, trans. James
Strachey (New York: Norton, 1966), 340, 472.

3. "If you have been able to comprehend it, you have comprehended
something else instead of God [. . .] but if it be God, you have not comprehended it" (Augustine, "Sermon 2 on the New Testament," trans. R. G. Mac-
Mullen, in *Nicene and Post-Nicene Fathers, First Series*, vol. 6, ed. Philip Schaff
[Buffalo, N.Y.: Christian Literature Publishing Company, 1888], para.16,
http://www.newadvent.org/fathers/160302.htm).

4. Søren Kierkegaard, *Philosophical Fragments: Or, a Fragment of Philosophy*, trans. Howard V. Hong and Edna H. Hong (Princeton: Princeton
University Press, 1985), 37.

5. In a now-infamous memo, Summers wrote, "shouldn't the World Bank be encouraging MORE migration of the dirty industries to the LDC? [. . .] I think the economic logic behind dumping a load of toxic waste in the lowest wage country is impeccable. [. . .] I've always thought that under-populated countries in Africa are vastly UNDER-polluted[;] their air quality is probably vastly inefficiently low compared to Los Angeles or Mexico City" (Larry Summers, cited in David Naguib Pellow, *Resisting Global Toxics: Transnational Movements for Environmental Justice* (Cambridge: MIT Press, 2007), 9.

6. Kenneth Surin, *Theology and the Problem of Evil* (Eugene, Ore.: Wipf and Stock, 1986), 83.

7. Emmanuel Levinas, "Transcendence and Evil," in *Of God Who Comes to Mind* (Stanford: Stanford University Press, 1998), 129, 128.

8. Pseudo-Dionysius, "The Mystical Theology," in *Pseudo-Dionysius: The Complete Works*, trans. Colm Luibheid (New York: Paulist Press, 1987), 997B–1000A.

9. Levinas, "Transcendence and Evil," 133–34.

10. Timothy Morton, *Hyperobjects: Philosophy and Ecology after the End of the World* (Minneapolis: University of Minnesota Press, 2013).

11. John Donne, "Batter My Heart, Three-Personed God," in *The Complete English Poems* (New York: Penguin, 1977), 314; Julian of Norwich, *Revelations of Divine Love*, trans. Elizabeth Spearing (New York: Penguin, 1999), 3; Regina Schwartz, *The Curse of Cain: The Violent Legacy of Monotheism* (Chicago: University of Chicago Press, 1998); Rita Nakashima Brock and Rebecca Ann Parker, *Proverbs of Ashes: Violence, Redemptive Suffering, and the Search for What Saves Us* (New York: Beacon Press, 2002), 18, 30.

12. J. Z. Smith, "Sacred Persistence: Toward a Redescription of Canon," in *Imagining Religion: From Babylon to Jonestown* (Chicago: University of Chicago Press, 1988), 43; cf. Russell T. McCutcheon, *Critics Not Caretakers: Redescribing the Public Study of Religion* (Albany, N.Y.: SUNY Press, 2001), 16–17.

13. Timothy David Knepper, *The Ends of Philosophy of Religion: Terminus and Telos* (New York: Palgrave Macmillan, 2013), 9. For a rejoinder to this argument, see Bradley Onishi, "The Beginning, Not the End: On Continental Philosophy of Religion and Religious Studies," *Journal of the American Academy of Religion* 85, no. 1 (2017).

14. Jacques Derrida, *Adieu to Emmanuel Levinas*, trans. Pascale-Anne Brault and Michael Naas (Stanford: Stanford University Press, 1999), 112.

15. Jacques Derrida, "On Forgiveness," in *On Cosmopolitanism and Forgiveness*, trans. Michael Hughes (New York: Routledge, 2001), 44.

16. Jacques Derrida, "Force of Law: The 'Mystical Foundation of Authority,'" in *Deconstruction and the Possibility of Justice*, ed. Drucilla Cornell, Michel

Rosenfeld, and David Gray Carlson, trans. Mary Quaintance (New York: Routledge, 1992), 24.

17. Édouard Glissant, *Poetics of Relation*, trans. Betsy Wang (Ann Arbor: University of Michigan Press, 2010), 11–14.

18. "The profound unity of his philosophy, his manifestation of Spirit as the identity of the finite and the infinite in God [. . .] all this is an echo from Eastern lands" G. W. F Hegel, *Lectures on the History of Philosophy, Volume 3: Medieval and Modern Philosophy*, trans. E. S. Haldane and Frances H. Simson (Lincoln: University of Nebraska Press, 1995), 252.

19. See Emmanuel Chukwudi Eze, "Georg Wilhelm Friedrich Hegel, 'Geographical Basis of World History,'" in *Race and the Enlightenment: A Reader* (New York: Wiley-Blackwell, 1997); Robert Bernasconi, "With What Must the Philosophy of World History Begin? On the Racial Basis of Hegel's Eurocentrism," *Nineteenth-Century Contexts* 22 (2000).

20. Hannah Arendt, *The Origins of Totalitarianism* (New York: Harcourt Brace, 1973), 177. For having brought this passage to my attention, I am indebted to Adam Stern, who undertakes a close reading of Arendt's racialized constructions in relation to the concept of survival in Adam Stern, "Hannah Arendt and the Phantom World of Colonialism," (Paper presentation, Annual Meeting of the American Academy of Religion, San Antonio, Tex., November 2016). See also Roy T. Tsao, "Arendt and the Modern State: Variations on Hegel in 'the Origins of Totalitarianism,'" *The Review of Politics* 66, no. 1 (2004).

21. David Hume, "The Natural History of Religion," in *Dialogues and the Natural History of Religion*, ed. J. C. A. Gaskin (Oxford: Oxford University Press, 1998), 23–24; Theodore Vial, *Modern Religion, Modern Race* (New York: Oxford University Press, 2016); Julia Kristeva, *This Incredible Need to Believe* (New York: Columbia University Press, 2010), 84. See also Mary-Jane Rubenstein, "Review of *This Incredible Need to Believe*, by Julia Kristeva," *Modern Theology* 26, no. 4 (October, 2010).

22. Toni Morrison, *Playing in the Dark: Whiteness and the Literary Imagination* (Cambridge: Harvard University Press, 1992), 5.

23. Morrison, *Playing in the Dark*, 46–47.

24. Morrison, *Playing in the Dark*, 43.

25. Cited in Charles Mills, "Non-Cartesian *Sums*," in *Blackness Visible: Essays on Philosophy and Race* (Ithaca, N.Y.: Cornell University Press, 1998).

26. See An Yountae, *The Decolonial Abyss: Mysticism and Cosmopolitics from the Ruins* (New York: Fordham University Press, 2016).

27. Mills, "Non-Cartesian *Sums*," 8.

ACKNOWLEDGMENTS

While all collaborative volumes are fruits of collective labor, not all germinate in such a mercurial political and intellectual season as this one has. Rather than suffering from problems of currency, this volume's relevance grew exponentially as it developed before and in the aftermath of the 2016 U.S. presidential election. For this reason, the editors are indebted to its contributors not only for the originality and rigor of their work, but also for the care with which they reexamined their thinking midway through a shifting cultural landscape. In particular, we are grateful for Mary-Jane Rubenstein's generative and timely afterword, which proved both methodologically instructive and politically therapeutic for the project as a whole.

The editors recognize the support of the Andrew W. Mellon Foundation grant for Collaborative Undergraduate Research in the Humanities, which made it possible for a number of undergraduate students at Allegheny College to contribute to the formation of this volume, including Valan Anthos, Milton Guevara, and Derek Sawer.

The editors thank Jody Falco and Angela Whalen of Guilford Press for granting permission to include an expanded version of Robert Stolorow's article, "A Phenomenological-Contextual, Existential, and Ethical Perspective on Emotional Trauma," which originally appeared in *Psychoanalytic Review* 102, no. 1 (2015): 123–38.

The editors deeply appreciate the editorial team at Fordham University Press for seeing this project to completion during a tumultuous time. Richard Morrison and Tom Lay were generous conversation partners as this volume took shape. John Garza and Eric Newman worked tirelessly during its mid-stage development. Two anonymous reviewers offered invaluable feedback that helped focus the volume considerably. Last, Nancy Rapoport's fastidious copyediting was a godsend.

Adorno, Theodor W. *Aesthetic Theory*. Translated by Christian Lenhardt. Edited by Gretel Adorno and Rolf Tiedemann. London: Routledge and Kegan Paul, 1984.

Agamben, Giorgio. *Infancy and History: On the Destruction of Experience*. Translated by Liz Heron. London: Verso, 2007.

———. *La Potenza del Pensiere: Saggi e Conferenze*. Vicenza: Neri Pozza, 2005.

———. *The Open: Man and Animal*. Translated by Kevin Attell. Stanford: Stanford University Press, 2004.

———. "Philosophical Archaeology." In *The Signature of All Things*, translated by Luca D'Isanto and Kevin Attell, 81–111. New York: Zone Books, 2009.

———. *Remnants of Auschwitz: The Witness and the Archive*. Translated by Daniel Heller-Roazen. New York: Zone Books, 2002.

———. *The State of Exception*. Translated by Kevin Attell. Chicago: University of Chicago Press, 2005.

———. "What Is an Apparatus?" In *What Is an Apparatus and Other Essays*, translated by David Kishik and Stefan Pedatella, 1–24. Stanford: Stanford University Press, 2009.

Ahmed, Sara. "A Phenomenology of Whiteness." *Feminist Theory* 8, no. 2 (2007): 149–68.

Alexander, Jeffrey C. "Toward a Theory of Cultural Trauma." In *Cultural Trauma and Collective Identity*, edited by Jeffrey C. Alexander, Ron Eyerman, Bernhard Giesen, Neil Smelser, and Piotr Sztompka, 1–59. Berkeley: University of California Press, 2004.

Alexander, Jeffrey, Ron Eyerman, Bernhard Giesen, Neil Smelser, and Piotr Sztompka, eds. *Cultural Trauma and Collective Identity*. Berkeley: University of California Press, 2004.

American Psychological Association. "About APA Division 12: Society of Clinical Psychology." http://www.apa.org/about/division/div12.aspx.

Amichai, Yehuda. *Open Closed Open: Poems*. Translated by Chana Bloch and Chana Kronfeld. New York: Harcourt, 2000.

Archard, David. *Children: Rights and Childhood*. London: Routledge, 1993.

Arendt, Hannah. *The Life of the Mind: Thinking*. Edited by Mary McCarthy. New York, Harcourt Brace Jovanovich: 1971.

———. "Nightmare and Flight." *Partisan Review* 12, no. 2 (1945): 259–60.

———. *The Origins of Totalitarianism*. New York: Harcourt Brace Jovanovich, 1973.

Ariès, Philippe. *Centuries of Childhood: A Social History of Family Life*. Translated by Robert Baldick. New York: Vintage, 1962.

Aristotle. *On Rhetoric: A Theory of Civic Discourse*. Translated by George A. Kennedy. Oxford: Oxford University Press, 1991.

———. "On the Soul." In *The Complete Works of Aristotle: The Revised Oxford Translation, Volume 1*, edited by Jonathan Barnes, translated by J. A. Smith, 641–92. Princeton: Princeton University Press, 1984.

Ashenden, Samantha. "The Persistence of Collective Guilt." *Economy and Society* 43, no. 1 (2014): 55–82.

Assmann, Aleida. *Shadows of Trauma*. New York: Fordham University Press, 2016.

Atwood, George E., and Robert D. Stolorow. *Structures of Subjectivity: Explorations in Psychoanalytic Phenomenology and Contextualism*, 2nd edition. New York: Routledge, 2014.

———. "Walking the Tightrope of Emotional Dwelling." *Psychoanalytic Dialogues* 26 (2016): 103–8.

Badiou, Alain. *Calme Bloc Ici-Bas*. Paris: P.O.L., 1997.

———. *Second Manifesto for Philosophy*. Translated by Louise Burchill. Cambridge: Polity Press, 2011.

Badiou, Alain, and Élisabeth Roudinesco. *Jacques Lacan Past and Present: A Dialogue*. Translated by Jason E. Smith. New York: Columbia University Press, 2014.

Baier, Kurt. "Guilt and Responsibility." In *Collective Responsibility: Five Decades of Debates in Theoretical and Applied Ethics*, edited by Larry May and Stacey Hoffman, 179–218. Lanham: Rowan and Littlefield, 1991.

Baldwin, James. *The Price of the Ticket: Collected Non-Fiction, 1948–1985*. New York: St. Martin's Press, 1985.

Balint, Michael. "Trauma And Object Relationship." *International Journal of Psychoanalysis* 50 (1969): 429–35.

Barth, Karl. *Theologian of Freedom*. Edited by Clifford Green. Minneapolis: Fortress Press, 1989.

Bartmanski, Dominik, and Ron Eyerman. "The Worst Was the Silence: The Unfinished Drama of the Katyn Massacre." In *Narrating Trauma: On the Impact of Collective Suffering*, edited by Ron Eyerman, Jeffrey C. Alexander, and Elizabeth Butler Breese, 237–66. New York: Routledge, 2016.

Belknap, Michal. *The Vietnam War on Trial: The My Lai Massacre and the Court-Martial of Lieutenant Calley*. Lawrence: Kansas University Press, 2002.

Bennett, Tony, Lawrence Grossberg, and Meaghan Morris, eds. *New Keywords: A Revised Vocabulary of Culture and Society*. Oxford: Blackwell, 2005.

Bernasconi, Robert. "With What Must the Philosophy of World History Begin? On the Racial Basis of Hegel's Eurocentrism." *Nineteenth-Century Contexts* 22 (2000): 171–201.

Bernstein, Richard J. *Radical Evil: A Philosophical Interrogation*. Cambridge: Polity Press, 2002.

Betcher, Sharon. *Spirit and the Politics of Disablement*. Minneapolis: Fortress Press, 2007.

Blanchot, Maurice. *The Writing of the Disaster*. Translated by Ann Smock. Lincoln: University of Nebraska Press, 1995.

Bohleber, Werner. "The Development of Trauma Theory in Psychoanalysis." In *Destructiveness, Intersubjectivity, and Trauma: The Identity Crisis of Modern Psychoanalysis*, 75–100. London: Karnac Books, 2010.

Bonhoeffer, Dietrich. *Ethics*. New York: Macmillan, 1955.

Boynton, Eric. "The Transcendence and Banality of Evil." In *I More Than Others: Responses to Evil and Suffering*, edited by Eric Severson, 116–26. Cambridge: Cambridge Publishing, 2010.

Brentano, Franz. *Psychology from an Empirical Standpoint*. Translated by Antos C. Rancurello, D. B. Terrell, and Linda L. McAlister. New York: Routledge, 1995.

Brock, Rita Nakashima, and Rebecca Ann Parker. *Proverbs of Ashes: Violence, Redemptive Suffering, and the Search for What Saves Us*. Boston: Beacon Press, 2001.

———. *Saving Paradise: How Christianity Traded Love of This World for Crucifixion and Empire*. Boston: Beacon Press, 2008.

Brown, Laura S. "Not Outside the Range: One Feminist Perspective on Psychic Trauma." In *Trauma: Explorations in Memory*, edited by Cathy Caruth, 100–12. Baltimore: Johns Hopkins University Press, 1995.

Buber, Martin, and Walter A. Kaufmann. *I and Thou*. New York: Scribner, 1970.

Buelens, Gert, Sam Durrant, and Robert Eaglestone, eds. *The Future of Trauma Theory: Contemporary Literary and Cultural Criticism*. New York: Routledge, 2013.

Bush, George W. "State of the Union Address, January 29, 2002." http://www.whitehouse.gov/news/release/2002/01/20020129-11html.

Butler, Judith. *Precarious Life: The Powers of Mourning and Violence*. New York: Verso Books, 2006.

———. *The Psychic Life of Power: Theories in Subjection*. Stanford: Stanford University Press, 1997.

Butler, Judith, and Athena Athanasiou. *Dispossession: The Performative in the Political*. Malden, Mass: Polity, 2013.

Canetti, Elias. *The Agony of Flies: Notes and Notatations*. Translated by H.F. Broch de Rothermann. New York: Farrar, Straus and Giroux, 1994.

Caputo, John D. *Against Ethics: Contributions to a Poetics of Obligation with Constant Reference to Deconstruction*. Bloomington: Indiana University Press, 1993.

———. *The Prayers and Tears of Jacques Derrida: Religion without Religion*. Bloomington: Indiana University Press, 1997.

Caputo, John D., and Michael J. Scanlon. "Introduction." In *God, the Gift, and Postmodernism*, edited by John D. Caputo and Michael J. Scanlon, 1–20. Bloomington: Indiana University Press, 1999.

Carr, Russell B. "Combat and Human Existence: Toward an Intersubjective Approach to Combat Related PTSD." *Psychoanalytic Psychology* 28 (2011): 471–96.

Caruth, Cathy. Introduction to *Trauma: Explorations in Memory*, edited by Cathy Caruth, 3–12. Baltimore: Johns Hopkins University Press, 1995.

———. *Literature in the Ashes of History*. Baltimore: Johns Hopkins University Press, 2013.

———. *Trauma: Explorations in Memory*. Baltimore: Johns Hopkins University Press, 1995.

———. *Unclaimed Experience: Trauma, Narrative and History*. Baltimore: Johns Hopkins University Press, 1996.

Cassin, Barbara. *Vocabulaire Européen des Philosophies: Dictionnaire des Intraduisables*. Paris: Le Seuil/Le Robert, 2004.

Cavell, Stanley. *Must We Mean What We Say? A Book of Essays*. Cambridge: Cambridge University Press, 1976.

Celan, Paul. "*Sprich Auch Du*." In *Selected Poems and Prose of Paul Celan*, translated by John Felstiner, 76. New York: Norton, 2001.

Chopp, Rebecca. *Converging on Culture: Contemporary Theologians in Dialogue with Cultural Analysis and Criticism*, edited by Sheila Davaney, Delwin Brown, and Kathryn Tanner. Oxford: Oxford University Press, 2001.

———. "Theology and the Poetics of Testimony." *Criterion* (Winter 1998), 2–12.

Cioran, E. M. *On the Heights of Despair*. Chicago: University of Chicago Press, 1992.

Clark, Janine. "Collective Guilt, Collective Responsibility and the Serbs." *East European Politics and Societies* 22, no. 3 (2008): 668–92.

Coates, Ta-Nehisi. *Between the World and Me*. New York: Spiegel & Grau, 2015.

Coleman, Monica A. *Making a Way Out of No Way: A Womanist Theology*. Minneapolis: Fortress Press, 2008.

Collins, Randall. *Violence: A Micro Sociological Theory*. Princeton: Princeton University Press, 2009.

Cone, James H. *The Cross and the Lynching Tree*. Maryknoll, N.Y.: Orbis Books, 2011.

Cook, Kevin. *Kitty Genovese: The Murder, the Bystanders, and the Crime That Changed America*. New York: Norton, 2014.

Coole, Diana, and Samantha Frost, eds. *New Materialisms: Ontology, Agency, and Politics*. Durham, N.C.: Duke University Press, 2010.

Craps, Stef. *Postcolonial Witnessing: Trauma Out of Bounds*. New York: Palgrave Macmillan, 2012.

Critchley, Simon. *Continental Philosophy: A Very Short Introduction*. Oxford: Oxford University Press, 2001.

Culbertson, Roberta. "Embodied Memory, Transcendence, and Telling: Recounting Trauma, Re-Establishing the Self." *New Literary History* 26, no. 1 (1995): 169–95.

Curran, Charles. "Where Have All the Dominant Theologians Gone?" *National Catholic Reporter* 41, no. 14 (February 4, 2005), 16.

Das, Veena. *Life and Words: Violence and the Descent into the Ordinary*. Berkeley: University of California Press, 2007.

Davis, Bret W. *Heidegger and the Will: On the Way to "Gelassenheit."* Evanston, Ill: Northwestern University Press, 2007.

de Saussure, Ferdinand. *Course in General Linguistics*. Edited by Charles Bally and Albert Sechehaye, in collaboration with Albert Reidleinger. Translated by Roy Harris. London: Duckworth, 1983.

DeMause, Lloyd. "The Evolution of Childhood." In *The History of Childhood: The Untold Story of Child Abuse*, edited by Lloyd deMause, 1–73. New York: Peter Bedrick Books, 1988.

Demby, Gene. "The Birth of a New Civil Rights Movement." *Politic Magazine* (December 31, 2014). http://www.politico.com/magazine/story/2014/12/ferguson-new-civil-rights-movement-113906.

Derrida, Jacques. *Adieu to Emmanuel Levinas*. Translated by Pascale-Anne Brault and Michael Naas. Stanford: Stanford University Press, 1999.

———. *Aporias*. Translated by Thomas Dutoit. Stanford: Stanford University Press, 1993.

———. "Faith and Knowledge: The Two Sources of 'Religion' at the Limits of Reason Alone." In *Religion*. Edited by Gianni Vattimo and Jacques Derrida, translated by Samuel Weber, 1–78. Stanford: Stanford University Press, 1998.

———. "Force of Law: The 'Mystical Foundation of Authority.'" In *Deconstruction and the Possibility of Justice*, edited by Drucilla Cornell, Michel Rosenfeld, and David Gray Carlson, translated by Mary Quaintance, 3–67. New York: Routledge, 1992.

———. *The Gift of Death*. Translated by David Willis. Chicago: Chicago University Press, 1995.

————. "Hospitality, Justice, Responsibility: A Dialogue with Jacques
    Derrida." In *Questioning Ethics: Contemporary Debates in Philosophy.* Edited
    by Mark Dooley and Richard Kearney, 65–82. New York: Routledge,
    1992.
————. "On Forgiveness." In *On Cosmopolitanism and Forgiveness,* translated
    by Michael Hughes, 27–60. New York: Routledge, 2001.
————. *Philosophy in a Time of Terror: Dialogues with Jürgen Habermas and
    Jacques Derrida.* Edited by Giovanna Borradori. Chicago: University of
    Chicago Press, 2003.
————. "Plato's Pharmacy." In *Dissemination.* Translated by Barbara Johnson,
    61–171. Chicago: University of Chicago Press, 1981.
————. *Points: Interviews 1974–1994.* Edited by Elizabeth Weber. Stanford:
    Stanford University Press, 1992.
————. *Specters of Marx: The State of Debt, the Work of Mourning and the New
    International.* Translated by Peggy Kamuf. New York: Routledge, 1994.
————. *The Work of Mourning.* Translated by Pascale-Anne Brault and
    Michal Naas. Chicago: Chicago University Press, 2001.
Derrida, Jacques, and Anne Dufourmantelle. *Of Hospitality.* Translated by
    Rachel Bowlby. Stanford: Stanford University Press, 2000.
Derrida, Jacques, and Maurizio Ferraris. *A Taste for the Secret.* Translated by
    Giacomo Donis. London: Polity, 2001.
Dews, Peter. *The Idea of Evil.* Malden, Mass: Blackwell Publishing, 2008.
Di Nicola, Vincenzo. "Ethnocultural Aspects of PTSD and Related Disor-
    ders Among Children and adolescents." In *Ethnocultural Aspects of Post-
    traumatic Stress Disorder: Issues, Research, and Clinical Applications,* edited by
    Anthony J. Marsella, Matthew J. Friedman, Ellen T. Gerrity, and Ray-
    mond M. Scurfield, 389–414. Washington, DC: American Psychological
    Association, 1996.
————. *Letters to a Young Therapist: Relational Practices for the Coming Commu-
    nity.* New York: Atropos Press, 2011.
————. "On the Rights and Philosophy of Children." *Transcultural Psychiatry*
    32, no. 1 (1995): 157–65.
————. *On the Threshold. Selected Papers of Vincenzo Di Nicola, MD, PhD.
    Volume I: Culture, Families and Culture Change.* New York: Atropos Press,
    2016.
————. *A Stranger in the Family: Culture, Families, and Therapy.* New York:
    Norton, 1997.
————. *Trauma and Event: A Philosophical Archaeology.* PhD diss., European
    Graduate School, 2012.
Dilthey, Wilhelm. *Selected Works: Vol. 3. The Formation of the Historical World
    in the Human Sciences.* Princeton: Princeton University Press, 2002.

Donne, John. "Batter My Heart, Three-Personed God." In *The Complete English Poems*, 314. New York: Penguin, 1977.

Dostoevsky, Fyodor. *The Brothers Karamazov*. Translated by Richard Pevear and Larissa Volokhonsky. New York: Farrar, Straus and Giroux, 1990.

Du Bois, W. E. B. *The Souls of Black Folk*. New York: New American Library, Inc., 1982.

Duvoux, Nicolas, and Pascal Sévérac. "Citizen Balibar: An Interview with Étienne Balibar," translated by Michael C. Behrent, *Books and Ideas* (November 26, 2012.)

Ellsberg, Daniel. *Secrets: A Memoir of Vietnam and the Pentagon Papers*. New York: Penguin, 2003.

Elsaesser, Thomas. "Postmodernism as Mourning Work." *Screen* 42, no. 2 (2001): 193–201.

Erickson, Kai. "Notes on Trauma and Community." In *Trauma: Explorations in Memory*, edited by Cathy Caruth, 183–99. Baltimore: Johns Hopkins University Press, 1995.

Evans, Brad, and George Yancy. "The Perils of Being a Black Philosopher." *New York Times Opinionator: The Stone* (April 18, 2016).

Eyerman, Ron, Jeffrey Alexander, and Elizabeth Breese, eds. *Narrating Trauma On the Impact of Collective Suffering*. Boulder: Paradigm Publishers, 2013.

Eze, Emmanuel Chukwudi. "Georg Wilhelm Friedrich Hegel, 'Geographical Basis of World History,'" In *Race and the Enlightenment: A Reader*, 110–49. New York: Wiley-Blackwell, 1997.

Falk, Richard. "An Interview with Richard Falk on Vietnam." In *The American Experience in Vietnam: A Reader*, edited by Grace Sevy, 241–56. Norman: University of Oklahoma Press, 1989.

Fanon, Frantz. *Black Skin, White Masks*. Translated by Charles Lam Markmann. New York: Grove Press, 1967.

Farley, Wendy. *Eros for the Other: Retaining Truth in a Pluralistic World*. University Park: Pennsylvania State University Press, 1996.

———. *Tragic Vision and Divine Compassion: A Contemporary Theodicy*. Minneapolis: Fortress Press, 1990.

———. *The Wounding and Healing of Desire: Weaving Heaven and Earth*. Louisville: Westminster John Knox Press, 2005.

Fassin, Didier, and Richard Rechtman. *The Empire of Trauma: An Inquiry into the Condition of Victimhood*. Translated by Rachel Gomme. Princeton: Princeton University Press, 2009.

Faulkner, Alison, and Phil Thomas. "Editorial: User-Led Research and Evidence-Based Medicine." *British Journal of Psychiatry* 180 (2002): 1–3.

Felitti, Vincent J., Robert F. Anda, Dale Nordenberg, David F. Williamson, Alison M. Spitz, Valerie Edwards, Mary P. Koss, and James S. Marks. "Relationship of Childhood Abuse and Household Dysfunction to Many of the Leading Causes of Death in Adults: the Adverse Childhood Experiences (ACE) Study." *American Journal of Preventive Medicine* 14, no. 4 (1998): 245–58.

Felman, Shoshana. "Education and Crisis, or the Vicissitudes of Teaching." In *Trauma: Explorations in Memory*, edited by Cathy Caruth, 13–60. Baltimore: Johns Hopkins University Press, 1995.

———. "The Return of the Voice: Claude Lanzmann's *Shoah*." In *Testimony: Crises of Witnessing in Literature, Psychoanalysis and History*, edited by Shoshana Felman and Dori Laub, 204–83. New York: Routledge, 1992.

Felman, Shoshana, and Dori Laub. *Testimony: Crises of Witnessing in Literature, Psychoanalysis, and History*. New York: Routledge, 1992.

Ferenczi, Sandor. "Confusion of Tongues Between Adults and the Child." In *Final Contributions to the Problems and Methods of Psycho-Analysis*, 156–67. London: Hogarth Press, 1933.

Figal, Gunter. *Objectivity: The Hermeneutical and Philosophy*. Translated by Theodore D. George. Albany: SUNY Press, 2010.

Fodor, Jerry A. *Psychological Explanation: An Introduction to the Philosophy of Psychology*. New York: Random House, 1968.

Foucault, Michel. *The Order of Things: An Archaeology of the Human Sciences*. New York: Pantheon, 1970.

Freud, Anna. *The Ego and the Mechanisms of Defense, Revised Edition*. Translated by Cecil Baines. New York: International Universities Press, 1966.

Freud, Sigmund. *Beyond the Pleasure Principle*. Translated and edited by James Strachey. New York: Norton, 1961.

———. *Civilization and Its Discontents*. Translated and edited by James Strachey. New York: Norton, 1961.

———. "The Dynamics of Transference." In *The Standard Edition of the Complete Psychological Works of Sigmund Freud, Volume XII (1911–1913): The Case of Schreber, Papers on Technique and Other Works*, translated and edited by James Strachey, 312–22. London: Hogarth, 1958.

———. "Fetishism." In *The Standard Edition of the Complete Psychological Works of Sigmund Freud, Volume XXI (1927–1931): The Future of an Illusion, Civilization and Its Discontents, and Other Works*, translated and edited by James Strachey, 152–57. London: Hogarth, 1961.

———. "Further Remarks on the Neuro-Psychoses of Defence." In *The Standard Edition of the Complete Psychological Works of Sigmund Freud, Volume III (1893–1899): Early Psycho-Analytic Publications*, translated and edited by James Strachey, 155–82. London: Hogarth, 1962.

————. "Inhibitions, Symptoms and Anxiety." In *The Standard Edition of the Complete Psychological Works of Sigmund Freud, Volume XX (1925–1926): An Autobiographical Study, Inhibitions, Symptoms and Anxiety, The Question of Lay Analysis and Other Works*, translated and edited by James Strachey, 77–175. London: Hogarth Press, 1959.

————. *Introductory Lectures on Psycho-Analysis*. Translated and edited by James Strachey. New York: Norton, 1966.

————. "The Neuro-Psychoses of Defence." In *The Standard Edition of the Complete Psychological Works of Sigmund Freud, Volume III (1893–1899): Early Psycho-Analytic Publications*, translated and edited by James Strachey, 45–59. London: Hogarth, 1962.

————. *New Introductory Lectures on Psycho-Analysis*. Translated and edited by James Strachey. New York: Norton, 1965.

————. *An Outline of Psycho-Analysis*. Translated and edited by James Strachey. New York: Norton, 1949.

————. *The Standard Edition of the Complete Psychological Works of Sigmund Freud, Volume VII (1901–1905): A Case of Hysteria, Three Essays on Sexuality and Other Works*, translated and edited by James Strachey. London: Hogarth, 1953.

————. "The Unconscious." In *The Standard Edition of the Complete Psychological Works of Sigmund Freud, Volume XIV (1914–1916): On the History of the Psycho-Analytic Movement, Papers on Metapsychology, and Other Works*, translated and edited by James Strachey, 159–204. London: Hogarth Press, 1957.

Gadamer, Hans-Georg. *Truth and Method*, 2nd ed. Translated by Joel Weinsheimer and Donald G. Marshall. New York: Continuum, 1975.

Gadamer, Hans-Georg, and Richard E. Palmer. *The Gadamer Reader: A Bouquet of the Later Writings*. Evanston, Ill: Northwestern University Press, 2007.

Galeano, Eduardo. *Open Veins of Latin America: Five Centuries of the Pillage of a Continent*. Translated by Cedric Belfrage. New York: Monthly Review Press, 1973.

Geddes, Jennifer. *Evil After Postmodernism*. London: Taylor and Francis Group, 2001.

Gerassi, John. *Talking With Sartre: Conversations and Debates*. Edited and translated by John Gerassi. New Haven: Yale University Press, 2009.

Gibbs, Robert. *Correlations: Rosenzweig and Levinas*. Princeton: Princeton University Press, 1992.

Gibson, James William. *The Perfect War: Technowar in Vietnam*. New York: Atlantic Monthly Press, 2000.

Giessen, Bernhard. "The Trauma of the Perpetrators: The Holocaust as the Traumatic Reference of German National Identity." In *Cultural Trauma and Collective Identity*, edited by Jeffrey C. Alexander, Ron Eyerman, Bernhard Giesen, Neil Smelser, and Piotr Sztompka, 112–54. Berkeley: University of California Press, 2004.

Gilligan, James. "Shame, Guilt, and Violence." *Social Research* 70, no. 4 (2003): 1149–80.

Ginsberg, Allen. "Footnote to Howl." 1988. http://www.poetryfoundation .org/poems-and-poets/poems/detail/54163.

Girard, René. "The Anthropology of the Cross: A Conversation with René Girard." In *The Girard Reader*, edited by James G. Williams, 262–88. New York: Crossroad Herder, 1996.

———. *The Scapegoat*. Translated by Yvonne Frecceru. Baltimore: Johns Hopkins University Press, 1986.

Glissant, Édouard. *Poetics of Relation*. Translated by Betsy Wang. Ann Arbor: University of Michigan Press, 2010.

Golden, Kristen Brown, and Bettina Bergo, eds., *The Trauma Controversy*. Albany: SUNY Press, 2009.

Goodman, Nancy R., and Marilyn B. Meyers, eds. *The Power of Witnessing: Reflections, Reverberations, and Traces of the Holocaust*. New York: Taylor & Francis, 2012.

Gordon, Avery. *Ghostly Matters: Haunting and the Sociological Imagination*. Minneapolis: University of Minnesota Press, 2008.

Grant, Ruth W. *Naming Evil, Judging Evil*. Chicago: University of Chicago Press, 2006.

Grossman, Dave. *On Killing: The Psychological Cost of Learning to Kill in War and Society*. New York: Back Bay Books, 2009.

Guibert of Nogent. "The Deeds of God through the Franks." In *Readings in World Christian History Volume 1: Earliest Christianity to 1453*, edited by John W. Coakley and Andrea Sterk, 324–33. Maryknoll, N.Y.: Orbis Books, 2004.

Gumbrecht, Hans Ulrich. *The Production of Presence: What Meaning Cannot Convey*. Stanford: Stanford University Press, 2004.

Hacking, Ian. "The Looping Effect of Human Kinds." In *Causal Cognition: An Interdisciplinary Approach*, edited by D. Sperber, D. Premack, and AJ Premack, 351–83. Oxford: Clarendon Press, 1995.

Halberstam, David. *The Best and the Brightest*. New York: Fawcett, 1993.

———. *The Making of a Quagmire: America and Vietnam in the Kennedy Era*. New York: Random House, 1965.

Hallie, Philip P. *Lest Innocent Blood Be Shed: The Story of the Village of Le Chambon, and How Goodness Happened There*. New York: Harper & Row, 1979.

Handscomb, Terrence. *Sinthôme: Mutant Automata in an Ill-founded World*. PhD diss., European Graduate School, 2011.

Hartman, Geoffrey H. *The Longest Shadow: In the Aftermath of the Holocaust.* Bloomington: Indiana University Press, 2002.

———. "Reading, Trauma, Pedagogy." In *The Geoffrey Hartman Reader,* edited by Geoffrey Hartman, and Daniel T. O'Hara, 291–99. Edinburgh: Edinburgh University Press, 2004.

Hashimoto, Akiko. "The Cultural Trauma of a Fallen Nation: Japan 1945." In *Narrating Trauma: On the Impact of Collective Suffering,* edited by Ron Eyerman, Jeffrey C. Alexander, and Elizabeth Butler Breese, 27–52. New York: Routledge, 2016.

———. *The Long Defeat: Cultural Trauma, Memory, and Identity in Japan.* New York: Oxford University Press, 2015.

Hegel, G. W. F. *The Encyclopaedia Logic, with the Zusätze: Part I of the Encyclopaedia of Philosophical Sciences with the Zusätze.* Translated by T. o. F. Geraets, W. A. Suchting, and H. S. Harris. Indianapolis: Hackett, 1991.

———. *Lectures on the History of Philosophy, Volume 3: Medieval and Modern Philosophy.* Translated by E. S. Haldane and Frances H. Simson. Lincoln: University of Nebraska Press, 1995.

Heidegger, Martin. *Being and Time.* Translated by Joan Stambaugh. Albany, N.Y.: SUNY Press, 2010.

———. *Being and Time.* Translated by John Macquarrie and E. Robinson. New York: Harper & Row, 1962.

———. *Contributions to Philosophy (Of the Event).* Translated by Richard Rojcewicz and Daniela Vallega-Neu. Bloomington: Indiana University Press, 2012.

———. "Plato's Doctrine of Truth." In *Philosophy of the Twentieth Century: An Anthology,* vol. 3, edited by William Barrett and Henry D. Aiken, 251–70. New York: Random House, 1962.

Heins, Volker, and Andreas Langenohl. "A Fire That Doesn't Burn? The Allied Bombing of Germany and the Cultural Politics of Trauma." In *Narrating Trauma: On the Impact of Collective Suffering,* edited by Ron Eyerman, Jeffrey C. Alexander, and Elizabeth Butler Breese, 3–26. New York: Routledge, 2016.

Herman, Judith. *Trauma and Recovery: The Aftermath of Violence—From Domestic Abuse to Political Terror.* New York: Basic Books, 1997.

Hersh, Seymour M. *My Lai 4: A Report on the Massacre and Its Aftermath.* New York: Random House, 1970.

———. "The Scene of the Crime." *The New Yorker* (March 30, 2015): 53–61.

Hoeller, Stephan A. *Gnosticism: New Light on the Ancient Tradition of Inner.* Wheaton, Ill.: Quest Books, 2002.

Holmes, Jeremy. "Countertransference Before Heimann: An Historical Exploration." *Journal of the American Psychoanalytic Association* 62 (2014): 603–29.

Horowitz, Gregg M. "A Late Adventure of the Feelings." In *The Trauma Controversy*, edited by K. Brown and B. Bergo, 23–44. Albany, N.Y.: SUNY Press, 2009.

———. *Sustaining Loss: Art and Mournful Life*. Stanford: Stanford University Press, 2001.

Hume, David. *Dialogues and the Natural History of Religion*. Edited by J. C. A. Gaskin. Oxford: Oxford University Press, 1998.

Husserl, Edmund. *Cartesian Meditations: An Introduction to Phenomenology*. Translated by Dorion Cairns. The Hague: Martinus Nijhoff, 1960.

———. *Ideas Pertaining to a Pure Phenomenology and to a Phenomenological Philosophy, Second Book*. Translated by Richard Rojcewicz and André Schuwer. Boston: Kluwer Academic Publishers, 2002.

———. *The Paris Lectures*. Translated by Peter Koestenbaum. Boston: Martinus Nijhoff, 1964.

Hwangbo, Kyeong. "Trauma, Narrative, and the Marginal Self in Selected Contemporary American Novels." PhD diss., University of Florida, 2004.

Ionesco, Eugene. *Fragments of a Journal*. Translated by Jean Stewart. London: Faber and Faber, 1968.

Jaenicke, Chris. *Change in Psychoanalysis: An Analyst's Reflections on the Therapeutic Relationship*. New York: Routledge, 2011.

———. *The Risk of Relatedness: Intersubjectivity Theory in Clinical Practice*. Lanham: Jason Aronson, 2008.

James, William. *A Pluralistic Universe*. Cambridge: Harvard University Press, 1977.

———. *The Varieties of Religious Experience: A Study in Human Nature*. New York: Longmans, Green, and Co., 1902.

Jones, Howard. *My Lai: Vietnam, 1968, and the Descent into Darkness*. New York: Oxford University Press, 2017.

Jones, Serene. *Trauma and Grace: Theology in a Ruptured World*. Louisville: Westminster John Knox Press, 2009.

Jordan, Mark D. *Telling Truths in Church: Scandal, Flesh, and Christian Speech*. Boston: Beacon Press, 2004.

———. "Writing-Terrors: A Dialectical Lyric." *Modern Theology* 30, no. 3 (2014): 89–104.

Kanstainer, Wulf. "Genealogy of a Category Mistake: A Critical Intellectual History of the Cultural Trauma Metaphor." *Rethinking History: The Journal of Theory and Practice* 8, no. 2 (2004): 193–221.

Kansteiner, Wulf, and Harald Weilnböck. "Against the Concept of Cultural Trauma or How I Learned to Love the Suffering of Others without the Help of Psychotherapy." In *Cultural Memory Studies: An International and*

Interdisciplinary Handbook, edited by Astrid Erll and Ansgar Nünning, 229–40. New York: Walter de Gruyter, 2008.

Kant, Immanuel. *Critique of the Power of Judgement*. Translated by Paul Guyer and Eric Matthews. Cambridge: Cambridge University Press, 2000.

Kaplan, Ann. *Trauma Culture: The Politics of Terror and Loss in Media and Literature*. New Brunswick, N.J.: Rutgers University Press, 2005.

Kauffmann, Jeffrey, ed. *Loss of the Assumptive World: A Theory of Traumatic Loss*. New York: Routledge, 2002.

Keefe-Perry, Callid. *Way to Water: A Theopoetics Primer*. Portland, Ore.: Cascade Books, 2014.

Keilson, Hans. "Sequential Traumatization of Children." *Danish Medical Bulletin* 27, no. 5 (1980): 235–37.

Keller, Catherine. *From a Broken Web: Separation, Sexism, and Self*. Boston: Beacon Press, 1986.

Keskgegian, Flora. *Time for Hope: Practices of Living in Today's World*. New York: Continuum, 2006.

Khan, Masud. "The Concept of Cumulative Trauma." In *The Privacy of the Self*, 42–58. Madison, Conn: International Universities Press, 1963.

Kierkegaard, Søren. *Fear and Trembling*. Translated and edited by Howard V. Hong and Edna V. Hong. Princeton: Princeton University Press, 1983.

———. *Fear and Trembling*. Translated by Alastair Hannay. New York: Penguin Books, 2006.

———. *Philosophical Fragments: Or, a Fragment of Philosophy*. Translated by Howard V. Hong and Edna H. Hong. Princeton: Princeton University Press, 1985.

Kisiel, Theodore. *The Genesis of Heidegger's Being and Time*. Berkeley: University of California Press, 1993.

Knepper, Timothy David. *The Ends of Philosophy of Religion: Terminus and Telos*. New York: Palgrave Macmillan, 2013.

Kohut, Heinz. *The Analysis of the Self*. Madison, Conn.: International Universities Press, 1971.

Kolko, Gabriel. *Anatomy of a War: Vietnam, the United States, and the Modern Historical Experience*. New York: The New Press, 1994.

———. *The Roots of American Foreign Policy: An Analysis of Power and Purpose*. Boston: Beacon Press, 1969.

Kristeva, Julia. *Powers of Horror: An Essay on Abjection*. Translated by Leon S. Roudiez. New York: Columbia University Press, 1982.

———. *This Incredible Need to Believe*. New York: Columbia University Press, 2010.

Krystal, Henry. *Integration and Self-Healing: Affect, Trauma, Alexithymia*. Hillsdale, N.J.: The Analytic Press, 1988.

Kubrick, Stanley, and Anthony Burgess. *A Clockwork Orange*. Los Angeles: Warner Bros, 1971.

Lacan, Jacques. "The Mirror Stage as Formative of the Function of the I." In *Écrits: A Selection*, translated by Alan Sheridan, 75–81. Bristol: Tavistock Publications, 1977.

LaCapra, Dominick. *Writing History, Writing Trauma*. Baltimore: Johns Hopkins University Press, 2001.

Ladd, Kevin L., and Daniel N. McIntosh. "Meaning, God, and Prayer: Physical and Metaphysical Aspects of Social Support." *Mental Health, Religion, and Culture* 11, no. 1 (January 2008): 23–28.

Laing, Ronald D. *The Divided Self: An Existential Study in Sanity and Madness*. London: Tavistock Publications, 1960.

Lake Williams, J. F. *An Historical Account of Invention and Discoveries in Those Arts and Sciences, Which Are of Utility or Ornament to Man, Vol I*. London: T. and J. Allamn, 1820.

Langer, Lawrence. *Versions of Survival: The Holocaust and the Human Spirit*. Albany, N.Y.: SUNY Press, 1982.

Lanzmann, Claude. "The Obscenity of Understanding: An Evening with Claude Lanzmann." In *Trauma: Explorations in Memory*, edited by Cathy Caruth, 200–20. Baltimore: Johns Hopkins University Press, 1995.

Laplanche, Jean, and J. B. Pontilis. *The Language of Psycho-Analysis*. Translated by Donald Nicholson-Smith. London: Hogarth Press, 1973.

Latane, Bibb, and John Darley. *The Unresponsive Bystander: Why Dosen't He Help?* New York: Appleton-Century-Crofts, 1970.

Laub, Dori. "Bearing Witness, or the Vicissitudes of Listening." In *Testimony: Crises of Witnessing in Literature, Psychoanalysis and History*, edited by Shoshana Felman and Dori Laub, 57–74. New York: Routledge, 1992.

———. "Truth and Testimony: The Process and the Struggle." In *Trauma: Explorations in Memory*, 61–75. Baltimore: Johns Hopkins University Press, 1995.

Laub, Dori, and Nanette C. Auerhahn. "Failed Empathy: A Central Theme in the Survivor's Holocaust Experience." *Psychoanalytic Psychology* 6 (1989): 377–400.

Lavey, Roberta, Tom Sherman, Kim Mueser, Donna Osborne, Melinda Currier, and Rosemarie Wolfe. "The Effects of Yoga on Mood in Psychiatric Inpatients." *Psychiatric Rehabilitation Journal* 28, no. 4 (Spring 2005): 399–402.

Layton, Lyn. "Psychoanalysis and Politics: Historicizing Subjectivity." *Psychiatry, Mental Health and Psychoanalysis* 11 (2013): 68–81.

Leer, Jonathan. "Inside and Outside the *Republic*." In *Plato's Republic: Critical Essays*, edited by Richard Kraut, 61–94. Lanham, Md.: Rowman & Littlefield, 1997.

Lem, Stanislaw. *The Investigation*. Translated by Adele Milch. New York: Avon Books, 1974.

Levi, Primo. *The Drowned and the Saved*. Translated by Raymond Rosenthal. New York: Vintage International, 1989.

———. *Survival in Auschwitz: The Nazi Assault on Humanity*. Translated by Stuart Woolf. New York: Collier Books, 1961.

———. *The Truce*. Translated by Stuart Woolf. Boston: Little, Brown, 1965.

Levinas, Emmanuel. *Collected Philosophical Papers*. Dordrecht, Netherlands: Martinus Nijhoff, 1987.

———. *Existence and Existents*. Translated by Alphonso Lingis. Pittsburgh: Duquesne University Press, 2001.

———. *Otherwise than Being or Beyond Essence*. Translated by Alphonso Lingis. Pittsburgh: Duquesne University Press, 1998.

———. "Peace and Proximity." In *Emmanuel Levinas: Basic Philosophical Writings*, edited by Adriaan T. Peperzak, Simon Critchley, and Robert Bernasconi, translated by Peter Atterton and Simon Critchley, 161–170. Bloomington: Indiana University Press.

———. "Reality and Its Shadow." In *Collected Philosophical Papers*, translated by Alphonso Lingis, 1–13. Dordrecht, Netherlands: Martinus Nijhoff, 1987.

———. "Time and the Other." In *The Levinas Reader*, edited by Sean Hand, 37–58. Oxford: Blackwell, 1989.

———. *Totality and Infinity: An Essay on Exteriority*. Translated by Alphonso Lingis. Pittsburgh: Duquesne University Press, 1969.

———. "Transcendence and Evil." In *Of God Who Comes to Mind*, edited and translated by Bettina Bergo, 122–34. Stanford: Stanford University Press, 1998.

———. "Useless Suffering." In *The Provocation of Levinas*, edited by Robert Bernasconi and David Wood, translated by Richard Cohen, 156–67. London: Routledge, 1988.

Lewy, Guenter. "Is American Guilt Justified?" In *The American Experience in Vietnam: A Reader*, edited by Grace Sevy, 257–76. Norman: University of Oklahoma Press, 1989.

Leys, Ruth. *Trauma: A Genealogy*. Chicago: University of Chicago Press, 2000.

Lifton, Robert Jay. *Home from the War: Learning from Vietnam Veterans*. New York: Other Press, 2005.

Lorde, Audre. *Sister Outsider: Essays & Speeches*. Berkeley, CA: Crossing Press, 1984.

Lucy, Niall. *A Derrida Dictionary*. Oxford: Blackwell Publications, 2004.

Lyotard, Jean-François. *The Differend: Phrases in Dispute*. Translated by Georges Van Den Abbeele. Minneapolis: University of Minnesota Press, 1988.

———. "Discussions, or Phrasing 'After Auschwitz.'" In *The Lyotard Reader*, edited by Andrew Benjamin, 360–92. Oxford: Blackwell, 1989.

———. *Heidegger and "The Jews."* Translated by Andreas Michel and Mark Roberts. Minneapolis: University of Minnesota Press, 1990.

———. *The Inhuman.* Translated by Geoffrey Bennington and Rachel Bowlby. Stanford: Stanford University Press, 1991.

———. *Postmodern Fables.* Translated by Georges Van Den Abbeele. Minneapolis: University of Minnesota Press, 1997.

Malka, Solomon. *Emmanuel Levinas: His Life and Legacy.* Pittsburgh: Duquesne University Press, 2006.

Malraux, André. *Man's Estate.* Translated by Alastair MacDonald. London: Methuen, 1948.

Marion, Jean-Luc. "The Saturated Phenomenon." Translated by Thomas A. Carlson. *Philosophy Today* 40, no. 1 (Spring 1996): 103–24.

Marlantes, Karl. *Matterhorn: A Novel.* New York: Grove Press, 2010.

———. *What Is It Like to Go to War?* New York: Grove Press, 2011.

Marty, Martin. "Under Many Influences." *Sightings* (February 14, 2005). https://divinity.uchicago.edu/sightings/under-many-influences -%E2%80%94-martin-e-marty.

"The Martyrdom of Perpetua and Felicity." In *Readings in World Christian History, Volume 1: Earliest Christianity to 1453.* Edited by John W. Coakley and Andrea Sterk, 30–36. Maryknoll, N.Y.: Orbis Books, 2004.

Matthews, Gareth B. *The Philosophy of Childhood.* Cambridge: Harvard University Press, 1994.

Matuštík, Martin Beck. *Radical Evil and the Scarcity of Hope: Postsecular Meditations* Bloomington: Indiana University Press, 2008.

May, Larry. *After War Ends.* Cambridge: Cambridge University Press, 2012.

McCarthy, Mary. *Medina.* New York: Harcourt Brace Jovanovich, 1972.

McCutcheon, Russell T. *Critics Not Caretakers: Redescribing the Public Study of Religion.* Albany, N.Y.: SUNY Press, 2001.

McNally, Richard J. "Posttraumatic Stress Disorder." In *Kaplan & Sadock's Comprehensive Textbook of Psychiatry, 9th ed., Vol. II*, edited by Benjamin J. Sadock, Virginia Alcott Sadock, and Pedro Ruiz, 2650–3560. Philadelphia: Lippincott, Williams and Wilkins, 2009.

———. *Remembering Trauma.* Cambridge: Belknap Press/Harvard University Press, 2003.

McNamara, Robert. *In Retrospect: The Tragedy and Lessons of Vietnam.* New York: Times Books, 1995.

Miller, Alice. "The Essential Role of an Enlightened Witness in Society." https://www.alice-miller.com/en/the-essential-role-of-an-enlightened -witness-in-society/.

Mills, Charles. "Non-Cartesian *Sums*." In *Blackness Visible: Essays on Philosophy and Race*, 1–19. Ithaca, N.Y.: Cornell University Press, 1998.

Mishra, Pankaj. "James Baldwin Denounced Richard Wright's 'Native Son' as a 'Protest Novel.' Was He Right?" *New York Times Sunday Book Review*, February 24, 2015.

Moltmann, Jürgen. *The Spirit of Life: A Universal Affirmation*. Minneapolis: Fortress Press, 1992.

Morag, Raya. *Waltzing with Bashir: Perpetrator Trauma and Cinema*. New York: I. B. Tauris, 2013.

Morgan Wortham, Simon. *The Derrida Dictionary*. London: Continuum, 2010.

Morgenson, Greg. *God Is a Trauma: Vicarious Religion and Soul-Making*. New York: Spring Publications, 1989.

Morris, David. *The Evil Hours: A Biography of Post-Traumatic Stress Disorder*. Boston: Houghton Mifflin Harcourt, 2016.

Morrison, Toni. *Beloved*. New York: Alfred A. Knopf, 1987.

———. *Playing in the Dark: Whiteness and the Literary Imagination*. Cambridge: Harvard University Press, 1992.

Morton, Timothy. *Hyperobjects: Philosophy and Ecology after the End of the World*. Minneapolis: University of Minnesota Press, 2013.

Mount Shoop, Marcia W. *Let the Bones Dance: Embodiment and the Body of Christ*. Louisville: Westminster John Knox Press, 2010.

———. "Safety and Vulnerability in a Dangerous and Fertile World: A Meditation on Incarnation." January 29, 2015. http://feminismandreligion .com/2015/01/29/safety-and-vulnerability-in-a-dangerous-and-fertile -world-a-meditation-on-incarnation/.

———. "Wandering Home Retreat 2016." http://marciamountshoop.com/ wh2016/.

Müller, Heiner. *Hamlet-Machine and Other Texts for the Stage*. Edited and translated by Carl Weber. New York: Performing Arts Journal Publications, 1984.

Mulvey, Laura. "Visual Pleasure and Narrative Cinema." *Screen* 16 (1975): 6–18.

Murray, Alex, and Jessica Whyte. *The Agamben Dictionary*. Edited by Alex Murray and Jessica Whyte. Edinburgh: Edinburgh University Press, 2011.

Neiman, Susan. *Evil in Modern Thought: An Alternative History of Philosophy*. Princeton: Princeton University Press, 2002.

Nietzsche, Friedrich. *The Genealogy of Morals*. New York: Random House, 1967.

Norwich, Julian of. *Revelations of Divine Love*. Translated by Elizabeth Spearing. New York: Penguin, 1999.

O'Brien, Tim. *The Things They Carried*. London: Flamingo, 1991.

Oliver, Kelly. *Witnessing: Beyond Recognition*. Minneapolis: University of Minnesota Press, 2001.

Oliver, Kendrick. *The My Lai Massacre in American History and Memory*. Manchester: Manchester University Press, 2006.

Olson, James, and Randy Roberts. *My Lai: A Brief History with Documents*. Boston: Bedford/St. Martin's Press, 1998.

Onishi, Bradley. "The Beginning, Not the End: On Continental Philosophy of Religion and Religious Studies." *Journal of the American Academy of Religion* 85, no. 1 (2017): 1–30.

Oppenheimer, Joshua. *The Act of Killing*. Copenhagen: Final Cut for Real, 2012.

Orange, Donna. *Climate Crisis, Psychoanalysis, and Radical Ethics*. London: Routledge, 2017.

———. *Emotional Understanding: Explorations in Psychoanalytic Epistemology*. New York: Guilford Press, 1995.

———. *Nourishing the Inner Life of Clinicians and Humanitarians: The Ethical Turn in Psychoanalysis*. London: Routledge, 2015.

Ornstein, Anna. "Survival and Recovery: Psychoanalytic Reflections." In *Progress in Self Psychology, Volume 19*, edited by Mark J. Gehrie, 85–106. Hillsdale: Analytic Press, 2003.

Pascal, Blaise. *Pensées and Other Writings*. Translated by Honor Levi. New York: Oxford University Press, 2008.

Pasolini, Pier Paolo. *Teorema*. Milano: Garzanti, 1968.

Pellow, David Naguib. *Resisting Global Toxics: Transnational Movements for Environmental Justice*. Cambridge: MIT Press, 2007.

Peperzak, Adriaan. "Giving." In *The Enigma of Gift and Sacrifice*, edited by Edith Wyschogrod, Jean-Joseph Goux, and Eric Boynton, 161–76. New York: Fordham University Press, 2002.

———. *To the Other: An Introduction to the Philosophy of Emmanuel Levinas*. West Lafayette, Ind.: Purdue University Press, 1993.

Pía Lara, María. *Rethinking Evil: Contemporary Perspectives*. Berkeley: University of California Press, 2001.

Pick, Daniel. *Faces of Degeneration: A European Disorder, c. 1848–1918*. Cambridge: Cambridge University Press, 1989.

Pineda-Madrid, Nancy. *Suffering and Salvation in Ciudad Juarez*. Minneapolis: Fortress Press, 2011.

Plato. *Complete Works*. Edited by John M. Cooper and D. S. Hutchinson. Indianapolis: Hackett Publishing, 1997.

———. *Republic*. Translated by Robin Waterfield. New York: Oxford University Press, 1993.

————. *The Theaetetus of Plato*, Translated by M. J. Levett. Indianapolis: Hackett Publishing, 1990.

Posner, Richard A. "Rational Choice, Behavioral Economics, and the Law." *Stanford Law Review* 50 (1997): 1551–75.

Prado, Adélia. *Poesia Réunida*. 2a edição. São Paulo: Editora Siciliano, 1991.

Pseudo-Dionysius. *Pseudo-Dionysius: The Complete Works*. Translated by Colm Luibheid. New York: Paulist Press, 1987.

Rambo, Shelly. *Spirit and Trauma: A Theology of Remaining*. Louisville: Westminster John Knox Press, 2010.

Rancière, Jacques. *Aesthetics and Its Discontents*. Translated by Steven Corcoran. Malden, Mass.: Polity, 2009.

————. *Malaise dan l'esthétique*. Paris: Galilée, 2004.

————. "The Paradoxes of Political Art," In *Dissensus: on Politics and Aesthetics*, translated by Steven Corcoran, 142–59. London: Continuum, 2011.

Rankine, Claudia. "The Condition of Black Life Is One of Mourning." *New York Times*, June 22, 2015.

————. "Q&A with Poet Claudia Rankine—Emerson College—Wed April 29 2015." YouTube Video. Posted June 21, 2015. https://www.youtube.com/watch?v=kugvV79R_io.

Ratcliffe, Matthew. *Experiences of Depression: A Study in Phenomenology*. Oxford: Oxford University Press, 2015.

Ray, Stephen. "Contending for the Cross: Black Theology and the Ghosts of Modernity." *Black Theology* 8, no. 1 (2010): 53–68.

Ricoeur, Paul. "Evil, a Challenge to Philosophy and Theology." In *Figuring the Sacred*, 249–61. Minneapolis: Fortress Press, 1995.

Ridenhour, Ron. "Jesus Was a Gook." In *Nobody Gets Off the Bus: The Vietnam Generation Big Book*, edited by Dan Duffy and Kalí Tal, 138–42. Woodbridge: Viet Nam Generation, 1994.

————. "Perspective on My Lai: 'It was a Nazi kind of thing.'" *Los Angeles Times*, March 16, 1993.

————. "What We Learned in Vietnam." *In These Times* (PBS Radio), March 3, 1997. www.ridenhour.org/about_ron.html.

Rivera, Mayra. *Touch of Transcendence: A Postcolonial Theology of God*. Minneapolis: Fortress Press, 2007.

Rogers, Todd, and Avi Feller. "Discouraged by Peer Excellence: Exposure to Exemplary Peer Performance Causes Quitting." *Psychological Science* 27 (2016): 365–74.

Rowling, J. K. *Harry Potter and the Goblet of Fire*. New York: Scholastic Press, 2000.

Rubenstein, Mary-Jane. "Review of *This Incredible Need to Believe*, by Julia Kristeva." *Modern Theology* 26, no. 4 (October, 2010): 666–69.

Sartre, Jean-Paul. Preface to Frantz Fanon, *The Wretched of the Earth*, 17–31. New York: Grove Press, 1968.

Savelsberg, Joachim, and Ryan King. *American Memories: Atrocities and the Law*. New York: Russell Sage Foundation, 2011.

Scarry, Elaine. *The Body in Pain: The Making and Unmaking of the World*. New York: Oxford University Press, 1987.

Scarsella, Hilary Jerome. "What's Love Got to Do with It? Theodicy, Trauma and Divine Love." *The Other Journal* 25 (2015): 100–5.

Schalk, David. *War and the Ivory Tower*. Lincoln: University of Nebraska Press, 2005.

Scheff, Thomas. "Aggression, Hypermasculine Emotions and Relations." *Irish Journal of Sociology*, no. 1 (2006): 24–39.

Schiller, Friedrich. *On the Aesthetic Education of Man*. Translated by Elizabeth M. Wilkinson and L. A. Willoughby. Oxford: Clarendon Press, 2005.

Schott, Robin May. *Feminist Philosophy and the Problem of Evil*. Bloomington: Indiana University Press, 2007.

Schrift, Alan. *Modernity and the Problem of Evil*. Bloomington: Indiana University Press, 2005.

Schwartz, Regina. *The Curse of Cain: The Violent Legacy of Monotheism*. Chicago: University of Chicago Press, 1998.

Sevy, Grace, ed. *The American Experience in Vietnam: A Reader*. Norman: University of Oklahoma Press, 1989.

Shatan, Chaim. "The Grief of Soldiers: Vietnam Combat Veterans' Self-Help Movement." *American Journal of Orthopsychiatry* 43, no. 4 (1973): 640–52.

Shay, Jonathan. *Achilles in Vietnam: Combat Trauma and the Undoing of Character*. New York: Scribner, 1994.

———. *Odysseus in America: Combat Trauma and the Trials of Homecoming*. New York: Scribner, 2003.

Sheehan, Neil. "Should We Have War Crimes Trials?" *New York Times Book Review*. March, 28, 1971.

Sherman, Nancy. *Afterwar: Healing the Moral Wounds of Our Soliders*. New York: Oxford, 2015.

Shue, Henry. *Climate Justice: Vulnerability and Protection*. Oxford: Oxford University Press, 2014.

Simon, Fritz B., Helm Stierlin, and Lyman C. Wynne. "Isomorphism." In *The Language of Family Therapy: A Systemic Vocabulary and Sourcebook*, edited by Fritz B. Simon, Helm Stierlin, and Lyman C. Wynne, 201–2. New York: Family Process Press, 1985.

Singer, Mel. "Shame, Guilt, Self-Hatred and Remorse in the Psychotherapy of Vietnam Combat Veterans Who Committed Atrocities." *American Journal of Psychotherapy* 58, no.4 (2004): 377–85.

Smith, Andrew Philip. *A Dictionary of Gnosticism*. Wheaton, Ill: Quest Books, 2009.

Smith, H. Shelton, Robert T. Handy, and Lefferts A. Loetscher. *American Christianity: An Historical Interpretation with Representative Documents*. New York: Scribner, 1960.

Smith, J. Z. . "Sacred Persistence: Toward a Redescription of Canon." In *Imagining Religion: From Babylon to Jonestown*, 36–52. Chicago: University of Chicago Press, 1988.

Sobrino, Jon. *The Principle of Mercy: Taking the Crucified People from the Cross*. Maryknoll, N.Y.: Orbis Books, 1994.

Socarides, Daphne D., and Robert D. Stolorow. "Affects and Selfobjects." *The Annual of Psychoanalysis* 12/13 (1984/85): 105–19.

Sontag, Susan. *AIDS and Its Metaphors*. New York: Farrar, Straus and Giroux, 1989.

———. *Illness as Metaphor*. New York: Farrar, Straus and Giroux, 1978.

———. *Regarding the Pain of Others*. New York: Penguin Books, 2003.

Spector, Ronald. *After Tet: The Bloodiest Year in Vietnam*. New York: Free Press, 1992.

Spiegel, Shalom. *The Last Trial: On the Legends and Lore of the Command to Abraham to Offer Isaac as a Sacrifice*. Reprint edition. Translated with an Introduction by Judah Goldin. New Preface by Judah Goldin. Woodstock, Vt.: Jewish Lights Publishing, 1993.

Spiegelberg, Herbert. *The Phenomenological Movement: A Historical Introduction*, 3rd rev. ed. Dordrecht, Netherlands: Kluwer Academic, 1994.

Stacewicz, Richard. *Winter Soldier: An Oral History*. Chicago: Twayne, 1997.

Stauffer, Jill, and Bettina Bergo, eds. *Nietzsche and Levinas: "After the Death of a Certain God."* New York: Columbia University Press, 2009.

Stern, Adam. "Hannah Arendt and the Phantom World of Colonialism." Paper presented at the Annual Meeting of the American Academy of Religion, San Antonio, Texas, November 2016.

Stolorow, Robert D. "The Phenomenology of Trauma and the Absolutisms of Everyday Life: A Personal Journey." *Psychoanalytic Psychology* 16 (1999): 464–68.

———. *Trauma and Human Existence: Autobiographical, Psychoanalytic, and Philosophical Reflections*. New York: Analytic Press, 2007.

———. "Undergoing The Situation: Emotional Dwelling Is More Than Empathic Understanding." *International Journal of Psychoanalytic Self Psychology* 9 (2014): 80–83.

———. *World, Affectivity, Trauma: Heidegger and Post-Cartesian Psychoanalysis*. New York: Routledge, 2011.

Stolorow, Robert D., and George E. Atwood. *Contexts of Being: The Inter-subjective Foundations of Psychological Life*. Hillsdale, N.J.: The Analytic Press, 1992.

———. "Deconstructing 'The Self' of Self Psychology." *International Journal of Psychoanalytic Self Psychology* 7 (2012): 573–76.

Stolorow, Robert D., George E. Atwood, and Donna M. Orange. *Worlds of Experience: Interweaving Philosophical and Clinical Dimensions in Psychoanalysis*. New York: Basic Books, 2002.

Surin, Kenneth. *Theology and the Problem of Evil*. Eugene, Ore.: Wipf and Stock, 1986.

Taylor, Charles. *Sources of the Self: The Making of the Modern Identity*. Cambridge: Harvard University Press, 1989.

Trezise, Thomas. "Unspeakable." *The Yale Journal of Criticism* 4, no. 1 (2001): 39–66.

———. *Witnessing Witnessing: On the Reception of Holocaust Survivor Testimony*. New York: Fordham University Press, 2013.

Tsao, Roy T. "Arendt and the Modern State: Variations on Hegel in 'The Origins of Totalitarianism.'" *The Review of Politics* 66, no. 1 (2004): 105–36.

Turkle, Sherry. "French Anti-psychiatry." In *Critical Psychiatry: The Politics of Mental Health*, edited by David Ingleby, 150–83. Harmondsworth: Penguin Books, 1981.

Turse, Nick. *Kill Anything That Moves: The Real American War in Vietnam*. New York: Picador, 2013.

van Manen, Max. *Researching Lived Experience: Human Science for an Action Sensitive Pegagogy*. 2nd edition. New York: Routledge, 2015.

Vasterling, Jennifer J., and Kevin Brailey, "Neuropsychological Findings in Adults with PTSD." In *Neuropsychology of PTSD: Biological, Cognitive, and Clinical Perspectives*, 178–207. New York: Guilford Press, 2005.

Vial, Theodore. *Modern Religion, Modern Race*. New York: Oxford University Press, 2016.

Vogel, Lawrence. *The Fragile "We": Ethical Implications of Heidegger's Being and Time*. Evanston, Ill.: Northwestern University Press, 1994.

von Trier, Lars. *Dogville*. Santa Monica: Lions Gate Entertainment, 2003.

Wajcman, Gérard. *L'object du siècle*. Paris: Verdier, 1998.

Walzer, Michael. *Just and Unjust Wars: A Moral Argument with Historical Illustrations*. New York: Basic Books, 1977.

Watkin, William. "*The Signature of All Things*: Agamben's Philosophical Archaeology." *MLN*, no. 129 (2014): 139–61.

Weaver, Gina. *Ideologies of Forgetting: Rape in the Vietnam War*. Albany, N.Y.: SUNY Press, 2010.

Weil, Simone. *Simone Weil Reader*, edited by George A Panichas. New York: McKay, 1977.

Westphal, Merold. "Levinas and the 'Logic' of Solidarity." *Graduate Faculty Philosophy Journal* 20, no. 2 (1998): 297–319.

White, Michael, and David Epston. *Narrative Means to Therapeutic Ends*. New York: Norton, 1990.

Wilbur, Richard. "Love Calls Us to the Things of the World." 2004. http://www.poetryfoundation.org/poems-and-poets/poems/detail/43048.

Williams, D. D. R., and Jane Garner. "The Case Against 'The Evidence': A Different Perspective on Evidence-Based Medicine." *British Journal of Psychiatry* 180 (2002): 8–12.

Williams, Delores S. *Sisters in the Wilderness: The Challenge of Womanist God-Talk*. Maryknoll, N.Y.: Orbis Books, 1993.

Williams, Raymond. *Keywords: A Vocabulary of Culture and Society*. London: Fontana, 1983.

Winnicott, Donald W. *Through Paediatrics to Psycho-Analysis*. New York: Basic Books, 1975.

Winthrop, John. "City on a Hill." In *Collections of the Massachusetts Historical Society* 7 *(Third Series)*, 31–48 (1838).

Wittgenstein, Ludwig. *Culture and Value*. Edited by G. H. von Wright. Translated by Peter Winch. Chicago: University of Chicago Press, 1980.

Wood, David. *What Have We Done. The Moral Injuries of Our Longest Wars*. Boston: Little, Brown and Company, 2016.

Woods, Angela. *The Sublime Object of Psychiatry: Schizophrenia in Clinical and Cultural Context*. Oxford: Oxford University Press, 2011.

Wright, Richard. *Black Boy*. New York: Perennial Classics, 1993.

Yancy, George. "Walking While Black in the White Gaze." *New York Times Opinionator: The Stone*, September 9, 2013.

Young, Iris Marion. *Responsibility for Justice*. Oxford: Oxford University Press, 2011.

Yountae, An. *The Decolonial Abyss: Mysticism and Cosmopolitics from the Ruins*. New York: Fordham University Press, 2016.

Yoder, John Howard. *The Politics of Jesus*. Grand Rapids: William B. Eerdmans Publishing Co., 1972.

Young, James E. *At Memory's Edge: After-Images of the Holocaust in Contemporary Art and Architecture*. New Haven: Yale University Press, 2000.

———. *The Texture of Memory: Holocaust Memorials and Meaning*. New Haven: Yale University Press, 1993.

Zamyatin, Yevgeny. "On Literature, Revolution, Entropy, and Other Matters." In *A Soviet Heretic: Essays by Yevgeny Zamyatin*, edited and translated by Mirra Ginsburg, 107–12. Chicago: University of Chicago Press, 1970.

Zizioulas, John D. *Being as Communion: Studies in Personhood and the Church*.
    Crestwood: St. Vladimir's Seminary Press, 1985.
Zummer, Thomas. "Arrestments: Corporeality and Mediation." In *Stitch
    & Split: Selves and Territories in Science Fiction*, curated by Constant vzw
    (2006), 1–13. http://data.constantvzw.org/s-a-s/16_zummer.pdf.

Eric Boynton is Professor and Chair of Philosophy and Religious Studies at Allegheny College, where he also serves as the Director of Interdisciplinary Studies. With Edith Wyschogrod and Jean-Joseph Goux, he edited *The Enigma of Gift and Sacrifice* (Fordham University Press, 2002), and with Martin Kavka, *Saintly Influence* (Fordham University Press, 2009). In addition to writings in these volumes, he has published articles and chapters on continental philosophy, the problem of evil and suffering, and aesthetics and film with venues in the philosophy of religion and contemporary theory.

Peter Capretto is a fellow in Theology and Practice at Vanderbilt University in the area of Religion, Psychology, and Culture. His publications on trauma, phenomenology, psychoanalysis, and the philosophy of religion have appeared in the *Journal of the American Academy of Religion*, *The Heythrop Journal*, *Journal of Religion and Health*, *Political Theology*, and other edited volumes, including *In the Wake of Trauma: Philosophy and Psychology for the Suffering Other* (Duquesne University Press, 2016). His writings are informed by his clinical work as a hospice chaplain, crisis counselor, and pastoral psychotherapist.

Tina Chanter is Professor of Philosophy and Gender at Kingston University, London. She is the author of *Whose Antigone? The Tragic Marginalization of Slavery* (SUNY Press, 2011), *The Picture of Abjection: Film Fetish and the Nature of Difference* (Indiana University Press, 2008), *Time, Death and the Feminine: Levinas with Heidegger* (Stanford University Press, 2001), and *Ethics of Eros: Irigaray's Re-writing of the Philosophers* (Routledge, 1995). She also edits the Gender Theory series at SUNY Press.

Vincenzo Di Nicola is Professor of Psychiatry and Philosopher-In-Residence at the University of Montréal, and works at the crossroads of children and families, culture and trauma. His books *A Stranger in the Family* (Norton, 1997) and *Letters to a Young Therapist* (Atropos, 2011) together offer an interdisciplinary synthesis of cultural psychiatry and family ther-apy. He pioneered transcultural child psychiatry, focusing on migration and trauma. After training in the Harvard Program in Refugee Trauma as a psychiatrist, he completed a PhD in philosophy in 2012. His forthcom-ing works include *On the Threshold* (Atropos), a two-volume selection of his writing, and *Psychiatry in Crisis* (Springer) with Drozdstoj Stoyanov.

Ronald Eyerman is Professor of Sociology and Co-Director at the Center for Cultural Sociology at Yale University. He has written several books within the theoretical framework of cultural trauma, the latest being *Is This America? Hurricane Katrina as Cultural Trauma* (University of Texas Press, 2015). His current research concerns the memory of the Vietnam War.

Donna Orange is Clinical Assistant Professor of Psychology in the Post-doctoral Program in Psychotherapy and Psychoanalysis at NYU. With both a PhD in philosophy and a PsyD, she regularly teaches at New York's Institute for the Psychoanalytic Study of Subjectivity and offers clinical consultations and supervision. Her recent books include *Thinking for Clini-cians: Philosophical Resources for Contemporary Psychoanalysis and the Humanistic Psychotherapies* (Routledge, 2010), *The Suffering Stranger: Hermeneutics for Everyday Clinical Practice* (Routledge, 2011), *Nourishing the Inner Life of Clini-cians and Humanitarians: The Ethical Turn in Psychoanalysis* (Routledge, 2016), and *Climate Crisis, Psychoanalysis, and Radical Ethics* (Routledge, 2016).

Shelly Rambo is Associate Professor of Theology at Boston University. Her work in constructive and systematic theology interrogates how classic themes in the Christian tradition inform contemporary issues on trauma, suffering, and violence. She is author of *Spirit and Trauma: A Theology of Remaining* (Westminster John Knox Press, 2010), as well as several articles and chapters on trauma and theology.

Mary-Jane Rubenstein is Professor of Religion at Wesleyan University, where she is also affiliated faculty in Feminist, Gender, and Sexuality Stud-ies and in the Science and Society Program. She is the author of *Strange Wonder: The Closure of Metaphysics and the Opening of Awe* (Columbia Uni-versity Press, 2009) and *Worlds Without End: The Many Lives of the Multi-verse* (Columbia University Press, 2014), and coeditor with Catherine Keller of *Entangled Worlds: Religion, Science, and New Materialisms* (Ford-ham University Press, 2017).

Hilary Jerome Scarsella is a doctoral student in theological studies at Vanderbilt University. Her interdisciplinary research brings trauma studies into conversation with religious and theological investigations of personal and cultural violence, systemic oppression, and human flourishing. She is director of Our Stories Untold, a solidarity organization for survivors of sexualized violence in Christian contexts. Her current research takes a special interest in trauma connected to sexual and gender-based violence, as well as in the ways that trauma of this sort intersects religious social practice.

ERIC SEVERSON is a philosopher specializing in the work of Emmanuel Levinas. He is author of the books *Levinas's Philosophy of Time* (Duquesne University Press, 2013) and *Scandalous Obligation* (Beacon Hill Press, 2011), and editor of several other works. He lives in Kenmore, Washington with his wife, Misha, and their three children, and teaches philosophy at Seattle University.

MARCIA MOUNT SHOOP is a constructive theologian working at the intersections of trauma, embodiment, and racial oppression in the Christian tradition. She is author of *Let the Bones Dance: Embodiment and the Body of Christ* (Westminster John Knox Press, 2010) and, with Mary McClintock-Fulkerson, *A Body Broken, a Body Betrayed: Race, Memory, and the Eucharist in White-Dominant Churches* (Cascade, 2015). She is pastor of Grace Covenant Presbyterian Church in Asheville, North Carolina.

ROBERT STOLOROW is a Founding Member at the Institute of Contemporary Psychoanalysis, Los Angeles, and the Institute for the Psychoanalytic Study of Subjectivity, New York. He received a PhD in Clinical Psychology in 1970 and in Philosophy in 2007. His four decades of rethinking psychoanalysis as a form of phenomenological inquiry are represented in his authored works, *World, Affectivity, Trauma: Heidegger and Post-Cartesian Psychoanalysis* (Routlege, 2011) and *Trauma and Human Existence* (Routledge, 2007), and eight other coauthored books.

GEORGE YANCY is Professor of Philosophy at Emory University. He is the author, editor, and coeditor of over eighteen books. His first authored book, *African-American Philosophers: 17 Conversations* (Routledge, 1998), received an honorable mention from the Gustavus Myers Center for the Study of Bigotry and Human Rights, and three of his edited books have received *CHOICE* outstanding academic book awards. He is editor of the Philosophy of Race Book Series at Lexington Books, and is known for his interviews and articles on the subject of race at *The Stone, New York Times*.